THE ARDEN SHAKESPEARE

GENERAL EDITORS:
RICHARD PROUDFOOT, ANN THOMPSON
and DAVID SCOTT KASTAN

A MIDSUMMER NIGHT'S DREAM

THE ARDEN SHAKESPEARE

ALL'S WELL THAT ENDS WELL	edited by G.K. Hunter*
ANTONY AND CLEOPATRA	edited by John Wilders
AS YOU LIKE IT	edited by Juliet Dusinberre
THE COMEDY OF ERRORS	edited by R.A. Foakes*
CORIOLANUS	edited by Philip Brockbank*
CYMBELINE	edited by J.M. Nosworthy*
DOUBLE FALSEHOOD	edited by Brean Hammond
HAMLET	edited by Ann Thompson and Neil Taylor
JULIUS CAESAR	edited by David Daniell
KING HENRY IV Part 1	edited by David Scott Kastan
KING HENRY IV Part 2	edited by A.R. Humphreys*
KING HENRY V	edited by T.W. Craik
KING HENRY VI Part 1	edited by Edward Burns
KING HENRY VI Part 2	edited by Ronald Knowles
KING HENRY VI Part 3	edited by John D. Cox and Eric Rasmussen
KING HENRY VIII	edited by Gordon McMullan
KING JOHN	edited by E.A.J. Honigmann*
KING LEAR	edited by R.A. Foakes
KING RICHARD II	edited by Charles Forker
KING RICHARD III	edited by James R. Siemon
LOVE'S LABOUR'S LOST	edited by H.R. Woudhuysen
MACBETH	edited by Kenneth Muir*
MEASURE FOR MEASURE	edited by J.W. Lever*
THE MERCHANT OF VENICE	edited by John Drakakis
THE MERRY WIVES OF WINDSOR	edited by Giorgio Melchiori
A MIDSUMMER NIGHT'S DREAM	edited by Harold F. Brooks*
MUCH ADO ABOUT NOTHING	edited by Claire McEachern
OTHELLO	edited by E.A.J. Honigmann
PERICLES	edited by Suzanne Gossett
SHAKESPEARE'S POEMS	edited by Katherine Duncan-Jones and H.R. Woudhuysen
ROMEO AND JULIET	edited by Brian Gibbons*
SHAKESPEARE'S SONNETS	edited by Katherine Duncan-Jones
THE TAMING OF THE SHREW	edited by Barbara Hodgdon
THE TEMPEST	edited by Virginia Mason Vaughan and Alden T. Vaughan
TIMON OF ATHENS	edited by Anthony B. Dawson and Gretchen E. Minton
TITUS ANDRONICUS	edited by Jonathan Bate
TROILUS AND CRESSIDA	edited by David Bevington
TWELFTH NIGHT	edited by Keir Elam
THE TWO GENTLEMEN OF VERONA	edited by William C. Carroll
THE TWO NOBLE KINSMEN	edited by Lois Potter
THE WINTER'S TALE	edited by John Pitcher

* Second series

THE ARDEN EDITION OF THE
WORKS OF WILLIAM SHAKESPEARE

A MIDSUMMER NIGHT'S DREAM

Edited by
HAROLD F. BROOKS

B L O O M S B U R Y
LONDON · NEW DELHI · NEW YORK · SYDNEY

Bloomsbury Arden Shakespeare

An imprint of Bloomsbury Publishing Plc

50 Bedford Square	1385 Broadway
London	New York
WC1B 3DP	NY 10018
UK	USA

www.bloomsbury.com

This edition of *A Midsummer Night's Dream*, by Harold E. Brooks,
first published by Methuen & Co. Ltd 1979
Reprinted 2004 and 2006 by Thomson Learning
Reprinted by Bloomsbury Arden Shakespeare 2009 (twice), 2010, 2012 (twice), 2013

The general editors of the Arden Shakespeare have been
W.J. Craig and R.H. Case (first series 1899-1944)
Una Ellis-Fermor, Harold F. Brooks, Harold Jenkins and
Brian Morris (second series 1946-82)

Present general editors (third series)
Richard Proudfoot, Ann Thompson, David Scott Kastan and H. R. Woudhuysen.

British Library Cataloguing-in-Publication Data
A catalogue record for this book is available from the British Library.

ISBN: PB: 978-1-9034-3660-8

Library of Congress Cataloging-in-Publication Data
A catalog record for this book is available from the Library of Congress

Printed and bound in India

CONTENTS

PAGE

PREFACE   ix

ACKNOWLEDGEMENTS   xii

ABBREVIATIONS AND REFERENCES   xiii

INTRODUCTION   xxi

I.   xxi

1. The text   xxi
2. Date and occasion: with consideration of the poetic style   xxxiv
3. Sources and antecedents   lviii

II. THE PLAY   lxxxix

1. The exposition   lxxxix
2. Design and plot   xciv
3. Characters and comedy   cii
4. Lyricism, music and dance   cxx
5. Setting: woodland and fairyland; moon   cxxv
6. The principal themes   cxxx

A MIDSUMMER NIGHT'S DREAM   1

APPENDIX I Source materials   129

APPENDIX II Four textual cruces   154

APPENDIX III The mislined verse in Q1, v. i.   163

APPENDIX IV Quince's Prologue (v. i. 108–16) rightly punctuated   165

PREFACE

A Midsummer Night's Dream has had a pre-eminent place in my affections ever since my first experience of the theatre: a matinée of Granville Barker's famous production, to which at the age of seven I was taken by my aunts, Dr Lillie and Miss Kathie Johnson. Round their Christmas hearth, shortly after, the family read the play aloud, taking parts: I read from Dr Lillie's copy of the handsome edition illustrated by Arthur Rackham. For these reasons among others I dedicate this edition to her and her sister, as well as to my wife who has been my fellow-Shakespearean for twenty years, and is the authority I invariably consult on Shakespeare's dramatic use of music.

I have referred in the Introduction and Commentary to one or two other productions besides Granville Barker's. I have profited, I hope, from documentation given me by his First Fairy, now Mrs Margaret Greenwood, of Ditchling, Sussex; and from talk with her and with a recent First Fairy, Miss Genevieve Allenbury, an observant and thoughtful actress, who told me also of the thought which had gone into the playing of Puck in the same 1975 production.[1] I have tried never to lose sight of performance as the end for which Shakespeare designed the piece (a first performance, I think probable, in the great hall of a mansion, with foreseen revival in the public theatre). I have not, however, included a stage history, though to do so has been a frequent (but not invariable) Arden practice. The space saved has helped to make possible an extensive treatment of the sources and antecedents of the *Dream*. In view of their number and variety, that seemed to have the prior claim. I regret not citing and placing in context Hazlitt's disappointment with the attempt to realize on stage the magical charm of the play,[2] and Pepys's notorious dismissal (29 September 1662):

1. In Regent's Park: cf. below, p. 110, n. 3.
2. *Characters of Shakespeare's Plays*, World's Classics edn, p. 108. But he appreciated the play as drama, nevertheless; cf. his protest in *The Examiner*, 21 January 1816: 'Shakespeare knew his job better as a playwright than to deserve such alteration' as the *Dream* had just received (and, one may add, has sometimes received since).

to the Kings Theatre, where we saw *Midsummer nights dreame*, which I have never seen before, nor shall ever again, for it is the most insipid ridiculous play that ever I saw in my life. I saw, I confess, some good dancing and some handsome women, which was all my pleasure.[1]

Any notion, however, that the *Dream* must fall short, for an audience, of what it offers the reader, has been refuted not too infrequently since Granville Barker's production. The stage history is not really difficult to assemble, and hence will be the less missed here.[2]

This apart, the present edition conforms to the Arden conventions, for example those governing modernization and the treatment of speech-heads and stage directions. They are by this time familiar: if a guide to them is wanted, the Introduction to the Arden *1 Henry IV*, with some allowance for differences between the two plays, will supply it.[3] It may be well, however, to specify the criteria for the inclusion of variant readings in the textual apparatus. The first Quarto being the copy-text, all departures from it are noted, and are easy to pick out because '*Q1*' is not then the symbol which follows the lemma-bracket. Such a notation as 'villagery] *Q1* (Villageree), *Hanmer*;' means that the authority for our reading is Q1, though it has the word in the form 'Villageree', Hanmer being the first to have it in ours. The First and Second

1. *Diary*, ed. R. C. Latham and W. Matthews, III. 208.
2. See *The London Stage . . . 1660–1800*, ed. Avery, Hogan, Beecher, *et al.*, 1960–5; C. B. Hogan, *Shakespeare in the Theatre, 1701–1800*, 1952, 57; G. C. D. Odell, *Shakespeare – from Betterton to Irving*, 1920; A. C. Sprague, *Shakespearian Players and Performances*, 1954; Harold Child, 'The Stage-History of *A Midsummer Night's Dream*' (to 1935), in the New Cambridge Shakespeare edn; Charles H. Shattuck on 'Stage History' in *The Riverside Shakespeare*, ed. G. Blakemore Evans; M. St Clare Byrne, 'Fifty Years of Shakespearian Production: 1898–1948', *Shakespeare Survey* 2, 1949; 'Shakespeare Productions in the United Kingdom', annually, 1950– , id. from Vol. 4 onward (except Vol. 17, 1964). For the whole context, see the references in Michael Jamieson, 'Shakespeare in the Theatre', *Shakespeare: Select Bibliographical Guides*, ed. S. Wells, 1973. Bernard Shaw reviewed Daly's 1895 production (*Our Theatres in the Nineties*, I, 178–84). For Barker's, 1914, see his own preface to the acting edition; the Savoy Theatre booklet, with an essay by Lawrence Housman and fourteen illustrations; and contemporary reviews (February), from the appreciative *Sunday Times* to the offended and carping *Globe*. Opposed views of Peter Brook's production, 1970, were put forward by Peter Thomson and J. R. Brown (with the second of whom I agree) in *Shakespeare Survey* 24, 1971. W. Moelwyn Merchant, in '*A Midsummer Night's Dream*: A Visual Re-creation' (*Early Shakespeare*, ed. Brown and Harris, 1961), studies stage settings, paintings, and engravings from 1692 (Purcell's *Fairy Queen*) to 1960 (Britten's opera), making them throw light on each other and on interpretations of the play.
3. Pp. lxxvi–lxxviii.

Quartos (1600, 1619) and the First Folio (1623) are collated in full, except that variant punctuation is recorded only if it affects the sense, and variant capitals and spelling only if they bear on a disputed reading. With the same proviso, mechanical errors about which there can be no doubt, such as wrong letters yielding no conceivably acceptable word, are ignored: the exception is illustrated by F's 'dxile' at III. ii. 386, which lends support to the emendation 'exil'd'. From editions subsequent to the First Folio, variants are cited selectively. Besides those adopted in our text, readings are given when they may be thought to merit consideration. Rarely, even when they do not, they may still be recorded if (because of the vogue they have had) not to notice them would occasion surprise. For each variant in these categories, only the edition which first introduced it is given; if the change had been previously suggested, the conjecture is given too.

The modern editor of a Shakespeare play is bound to have been anticipated in his observations more often than he is aware. When I am conscious of saying what has been said before, I have done my best to make due acknowledgements. By no means all of them are of actual debts. It has not been practicable to distinguish from debts the not infrequent instances where I had first formed my view (perhaps when teaching the play), and then been encouraged by finding in print, prior to this edition, a view like my own. But very many of my references are to scholars and critics for whose guidance or suggestions I am warmly grateful.

The present edition is not in any way based on the old Arden: I have sometimes drawn, however (with acknowledgement), upon Cuningham's annotations there. For the clearing of textual and interpretative difficulties I am of course repeatedly indebted to the eighteenth- and nineteenth-century editors, to whose labours the Furness Variorum (1895) – used with discretion – is a valuable guide. Among subsequent editions, I have had most help from those by G. L. Kittredge, Peter Alexander, and Stanley Wells (in the New Penguin series); with the New Cambridge Shakespeare edition (1924), still of use despite hypotheses of Dover Wilson's which I have brought evidence and argument to refute.

I owe most of all to the published work of Granville Barker, E. K. Chambers, W. W. Greg, M. W. Tilley, Geoffrey Bullough, Kenneth Muir, Nevill Coghill, C. L. Barber, Katharine M. Briggs, Muriel C. Bradbrook, and G. K. Hunter. In Alexander Leggatt's chapter, and in articles by Ernest Schanzer, R. W. Dent, and J. L. Calderwood, I have been delighted to meet with interpretations, expressed often with particular felicity, which strengthen me in my own. I have found much to agree with in D. P. Young's full-length book on the play, while in Stephen Fender's short one I alternate between agreement and dissent.

I have had the advantage of conversation or correspondence with Mr David Jenkins, Librarian of the National Library of Wales, Dr Frances Yates, Dr Katharine Briggs, Dr William Urry, Dr Stanley Wells, Dr Gerald Cockshott, Professors Marvin Spevack, Kenneth Muir, W. A. Armstrong, J. C. Maxwell, W. J. N. Rudd, and C. L. Barber (of the University of Leeds), and particularly with Professor Henning Krabbe, and with Professor Anthony Hammond who examined for me the disputed date on the original MS. of *John a Kent*. I am glad of this opportunity to thank them, and also the staffs of the Birkbeck College and University of London Libraries, and of the British Library. Once again an Arden edition has had the benefit of Mrs Magdalen Pearce's expert copy-editing; and I am also much indebted to Mrs Esther West for typing the copy.

Dr Agnes Latham read the edition in page proof: for her help and that of my fellow General Editors, Brian Morris and Harold Jenkins, I am most grateful. What I owe to Harold Jenkins is beyond all acknowledgement. That he has brought to the edition all his accustomed care in everything one might hope from a General Editor goes almost without saying. But in addition he has discussed with his unfailing clarity and balanced judgement all difficulties – not few – on which I have asked his advice. Occasionally, but with hesitation, I have rejected it. I am, of course, responsible for all blemishes which remain.

Birkbeck College, University of London   HAROLD F. BROOKS
March 1979

ACKNOWLEDGEMENTS

The author and publishers would like to thank the Centaur Press and acknowledge consultation of *Shakespeare's Ovid: being Arthur Golding's Translation of the Metamorphoses*, ed. W. H. D. Rouse (1961); William Heinemann Ltd: the Loeb Classical Texts, for permission to include selections from F. J. Miller's translations from Seneca (1917); and Constable & Co. Ltd for selections from *Seneca His Tenne Tragedies*, Tudor Translation Series, ed. Charles Whibley (1927).

ABBREVIATIONS AND REFERENCES

The abbreviated titles of Shakespeare's works are those in C. T. Onions, *A Shakespeare Glossary*, 2nd edn, 1919. Passages quoted or cited are from the volumes of the new Arden Shakespeare or, where the relevant volume is still to come, from the complete Tudor Shakespeare, ed. Peter Alexander (Collins, 1951).

Throughout, this edition gives in the Introduction the Latin of Senecan passages; Elizabethan and modern translations in Appendix I.

I. EDITIONS

Q1	*A Midsommer nights dreame . . . Written by William Shakespeare . . .* Imprinted for Thomas Fisher . . . 1600 [First Quarto].
Q2	*A Midsommer nights dreame . . . Written by William Shakespeare . . .* Printed by Iames Roberts 1600 [really by William Iaggard, 1619] [Second Quarto].
F	*Mr. William Shakespeares Comedies, Histories, & Tragedies,* 1623 [First Folio].
F2	*Mr. William Shakespeares Comedies, Histories & Tragedies,* 1632 [Second Folio].
F3	*Mr. William Shakespear's Comedies, Histories, and Tragedies . . . The third Impression,* 1664 [Third Folio].
F4	*Mr. William Shakespear's Comedies, Histories, and Tragedies . . . The fourth Edition,* 1685 [Fourth Folio].
Rowe	*The Works of Mr. William Shakespear . . . Revis'd and Corrected By N. Rowe Esq.,* 1709 [Rowe², a 2nd edn, 1709].
Rowe³	*The Works of Mr. William Shakespear . . . Revis'd and Corrected by N. Rowe Esq.,* 1714.
Pope	*The Works of Shakespear . . . Collected and Corrected . . . by Mr. Pope,* 1723.
Theobald	*The Works of Shakespeare . . . Collated with the Oldest Copies, and Corrected; with Notes . . . By Mr. Theobald,* 1733.
Theobald²	*The Works of Shakespeare . . . Collated . . . and Corrected: With Notes . . . By Mr. Theobald. The Second Edition,* 1740.
Hanmer	*The Works of Shakespear . . . Carefully Revised and Corrected by the former Editions.* [ed. Thomas Hanmer] Oxford, 1744.
Warburton	*The Works of Shakespear. The Genuine Text . . . settled . . . By Mr. Pope and Mr. Warburton,* 1747.
Johnson	*The Plays of William Shakespeare . . . To which are added Notes by Sam. Johnson,* 1765.

Capell	*Mr. William Shakespeare his Comedies, Histories, and Tragedies* [ed. Edward Capell, 1768].
Steevens	*The Plays of William Shakespeare . . . To which are added notes by Samuel Johnson and George Steevens,* 1773 [Variorum '73].
Var. '78	*The Plays of William Shakespeare . . . The Second Edition, Revised and Augmented,* 1778 [Steevens²].
Rann	*The Dramatic Works of Shakespeare . . . with notes by Joseph Rann.* Oxford, 1787.
Malone	*The Plays and Poems of William Shakespeare . . . with . . . notes by Edmond Malone,* 1790.
Var. '93	*The Plays of William Shakespeare . . . The Fourth Edition.* 1793 [Steevens³].
Var. '03	*The Plays of William Shakespeare . . . The Fifth Edition. Revised and augmented by Isaac Reed,* 1803.
Var. '13	*The Plays of William Shakespeare . . . Revised and augmented by Isaac Reed. . . . The Sixth Edition,* 1813.
Var. '21	*The Plays and Poems of William Shakespeare . . .* [*with*] *a life of the poet . . . by the late E. Malone . . .* [*ed. J. Boswell*] 1821 ['Boswell's Malone'].
Harness	*The Dramatic Works of William Shakespeare; with notes . . . By the Rev. William Harness,* 1825.
Singer	*The Dramatic Works of William Shakespeare with Notes . . . by Samuel Weller Singer,* 1826.
Knight	*The Pictorial Edition of the Works of Shakspere. Edited by Charles Knight. Vol. 1, Comedies,* [1839].
Collier	*The Works of William Shakespeare . . . with the various readings,* [*and*] *notes . . . by J. Payne Collier, Vols 2 and 9,* 1842.
Collier²	*The Plays of Shakespeare: The text regulated by the old copies, and by the recently discovered Folio of 1632, containing early manuscript emendations. Edited by J. Payne Collier,* 1853.
Halliwell	*The Complete Works of Shakspere revised . . . by J. O. Halliwell. Comedies.* London and New York, Vol. 1, [1852].
Halliwell²	*The Works of William Shakspere . . . from a New Collation of the Early Editions . . . by James O. Halliwell, Vol. 5,* 1856.
Singer²	*The Dramatic Works of William Shakespeare . . . revised by Samuel Weller Singer, Vol. 4,* 1856.
Dyce	*The Works of William Shakespeare. The Text revised by the Rev. Alexander Dyce, Vol. 2,* 1857.
Grant White	*The Works of William Shakespeare . . . edited by Richard Grant White.* Boston, 1857.
Collier³	*Shakespeare's Comedies, Histories, Tragedies, and poems. Edited by J. Payne Collier, Vol. 2,* 1858.
Staunton	*The Plays of Shakespeare. Edited by Howard Staunton, Vol. 1,* 1858.
Delius	*Shakspere's Werke. Herausgegeben und erklärt von N. Delius, Vol. 5, Elberfeld (the Dream, 1859),* 1858.
Camb.	*The Works of William Shakespeare. Edited by William George Clark and John Glover* [Vols. 2–9 edited by W. G.

	Clark and W. Aldis Wright]. The Cambridge Shakespeare, Cambridge and London, Vol. 2, 1863–6.
Dyce²	*The Works of William Shakespeare . . . Second Edition*, 1863–7
Globe	*The Works of William Shakespeare. Edited by W. G. Clark and W. Aldis Wright*. Cambridge and London, 1864.
Keightley	*The Plays of William Shakespeare. Carefully edited by Thomas Keightley*, 1864.
Rolfe	*A Midsummer Night's Dream . . . edited . . . W. J. Rolfe*, 1877.
Wright, W. Aldis	*A Midsummer Night's Dream, edited by W. A. Wright* (Clarendon Press), 1877.
Hudson	*The Complete Works of William Shakespeare . . . edited by the Rev. Henry Hudson*, Boston, Vol. 3, 1881.
Grant White²	*Mr. William Shakespeare's Comedies, Histories, Tragedies and Poems. The text newly edited . . . by Richard Grant White. I. Comedies*, 1883.
Deighton	*A Midsummer Night's Dream, with notes by K. Deighton*, 1891.
Verity	*A Midsummer Night's Dream, ed. A. W. Verity* (Pitt Press), 1893.
Furness	*A Midsummer Nights Dream Edited by Horace Howard Furness* (A New Variorum Edition of Shakespeare), 1895.
Chambers, E. K.	*A Midsummer Night's Dream, edited by E. K. Chambers* (Warwick Shakespeare), 1897.
Cuningham	*A Midsummer-Night's Dream Edited by Henry Cuningham* (Arden Shakespeare) 1905; (with some revisions) 1930.
Durham	*Midsummer Night's Dream, edited by W. H. Durham* (The Yale Shakespeare), 1918.
N.C.S.	*A Midsummer-Night's Dream [edited by] Sir Arthur Quiller-Couch and John Dover Wilson*. (New Cambridge Shakespeare) 1924; (with some revision) 1968.
Kittredge	*A Midsummer Night's Dream, edited by G. L. Kittredge*, 1939.
Alexander	*William Shakespeare. The Complete Works . . . edited . . . by Peter Alexander*, 1951.
Sisson	*William Shakespeare. The Complete Works . . . Edited by Charles Jasper Sisson*, [1954].
Munro	*The London Shakespeare . . . edited by . . . John Munro*, Vol. 1, 1958.
Clemen	*A Midsummer Night's Dream Edited by Wolfgang [H.] Clemen* (Signet Classic Shakespeare), 1963.
Wells	*A Midsummer Night's Dream Edited by Stanley Wells* (New Penguin Shakespeare), 1967.
Wright, M.	*A Midsummer Night's Dream Edited from the Quarto of 1600 by Martin Wright* (Shakespeare Workshop: old-spelling edn), 1968.
Riverside	*The Riverside Shakespeare* (textual editor, G. Blakemore Evans), 1974.

2. TEXTUAL COMMENTARIES

Thirlby   [Styan Thirlby, conjectures adopted by Theobald, 1733;
                     others published in J. Nichols, *Literary Illustrations of
                     the Eighteenth Century*, 1817.]
Tyrwhitt   [Thomas Tyrwhitt] *Observations and Conjectures upon some
                     Passages of Shakespeare*, Oxford, 1766.
Walker   W. S. Walker, *A Critical Examination of the Text of
                     Shakespeare* [ed. W. N. Lettsom), 1860.
Daniel   P. A. Daniel, *Notes and Conjectural Emendations of certain
                     Doubtful Passages in Shakespeare's Plays*, 1870.
Kinnear   B. G. Kinnear, *Cruces Shakespearianae*, 1883.
Sisson²   C. J. Sisson, *New Readings in Shakespeare*, Cambridge,
                     1956.

3. OTHER WORKS

Abbott   E. A. Abbott, *A Shakespearian Grammar*, 1901 (1869).
Alexander   Peter Alexander, *Shakespeare's Life and Art*, 1939.
Apuleius   *The Golden Asse, conteininge the Metamorphosie of Lucius
                     Apuleius*, tr. Wm. Adlington, 1566.
Barber   C. L. Barber, *Shakespeare's Festive Comedy*, 1959.
Barker   H. Granville Barker, *Prefaces to Shakespeare*, Vol. VI, ed.
                     Edward M. Moore, 1974.
Borinski   Ludwig Borinski, 'Shakespeares Comic Prose', *Sh.S.* 8,
                     1955.
Bradbrook.   Muriel C. Bradbrook, *The Growth and Structure of
 Elizabethan Comedy   Elizabethan Comedy*, 1955.
Bradbrook,   Muriel C. Bradbrook, *Shakespeare and Elizabethan Poetry*,
 Shakespeare   1951.
Briggs, *Dictionary*   Katharine M. Briggs, *Dictionary of British Folk Tales*,
                     Part B., 1971.
Briggs, *Fairies*   Katharine M. Briggs, *Fairies in Tradition and Literature*,
                     1967.
Briggs, *Puck*   Katharine M. Briggs, *The Anatomy of Puck*, 1959.
Brooke   Stopford A. Brooke, *On Ten Plays of Shakespeare*, 1930
                     (1905).
Brown   John Russell Brown, *Shakespeare and his Comedies*, 1957.
Bullough   Geoffrey Bullough (ed.), *Narrative and Dramatic Sources of
                     Shakespeare*, Vol. I, 1957.
Byrne   Muriel St. Clare Byrne, *Elizabethan Life in Town and
                     Country* (revised edn), 1961.
Calderwood   J. L. Calderwood, '*A Midsummer Night's Dream*: The
                     Illusion of Drama', *MLQ*, 1965.
Chambers,   E. K. Chambers, *The Elizabethan Stage*, 1923.
 Elizabethan Stage
Chambers, *Gleanings*   E. K. Chambers, *Shakespearean Gleanings*, 1946.
Chambers,   E. K. Chambers, *William Shakespeare: A Study of Facts
 Shakespeare   and Problems*, 1930.
Chaucer   Geoffrey Chaucer, *Works*, ed. F. N. Robinson (2nd edn,
                     revised), 1957.
Chaucer   Geoffrey Chaucer, *The Knight's Tale* from *Woorkes*, ed.
 (Appendix I)   Thynne and Stow, 1561.

Clemen	Wolfgang H. Clemen, introduction to *MND*, Signet edn, 1963.
Coghill	Nevill Coghill, *Shakespeare's Professional Skills*, 1964.
Coghill[2]	Nevill Coghill, 'Shakespeare's Reading in Chaucer', *Elizabethan and Jacobean Studies presented to [F.P.] Wilson*, ed. H. Davis and Helen Gardner, 1959.
Craik	T. W. Craik, *The Tudor Interlude*, 1967.
Crane	Milton Crane, *Shakespeare's Prose*, 1951.
Dent	R. W. Dent, 'Imagination in *A Midsummer Night's Dream*', *Sh.Q.*, 1964.
Doran	Madeleine Doran, *Shakespeare's Dramatic Language*, 1976.
Dover Wilson	J. Dover Wilson, *Shakespeare's Happy Comedies*, 1962.
Early Shakespeare	J. R. Brown and Bernard Harris (eds), *Early Shakespeare* (Stratford-upon-Avon Studies 3), 1961, 1967 (revised).
E.E.T.S., e.s., o.s.	*Early English Text Society*, extra series, ordinary series.
Evans	Bertrand Evans, *Shakespeare's Comedies*, 1960.
Fender	Stephen Fender, *Shakespeare: A Midsummer Night's Dream*, 1968.
Golding	*Shakespeare's Ovid: being Arthur Golding's Translation of the Metamorphoses*, ed. W. H. D. Rouse, 1961.
Golding (Appendix I)	Arthur Golding, *The XV Bookes of P. Ouidius Naso, entytuled Metamorphosis*, translated, 1567.
Gorgious Gallery	*A Gorgious Gallery of Gallant Inventions*, 1578.
Gouernour	Sir Thomas Elyot, *The Boke of the Gouernour* (1531), ed. Foster Watson (Everyman), 1907.
Greg	W. W. Greg, *The Shakespeare First Folio*, 1955.
Greg, *Documents*	W. W. Greg, *Dramatic Documents from the Elizabethan Playhouses*, 1931.
Gwynn Jones	T. Gwynn Jones, *Welsh Lore and Folk Custom*, 1930.
Hart	Alfred Hart, *Shakespeare and the Homilies*, 1934.
Hemingway	S. B. Hemingway, 'The Relation of *A Midsummer Night's Dream* to *Romeo and Juliet*', *MLN*, 1911.
Henslowe	Philip Henslowe, *Diary*, ed. W. W. Greg, 1904–8.
Henslowe[2]	Philip Henslowe, *Diary*, ed. R. A. Foakes and R. T. Rickert, 1961.
Hinman	Charlton Hinman, *The Printing and Proof-Reading of the First Folio of Shakespeare*, 1963.
Hughes	Felicity A. Hughes, 'Psychological Allegory in *The Faerie Queene* III. xi. xii', *RES*, May 1978.
Hulme	Hilda M. Hulme, *Explorations in Shakespeare's Language*, 1962.
Hunter	G. K. Hunter, *John Lyly: The Humanist as Courtier*, 1962.
Hunter, Joseph	*New Illustrations of the Life, Studies and Writings of Shakespeare*, 1845.
Huon	*Huon of Burdeux*, tr. Lord Berners, ed. S. L. Lee, E.E.T.S., e.s., xl, 1882.
Kennedy	Judith M. Kennedy (ed.), *B. Yong's Translation of George de Montemayor's 'Diana' and Gil Polo's 'Enamoured Diana'*, 1968.
Kermode	Frank Kermode, 'The Mature Comedies', *Early Shakespeare*, 1967 (1961).
Kökeritz	Helge Kökeritz, *Shakespeare's Pronunciation*, 1953.

Latham	M. W. Latham, *The Elizabethan Fairies*, 1930.
Leggatt	Alexander Leggatt, *Shakespeare's Comedy of Love*, 1974.
Long	John H. Long, *Shakespeare's Use of Music: The Comedies*, 1955.
Lyly	John Lyly, *Works*, ed. R. Warwick Bond, 1902.
McManaway	J. G. McManaway, 'Recent Studies in Shakespeare Chronology', *Sh.S.* 3, 1950.
Madden	D. H. Madden, *The Diary of Master William Silence*, 1907.
Marlowe	Christopher Marlowe, 'Hero and Leander'; *Works*, ed. C. F. Tucker Brooke, 1910 (1946).
Mirror	*The Mirror for Magistrates*, ed. Lily B. Campbell, 1938.
Mirror, *Parts Added*	*Parts Added to The Mirror for Magistrates*, ed. Lily B. Campbell, 1946.
Montemayor	Jorge de Montemayor, *Diana* (revised 1561), tr. B. Yong, 1598: see Kennedy.
Mouffet	Thomas Mouffet, *Of the Silkewormes, and their Flies*, 1599.
M.S.R.	Malone Society Reprint.
Muir[1]	Kenneth Muir, *Shakespeare's Sources: Comedies and Tragedies*, 1957.
Muir[2]	Kenneth Muir, *The Sources of Shakespeare's Plays*, 1977.
Munday	Anthony Munday, *John a Kent and John a Cumber*, M.S.R.
Nashe	Thomas Nashe, *Works*, ed. R. B. McKerrow, revised F. P. Wilson, 1966.
N.C.S.	New Cambridge Shakespeare, ed. A. T. Quiller Couch and J. Dover Wilson, etc.
Nemerov	Howard Nemerov, 'The Marriage of Theseus and Hippolyta', *Kenyon Review*, 1956.
New Companion	K. Muir and S. Schoenbaum (eds), *A New Companion to Shakespeare Studies*, 1971.
Nichol	J. Nichol, *The Progresses and Public Processions of Queen Elizabeth*, 1788.
Noble	Richmond Noble, *Shakespeare's Biblical Knowledge*, 1935
Noble, *Song*	Richmond Noble, *Shakespeare's Use of Song*, 1923.
North	Sir Thomas North, *The Lives of the Noble Grecians and Romans, compared together by . . . Plutarke . . . translated . . . into French by James Amyot, and . . . into English by Thomas North*, 1595 (1579).
OED	*Oxford English Dictionary*.
Olson	Paul A. Olson, 'A Midsummer Night's Dream and the Meaning of Court Marriage' *ELH*, 1957.
Onions	C. T. Onions, *A Shakespeare Glossary* (2nd edn, revised), 1919.
Pettie	George Pettie, *The Petite Pallace of Pettie his Pleasure*, 1576.
Polo	Gil Polo, *Diana Enamorada* (1564), tr. B. Yong 1598; see Kennedy.
Puttenham	George Puttenham, *The Arte of English Poesie*, ed. G. Willcock and A. Walker, 1936.
Reed	Robert R. Reed, 'Nick Bottom, Dr. Faustus, and the Ass's Head', *N. & Q.*, 1959.
Rhys	John Rhys, *Celtic Folklore, Welsh and Manx*, 1901.

Robinson, Clement (etc.)	*A Handeful of Pleasant Delites*, 1584.
Robinson, J. W.	J. W. Robinson, 'Palpable Hot Ice: Dramatic Burlesque in *A Midsummer Night's Dream*', *S.Ph.*, 1964.
Salingar	Leo Salingar, *Shakespeare and the Traditions of Comedy*, 1974.
Schanzer	Ernst Schanzer, 'The Moon and the Fairies in *A Midsummer Night's Dream*', *UTQ*, 1955.
Schmidt	Alexander Schmidt, *Shakespeare Lexicon* (revised G. Sarrazin), 1923.
Scot, *Witchcraft*	Reginald Scot, *The discoverie of witchcraft*, 1584 (and cf. id. ed. Brinsley Nicholson, 1886, repr. 1973).
Scragg	Leah Scragg, 'Shakespeare, Lyly, and Ovid: The Influence of "Gallathea" on "A Midsummer Night's Dream" ', *Sh.S.*, 30, 1977.
Seneca	*Seneca's Tragedies* (with tr. by F. J. Miller), Loeb Classical Library, 1917.
Seneca, ed. Newton	Thomas Newton (ed.) *Seneca His Tenne Tragedies* (1581), Tudor Translations Series, 1927.
Seng	Peter J. Seng, *Vocal Songs in the Plays of Shakespeare*, 1967.
Shakespeare's England	*Shakespeare's England. An Account of the Life and Manners of his Age*, ed. Sidney Lee and C. T. Onions, 1916.
Sidney	Sir Philip Sidney, *The Countess of Pembroke's Arcadia* (1590), ed. Albert Feuillerat, 1922.
Siegel	Paul N. Siegel, '*A Midsummer Night's Dream* and the Wedding Guests', *Sh.Q.*, 1953.
Spenser	Edmund Spenser, *The Shepheardes Calender* (1579), ed. W. L. Renwick, 1931.
Spenser[2]	Edmund Spenser, *Works*, ed. R. Morris (Globe), 1869 (1929).
Spurgeon	Caroline Spurgeon, *Shakespeare's Imagery and what it tells us*, 1935.
S.R.	Stationers' Register.
Thompson	Ann Thompson, *Shakespeare's Chaucer*, 1978.
Thomson, J.	J. Thomson, 'A new Sonet of Pyramus and Thisbie', see Robinson, Clement.
Tilley	M. P. Tilley, *A Dictionary of the Proverbs in England in the Sixteenth and Seventeenth Centuries*, 1950.
Turner	Robert K. Turner, Jnr, 'Printing Methods and Textual Problems in *A Midsummer Night's Dream* Q1', *S.B.*, 1962.
Vickers	Brian Vickers, *The Artistry of Shakespeare's Prose*, 1968.
Welsford	Enid Welsford, *The Court Masque*, 1927.
Wilson	See Dover Wilson; see N.C.S.
Wilson, F. P.	F. P. Wilson, *Shakespearian and other Studies*, ed. Helen Gardner, 1969.
Wilson Knight	G. Wilson Knight, *The Shakespearian Tempest*, 1932 (1953).
Wright, M.	Martin Wright, *Notes on A Midsummer Night's Dream* (Shakespeare Workshop), 1968.
Young	David P. Young, *Something of Great Constancy, The Art of A Midsummer Night's Dream*, 1966.

4. PERIODICALS

E. & S.	*Essays and Studies.*
ELH	*ELH: English Literary History.*
JEGP	*Journal of English and Germanic Philology.*
MLN	*Modern Language Notes.*
MLQ	*Modern Language Quarterly.*
MLR	*Modern Language Review.*
N. & Q.	*Notes & Queries.*
Ph.Q.	*Philological Quarterly.*
RES	*Review of English Studies.*
S.B.	*Studies in Bibliography.*
Sh.Q.	*Shakespeare Quarterly.*
Sh.S.	*Shakespeare Survey.*
S.Ph.	*Studies in Philology.*
UTQ	*University of Toronto Quarterly.*

INTRODUCTION
I.

The first edition of *A Midsummer Night's Dream* was published in 1600 by Thomas Fisher, in whose name the play was entered, shortly before, in the Stationers' Register:

> 8 Octobris [1600]
> Thomas Fyssher./Entred for his copie vnder the handes of Master Rodes/and the Wardens A booke called A mydsommer nightes Dreame. vj^d.

Since this First Quarto (Q1), besides being registered in the regular way, contains a good text, it is reasonable to suppose that the publication was authorized by Shakespeare's company. The title-page reads:

> A/Midsommer nights/dreame./As it hath been sundry times pub-/*lickely acted, by the Right honoura-*/ble, the Lord Chamberlaine his/ seruants./Written by William Shakespeare./[Fisher's device, McKerrow 321]
> Imprinted at London, for *Thomas Fisher*, and are to/be soulde at his shoppe, at the Signe of the White Hart,/in *Fleete streete*. 1600.

A Second Quarto (Q2) purported to be 'Printed by Iames Roberts, 1600', but was actually printed in 1619 by William Jaggard,[1] subsequently the printer, and joint publisher with Edward Blount, of the first collected edition of Shakespeare's plays, the First Folio (F), in 1623. Shakespeare having died in 1616, two of his leading fellow-actors, Heminge and Condell, were responsible for the collection,[2] printed in part from, or with the aid of, playhouse texts which they made available, and in part from Quartos of single plays, already published. The First

---

1. The false-dated Pavier Quartos of 1619 are described by Sir Walter Greg. *The Shakespeare First Folio* (1955), pp. 9–17; p. 11, n. 3 summarizes the research, by A. W. Pollard, W. Neidig, and Greg himself, which established the facts.

2. On their responsibility and its limits, see Greg, pp. 3, 17, 77 f. Other references to him in this section are to the same volume.

Folio text of the *Dream* derives, as we shall see, from both these sorts of material.[1]

The First Quarto is of the very highest textual authority, since it bears many marks of having been printed from the author's 'foul papers': that is, his autograph draft (in this instance evidently in its final state; simply not a fair copy). Certainly it was not printed from the prompt-book which would be transcribed from the autograph.

The stage-directions of the Q1 text would not have been satisfactory for regulating performance—the function of a prompt-book. The Q1 exits are some twenty short of those an editor finds essential. It is true that even in texts evidently printed from prompt-books, not all exits are marked: some are overlooked, for example, in the Folio *As You Like It*. 'An actor', Agnes Latham observes, 'can be trusted to get himself off the stage when he is no longer required'; so 'Exits do not concern the prompter in the same way as entrances'.[2] The prompter would have been ill-served, however, in the *Dream*, without exits for Philostrate at I. i. 15; Oberon at II. ii. 33 and III. ii. 395; and Pyramus and Thisbe at V. i. 202; and the brief reappearances of Snout and Quince at III. i. 108, 112 would hardly be quite clear without Snout's exit (112). Nor is it only exits that are wanting. There is no entry for Lysander at III. ii. 412, where again there is complexity of exits and reappearances: none for Philostrate at V. i. 105, or Thisbe at V. i. 310; and no indication that when Theseus, Hippolyta and Philostrate enter to begin V. i they have attendants.

Errors and ambiguities attributable to the author, when they are such as would not have survived rehearsal, are a further sign of foul-paper texts. The entrance for Puck, as well as Oberon, at the start of III. ii instead of at l. 3, may be an error of this kind; or it may only mean that, Oberon having preceded him, he comes on at a distance before his master perceives him.[3] There can be no similar explanation for Helena's inclusion in the entry at I. i. 19, when her real point of entry is at l. 179. Evidently this is an error of Shakespeare's, in whose mind the four lovers go together; and so is the aberration in the opening entry of IV. ii, which brings on both Flute and Thisbe, Shakespeare having

---

1. In what follows, I am greatly indebted to Greg on the Q1 and F texts of the *Dream*, pp. 240–7; and though I have examined all the evidence independently, am reassured to find my conclusions so largely the same as his.

2. *AYL*, Arden edn, (1975) p. xv.

3. But F, perhaps with prompt-book authority, does alter the entry to l. 3. See Greg, pp. 241, 245.

temporarily forgotten that they are the same person. There are ambiguities, too, which the bookholder (prompter)[1] would have been obliged to resolve. Unless at III. i. 48 *Sn.* was the compositor's abbreviation of a fuller speech-prefix in the copy, a prompter would have wanted to know whether Snout or Snug was to speak. The generic titles sometimes given to characters in the QI text would not have sufficed him; especially not at the start of IV. ii, where 'and the rabble' does not reveal that only Snout and Starveling come on with Quince and Flute/Thisbe—Snug as well as Bottom joining them later.

Imperfectly specific directions are an acknowledged sign of foul-paper copy, since for performance, and therefore at the prompt-book stage, decisions must have been arrived at.[2] Besides 'and the rabble' (a delightful specimen of author's language) our First Quarto has, in its opening direction, 'with others'. 'Enter the Clownes' to begin III. i, and 'Enter Lovers', v. i. 27,[3] are further instances, though there no uncertainty could result.

Variation in the designations of characters, as with 'Clownes' and 'rabble' denoting in groups persons elsewhere individually named, has been recognized as indicating foul-paper copy ever since McKerrow pointed out how it would inconvenience a prompter, and how naturally it would come to a dramatist, thinking of his stage-people now in this way, now in that.[4] Until at v. i. 107, when 'Pyramus and Thisbe' is about to begin, the speech-prefixes for the ducal pair have been *The.* or *Thes.*, and *Hip.* But 'Let him [sc. the Prologue] approach' is prefixed *Duk.* After four further speeches by *The.* and the first dialogue in which *This.* takes part, Theseus (at l. 204) is again *Duk.*, and Hippolyta (at l. 207) is *Dutch.*; and to their final exit these titles (in one form or another) continue. Did Shakespeare, beginning the Burlesque, foresee possible confusion between *The.* or *Thes.*, and *This.*, revert to his normal prefix while no confusion could arise, and only change again to *Duk.* (and concomitantly to *Dutch.*) when *This.* had started to occur? Bottom (it is safe to assume) was written for Will Kempe, the famous clown of the company, and in IV i. is 'Clowne' at his entry; *Clown.*, *Clow.* or *Clo.* in the speech-prefixes, till he falls asleep; and *Clo.* when he awakes. As Dogberry, Kempe

1. On the bookholder, see Greg, p. 100, n. B.

2. Cf. Greg, pp. 135 f.

3. Presuming the duplication, by adding their names, was not his (Greg, p. 241).

4. 'A Suggestion regarding Shakespeare's Manuscript', *RES* (1935); Greg, pp. 113 f.

was later to be denominated *Andrew* in one prefix (meaning Merry Andrew = Clown), and *Kempe* in the rest of that scene. Oberon is named in an entry only at II. ii. 25; at II. i. 59, III. ii. 0, and v. i. 376 he is 'King . . . of Faeries', and at IV. i. 0, following 'Queene of Faieries', 'the King'. In speech-prefixes, however, he is *Ob.* or some other form of his name, throughout. On her first entry Titania is at once addressed by name: but at II. i. 59, IV. i. 0, and v. i. 376 S.D. she is 'Queene of Fairies'; only at II. ii. 0 is she 'Tytania Queene of Fairies', and there Greg notes the possibility that 'Tytania' was added by the bookholder. In II. i and II. ii her speech-prefixes conform to the entries, and designate her as Queen; but in the later scenes they are once *Tytania* and otherwise an abbreviation of it.

The most striking variations are between 'Puck' and some version of 'Robin Goodfellow'.[1] These can readily be understood as corresponding each to the aspect of the character then uppermost in Shakespeare's mind. In his dialogue with the Fairy, he is being introduced as the Robin Goodfellow of folklore, so he has that name in the entry II. i. 0, and is *Robin* or *Rob.* in the speech-prefixes. Preparatory to instructing him about the love-juice, Oberon summons him as 'my gentle Puck' (II. i. 148), and to the end of the scene he is *Puck* in the speech-prefixes. He continues so in his next entry and speech at II. ii. 64 f., where he is acting on those instructions; his role as Oberon's minister is plain in his exit-line:

> For I must now to Oberon.

When in III. i he intervenes in the clowns' rehearsal, claps the ass-head on Bottom, and describes the dance he will lead the rest, he is acting on his own initiative, in the vein of Robin, performing two of the pranks, shape-shifting and pixie-leading, ascribed to him in the dialogue with the Fairy. Naturally, as there, he is 'Robin' in his entry (III. i. 72), and the same in abbreviated forms in the speech-prefixes at ll. 73, 84 and 101. He is still 'Robin Goodfellow' when at the start of the next scene

---

1. See below, p. xl. 'We do not need to follow Fleay in the belief that they indicate different periods of composition rather than the habitual inconsistency of the author.' Dover Wilson *did* follow him, and on other plays argued similarly from similar evidence; but 'such an explanation is obviously inapplicable, for instance, in the case of *Romeo and Juliet*, whereas McKerrow's theory covers all cases' (Greg, pp. 241, 114, n. 1. I do not, however, find that 'in the text and in the prefixes of a single scene (III. ii)' 'the names are used *indifferently*'. Cf. p. 241; italics mine).

the stage-direction combines his entrance with Oberon's: but when he reports (III. ii. 6, 38)

My mistress with a monster is in love

and his anointing an Athenian's eyes—sequels which conclude, he supposes, the events anticipated by Oberon and himself in II. i—he speaks once more as Puck, as he did there. He does so still in his comment (III. ii. 42) on the entry of Demetrius and Hermia, which begins the recognition of his mistake. On Oberon's scolding him for it, however, he replies (rather surprisingly) as Robin (ll. 92, 100), possibly because his role as mischief-maker is in question. In the dialogue preparatory to the fog scene, once more the concern is with Oberon's instructions, and he (III. ii. 347, 378) is 'Puck'. In the fog scene itself (ll. 402, 403, 407, 412, 420 S.D., 425, 437, 448), though he is carrying out the new instructions, it is by Robin Goodfellow's trick of pixie-leading, to the accompaniment (l. 421) of his traditional 'Ho, ho, ho!'; and accordingly he is Robin. Finally when 'sent . . . before' at v. i. 356 on his mission as Oberon's and the fairies' harbinger, he enters and speaks as 'Puck'; but he addresses the audience in the Epilogue in the folk-lore character familiar to them: the epilogue-prefix is *Robin*, and the last line promises:

Robin shall restore amends.

Yet in the course of his address he has called himself 'the Puck' and 'an honest Puck' (l. 417). By this time, no doubt, both appellations, 'Robin' and 'Puck', were always present in Shakespeare's mind.

With the foregoing explanation of how they came to alternate in the Q1 text—an explanation on the straightforward lines of McKerrow's general interpretation of such evidence—theories attributing them to heterogeneous copy, and composition at different periods, fall to the ground.

From the foul papers, it is evident, a number of Shakespeare's spellings reached Q1. That they are his, we can be virtually certain when they can be paralleled from the pages contributed by 'Hand D' to *Sir Thomas More*, confidently believed to be in his autograph,[1] and when at the same time they can be contrasted in Q1 with other spellings of the same words, which we may

---

1. See *Shakespeare's Hand in 'Sir Thomas More'*, ed. A. W. Pollard; especially, for the spellings, VII, Greg's 'Special Transcript of the Three Pages', and IV with appendix, J. Dover Wilson, 'Bibliographical Links between the Three Pages and the Good Quartos'.

suppose to be the compositor's.[1] By these criteria, Shakespeare was responsible for 'heare', found twice as against 'here' (37 times) and 'heere' (12); 'fower', 'scowle' (cf. 'hower(s)' and 'scrowle', not in Hand D, and the second word not elsewhere in Q1), and 'howe' (for 'ho'); and likewise 'waigh'. Against the otherwise invariable 'doe' in Q1, 'dooe' occurs once, and once 'foredoone'; Hand D has 'doon'. It bears witness to Shakespeare's fondness for 'oo'; its 'afoord' suggests that in Q1 'hoord' and 'boord' are Shakespearean, though Q1 has no alternative spellings to contrast with them. Q1's 'approue' and 'remou'd' do contrast with the no doubt Shakespearean 'prooue', 'prooud' and 'mooue'. So do its 'mourne', 'would', 'should' with Hand D's 'moorne', 'woold', and 'shoold'; and that contrast, though these Hand D spellings do not occur in Q1, strengthens the presumption that 'hoord', 'boord', 'prooue', 'prooud', and 'mooue', and 'shooes' too, are Shakespeare's. His also, we may assume, are 'cowardize', 'practiz'd' and 'mouzd', comparable with 'prentizes' in Hand D, and distinct from 'marchandise', 'enterprise', 'mispris'd', 'reremice', and 'mouse' elsewhere in Q1. At II. i. 55 (see n.) the form 'loffe' is clearly adopted by Shakespeare for a particular (local) effect: 'coffe' (l. 54) is probably his also. To the fifteen Shakespearean spellings so far listed, Dover Wilson in N.C.S. would add, with some support from other Good Quartos, 'of' (for 'off'), 'warnd' (for 'warn't', warrant) and 'maruailes'.[2] With perhaps twenty authorial spellings in Q1, we see yet again how close it takes us to the original MS.

Greg detected signs that the bookholder had looked over the foul papers preparatory to transcribing the prompt-book, and had made a few 'desultory jottings', duplications in stage-directions:

1. A single compositor throughout, to judge by his consistency in the spellings doe, goe, hee (frequently mee, shee, wee), here or heere, eyes, daies, -nesse, -lesse; a verdict in which Robert K. Turner Jr concurs; see, for a meticulous analysis of the presswork, his 'Printing Methods and Textual Problems in *A Midsummer Night's Dream*, Q1', *Studies in Bibliography*, xv, pp. 33–55. He concludes that the compositor began with Sheet B and set A last; the setting was by formes, outer forme first, except that in Sheet C an attempt was made to set seriatim (that is in the order of the copy): there, the pages within each forme were so set. Irregularities in the process of distributing the type point to occasions when typesetting slowed down, and suggest that there the copy was difficult. The evidence is favourable to 'late stage foul papers' (p. 55) being the copy; but such attempt, carefully guarded, as Turner makes to correlate it with Dover Wilson's revision theories, must fall with them.

2. Pp. 79, 112, 116, 121, 148 (1971 reprint).

The addition of the lovers' names at v. i. 27 must surely be his; he may have added 'Tytania' . . . at II. ii. 0. There is evident duplication at IV. i. 137; Shoute within: they all start vp. Winde hornes', where it looks as if 'Winde hornes' were the addition . . .

He continues:

In that case 'Winde horne' at l. 101 may also be due to the book-keeper, and so may the notes 'Ly downe' (III. ii. 87) and 'Sleepe' (l. 436).[1]

In mentioning this possibility, he is not, of course, subscribing to 'the old superstition that the author writes directions in indicative and the prompter in the imperative mood',[2] a superstition against which, with McKerrow, he protests. Directions in stage-terms are at least as likely to come from Shakespeare, man of the theatre, as from the prompter. To Shakespeare, a 'Shoute' is 'within' the tiring-house, though for the audience it is without— outside the visible scene. Similarly, in the wood, the Fairy enters 'at one doore, and Robin Goodfellow at another'; the same terminology is used for the first entrance of Titania and Oberon: the doors are those of the tiring-house façade or a hall-screen. Once more in Q1 we are close to Shakespeare—and here, to his stage.

The Second Quarto will not detain us long. It was set up from Q1, of which, except for the first five leaves of Sheet G, it is a page-for-page reprint. If further bibliographical evidence of its derivation were needed, one would cite its reproduction of such peculiarities as the spelling 'wodde' for 'wood' (I. i. 247) and the omission of 'Enter' before 'Robin *and* Demetrius' (III. ii. 420); its printing of '*The*. In himselfe he is' (I. i. 53), '*Enter* Snout' (III. i. 108), '*Enter* Lysander' (III. ii. 400), '*Enter* Thisbie' (v. i. 185), and '*Lyon*. Oh', (v. i. 254) just as Q1 has them, tucked in on the same line as the end of the preceding speech; its agreement with Q1 in capitalizations which are not simply those to be expected; and above all its concurrence in thirty-five of the speech-prefixes where Q1 varies the form of abbreviation. In II. i, for example, where Q1 has '*Ob*.' three times, then '*Oberon*', '*Ob*.' four times more, then '*Oberon*' again; and, also exceptionally, for Demetrius' sixth speech, '*Demet*.', Q2 follows suit. Full collation shows that it repeats all but thirteen of the verbal errors made in Q1. It corrects prose set as verse at III. i. 93 ff., but not at v. I. 184. A

1. Greg, p. 241 (line numbers conformed to this edn).
2. *Id*., pp. 123 f.; cf. 122.

half-hearted attempt is made to rectify some of the misdivided verse in v. i between ll. 5 and 83, but most of it, like the misdivided ll. 115 f. in II. i, is reprinted as it stands.

It is clear that Q2 owes nothing to any fresh evidence of what Shakespeare wrote. Of its thirteen corrections, four eliminate obvious 'literal' misprints. In the remainder the errors announce themselves: the misreading of 'waves' for 'wanes', and of *Cet.* for *Bot.*; the displacement of 't' from 'comfcr' to 'bet', the omission of an 'o' from 'good', and of 'to' before 'expound' where the sense requires it; a mistake of number in 'gentleman'; a failure to repeat 'is' after 'this'; an assimilation of 'is' to 'knit', yielding 'it'; and a catching of 'yet' from earlier in the phrase. They needed nothing beyond the context in Q1 itself either to draw attention to them or to indicate the proper correction. Apart from the 'accidentals' of spelling and the like, Q2 differs from Q1 only through the guesswork which furnished these corrections, and by over sixty new errors of the printing-house. Since it derives from the author only through Q1, its readings have no independent authority. Its significance lies in its transmission of the First Quarto text, in a blemished form, to the First Folio.

So far as the Folio text was taken from Q2, it is a third-hand version, deteriorated further, of what we have in Q1. But unlike Q2 it presents some readings, not obvious emendations by guess, which do not derive from Q1. They are mostly stage-directions, and these must have their source in a theatre manuscript, other than Shakespeare's foul papers.

In the Folio, the *Dream* was printed from a copy of Q2.[1] The evidence is of several kinds. At III. i. 7, after '*Bot. Peter quince?*' Q2 substitutes '*Peter.*' for Q1's *Quin.*; it reverts to *Pet.* for ll. 85, 93, 99 and 113, and at l. 112 has '*Enter Peter quince*' (Q1 '*Enter Quince*').[2] F follows Q2 in all these variants. At III. ii. 145, both

1. The typesetting is analysed by Charlton Hinman, *The Printing and Proof Reading of the First Folio of Shakespeare* (1963), Vol. II, pp. 415–26. He finds that Compositor B set pp. N1^r, N1^v, N2^v, O3^r (I. i. 1–205; I. ii. 80—II. i. 97; v. i. 198–331); Compositor C, N2^r, N3^r, N3^v N5^v, O1^r, O2^r, O2^v, O3^v (I. i. 206—I. ii. 79; II. i. 98—II. ii. 73; III. ii. 87–210; III. ii. 458—v. i. 197; v. i. 332–424); Compositor D, N4^r, N4^v, N5^r, N6^r, and N6^v col. a (II. ii. 74—III. ii. 86; III. ii. 211–393). N6^v col. b (III. ii. 394–457) may have been set by him or by Compositor A. The three press-variants (Hinman, I. 260 f.) do not affect the text.

2. The abnormal prefix originates on D1^r. Bottom's '*Peter quince*' supports Dover Wilson's diagnosis of the cause, a shortage of capital Qs; undoubtedly it prompted the resort to '*Peter*', '*Pet.*', which continues on D2^v. These are two pp. of the outer forme; in between them, D1^v, D2^r, belonging to the inner forme, have '*Quin.*' (eight times). Sheet D, then, was set by formes, D2^v

have the abbreviation *Hell.* (Q1 *Hel.*), unique in each. On fifteen further occasions they have identical abbreviations in speech-prefixes, differing from Q1's and from some of their own. Hence we can be confident that the tucking-in of '*Enter* Snowt' (III. i. 108) rather than giving it the normal line of its own, and the printing of prose as verse at v. i. 184, come in F from Q2, even though they originated in Q1. The Folio has several instances of progressive corruption. At I. i. 239 Q1 reads 'is so oft'; Q2 inadvertently omitted 'so'; F, lamely attempting to mend the metre, miscorrects to 'is often'. Q2, at IV. i. 177, undoes the Q1 inversion 'more will hear', reading 'will hear more'; F worsens the corruption with 'shall hear more'. There are less striking instances at III. ii. 374, 379. Lysander's sentence at IV. i. 154 is left incomplete because Egeus interrupts him; not realizing this, Q2 completes it by supplying a verb: 'be'. The Folio repeats this and over fifty of its other corruptions: good examples are Q2's 'silly foal' for 'filly foal' (misreading long 's'), 'hoared headed' for 'hoary headed' (by assimilation), 'followed' for 'following' (caught from the line above), and 'hearken' for 'listen' (a compositor's synonym).[1]

This last exemplifies the usefulness of Q2. If we did not know that 'hearken' originated there, we might wonder whether F obtained it from the theatre-document undoubtedly drawn upon in the F text. Dover Wilson believed that this document was none other than the Q2 from which F was set up: it had, he thought, been used as a prompt-book, and reached Jaggard's compositors bearing the alterations and supplementations of the bookholder himself. With the powerful support of Greg, I consider this improbable.[2] One can scarcely conceive a bookholder being content to control performance from a Q2 so imperfectly brought into line with his requirements as the F text

---

immediately after D1r, and not seriatim. So, no doubt, was the whole of Q2; an easy method with a page-for-page reprint.

1. II. i. 46, 107; IV. i. 162; V. i. 230.

2. Greg, pp. 245 f. As a second best, Wilson allowed the view we accept, that Q2 was *compared* with the prompt-book. Later (see e.g. N.C.S., 1971 reprint, p. 157) to meet Greg's objection yet still link F with a Quarto used as prompt-copy, he suggested that a First Quarto was so used (adequately annotated, we are to presume), F's Q2 being imperfectly compared with this (hypothetical) Q1. Though a few instances are known of Quartos becoming prompt-books (see C. J. Sisson, 'Shakespeare Quartos as Prompt-Copies', *RES* (1942) and Greg's discussion, pp. 159–61 and nn.), this hypothesis is too like an expedient for saving a pet idea.

shows its copy to have been.[1] Few of the features taken to rule
out the prompt-book as source of Q1 were corrected; the bookholder would hardly have left standing the unspecific 'with
others' (I. i. 0), 'Enter the Clownes' (III. i. 0), and 'Clowne'
for 'Bottom' (IV. i. 0); nor failed to supply two of the entries
and all five of the exits whose absence (we noted) was likely to
incommode him; nor, introducing an exit for Wall, written *Exit
Clow*. At the beginning of IV. ii the error of a speech for Flute next
to one for Thisbe is rectified; but 'Flute, Thisby', remains in the
entry, contrary (one presumes) to the prompt-copy.[2] That points
to an annotator of the Quarto who was not turning it into
prompt-copy, but was comparing it with the prompt-book in
order to prepare it as copy for the printer. He missed some
prompt-book corrections and additions, observed and adopted
others. He took 'Enter Piramus with the Asse head' from the
prompt-book, but inserted it in his Q2 nine lines too late; a
mistake the bookholder, even if he had made it, would have been
obliged to put right. The whole mingling seen in F, when it is
compared with Q2, of correction and the want of it, leads to the
same conclusion: for the benefit of the Folio edition, a copy of
Q2 was annotated from a prompt-book, but cannot be said to
have been closely collated with it: the annotator paid little
attention to dialogue, his main concern being with stage-
directions, and even there his attention faltered, though he did
effect improvements.

If absolute proof were lacking, prompt-book origin could still
safely be presumed for much of the annotator's work on the
directions: Greg notes an unquestionable instance in '*Sleepers Lye
still*' (IV. i. 101 S.D.), 'a warning to wait for the second "Winde
hornes" before stirring'.[3] Proof, however, exists in the direction
at the entry of the actors in 'Pyramus and Thisbe' (v. i. 125 S.D.):
'*Tawyer with a trumpet before them*'. For William Tawyer, as we
know from the record of his burial, was 'Mr. Heminges man'.[4]
At '*Enter the Prologue*' (v. i. 107 S.D.), '*Flor* [ish of] *Trum* [pets]',
and no doubt the addition '*Quince*', are from the playhouse; and
'*the Asse head*' (III. i. 97 S.D.) has reasonably been claimed as playhouse language, referring to *the* ass-head among the company's
properties.[5]

The prompt-book consulted in preparing copy for the Folio was
clearly not without alterations from the text in the prompt-copy as

1. Greg, pp. 244 f.   2. *Id.*, p. 245.   3. *Loc. cit.*
4. June 1625, at St Saviour's, Southwark; discovered by Halliwell.
5. Furness, p. xv.

originally transcribed from Shakespeare's autograph. Theoretically, some changes might have been authorized by him; but at least the majority were no doubt made without authority, whether in the original prompt-book or in a new one, if a new one was transcribed from it. But whatever unauthentic changes had accumulated in it, the prompt-copy which supplied some Folio readings did derive by a process of transcription from Shakespeare's autograph. That process was independent of Q1. Accordingly, in respect of readings which the Folio can be presumed to have taken from the prompt-copy, F is an independent witness to what may have stood in the autograph. In the line of descent described it is the earliest extant witness, and in respect of those readings, and of those alone, it is therefore a substantive (that is, an evidential) text—as Q1 is for the play as a whole. Such authority as F therefore has is weakened, however, by the annotator's demonstrable negligence and clumsiness. Besides misplacing Bottom's entry 'with the Asse head', he introduces stage-directions at III. i. 51, v. i. 150, without noticing that they duplicate those in Q2 at III. i. 72, v. i. 153, and that the first is wrong. Still worse, at IV. i. 44 he has Oberon enter, and at III. ii. 344, Oberon, and Puck, when they are on stage already;[1] and he mistakes Titania's summons by name of the four fairies for an additional stage-direction, so that his own reads '*Enter* Pease-blossome, Cobweb, Moth, Mustard-seede, *and four* Fairies', and Titania's line is cancelled.[2] His neglect of dialogue further limits the possible authority of F. This is significant for F's readings at III. ii. 220 and v. i. 189: 'passionate' where Q1 has a palpable omission, and 'knit up in thee' where Q1 has the impossible 'knit now againe'. If these are sheer inventions, they are happier than we are accustomed to in Bad Quartos and in emendations by guess in Shakespearean Good Quartos and the Folio. Yet if they are retrievals from prompt-copy, why are there not more? That the annotator's eye might fall upon dialogue may be suggested by F's 'choise of merit' for the Quartos' 'choise of friends' (I. i. 139): 'merit' is not easy to account for (see Appendix II. 1) except as a Shakespearean first thought, and if it is, can hardly have reached F otherwise than from the prompt-book. If in the prompt-book the text at v. i. 204 was already simplified to 'wall downe', that

1. Greg, pp. 244 f., demonstrating that 'the revision [of the S.D.s] is spasmodic and that 'incompetence appears throughout'.

2. The mistake was facilitated by Q2's version of Titania's words, corrupted to '*and Mustard-seed*' from Q1's 'and *Mustard-seede*': Dover Wilson, N.C.S., p. 154 f.

would be the source of the annotator's 'correction' of Q2's 'Moon vsed'; his 'wall' appears to have been misread as 'rall' by the F compositor and regarded as a correction of the last two letters of 'Moon', so that he set up 'morall downe' (see Appendix II. 4). It seems more likely, however, that faced with the unintelligible 'Moon vsed' in Q2, the annotator, without benefit of prompt-book copy, made his correction, 'wall', by guess from the context. If so, he was perfectly prepared to guess, even when he could have consulted the prompt-book, and 'passionate' and 'up in thee' may be other guesses of his, though there the contexts offered little hint.

A further subtraction has to be made from the authority of F's text, even where its source is prompt-copy. The prompt-book itself is unlikely still to have represented in all respects the kind of performance for which Shakespeare designed the play, or to which he may have slightly adapted it. The substitution of Egeus for Philostrate in Act v, at odds with Theseus' enquiry for 'our usual manager of mirth' and damaging the metre at l. 38, was made apparently to save a speaking-part (Philostrate is mute in I. i.):[1] it is a change Shakespeare cannot have wished for, though he might acquiesce in it as an expedient. The same may be said of the one or more intervals introduced in a play conceived and originally performed as a continuous action. The F stage-direction between Act III and Act IV, 'They sleepe all the Act' reproduces a prompt-book note about an actual break in per-formance: the Act' is not the literary term, but means the 'Act-interval'. The awkward procedure of having the lovers lie asleep in the sight of the audience throughout this interval, results from the original continuity of action which is being interrupted. The ph ase 'all the Act' suggests an interval of some length, 'probably', Greg adds, 'with music'. If so, 'we may reasonably surmise', he continues, that the revival concerned was 'at the Blackfriars house'.[2] According to Richard Hosley it was 'about 1609', after Shakespeare's company 'had begun per-forming at the Blackfriars' (a private theatre) 'as well as at the Globe', that 'the custom of inter-act music seems to have spread from the private to the public playhouses', which at first had not

1. Capell attributed it to the actor of Egeus doubling, 'in this act', for Philostrate, and, with the limitation to Act v, Greg (p. 243) is disposed to concur. His statement that in I. i the two characters are 'on' together is not strictly accurate: but on departing as Philostrate the actor would have to return as Egeus only four lines later, a remarkable feat unless he were (im-probably) far upstage.

2. Greg, pp. 243 ff.

employed act-intervals.[1] In 1604 the company spoke of the 'not received custome of musicke in our Theatre'[2] (by then, the Globe). If the revival of the *Dream* matched by the prompt-book was in 1609 or later, Shakespeare may not have been closely associated with it. Exceptional characteristics of the texts of *Antony and Cleopatra* and *Coriolanus* (*c.* 1607–8) have been thought to suggest that he did not expect to be on hand when those plays were produced.[3] (But it will be obvious that in these surmises one is building hypothesis upon hypothesis.)

In the First Quarto an editor has a text of high authority to follow. Free, of course, from the accumulated printing-house corruptions in the Folio (which adds to the fifty and upward—excluding mislineations—repeated from Q2, over fifty of its own), it is a gratifyingly clean text, but not so clean as to cast doubt on its having been printed from Shakespeare's autograph final draft. As we have seen, it reproduces several errors for which he was evidently responsible, as he seems likely to have been for the syntactical hiatus at III. i. 78–80. Another crux, at III. ii. 257–9 ('No, no; heele / seeme to breake loose', etc.), might possibly go back to a tangle in the foul papers (see Appendix II. 2, 3). A third, 'Moon vsed', turns out to be (almost certainly) the result of a conscientious attempt by the compositor to decipher the pen-strokes he had before him, and that (we have supposed) may also be the explanation of his 'now againe' (v. i. 189). The only other real crux in Q1 is Puck's phrase 'at our stampe' (III. ii. 25), which may be correct but remains puzzling.[4] In the present edition, it has been found necessary to depart from Q1 in just over fifty verbal readings, besides nine punctuations affecting the sense, one transposition of a pair of lines, a number of line-divisions, and a very few places where verse was set as prose or prose as verse. Apart from the authorial lapses, and the cruces,

1. 'The Playhouses and the Stage', *A New Companion to Shakespeare Studies* (1971), ed. Muir and Schoenbaum, p. 33.

2. Induction, Marston's *Malcontent*, quoted Greg, p. 144, n. 4.

3. Dover Wilson (ed.), *Coriolanus* (facsimile) (1928); Greg, *Editorial Problem* (1942), pp. 147 f.

4. II. i. 101, 'want their winter here', and v. i. 263, 'golden glittering beams' might perhaps be added. In the second, the compositor's erroneous 'beams' leaves us without textual authority for the genuine word. In the first, different solutions have been proposed by good scholars; but of those which might be acceptable, none postulates more than a simple misreading in the Q1 text, and some would defend it as it stands. Now that probable sources for the phrases as emended by reading 'cheer' and 'gleams' have been found (in the November eclogue of *The Shepheardes Calender*, and in *Diana Enamorada*: see Commentary) these cruces may reasonably be regarded as no longer obstinate.

the faults are unsurprising errors of the press, almost all of the kinds that compositors are prone to; even in the less obvious corruptions such as 'strange companions' (I. i. 219, for 'stranger companies') the emendation is confirmed because the probable cause of the corruption can be recognized. In such instances, and in some of the more obvious ones, the probable cause is signified in the Commentary.[1]

2. DATE AND OCCASION: WITH CONSIDERATION OF THE POETIC STYLE

There are three principal indications of the date when *A Midsummer Night's Dream* was composed. Taken together, they point to 1595 or 1596. One is a topicality; another, the style, or styles, of the play itself; but only the third is incontrovertible evidence, fixing the *terminus ad quem*, the date by which it had certainly become known. It had reached performance in time for mention by Francis Meres in his *Palladis Tamia*, 1598, where it is included in his list of twelve Shakespeare plays.[2] *Palladis Tamia* was entered in the Stationers' Register on 7 September 1598.

It is highly probable that when he wrote the *Dream* Shakespeare knew of an episode which occurred at the Scottish court in 1594. If so, that yields a *terminus a quo*: the *Dream* could not be earlier than the baptismal feast of Prince Henry, 30 August 1594, and probably not than the account of it in *A True Reportarie*, registered with the Stationers on 24 October. At the feast, while King James was at dinner, a chariot was drawn in by a blackamoor.

> This chariot should have been drawne in by a lyon, but because his presence might have brought some feare to the nearest, or that the sights of the lights and the torches might have commoved his tameness, it was thought meete that the Moor should supply that room.[3]

Bottom and his fellows, likewise planning a performance before

1. Cf. I. i. 10, 24, 26, 27, 136, 187, 216, 219; II. i. 61, 78, 79, 190; II. ii. 38; III. i. 48, 65, 83, 188; III. ii. 85, 213, 250; IV. i. 81, 127, 171, 208; V. i. 34, 299, 337, 358 nn.

2. Shakespeare, says Meres, is the most excellent of English dramatists in both comedy and tragedy: 'for Comedy, witnes his *Gentlemen of Verona*, his *Errors*, his *Loue labors lost*, his *Loue labours wonne*, his *Midsummers night dreame*, & his *Merchant of Venice*' (E. K. Chambers, *William Shakespeare*, 1930, II, pp. 193–5; I, pp. 244 f.).

3. *Somers Tracts*, Vol. II, p. 179; Malone called attention to the occurrence (but as an 'odd coincidence'). Cf. Cuningham, p. xxxi; Peter Alexander, *Shakespeare's Life and Art* (1939), pp. 105 f.

their sovereign, anticipate the fear that bringing in 'a lion among ladies' may produce, and likewise modify their plan in order to avoid it. It seems harder to dismiss this parallel as coincidence, than with E. K. Chambers and Peter Alexander to accept the Scottish incident as having lodged in Shakespeare's mind.[1] Supposed topicalities are often weak evidence. But here it is not a question of some passing allusion the audience may have been expected to pick up: indeed, it is not primarily a question of them at all, but of the dramatist: for the boggling over the lion is organic to the play. The device adopted to meet the 'difficulty' contributes in spectacle as well as speech to the farcical nature of 'Pyramus and Thisbe': and the artisans' anxiety is part of a major joke: their fear of creating too much dramatic illusion, when it is obvious they will create far too little. The Scottish lion-incident may reasonably be reckoned among Shakespeare's sources of inspiration for his artisan-plot.

No other probable or even certain source offers reliable help in dating the play. Possibly relevant are the new edition of North's Plutarch, and Spenser's *Epithalamion*, both published in 1595 (*Epithalamion* no doubt in the first months; it was registered with the Stationers on 19 November 1594). No debt to North has so far been found in Shakespeare earlier than the date-range of the *Dream*; the new edition was published by his friend Field and may have been the one Shakespeare used: but we cannot show it was.[2] *Epithalamion* would match his theme, and offers more than one parallel, but none is decisive. In the stanza before the consummation of Spenser's marriage is symbolically depicted (with 'an hundred little winged loves' flying about the bed), he exorcizes the terrors of the night. Just before the fairies enter to bless the bride-beds, Puck describes some of the terrors: this and his former description of nocturnal ghosts and damnèd spirits bear a general resemblance to Spenser's.[3] Like Puck, Spenser includes the screech owl; he refers to 'damnèd ghosts', 'hobgoblins', and (though as an evil spirit) 'the Pouke'. But there are no echoes of phrase; the subject is a familiar *topos*; the placing next to happy consummation was likely, for aesthetic and moral contrast, to appeal to each poet; and Spenser's recital of night terrors embraces so many that the surprise would be if it did not include some that Puck also speaks of. The parallel does not,

1. Chambers, *op. cit.*, Vol. 1, p. 360; Alexander, *loc. cit.*
2. Furness, p. 267; Alexander, p. 105.
3. N.C.S., pp. x f., sets the passages side by side, noting Spenser's as an exorcism, and Puck's as 'a pretty purgation'; but goes into no further detail.

however, stand quite alone. In the *Dream* the Moon reigns queen of fertility no less than of virginity; in *Epithalamion*, Cynthia's blessing is sought for what pertains to Lucina (more often identified with Juno than with the Moon-goddess): conception and childbirth.[1] Wolves are to be chased from 'coming near' the place where on the wedding morning the bride lies asleep, as 'Newts and blindworms' are to 'come not near' the sleeping Titania; and nymphs are adjured to

> Behold your faces as the christal bright

in the 'waters which your mirror make': so in the *Dream*, Phoebe will

> behold
> Her silver visage in the watery glass.[2]

In the same volume with *Epithalamion* appeared *Amoretti*, where in Sonnet LXXI we find Oberon's woodbine and eglantine; and extending from start to finish in LXXIX, word-play upon 'fair', such as we have from Helena (I. i. 181 f.); the unusual sense she gives to it in 'Demetrius loves your fair' (fairness, beauty) may have an antecedent in Spenser's 'all other fair' (fairnesses, beauteous objects or creatures). Spenser plays on the word, for three lines, in 'Astrophel' also,[3] an elegy on Sidney, which is likewise of 1595. Perhaps no Elizabethan poet could easily refrain. Yet in combination the parallels, seven in a single volume, may not be wholly without force. Little can attach to the only one discovered in the last three books of *The Faerie Queene*, published 1596.

> Through hills and dales, through bushes and through briars[4]

In itself it is close to the Fairy's lines (II. i. 3 f.) as she begins the first woodland scene; but the coupled words were probably common coin, and if Shakespeare echoed this line it is strange that he did not echo others.

It is natural, and probably right, to see topicality in Titania's great speech on the foul weather and dislocation of the seasons.[5]

---

1. See below, pp. lxxv, n. 1, cxxix f.
2. *Epithalamion*, ll. 63 f., 69 f.; *MND*, I. i. 209 f., II. ii. 11 f.
3. Ll. 55–7.
4. VI. viii. 32; cited Halliwell (see Furness, p. 249).
5. See Chambers, *op. cit.*, Vol. I, p. 360 and the detailed account of the succeeding dearth, especially in Stratford and south-west Warwickshire, II. 99–101. Furness (pp. 249–53) gives the views (some sceptical) of investigators up to Fleay (1886), with their quotations from Dr King's *Lectures* (printed by

Memorably foul weather was experienced in 1594 from March onward, continuing, except (according to Stowe) for a remission in August, to the end of the year, and followed by bad, wet summers in 1595 and 1596. In his memoranda, Simon Forman noted that the summer was cold enough for winter:

> June and July were very wet and wonderfull cold like winter, that the 10 dae of Julii many did syt by the fyer, yt was so cold; and so was yt in Maye and June . . . There were many gret fludes this summer, and about Michelmas, thorowe the abundaunce of raine that fell sodeinly.[1]

Stowe records that 'notwithstanding' the miserable summer, 'in . . . August there followed a faire harvest'.[2] That did not prevent grain from rising to an exorbitant price (it remained excessively high throughout 1594–8). That, however, was attributed to the malpractices of cornholders. But commodities can hardly be cornered when they are plenty: there must have been a natural dearth to give the cornholders their chance. There is no significant discrepancy (such as Aldis Wright saw here[3]) between Titania's account and Stowe's, at least when we remember how much of Titania's is of literary origin, from Ovid, Seneca, and *The Shepheardes Calender*, and need not be expected to fit the historical facts.[4] Its topicality (if we accept that it is topical) lies in its general reference to such unseasonable rain and cold, with consequent devastation and wretchedness, as men do not readily forget. 'A colder time', wrote Thomas Churchyard, 'in world was never seen.' His description, in *A Musicall Consort . . . called*

Strype), Stowe, and Dr Simon Forman's 'Diary'. Steevens in 1773 asserted an allusion; but not till 1793, when he quoted Churchyard (see below), did he date it credibly (in 1595). Among twentieth-century editors, Cuningham and N.C.S. accept the allusion; Stanley Wells (Penguin edn) repudiates it; Martin Wright, like Alexander, *loc. cit.*, is willing to believe in it.

1. MS. Ashmole 384; quoted Halliwell in his edition of the *Dream* (1841), p. 6.
2. *The Annales of England* (1600 edn) quoted, with the rest of his account, by Halliwell, p. 8.
3. Edn of the *Dream* (1877) p. vi.
4. This is also the answer to Wells's objection (Penguin edn, p. 12) that 'Titania speaks of unusually fine winters as well as bad summers'. The unseasonable winters do not correspond to recent weather, because they come from the utter confusion of seasons which Seneca's Medea boasts of having effected. But the bad summer of 1594 was seen in terms of an aberration in the seasonal cycle: Forman describes it as winter-like; to Churchyard it suggests Nature scorning her proper course. Why should not fact supply Shakespeare with part of his picture of cosmic disorder, while literature heightened that part and supplied the rest? See below, II. i. 88–116 nn.

Churchyard's Charitie, 1595 (at some time after what a sidenote in the volume calls 'this last Aprill'), has points of resemblance with Shakespeare's. In Shakespeare, the rivers have 'overborne their continents'; in Churchyard

> The winter's waste, drives water o'er the brim.

In Churchyard,

> Nature thinks scorne to do her dutie right
> Because we have displeased the Lord of light.[1]

In Shakespeare the seasonal order of nature is in confusion, because the moon, the Lady of light in the *Dream*, has been angered. It would not astonish me if Shakespeare knew this poem, dedicated to Essex.[2]

Rejecting the idea that

> the death
> Of learning, late deceas'd in beggary (v. i. 52 f.)

alludes to that of Robert Greene, E. K. Chambers thought that 'If any particular death was in mind, Tasso's, on 30 April 1595,' was 'more plausible'. The sidenote in Churchyard, mentioned above, shows it registered in England: 'Torquato Tasso an Italian knight and poet laureat . . . departed from oblivion to immortalitie this last Aprill 1595, whose memorie shall never vanish.'[3] The supposition that, with characteristic magnanimity, Shakespeare alluded to his old assailant Greene, who died in notoriously abject poverty in 1592, is not impossible:[4] as 'Utrius . . . Academiae in artibus Magister'[5] (M.A. of Cambridge and incorporated at Oxford) he might have some title to stand for 'learning'; though—one must agree with Chambers—he could hardly rank as an orthodox type of it.[6] There is, of course, no compelling reason why learning's decease in beggary should be other than allegorical. The scholar's destitution for want of due patronage was a perennial topic. But though in the 'satire keen

1. Pp. 22, 42; the famine is mentioned on p. 18.

2. Though the resemblances may be fortuitous, the 'fall of leaf' (A1ᵛ), 'We quickly can . . . seeme shadow in a glasse' (p. 8), and 'no chinks to spend' (p. 17) remind one of *R2*, III. iv. 49, IV. i. 292 f., *Rom.*, I. v. 115. 'Chinks' = cash is, however, in Holinshed (*OED*); 'fall of the leaf' in *Shepheardes Calender*.

3. Chambers, *op. cit.*, Vol. I, p. 360; Churchyard, p. 42.

4. It originated with Charles Knight (Furness, p. 257).

5. So described on the title-page of *Greenes Mourning Garment* (1590), *Greenes Farewell to Folly* (1591) and his *Philomela* (1592); and repeatedly on others as M.A. of Cambridge.

6. Chambers, *loc. cit.*

and critical', with the Nine Muses mourning 'the death of Learning' Shakespeare was probably not asking his audience to see an existing work, he is likely to have had two in mind. In the *Dream* he repeatedly remembers *Hero and Leander* (left unfinished at Marlowe's death, licensed for publication in September 1593, but apparently not published till 1598) and here is no doubt remembering Marlowe's myth of Mercury condemned ever to kiss poverty,

And to this day is everie scholler poore.[1]

But Marlowe says nothing of the Muses; and the old suggestion that Shakespeare is thinking of Spenser's 'Teares of the Muses' in his *Complaints*, 1591, has been too hastily dismissed. It has been objected that Spenser's poem is not a satire,[2] but a complaint is first cousin to one, and satire is not absent from the 'Teares'. In her complaint, each Muse except Erato and Polyhymnia employs the formula 'Therefore I mourn' or a close variant of it; and of the first six all but Euterpe name 'learning' as the victim.

That there is topical reference in Oberon's description of the mermaid and the shooting stars is tolerably apparent; evidently, too, it reflects Shakespeare's acquaintance with the kind of elaborate courtly entertainment which combined a mythological water-pageant with fireworks, rather like those presented to Elizabeth by Leicester at Kenilworth and the Earl of Hertford at Elvetham. But 'there is a generic quality about such pageants'[3] and Shakespeare may not have had any particular one in view. If he had, Leicester's—so far back as 1571—is not likely to have been the one; and such case as can be made for Hertford's (1591) is not very persuasive. The attempts to decode the allegory of the mermaid and the stars must be accounted failures; whether, rightly interpreted, it would yield evidence on the date of the play, we do not know.[4]

Having gleaned what evidence probable or possible sources and topical references afford,[5] we can return to our three main

1. II. 386 ff., 469-71.

2. The objection is Charles Knight's, to the notion first mooted by Warburton. Aldis Wright was prepared to believe that Shakespeare, without intending an allusion, had from Spenser's poem a hint for the title he invented.

3. Chambers, *op. cit.*, p. 358.

4. See below, p. lxvii f.; Chambers, 'The Occasion of *A Midsummer Night's Dream*', *Shakespeare Gleanings* (1946), pp. 63 f. (and *A Book of Homage to Shakespeare*, ed. I. Gollancz, 1916); Furness, II. i. 153-75, n. (much of it to be discounted).

5. The significance of the production, as new, by the Admiral's Men, 3

indications of the play's date, and consider the one postponed till now; the place of the *Dream* among Shakespeare plays assignable to 1594–8, as judged by its style (or styles).

Diversity of style was the second main ground—the first being the alternation of 'Puck' and 'Robin'—on which Dover Wilson divided the Q1 text of the *Dream* between three periods of composition.[1] We have seen reason to reject the first, bibliographical argument; the stylistic argument will prove equally fallacious, and the hypothesis of threefold date, never widely accepted, should now be laid finally to rest. To recognize the *Dream* as substantially of one date does not entail denying all revision. What has been generally accepted, and rightly, is Dover Wilson's brilliant detection of marginal revisions in v. i. 1–83, especially his identifying as an addition the lines about the imagination of the poet. His analysis of the mislined verse explains it as the result of the compositor's unskilful attempt to insert into the text as first written, coherent as that was in sense and versification, the equally coherent additions which had been crowded into the margin. Yet an inspired afterthought may come to an author after five minutes just as well as after four years: Wilson's conviction that the lines on the poet are of much later date than those on the lunatic and the lover comes mainly from his impression

---

December 1594, of *The Wise Man of West Chester* (Chambers, *Elizabethan Stage*, Vol. III, p. 446) depends upon (1) whether it is Munday's *John a Kent and John a Cumber*, and (2) whether that play is a source of the *Dream*, a question considered below, pp. lxiv–vi; and cf. pp. lxxxiii f. A few faint possibilities may be added. Shakespeare's attention might have been drawn to two of the sources he used by the Admirals' productions of *Palamon and Arcite* (new), 18 September 1594, and *Huon of Bordeaux* (revised), 28 December 1593 (Chambers, *op. cit.*, Vol. II, pp. 95, 143, 364). If (see below, p. lvi. f.) the *Dream* was written for 19 February 1596, but not if *c.* 26 January 1595, *2 Hercules*, produced 23 May 1595, might be relevant. Chambers (*Shakespeare*, Vol. I, p. 360) notes that supposing it were Thomas Heywood's *Silver Age* it shared with the *Dream* the error of making Hercules a hero of the battle with the Centaurs. Unfortunately, that is how anyone would read Ovid's account, unless with modern classicists like Niall Rudd they saw Tlepolemus as meant to be mistaken: Shakespeare and Heywood would be likely to read it so, each on his own account. Finally, it may even be that Puck's prank as the three-legged stool was included on the hint of a suitor's practical joke on an old woman, Mrs Mascall the tripe-wife, reported in April 1595: 'coming behind her' he 'pulled the stool from her, when down fell she,' while he cried ' "Keep the widow waking" '. The day before she had been at a talkative drinking-party at one of her sisters (G. B. Harrison, *A Second Elizabethan Journal*, p. 19).

1. N.C.S., pp. 91 ff.; and see below, pp. xli f., lii f.

of their style.[1] 'They are a little more freely written' is as far as Chambers will go; they are 'no doubt', says Greg, 'as a whole more poetical and lively than the original speech, which they serve to brighten up', but 'Shakespeare may have introduced them for that very purpose on reading the scene over soon after it was written'.[2] He would have had an even stronger motive, which might have come into play from the time he finished the first draft of the speech. Imagination and illusion form a master-topic in the conclusion of the *Dream*, and not only in relation to actuality, but to the art of drama and poetry as well; a concern to which the addition links the speech as none of its existing lines did. The subject itself would be likely to inspire a more soaring style,[3] as subjects dear to Shakespeare do in *Richard II*. He who in 1595 could write Gaunt's hymn of praise to England and Carlisle's prophecy of civil strife could at no distant date have written the lines in the *Dream* on the poetic imagination. If (as, to anticipate, I believe) the play was composed originally for a wedding in a noble household, there would hardly be a long delay before its revival on the public stage, when it is likely that the fairy masque would have to be omitted. Puck's epilogue presumably took its place,[4] and it may be that the expansion in v. i. 1–83 was undertaken at that juncture, partly to help compensate for the shortening.

To Dover Wilson (encouraged by Walter de la Mare)[5] the style of the young lovers, compared especially with the lyrical poetry of the play, was much inferior in skill and merit; a survival, he concluded, of immature work from 1592. Both premise and argument are open to a number of general objections. If there had been such refashioning as the stylistic differences were alleged to indicate, it would, Greg felt sure, 'have left more bibliographical traces than are now apparent'. Chambers thought the 'differences of style between the lover scenes and the fairy scenes, . . . such as they are' were 'sufficiently explained by the

1. N.C.S., pp. 80–6; on the style, see pp. 83, 85. I give the mislined verse, Appendix III.

2. Chambers, *Shakespeare*, Vol. I, p. 360; Greg, p. 242.

3. Greg, *loc. cit.*

4. Greg, *loc. cit.*; he adds: 'There would be nothing surprising in finding both in the foul papers, and we should expect to find them in the order in which they were written.'

5. For the references to them in this paragraph, see Dover Wilson in N.C.S., pp. 85 f., 91 f., 125, 127–9, 141; his *Shakespeare's Happy Comedies* (1962), pp. 207–19, reprinted from *Tribute to Walter de la Mare* (1948); and de la Mare's introduction to the *Dream*, ed. C. Aldred (1933), reprinted in his *Pleasures and Speculations* (1940).

differences of subject matter'.[1] The *Dream* is a play, and its styles
are suited to their dramatic functions: a consideration to which
the revisionist argument pays no heed. Among the lovers' scenes,
for example, Dover Wilson himself exempted the grand quarrel
(III. ii. 195–344) from the imputation of early immaturity: he
believed it to have been transcribed from a 1594 original in 1598,
and revised in the process. But its less formal and more animated
style springs from the emotional crescendo, corresponding to
the dramatic situation. Wilson censured most of the lovers'
utterances as stiff and pestered with antithesis: it was evidently
the rhetoric, in the comparatively stiff form it still has in the
Dream, which particularly displeased him and de la Mare.[2]
Neither they, nor (so far as I am aware) their critics, looked for
stylistic comparisons outside the *Dream* itself. Yet the decisive
test is whether the range of Shakespeare's writing elsewhere, in
or about 1595, resembles the range in the *Dream*; and especially
whether it includes similar rhetoric. In answering that question
one is at the same time marshalling the stylistic evidence for
dating the *Dream c.* 1595, in close proximity to plays which in style
it resembles.

Before proceeding to the comparison, something should be said
of Shakespeare's dramatic output in the years 1594–8, so far as
is relevant to the place of the *Dream*. Prior to the limit fixed by
Palladis Tamia, 1598, Shakespeare since the summer of 1596
had written *The Merchant of Venice*, both parts of *Henry IV*, and
The Merry Wives of Windsor.[3] However fluently his mind and hand
went together, it is hard to imagine him writing the *Dream* then
as well. In these plays, the only passage of lyricism comparable
with those in the *Dream*, and in *Romeo and Juliet*, *Richard II*, and
Love's Labour's Lost, is the scene of music, moonlight and starlight
at the final return to Belmont. No doubt lyricism would be un-

1. Chambers, *op. cit.*, p. 361; Greg, p. 243. He thinks (p. 242) the young
lovers 'rather tiresome', and Shakespeare, when concerned with them, naturally
'writing in a flatter, and more conventional and seemingly earlier manner'.
His inability to accept Wilson's view of the style is welcome; but, as will be
seen, I deny the manner is even 'seemingly earlier'; nor can I believe the lovers
were at all tiresome to Shakespeare.

2. Their taste for the lyricism—de la Mare, after all, was the most exquisite
romantic lyrist of his day—seems to have precluded all sympathy with Elizabethan rhetoric. They quote a line or two as immaturely bad; but even if one
agreed about the badness, at what date did Shakespeare become incapable of
a bad line? Bernard Shaw thought 'In a most hideous and dreadful manner' so
bad that when Ellen Terry spoke it as Imogen he believed for the moment
that she had improvised it.

3. Chambers, *op. cit.*, Vol. I, pp. 267 f.; Alexander, p. 103.

looked for in the Falstaff plays, so different from the *Dream* in form and subject; yet *Richard II*, no less a history-play than the *Henry IV*s, and presenting the first part of the same historical and dramatic sequence, has much lyricism; presumably because that was a mode congenial to Shakespeare at the time. Thus Shakespeareans are on strong ground when they agree in positing a 'lyrical group' of plays, comprising (besides the *Dream*) *Richard II*, *Romeo* and *Love's Labour's Lost*. *Richard II* can be dated, with fair certainty, in 1595.[1] For *Love's Labour's Lost* the Arden editor proposed Autumn 1593; the evidence he assembled could support 1594, or very early 1595, the date cautiously favoured, after a searching discussion, by Geoffrey Bullough.[2] I have found more parallels in the *Dream* with *Love's Labour's Lost* and *Romeo* than with any other plays. Whether *Romeo* precedes or follows the *Dream* cannot be firmly determined, though there are signs that it is the earlier.[3] The parallels diminish as the *Dream* goes on: their prominence nearer the start reminds me of the echoes of *Julius Caesar* in *Hamlet* which show Shakespeare's previous tragedy lingering in his mind. In *Romeo* the vivid comparison of love to the lightning springs immediately from the situation: 'this contract to-night'. It is the sudden, unadvised rashness of the contract which prompts Juliet's foreboding and probably the image from Lyly's *Euphues* (II. 209, 16–19), illustrating the maxim 'nothing violent, can bee permanent'. The same comparison, no less vivid, in the first scene of the *Dream*, concerns the transience of 'bright things', not violent ones, and is a general reflection, natural climax though it may be to a speech on the hazards besetting love. Both less bound up in the situation and

1. J. G. McManaway, 'Recent Studies in Shakespeare Chronology', *Sh.S.*, 3 (1950), p. 26. The probable debt to Daniel's *Civil Wars* would place it after *c.* November 1594, and what was most likely an invitation to a private performance, before 7 December 1595. Chambers, *op. cit.*, p. 351, and P. Ure, Arden edn, pp. xxix f., xlii–iv, accept 1595, though with less assurance than McManaway.

2. *Narrative and Dramatic Sources of Shakespeare*, Vol. I, pp. 428–32. The part of Navarre, he points out, would hardly have been written during Henry of Navarre's unpopularity in England, which lasted from July 1593 till autumn 1594; after the Gray's Inn Christmas Revels, 1594–5, where Shakespeare's company seem to have performed *The Comedy of Errors*, the Muscovite masque could have been a reminiscence of the mock-Russian embassy at the Revels, which arrived on Twelfth Night. Bullough allows the possibility of revision.

3. Chambers, *op. cit.*, Vol. I, pp. 345 f., would 'put it in 1595'. It must have been in the acting repertory in time for the reconstruction by memory of the text piratically published in 1597. McManaway, *loc. cit.*, considers 'either 1595 or 1596 . . . an acceptable date'.

further from the probable source, it is the *Dream* version which is likely to be the echo. In the same dialogue there may be evidence in the Folio variant at l. 139 that Shakespeare was remembering *Romeo*. It instances as an obstacle to true love 'the choice of merit' (Q1 'friends'), a reading I have tentatively explained as Shakespeare's first thought, recalling Capulet's insistence on the merits of Paris, for which he chose him to be Juliet's husband.[1] It has often been noted that 'Pyramus and Thisbe' burlesques a story which corresponds to Romeo and Juliet's: lovers disregarding parental opposition, meeting in secret and, through mistiming at a rendezvous, coming to a tragic end, the heroine killing herself over the hero's dead body. For those who believe (as I do not) that Shakespeare, dissatisfied with *Romeo*, was mocking or criticizing it, that of course settles the question of priority.[2] But *Romeo* or no *Romeo*, Shakespeare needed a burlesque counterpart to the defiance of the parental ban by Hermia and Lysander, and their attempted runaway match: tragical, to demonstrate awareness of the alternative tragic outcome; farcical, to avert the omen in a play celebrating love and happy marriage. For this he took Ovid's story. It has been shrewdly observed by C. L. Barber[3] that the inclusion of the parents in Quince's original casting, and the assurance that 'the wall is down which parted their fathers', may reflect the prominence of the reconciliation scene, and the Capulets' lamentation scene, in *Romeo*; these have no equivalent in the tale of Pyramus. Yet Shakespeare, even if he had Romeo's story also in view, had known it in Brooke's narrative poem *Romeus* at least since he wrote *3 Henry VI*.[4] Necessarily derived from the play and not the poem would be any reminiscence (such as Muriel Bradbrook and Barber suspect), in the artisans' trouble about bringing in a wall, of the difficulty in the staging of the Capulets' orchard wall that Romeo leaps over.[5]

1. See Appendix II. 1.

2. Cf. Kenneth Muir, *The Sources of Shakespeare's Plays* (1977), p. 77. S. B. Hemingway, 'The Relation of *A Midsummer Night's Dream* to *Romeo and Juliet*', *MLN*, 26 (1911) thought Shakespeare in reaction from 'excessive emotionalism' and even 'shaking himself free from ideals of romantic love': but these are not fair impressions of the plays as wholes. Hemingway's other arguments show their relationship, but not the direction of indebtedness.

3. *Shakespeare's Festive Comedy*, p. 152, n. 25.

4. *3H6*, v. iv. 3–31, with Dover Wilson's and Cairncross's notes in their editions.

5. Barber, *loc. cit.*; M. C. Bradbrook, *Elizabethan Stage Conditions*, p. 39. Not that Romeo's wall will have given trouble; a practicable wall on stage was within normal competence; see T. W. Craik on Wall in the *Dream* and the wall in *Susanna* (*c.* 1569), *The Tudor Interlude*, pp. 17f., cf. p. lxxxiii, and III.i.61 n. below.

Finally it is natural to suppose that the diminutive fairies peopled Mercutio's imagination before, more boldly, Shakespeare asked his audience to imagine them peopling the scene itself. So much falls into place if he had recently dramatized Brooke's story, that I incline to think he had. If so, it might have helped to remind him of the similar tale of Pyramus and Thisbe (and Thisbe is mentioned in *Romeo*)[1] as suiting his need for a counterpart, in a contrasting key, to Lysander and Hermia's situation. What cannot be doubted, whichever play is the earlier, is the close relationship between them.

Stylistically, the group is linked not only by the lyricism from which the critics have named it (and to which we shall return), but also by its rhetoric, the art of which is not concealed but displayed. This is the most finished version of the rhetoric found in earlier plays, which, however, have not the lyricism: later, both lyricism and rhetoric are incorporated further 'into the tissue of living dramatic speech'.[2] It is the presence of both, at a particular stage of their development, which characterizes these plays of the mid-1590s.

Throughout the four plays, Shakespeare is still patterning his diction in verse by salient use of the rhetorical 'schemes'. *Richard II* and *Romeo*, no less than many passages in the *Dream*, abound in a great variety of them. There is space here only for examples from the *Dream* itself (to which I shall append the technical names); my footnotes will make it easy to compare them with their like in the other plays.

Hermia's vow (i. i. 169 ff.) has a series of phrases beginning identically (anaphora), and three of them of the same length (isocolon):[3]

> . . . by Cupid's strongest bow,
> By his best arrow with the golden head,
> By the simplicity of Venus' doves,
> By that which knitteth souls and prospers loves . . .

1. The two love-tragedies are coupled in George Pettie's *Petite Pallace of Pettie his Pleasure* (1576): parents' tyranny 'brought Pyramus and Thisbe to a woful end, Romeo and Julietta to untimely death' (quoted Bullough, Vol. 1, p. 374).

2. Brian Vickers, 'Shakespeare's Use of Rhetoric', *A New Companion*, p. 91. For the rhetorical 'schemes', I rely on this essay, Vickers's *Classical Rhetoric in English Poetry* (1970) and Sr. Miriam Joseph, *Shakespeare's Use of the Arts of Language* (1947), and have consulted Abraham Fraunce, *The Arcadian Rhetorike* (1588), and George Puttenham, *The Arte of English Poesie* (1589), ed. G. Willcock and A. Walker (1936).

3. Cf. *R2*, II. i. 40–3, 45–6, 50–1, III. iii. 105–10; *Rom.*, II. i. 17–19, IV. v. 86–9.

With isocolon, Helena matches word against word (parison) at
III. ii. 155 f.:

> You both are rivals, and love Hermia;
> And now both rivals to mock Helena;

and without it when she retorts to Demetrius'

> But I shall do thee mischief in the wood

with

> Ay, in the temple, in the town, the field,
> You do me mischief. (II. i. 237–9)[1]

Lines or phrases end with the same word (epistrophe)[2] at I. i.
27–9, V. i. 19 f., and II. i. 188, 191–2:

> I love thee not, therefore pursue me not . . .
> Thou told'st me they were stol'n into this wood;
> And here am I, and wood within this wood . . .

There is repetition of words in inverted order (antimetabole)[3] in

> Some true love turn'd, and not a false turn'd true; (III. ii. 91)

and in

> *Her.* I would my father look'd but with my eyes.
> *The.* Rather your eyes must with his judgement look (I. i. 56 f.)

it is combined with anadiplosis—giving the word which ends one
clause the first, or near the first, position in the next. Repetition
of a word within the same phrase (ploce) is seen in 'confounding
oath on oath' (III. ii. 93), and 'truth kills truth' (III. ii. 129).[4] A
phrase or word repeated in immediate succession (epizeuxis)[5] is
used with great dramatic aptness in Helena's reproach (II. ii.
124):

> Is't not enough, is't not enough, young man . . .?

and Egeus' characteristic outburst:

> Enough, enough, my lord; you have enough!
> I beg the law, the law upon his head!
> They would have stol'n away, they would, Demetrius.
> (IV. i. 153 ff.)

1. Cf. *R2*, IV. i. 194–8; *Rom.*, II. iii. 171–6.
2. Cf. *R2*, III. iii. 15–17, IV. i. 133–5; *Rom.*, I. iii. 78 f., III. v. 92–3.
3. Cf. *R2*, II. i. 74, 107 f.; *Rom.*, I. i. 180, II. ii. 14 f., III. iii. 87, V. i. 16 f.
4. Cf. *R2*, II. iii. 86, IV. i. 141, V. i. 82; *Rom.*, II. iii. 86, 157, III. i. 157.
5. Cf. *R2*, III. ii. 86, III. iii. 154; *Rom.*, II. ii. 33, II. iii. 139, III. ii. 61, 72.

At III. ii. 131 a line begins and ends with the same word (epano-lepsis).[1]

> Weigh oath with oath, and you will nothing weigh.

In retort or pertinent reply, it is natural to pick up the last word spoken (anadiplosis).[2] So Helena's 'then be content' provokes Lysander's 'Content with Hermia?' (II. ii. 109 f.). In yet another figure of repetition (polyptoton)[3] the second word is not identical with the first, but is from the same root, as in

> I follow'd fast; but faster he did fly. (III. ii. 416)

When the two words of this sort are of different meaning, we have one of the punning figures, paronomasia:[4]

> For lying so, Hermia, I do not lie, (II. ii. 51)

or

> The one I'll slay, the other slayeth me (II. i. 190)

(the second slaying being a commonplace of love-metaphor). The simplest kind of pun (antanaclasis) is upon two words of the same form but different sense;[5] so Demetrius is 'wood within this wood' (II. i. 192), and Lysander is accused of having 'with faining voice' serenaded Hermia with 'verses of feigning love' (I. i. 31). The *Dream* offers no perfect instance of picking up a word and giving it a different application (asteismus), as Richard does with Bolingbroke's 'Convey him to the Tower':

> O good! Convey! Conveyers are you all (IV. i. 316 f.);[6]

the nearest I have found is Demetrius' retort, 'So should the murder'd look', to Hermia's 'So should a murderer look' (III. ii. 57 f.). Without resort to verbal echoing, two senses may be punned on: this is syllepsis, Richard III's 'two meanings in one word'.[7] Sometimes a metaphor, such as Hermia's 'want of rain',

---

1. Cf. *R2*, II. i. 74, v. ii. 67 f., v. iii. 43 f.; *Rom.*, I. i. 180.

2. Cf. *R2*, III. iii. 180–2, 199–201, IV. i. 152 f., v. ii. 83; *Rom.*, III. iii. 11 f., IV. i. 29 f. This and other figures of repetition assist a playwright in that necessity for good dramatic dialogue, 'making the people answer each other' (W. B. Yeats on his revision of 'The Shadowy Waters', *Letters*, ed. Allan Wade (1954), p. 453). They are frequent in real-life argument or emotional exchanges.

3. Cf. *R2*, III. 15–17, IV. i. 117–20; *Rom.*, II. ii. 125 f., III. v. 29 f., IV. v. 37.

4. Cf. *R2*, III. iv. 62–5; *Rom.*, I. v. 98.

5. Cf. *R2*, II. ii. 44–7, III. iii. 140 f., III. iv. 7 f., IV. i. 281–8; *Rom.*, I. iv. 9 f., III. v. 29 f.

6. Cf. *R2*, v. i. 34 f. (with anadiplosis); *Rom.*, I. iv. 19–21.

7. Cf. *R2*, III. iv. 4 f., 72; *Rom.*, II. v. 74.

referring to the tears she is not shedding (I. i. 130), may be felt as a pun of this kind.

The 'schemes' are not the only forms of rhetoric common to the *Dream*, *Romeo*, *Richard II* and likewise *Love's Labour's Lost*. Aphorisms are numerous in the *Dream* as in the others:[1] gnomic sayings such as

> Things base and vile, holding no quantity,
> Love can transpose to form and dignity (I. i. 232 f.)

are not appropriated solely to the young lovers: Theseus' wisdom often takes aphoristic form, and even Bottom has his 'reason and love keep little company together nowadays. The more the pity, that some honest neighbours will not make them friends' (III. i. 138 ff.). Antithesis is a favourite figure;[2] there are a number of instances in lines quoted already to illustrate the 'schemes'. Another is Helena's

> The more my prayer, the lesser is my grace (II. ii. 88);

but like aphorism, antithesis is not the exclusive property of the young lovers: Puck, for instance, has

> Their sense thus weak, lost with their fears thus strong
> (III. ii. 27),

quite as mannered a phrase as any the lovers use. Helena's 'devilish-holy fray' (III. ii. 129) is an oxymoron comparable with Juliet's 'fiend angelical . . . A damned saint' (III. ii. 75–9); and, for paradox,[3] take Lysander's 'Nature shows art' (II. ii. 103). There is a fine example of pseudo-logic[4] in Helena's self-justification to Demetrius (II. i. 221–6), which has the air of being logically argued, though it is pure fanciful lovers' hyperbole. Another sentence of hers in the same scene (ll. 195–7), likewise fanciful, has the form of a logical distinction:

> You draw me, you hard-hearted adamant—
> But yet you draw not iron, for my heart
> Is true as steel.

1. Cf. *R2*, I. iii. 275–8, 294–9, II. i. 5–8, 11–13; *Rom.*, I. ii. 131, II. ii. 1, II. iii. 9 f., 17–20.
2. Cf. *R2*, II. ii. 27, 36, 80 f., III. ii. 58–62; *Rom.*, I. v. 136 f.
3. Cf. *R2*, II. ii. 36–40, IV. i. 196–9; *Rom.*, I. ii. 174–9.
4. When Richard attempts (v. v. 1 ff.) to argue a likeness between his prison and the world, he admits to himself beforehand that it can be no better than a tour-de-force: 'Yet I'll hammer it out'. Cf. *Rom.*, II. ii. 16–22.

That could equally well be described as a conceit.[1] At I. i. 186–9
she embroiders her conceit of wishing that favour could be
caught like sickness. Lysander's conceit, of her eyes as 'love's
richest book' (II. ii. 121), has its counterpart in *Romeo*, where
Paris is described (I. iii. 82) as 'this precious book of love'.
Similarly, Demetrius' rapturous conceit on Helena's beauty:

> That pure congealed white, high Taurus' snow,
> Fann'd with the eastern wind, turns to a crow
> When thou hold'st up thy hand (III. ii. 141 ff.)

is akin to Romeo's simile for Juliet at the ball (I. v. 46):

> So shows a snowy dove trooping with crows.

In each of the three plays there is a passage where the conceit is
taken to the furthest point of extravagance. The mildest is
Richard's whimsical proposal (III. iii. 164–9) that he and Aumerle
should 'play the wanton with [their] woes', and 'make [their] tears
fret [them] a pair of graves'. Yet more extravagant is Juliet's
notorious fancy of cutting Romeo out in little stars (III. ii. 21–5).
In the *Dream* (where there is the excuse that it is a figure of the
impossible) Hermia exclaims:

> . . . I'll believe as soon
> This whole earth may be bor'd, and that the moon
> May through the centre creep, and so displease
> Her brother's noon-tide with th'Antipodes. (III. ii. 52 ff.)

In all three of these speeches, and in the pilgrim conceit passed
to and fro between Romeo and Juliet (I. v. 91 ff.), the image is
elaborated. To pursue a metaphor, or to furnish parallel illustrations of a single idea, has been noted as characteristic of Shakespeare's rhetoric at this stage and earlier.[2] Though the *Dream* has
no worked-out metaphor to equal Richard's of himself as a
hermit (III. iii. 147 ff.) or as Time's numbring clock' (v. v. 50 ff.),
Demetrius briefly pursues the metaphor of 'debt that bankrupt
sleep doth sorrow owe' (III. ii. 84–7); and Helena (II. i. 203–10),
after declaring herself his spaniel, spells out the corollaries. In
ll. 231–3 she emphasizes the unnaturalness of the woman having
to run after the man, and her own desperate resolve to do so, by
three images in parallel:

---

1. Cf. *R2*, II. i. 74–82, III. ii. 160–70, v. v. 50 ff.; *Rom.*, v. iii. 102–5.
2. George Rylands, 'Shakespeare the Poet', in Granville Barker and G. B.
Harrison (eds), *A Companion to Shakespeare Studies* (1934), p. 100. Cf. *R2*, IV. i.
184–9, v. i. 11–15; *Rom.*, II. ii. 178–84, IV. i. 77–85.

> Apollo flies, and Daphne holds the chase;
> The dove pursues the griffin, the mild hind
> Makes speed to catch the tiger.

A common feature of the verse of the four plays is the occasional use of stichomythia.[1] It is at its most frequent in *Love's Labour's Lost*. After the exchanges between Rosaline and Katharine at v. i. 19 ff., the Princess comments:

> Well bandied both: a set of wit well play'd.

That is often the tone and style of stichomythia, as it is earlier in the banter (II. i. 183 ff.), mainly in rhyme and partly in half-lines, between Berowne and Longaville on the one hand and Rosaline and Boyet on the other. At II. i. 95 ff., between the Princess and the King, and in *Richard II*, I. iii. 258 ff., between Bolingbroke and his father, and in the *Dream*, II. ii. 83–6, between Demetrius and Helena, the form is a vehicle for graver disagreement or conflict; still more is it so in Gaunt's death-bed reproaches to Richard (II. i. 90 ff.) with the typically riddling epigram:

> *Richard.* Thou now a-dying sayest thou flatterest me.
> *Gaunt.* O no, thou diest, though I the sicker be.

Juliet's fencing with Paris when they meet at Friar Laurence's cell is sustained in stichomythia for eighteen lines (IV. i. 18–26, 28–36); the Friar and Romeo briefly employ it at III. iii. 61–6. It can be used apart from repartee, as in the parting between Richard and his Queen (v. i. 81 ff.), and the sympathetic dialogue between Helena and Hermia when they first meet (I. i. 194 ff.) in the *Dream*. Though in itself stichomythia is by no means a lyric form, Shakespeare fills it with lyric emotion in Hermia's responses to Lysander on the tribulations of true love (I. i. 135 ff.).

The lyricism of the four plays is partly of feeling, partly in forms of expression. The amount of rhyme in each has often been remarked: many speeches are in rhymed couplets which later or earlier would have been in blank verse. They are particularly numerous in the *Dream*, where the regular dialogue has some ten extended passages of this kind, totalling just over four hundred lines. Lyric measures, from Dumain's ode in *Love's Labour's Lost* to the fairies' short couplets in the *Dream*, are among the verse-forms in all four plays. Rhymes patterned in quatrains, or

---

1. In Shakespeare, it derives from Seneca. He has used it from much earlier (cf. e.g. *R3*) and as late as *Ant.* will use it for a special purpose, Antony and Cleopatra's first entrance.

alternatively like the last six lines of a Shakespearean sonnet, recur in all of them. In the *Dream*, at ii. ii. 35 ff., Lysander's proposal that, since they are lost, he and Hermia should rest till day, is couched in a quatrain. Protesting love to Helena, he speaks in the six-line pattern at iii. ii. 122 ff., and she replies in the same form. It is used again by the girls when they sink down exhausted (iii. ii. 431 ff., 442 ff.).[1] Berowne and the King use it in *Love's Labour's Lost*, and actual sonnets by the King, Berowne, and Longaville are read aloud. In *Romeo* there is the often-quoted sharing of a sonnet between the destined lovers when they first converse. As a fairy play, the *Dream* has its fairy songs and dance-music. Besides the spoken lyrics, *Love's Labour's Lost* has three songs and the snatch shared between Berowne and Rosaline. There are no songs in *Richard II*; nor yet in *Romeo*, where they would have been in tune with the play's romance—but until Lady Mortimer's Welsh song in *1 Henry IV*, no one sings in Shakespeare outside romantic comedy. If not song, *Romeo* has dancing to music at Capulet's ball.

Both in form and feeling, *A Midsummer Night's Dream* is the most lyrical of all Shakespeare's plays, not excepting even *The Tempest*. The reflections upon imagination and dreaming, the evocation of fairyland, of the moonlit wood, and of the moon as presiding divinity, are often lyrical in feeling, as are the recollections of Hermia's and Helena's girlhood friendship, the early morning hunting-scene, and at times the words of romantic love —'Love, whose month is ever May'.[2] Romantic love glows and flames with lyrical passion in *Romeo*; in *Love's Labour's Lost* lyrical emotion suffuses (to take the pre-eminent instance) Berowne's great tribute to love's educative power. In *Richard II* it is a quality of Richard's imagination, but is not confined to him; nor, among Gaunt's speeches, to the eulogy of England. The realms of political conflict, and Verona streets, do not offer the same opportunity as the *Dream* to the poet's 'natural magic'— the magic of

> I know a bank where the wild thyme blows.

Yet even in *Richard II* he can write

> Who are the violets now
> That strew the green lap of the new-come spring? (v. ii 46 f.)

---

1. Cf. *R2*, ii. i. 9 ff., iii. ii. 76 ff.; *Rom.*, i. ii. 88 ff.
2. *LLL*, iv. iii. 100; the *Dream*, by iv. i. 131–3, is associated with 'the rite of May'.

and in *Romeo* depict

> the bud bit with an envious worm,
> Ere he can spread his sweet leaves to the air,
> Or dedicate his beauty to the sun. (I. i. 149 ff.).

That, like the rose withering on the virgin thorn, has the accent of the sonnets to the fair young man; and in *Richard II*, I. iii. 214,

> Four lagging winters and four wanton springs

calls to mind from Sonnet 104

> Three winters cold
> Have from the forests shook three summers' pride
> Three beauteous springs to yellow autumn turn'd ...
> Three April perfumes in three hot Junes burn'd.

These touches in *Richard II* and *Romeo* show us a Shakespeare both able and likely, *c.* 1595, to write such poetry as he gave Helena in

> Your eyes are lode-stars, and your tongue's sweet air
> More tuneable than lark to shepherd's ear,
> When wheat is green, when hawthorn buds appear,
>   (I. i. 183 ff.)

and Hermia, when she speaks of

> the wood, where often you and I
> Upon faint primrose beds were wont to lie. (I. i. 214 f.)

In a history play, a tragedy, and a comedy with fairies in it, stylistic decorum will not be identical; but allowance being made for that, the range of poetic styles in the *Dream* is their range also in *Romeo* and *Richard II*.[1] It includes the formal rhetoric which, in the *Dream*, de la Mare and Dover Wilson thought alien and inferior to the rest. For Shakespeare and his audience that would not be so. The classic appreciation is Gladys Willcock's.[2] At this stage of Shakespeare's stylistic development 'strongly patterned language tends to occur in emotional contexts ... Strong feelings such as scorn or indignation will often find pointed schematic expression.' As the *Dream* illustrates, 'the

---

1. In *Shakespeare's Dramatic Language* (1976), Ch. 1, Madeleine Doran compares the three plays in terms of the style they share, and of the distinctive variation of it in each.

2. 'Shakespeare and Elizabethan English', *Sh.S.*, 7 (1954), pp. 16 f. 'Language was the principal approach to Art; ... this approach ... sought to unite grave affairs, even passion, with open artifice and verbal play.'

patterns are used to strike the note of love . . .'[1] 'It is the young men'—and in the *Dream* the young women—'whose feelings sweep them into the schemes . . . The young people display . . . obvious artifice, and this artifice they pursue, not because they do not have feelings but because they have.' Their rhetoric, moreover, establishes them as lovers accomplished in the idiom of court: it links them 'with the sonneteering world'. There is every reason to suppose that the formal rhetoric in the *Dream* was seen by Shakespeare and those for whom he wrote as the right partner for the lyricism. He improved on it, as a dramatic vehicle, later: but so he did on the lyricism, ideal though that is for the present play. Together, they characterize his style in the mid-1590s.

Most scholars are agreed that the *Dream* was designed to grace a wedding in a noble household. The one or two sceptics[2] provide a useful reminder that—as the others freely acknowledge —there is no proof of this. But so long as the distinction between fact and probability is made clear, there is nothing unscholarly in giving proportionable credence to probability. The *Dream* has many marks of a wedding play. The owner of 'this palace', blest by the fairies with the promise that he

> Ever shall in safety rest,

is likely to have been identifiable, not with Theseus alone, but also with the owner of a mansion where in actual fact there was on the occasion a 'best bride-bed'. The theme of the play is love

1. It is not 'the natural language of lovers', but the poetry of love's imaginative emotion, 'amplified into tropes, formal figures, and copious varying' (Doran, p. 11).

2. Of these, W. J. Lawrence's theory, in *Shakespeare's Workshop* (1928), was traversed by Chambers, *op. cit.*, Vol. 1, p. 361 (along with Edith Rickert's even wilder one, 'Political Propaganda and Satire in *A Midsummer Night's Dream*', *MP*, 21 (1923–4). Stanley Wells (Penguin edn, pp. 13 f.) raises more plausible doubts, and states his conclusion temperately: 'To me . . . it seems credible that *A Midsummer Night's Dream* was always intended for the public theatres'. I think so too, but only in the sense that Shakespeare would not mean the play to be laid aside after its one wedding performance. Wells contends that stage directions for entrances 'at one door' and 'at another' suggest he 'had in mind the structure of the public theatres'; but the screen of a great hall had likewise two doors. 'If Shakespeare's company could at any time muster enough boys for public performances' (and sundry public performances we know from the Q1 title-page there were) 'it could', he argues, 'have done so at the start'. But it is one thing to plan for resources you know will, exceptionally, be available, and then surmount the difficulty of a revival which takes you beyond those you normally possess; and another to plan from the start to exceed those normal resources. Why should you?

consummated in marriage. It is announced in the opening phrase: 'our nuptial hour / Draws on apace'; and its human action concludes with Theseus' summons, 'Lovers, to bed'. Romantic comedies do end with marriage; but that does not mean the *Dream* is no more apt than others to have been part of a wedding entertainment.[1] Among Shakespeare's, only one, concluding with the masque of Hymen, is at all suitable: comparison with the rest simply brings out what E. K. Chambers called the 'hymeneal' character of the *Dream*.[2] Even in *As You Like It*, though as J. R. Brown has shown, 'love's order' may be a principal branch of its central theme, there are by his account two others, 'social disorder', and 'Arden's subjective order'.[3] Certainly it is not focused exclusively on the theme of love leading to marriage, to which in the *Dream* everything relates, and more organically than is perhaps always realized.[4] The *Dream* appears purpose-built to suit the subject and occasion, which—as in *Love's Labour's Lost*, also evidently designed in the first place to be acted in private before noble patrons—furnished the foundation Shakespeare usually took from some written source. That both these plays were designed for occasions of that sort is further supported by what G. K. Hunter has observed in his fine comparative study of Shakespeare's early comedies and the court comedies of Lyly. '*Love's Labour's Lost* and *A Midsummer Night's Dream* are ... Lylian in their construction, and [are] so in marked contrast to the preceding plays.' They 'mark a change', he on the whole believes, 'largely because [their] occasion ... is aristocratic rather than popular'.[5]

For a private entertainment a shortish play might be wanted;

1. As Wells implies.

2. In *Gent.*, for example, the concurrent friendship theme is so important that, momentarily, true love is to be sacrificed to it; in *Mer.V.* the love-and-marriage theme culminates in mid-play; in *Ado* a bride is repudiated at the altar. The taming of a shrew, with two uncooperative wives at the wedding feast, would not fit marriage festivities. Obviously the *Dream* is 'hymeneal' in a way these comedies are not. Its hymeneal qualities are well brought out by Paul N. Siegel, '*A Midsummer Night's Dream* and the Wedding Guests', *Sh.Q.*, IV (1953), even though he cannot avoid all the hazards of imaginative reconstruction. A contemporary context of ideas in which P. A. Olson believes the *Dream* has its place is learnedly explored in his '*A Midsummer Night's Dream* and the meaning of Court Marriage', *ELH*, XXIV (1957).

3. *Shakespeare and his Comedies*, p. 153.

4. See below, pp. lxxxix n. 2, cxxx–xxxvi.

5. *John Lyly*, p. 318. He does not omit to show (pp. 319 f.) how 'with all [its] similarities to Lyly, *A Midsummer Night's Dream* remains obviously in the line of the earlier plays ... Shakespeare imitates Lyly yet remains true to himself'.

and the text of the *Dream* is on the shorter side, though in performance the songs and dances would lengthen it. The songs and the availability of boys as fairies to sing them and to take the parts of Peaseblossom, Cobweb, Moth and Mustardseed—indeed the whole lavish provision of music—suggest that Shakespeare could reckon on resources beyond those he normally had in the public theatre. So far as singing 'fairies' went, similar resources were to be needed in the final scene of *The Merry Wives of Windsor*, another play composed, it seems, for a private occasion. The requisite boys, in both plays, may have come from the same establishment.[1]

It seems likely that Queen Elizabeth was present when the *Dream* was first acted. It is so constructed as to bring in, to good dramatic purpose, two compliments that would fall gratefully upon her ear. She delighted in homage paid her as the Virgin Queen, and receives it in the myth-making about the Imperial votaress. She valued herself on the love of her subjects and in knowing how to cherish it; and as Theseus describes how, when great clerks broke down in their speeches of welcome,

> Out of this silence yet I pick'd a welcome,

since

> Love . . . and tongue-tied simplicity
> In least speak most, to my capacity,

she would recognize the tribute to her own behaviour and to the spirit that animated it.[2] It is not impossible to imagine the compliments as paid her *in absentia*; they would then reach her by hearsay or at a revival of the play at court; but it is more natural to imagine that Shakespeare knew she would hear them at the original performance.

If, on the strength of the previous discussion, *A Midsummer Night's Dream* can be dated in the period 1594 (not before autumn) to 1596, some of the occasions proposed for that performance can be ruled out. The marriages of Henry, Lord Herbert and Anne Russell in 1600,[3] and Southampton and Elizabeth Vernon in 1598, are too late. That of the Countess of Southampton and Sir Thomas Heneage on 2 May 1594 is just too early, and Frances, Lady Sidney's to the Earl of Essex in 1590 too early by far. Besides, Southampton's was clandestine, and landed him

---

1. See below, p. lvii.   2. See II. i. 158 n., v. i. 93 n.; below, p. lxvi.
3. An extant 'account of the Herbert wedding . . . tells of a mask . . . but of no play' (Chambers, *Shakespeare*, Vol. 1, p. 361).

in the Tower; those of his mother and the Countess of Essex also brought the bridegrooms into disfavour with the Queen. The choice lies, as Chambers says, between two other marriages.[1]

The earlier, on 26 January 1595, between Elizabeth Vere and William, Earl of Derby, was solemnized at Greenwich where the court then was; the Queen is known to have honoured with her presence the wedding festivities at Burghley House in the Strand. Elizabeth Vere was Lord Burghley's granddaughter and one of the Queen's maids of honour.[2] If the *Dream* were composed for this wedding, the tenuous possibilities of any connection with *Churchyard's Charitie* or Tasso's death must be dismissed, and the parallels with *Epithalamion* and *Amoretti* ascribed to coincidence. Further, the *Dream* must antedate *Richard II*, and in all probability *Romeo* as well.

Partly from these considerations, I concur with Peter Alexander[3] in taking the likelier occasion to be the marriage of Elizabeth Carey and Thomas, the son of Henry, Lord Berkeley, on 19 February 1596.[4] It evidently took place from the mansion of the bride's father, Sir George Carey, in Blackfriars. No other details being known, it cannot be established that the Queen was there; the court was at Greenwich, but she could have come to Blackfriars by water as easily as in January 1595 she came to the Strand. She would have motives for doing so; Elizabeth Carey was (like Elizabeth Vere) one of her goddaughters, and was, moreover, granddaughter of Henry, Lord Hunsdon, the Queen's Lord Chamberlain and cousin, whose son, Elizabeth Carey's father, Sir George, evidently stood high in her regard.[5] The connection of Shakespeare and his fellows with the Careys was far closer than any they had with the Stanleys, Earls of Derby. True, some of the company (but perhaps not including Shakespeare) had been members of Strange's (subsequently Derby's) Men, whose patron was Ferdinando, Lord Strange; he died Earl of Derby on 16 April 1594, nine months before his younger brother William's marriage. But at the time of that

1. *Id.*, i. 358 f.

2. *Ibid.*; and his *Gleanings*, pp. 61–6.

3. *Shakespeare's Life and Art*, p. 105.

4. If so, it was planned after the autumn of 1595, when 'a family chronicler tells us that affection between [the couple] began' (Chambers, *Shakespeare*, Vol. I, p. 359; *Gleanings*, p. 67, citing T. Smyth, *Lives of the Berkeleys*, Vol. II, pp. 383, 395). For the rest of this paragraph, see Chambers, *Shakespeare*, Vol. I, pp. 358 f.; *Elizabethan Stage*, Vol. II, pp. 192, 194 f.; A. R. Humphreys (ed.), *1H4*, p. xiv; Greg, p. 232 n. A, correcting Chambers' '17 March'.

5. See H. J. Oliver (ed.), *Wiv.*, p. xlvi.

marriage, and from shortly after Ferdinando's death, Shakespeare's company were already Lord Hunsdon's, and so they continued not only till Henry, Lord Hunsdon's death on 22 July 1596, but under Sir George's patronage thereafter. When, after a short interval,[1] on 17 April 1597 he received his father's office of Lord Chamberlain, they became the Lord Chamberlain's Men. There can be little doubt that it was for the Garter Feast of 23 April 1597, where Sir George was one of the Knights newly elected, that Shakespeare wrote *The Merry Wives of Windsor*.[2] For the scene at Herne's Oak he once more needed additional boys to impersonate fairies (pretended ones this time), and able to sing: Sir George maintained as part of his household a musical establishment from which they could have been drawn, and probably were. It is likely enough that Shakespeare had met the similar but more extensive need in the *Dream* from the same source. Sir George was a notable patron of music. In March 1596 he undertook to give a musical education to Robert Johnson, afterwards for ten years a composer for Shakespeare's company; and in 1597 John Dowland thanked Sir George for upholding his 'poore fortunes', and Lady Carey with him for their 'honourable favours'.[3] A play of which so much music is an integral part would be well calculated to please the bride's father at Elizabeth Carey's wedding.

The hypothesis which fits the largest number of facts and probabilities—though it must remain a hypothesis—is that *A Midsummer Night's Dream* was composed in the winter of 1595-6, for the Carey wedding on 19 February, and was subsequently, as the 1600 Q1 title-page testifies, 'Sundry times publickely acted'. In any event, it can be dated with confidence between autumn 1594 and spring 1596, and with certainty before 1598.

1. William, Lord Cobham (d. 5 March 1597) had succeeded Sir George's father.

2. H. J. Oliver (ed.), *Wiv.*, pp. xlv f., after J. L. Hotson. The Queen attended the Feast: tradition credits her with having, as it were, commissioned the play by her express wish to see Falstaff in love. The whole history of Shakespeare's company and the Hunsdons suggests a firm and active relationship. On 6 March 1600 they gave a private performance of *Henry IV* for Sir George, presumably at his Blackfriars house. Premises abutting on that house were acquired by James Burbage, their impresario, on 4 February 1596, a fortnight before Elizabeth Carey's marriage, though his plans to use them as a public theatre were vetoed (Chambers, *Elizabethan Stage*, Vol. II, pp. 204, 501, 503 f.).

3. Chambers, *Shakespeare*, Vol. I, p. 359, Vol. II, p. 86; John H. Long, *Shakespeare's Use of Music* (1955), pp. 3, 87, 103.

3. SOURCES AND ANTECEDENTS

That there was any comprehensive source for *A Midsummer Night's Dream* is altogether unlikely. There was evidently none, either, for *Love's Labour's Lost*, which, like the *Dream*, has every appearance of being composed in the first place for a private occasion: in each instance a subject appropriate to the occasion seems to have supplied the unifying factor in the play.[1] In respect of the source-materials of the *Dream* the subject of love fulfilled in marital union acted (one can presume) as the assembling and organizing agent, resembling the powerful magnet which attracts pieces of metal into the pattern of its field of force, or the crystal suspended in a supersaturated solution, which grows by giving to what it takes from the liquid its own crystalline form. The super-saturated solution existed in Shakespeare's mind. Literary sources, it has been admirably said, 'are, rightly speaking, the whole relevant contents of the writer's mind as he composes, and no account of them can be complete'.[2]

This applies with especial force to the topicalities and the courtly and popular traditions which the play reflects. When the sources lie in works Shakespeare had read or knew perhaps from performance, and which we ourselves can read, we are in a stronger position: the close comparisons we can make enable us to reach an informed opinion of the indebtedness. Most of his chief sources of this kind (with, I believe, a major and a minor exception) have been generally recognized, though two likely ones, because their availability to him is uncertain, are in dispute.[3]

He drew, no one seriously doubts or need doubt, upon a dozen identifiable works, including more than one of Chaucer's and several by John Lyly: the evidence consists in features, large and small, to which attention is called in the extracts from sources and in the commentary in the present edition. In this introduction I shall single out a few, mostly of the small but generally of the decisive sort. The life of Theseus in North's Plutarch[4] furnished the names of his earlier loves: Ariadne, Aegles,

---

1. 'It is probable that the main lines' of the *Dream*, 'the marriages, the fairies coming to give their blessing, the townsmen to give their play, were all suggested to Shakespeare by the very nature of his task'. Alexander, p. 106; see further, below, pp. cxxx–xxxvi; cf. lxxxix n. 2.
2. A. R. Humphreys (ed.), *1H4*, p. xxi.
3. See below, pp. lxiv, lxvi.
4. Below, Appendix I. 2; Bullough, Vol. I, pp. 368 f. and Text II.

Perigenia, and Antiopa. From Chaucer's *Knight's Tale*[1] Shakespeare three times echoes the phrase 'to doon his observaunce to May'; and from *The Legend of Good Women* he echoes in 'Pyramus and Thisbe' the apostrophe to the 'wikkede wal', the reference to its 'lym' and 'ston', and the wording 'with blody mouth' in the description of the lion.[2] 'Pyramus and Thisbe' is patently from Golding's version in his translation of Ovid's *Metamorphoses*, and employs Golding's word 'cranny'.[3] Outside the artisans' play, this favourite volume of Shakespeare's contributes notably to the hunting scene and to Titania's description of the 'progeny of evils' resulting from the quarrel between herself and Oberon.[4] The name Titania is not in Golding: Shakespeare had it from the original Latin, where Ovid uses it once for Diana and twice for Circe:[5] moon-goddess, and shape-shifter, each associated with a leading motif in the play. Shakespeare would know of Oberon from several sources, but it is in *Huon of Burdeux* that he is fairy king of a wood where travellers are bound to lose themselves and encounter his magic power; this, too, is an Oberon who distinguishes himself from evil creatures of the supernatural world, as Shakespeare's does with 'we are spirits of another sort', and whose assistance (as he tells Huon) is indispensable to a happy outcome.[6] Shakespeare could scarcely be ignorant of the most famous of all stories of a man metamorphosed by enchantment into an ass, *The Golden Ass* of Apuleius, which had been translated by William Adlington (1566).[7] As Dover Wilson pointed out, a modulation of the coarse love made to the ass by a lascivious matron, into the key of the blandishments lavished upon him by a charming captive princess, would yield something like Titania's courtship of Bottom. The blandishments include promises to 'bring thee every day . . . the kernels of nuts', and to 'deck thee'

1. Appendix I. 1; Bullough, *loc. cit.* and Text I. The debts are greater and more significant than Ann Thompson indicates n her frequently helpful *Shakespeare's Chaucer* (1978): cf. below, pp. lxi, lxxvii–xxx, lxxxiii–v.

2. Cf. Bullough, Vol. I, p. 374 and v. i. 130, 142 and nn., 160.

3. Appendix I. 7; Muir, *Sources*[2], p. 69; Bullough, Vol. I, p. 374 and Text IX.

4. Below, pp. lxxxv f., cxxvii f.; Appendix I. 3.

5. *Metamorphoses*, XIV, 382, 438; III. 173; Kittredge (ed.), *Sixteen Plays of Shakespeare*, p. 148, n. 3.

6. Appendix I. 5; Bullough, Vol. I, pp. 370 f. Beasts bray in his wood (cf. III. i. 105, 194). Cuningham (ed.), *MND*, p. xxxix, refers II. i. 232, III. i. 31 to *Huon*, Ch. xxx, p. 425.

7. Bullough, Vol. I, p. 372 and Text VI; Muir, *Sources*[2], p. 68; see Dover Wilson, *Shakespeare's Happy Comedies*, pp. 215–19 (but rejecting his hypotheses of an earlier form of the *Dream*, and a source-play). Apuleius is referred to in a part of Scot, *Discoverie of Witchcraft*, Shakespeare clearly drew upon; v. i. 91, v. iv. 99.

and 'bravely dress the hair of thy forehead'. Titania has a fairy
who shall 'fetch' Bottom 'new nuts'; she sticks 'musk-roses in his
sleek smooth head'; he finds himself 'marvellous hairy about
the face', and Oberon observes she has 'his hairy temples rounded/
With coronet of fresh and fragrant flowers'. At the moment of
metamorphosis, Apuleius' 'hair did turn in ruggedness' and his
'tender skin waxed tough'. It is possible that Shakespeare picked
up this last phrase and that it emerged, transferred in application,
when Bottom declares himself 'such a tender ass'. In the inset
story of Cupid and Psyche, Venus plans to take a jealous vengeance by having Psyche fall in love with 'the most vile' creature
living; as 'jealous Oberon' plans Titania shall, with her eyes
bewitched,

> Wake when some vile thing is near.

Apuleius, and an English sailor in a story told from Bodin by
Reginald Scot in *The discoverie of witchcraft*, 1584,[1] have their
whole bodies changed into the ass-form. But because at v. v. 99
Scot is speaking of the sailor eating hay, he there calls him
'Bodin's asseheaded man'. Elsewhere in Scot's book (treated
with the same scorn, as sheer superstition) Shakespeare would
find recipes for setting 'an horse or an asses head upon a man's
shoulders', or at least for creating an illusion that this had been
done. From the chapters about the 'English man' he picked up
the term 'provender' in conjunction with 'hay': Scot cites 'that
foolish fable of *Praestantius* his father, who . . . did eate provender
and haie among other horsses'. In the *Dream*, the fairy recognizes
Robin Goodfellow as 'that knavish sprite', and Oberon suspects
that perhaps he has been committing his 'knaveries' on purpose.
Scot, among a number of references to him, associating him with
'hob gobblin' and other bugbears of popular belief, writes of 'the
knaverie of Robin Goodfellow' and asserts that 'By this time all
kentishmen know (a few fooles excepted) that Robin Goodfellow
is a knave'. He attributes to him the exclamation 'What have we
here?', which becomes, in Shakespeare, Puck's 'What hempen
homespuns have we swaggering here?' on coming upon the
artisans' rehearsal. He reports the good that is believed of him
as well as the bad: his 'grinding of malt or mustard', and his
'sweeping of the house at midnight' which Puck arrives to do in
the conclusion of the play. Scot even offered a hint for his

---

1. Appendix I. 6, which adds to Bullough, Vol. I, pp. 372 f. and Text VII. For
the 'kentishmen' and the 'ventriloqua of Westwell', see Scot, XVI. vii. 483 and
VII. ii. 130 f.; for the rest of the paragraph Appendix I. 6. Cf. pp. lxv, lxxxiii.

ventriloquism, in the story of Mildred of Westwell. In the same breath with Robin he mentions 'the puckle', though he does not identify the two.

Debts in the *Dream* to the *Diana* of Montemayor and to John Lyly cause no surprise. The *Diana* was a principal source of *Two Gentlemen of Verona*. *Love's Labour's Lost*, however different from any play by Lyly, is reminiscent of him in various respects; *Endimion*, for example, furnished in Sir Tophas a starting-point for Armado: and shortly after writing the *Dream*, Shakespeare was to set Falstaff parodying *Euphues* and *Campaspe*.[1]

To the Chaucerian sources of the *Dream* should be added *The Merchant's Tale*. Tyrwhitt suggested that Pluto and Proserpina, its king and queen of fairy, were progenitors of Oberon and Titania; and Geoffrey Bullough has shown good reason to think him right. The notion of Bottom embraced by the fairy queen may have germinated from the *Tale of Sir Thopas*.[2]

A source which so far as I am aware has been overlooked is Spenser's *Shepheardes Calender*.[3] From the appropriate months of November and December it contributes to Titania's foul-weather speech; from the same two months, through references to what they have lost or destroyed, and directly from May, June, and August, it contributes to the sylvan beauty of the setting. It has the 'hawthorn buds' and 'flowrets' Helena and Oberon speak of: the first in May, the second in November and also in February. In December, 'the fragrant flowres' would constitute for Shakespeare an associative link between the *Calender* and two other sources. His

> With coronet of fresh and fragrant flowers

comes verbatim from Golding's

> . . . with a crowne of fresh and fragrant flowers

1. For *Diana* and its sequel, tr. B. Yong, see below, pp. lxiv. n. 1, lxxxi, cxxv. n. 2; Furness, pp. 283–6; Clifford Leech (ed.), *Gent.*, xli. ff.; for Lyly, below, pp. lxxx f.; Hunter, p. 317 (which, without denying the common ancestry in the Commedia dell' Arte, corrects R. David (ed.), *LLL*, p. xxxv); *1H4*, II. iv. 395–7, 402–9 and Humphreys's nn.

2. Bullough, p. 370: the major features of the tale significant for Shakespeare are 'fairy monarchs commenting on human life and taking sides for and against mortals while quarrelling among themselves'; 'the theme of marriage associated with [them]'; and 'discussion of the ethics of marriage and the relation between the sexes'. Coghill, *Shakespeare's Professional Skills*, p. 56, compares Bottom as Titania's beloved with what Chaucer's burlesque and bourgeois knight errant Sir Thopas anticipates: 'Me dremed al this night, pardee,/An elf-queene shall my lemman be.' (*Canterbury Tales*, VIII. 787 f.)

3. See II. i. 88 ff. and nn.; III. ii. 388 n.; I. i. 185, 209, II. i. 252, IV. i. 51–5 n.

and as in December in the *Calender* the 'fragrant flowres' are
withered, so in Montemayor's *Diana* 'winter' will despoil the
meadow 'of fresh and fragrant flowers'. Spenser's 'flowers' are
dewed with 'teares', and through association with

> The kindly dewe drops from the higher tree
> And wets the little plants,

this calls up the November eclogue, where the poetical word
'flouret' is highlighted by E. K.'s gloss. Hence in the *Dream* the
collocations when Oberon describes 'that dew' which

> Stood now within the pretty flowerets' eyes
> Like tears.

Spenserian, too, whether from the *Calender* or *Amoretti* or both, is
the eglantine; and whether from the *Calender* or *Epithalamion* or
both, the image of 'Phoebe' beholding

> Her silver visage in the watery glass.

In the August eclogue

> Dame Cynthia's silver raye . . .
> Upon the glyttering wave doth playe,

which evidently brought to mind, from 'June', the 'christall
faces' of fairies, Graces, and nymphs who assemble 'when
Phoebe shineth bright'. Together, the two passages furnish
Shakespeare with 'Phoebe' and 'silver'; and through 'faces',
'wave', and 'christall', with 'visage', 'watery', and 'glass', besides
the image as a whole in correspondence with the one in 'August'.
The reference, in 'June', to fairies, distinguishes them, as *Epithalamion* does, from evil creatures of the night: this is the most
important of all among the parallels between Spenserian poems
and the *Dream*.

The *Calender* is a minor neglected source of the *Dream*: Seneca
is a major one.[1] Naturally, Shakespeare's debt to Seneca in tragedy
and tragical history has been recognized; but a dramatist who
remembers him in such plays does not lose his familiarity with
him because he is writing comedy. Shakespeare could have
decided that Seneca offered nothing in keeping with that genre;
but clearly he found it otherwise. In the *Dream*, the principal
debts are to Medea's invocation of Hecate (*Medea*), and ex-
tensively to the *Hippolytus*; both works, judging from his use of
them elsewhere as well as here, were favourites with Shakespeare.

---

1. For translations, see Appendix 1. 4; for the Latin, the nn. which follow.

The most striking parallel is between Seneca's seascape with Cupid all armed (*Hippolytus*), and Shakespeare's in the vision which Oberon relates to Puck.[1] More than local, however, is the resemblance to Phaedra's of Helena's self-abasement in love, and her desperate resolves.[2] Fullest of suggestion, perhaps, is the prayer of Phaedra's nurse that three-formed Hecate, bright orb of heaven, glory of the night, great goddess of the woods and groves, will ensnare the mind of Hippolytus so that he may turn back into the fealty of love.[3] In a play which makes its supernatural agents runners beside the triple Hecate's team, Demetrius, in woods of which the moon is regent, is turned back into the fealty of his original love for Helena by having his mind supernaturally ensnared. The *Hippolytus* opens with a hunting scene which evidently contributed to Shakespeare's; as Medea's invocation did to the picture of cosmic disorder, and (probably) the plague in *Oedipus* to that of the afflictions in the countryside.[4]

1. ipsumque Phoebum, tela qui nervo regit,/figit sagitta certior missa puer/volitatque caelo pariter et terris gravis./*Nutrix.* Deum esse amorem turpis et vitrio furens/finxit libido, quoque liberior foret/titulum furori numinis falsi addidit/natum per omnes scilicet terras vagum/Erycina mittit, ille per caelum volans/proterva tenera tela molitur manu/regnumque tantum minimus e superis habet./vana ista demens animus ascivit sibi/Venerisque numen finxit atque arcus dei . . . *Chorus* . . . qua terra salo/cingitur alto quaque per ipsum/ candida mundum sidera currunt,/ haec regna tenet puer immitis/spicula cuius sentit in imis/caerulus undis grex Nereidum/flammamque nequit relevare mari./ . . . amat insani belua ponti/ . . . [Cupid] iubet caelo superos relicto/ . . . habitare terras.

2. Hunc in nivosi collis haerentem iugis,/et aspera agili saxa calcantem pede/sequi per alta nemora, per montes placet./*Nutrix.* Resistet ille seque mulcendum dabit/ . . . ? tibi ponet odium, cuius odio forsitan/persequitur omnes?/ . . . Fugiet./*Phaedra.* Per ipsa maria si fugiet, sequar./ . . . mei non sum potens./te vel per ignes, per mare insanum sequar/rupesque et amnes, unda quos torrens rapit:/quacumque gressus tuleris hac amens agar—/iterum, superbe, genibus advolvor tuis./ . . . Hippolyte, nunc me compotem voti facis;/sanas furentem. maius hoc voto meo est/ . . . manibus immoriar tuis.

3. Regina nemorum . . . /o magna silvas inter et lucos dea/clarumque caeli sidus et noctis decus,/ cuius relucet mundus alterna vice,/Hecate triformis . . . /animum regentem tristis Hippolyti doma;/ . . . amare discat, mutuos ignes ferat./innecte mentem . . . /in iura Venus redeat.

4. *Hippolytus*: Ite, umbrosas cingite silvas/summaque montis iuga, Cecropii!/ . . . planta lustrate . . . /quae . . . /subiecta iacent. Thriasiis/ vallibus . . . At vos laxas canibus tacitis/mittite habenas; . . ./ . . . et pugnaces/tendant Cretes fortia trito/vincula collo./at Spartanos (genus est audax/avidumque ferae) nodo cautus/propiore liga. veniet tempus,/cum latratu cava saxa sonent:/nunc demissi nare sagaci/captent auras lustraque presso/ quaerant rostro, dum lux dubia est/dum signa pedum roscida tellus/impressa tenet.

Medea: Nunc. . ., noctium sidis, veni/pessimos induta vultus, fronte non una minax./Tibi . . . / . . . mundus lege confusa . . . / . . . temporum flexi vices:/

In seeking to identify Shakespearean sources it is reassuring to
know that a work in question was available in print. All the same,
he read some in manuscript: Marlowe's sestiads of *Hero and
Leander* and Yong's translation of *Diana* and *Diana Enamorada* we
know to have been in existence though unpublished.[1] Accordingly
it is not a grave objection to the claim that 'Pyramus and Thisbe'
parodies, among other inept versions of the story, Thomas
Mouffet's in *Of the Silkewormes, and their Flies*, that if so, Shakespeare must have read it in manuscript. It was published only in
1599, 'but it is likely', writes Kenneth Muir, 'to have been
written some years earlier, perhaps as early as 1589'. The
parallels he adduces are fully sufficient, it appears to me, to show
that one author is echoing the other;[2] and it is unlikely that
Mouffet, in what he designed as a serious poem, would borrow
from a burlesque. If Shakespeare used Mouffet, it was for the
single purpose of parody in his 'Pyramus'.[3] If he was influenced
by Anthony Munday's play *John a Kent and John a Cumber*,[4] that
influence operated at many points: its importance would lie in
having helped to suggest the combination of a considerable

aestiva tellus floruit cantu meo,/coactu messem vidit hibernam Ceres./ . . .
Video Triviae currus agiles,/ . . . agitat . . . quos facie/lurida maesta, . . . / . . . sic
face tristem/pallida lucem funde per auras,/horrore novo terre populos/ . . .
Oedipus: fecimus caelum nocens/ . . . gravis et ater incubat terris vapor./ . .
denegat fructum Ceres/adulta, et altis flava cum spicis tremat,/arente culmo
sterilis emoritur seges./ . . . Prima vis tardas tetigit bidentes;/laniger pingues
male carpsit herbas./ . . . Incubant agris pecudes relictae;/taurus armento
pereunte marcet; . . . /omnia nostrum sensere malum . . . / . . . aegro/rubor in
vultu, maculaeque caput/sparsere leves; tum vapor ipsam/corporis arcem
flammeus urit/ . . .

1. Marlowe d. 30 May 1593; *Hero and Leander* was entered in S.R. 28 Sept.
1593; Yong completed his translation in May 1583 (Kennedy, ed. cit., p. xxxi).
For debts to Marlowe, see I. i. 78, 170, 189, II. i. 39, III. ii. 355, 357, 379, v. i. 36,
40, 41, 53 nn.; for parallels with Yong (not all debts), I. i. 235, II. i. 169–72,
214, II. ii. 103, 110 ff., 114 f., 117, 131, III. i. 105 f., III. ii. 3, 141 f., 170, 187 f.,
190, IV. i. 51–4, 72 f., 80 f., 174 f., 183 f., 193, IV. ii. 13, v. i. 263, 274–6 nn.
2. See Muir, *Sources²*, pp. 73–6 and nn. 25–8.
3. Except that 'Hop in his walks . . .,/Feed him' (III. i. 158 f.) probably picks
up a phrase of Mouffet's; perhaps because his two preceding lines: 'Transforme
thy selfe into a courser brave,/What cannot love transforme itself into?' chimed
with the transformation of Bottom. The courser might form an association-link
with Scot's man-horse who ate 'provender', as Bottom would like to. Muir
recognizes that if Mouffet's lines actually went towards suggesting Bottom's
transformation, it would be in combination with other sources. Further debts
he thinks possible, outside the Pyramus story, leave me, with Bullough, un-
convinced: in particular, there are likelier origins for v. i. 1, 4, 21 f., 49. See
Muir, *loc. cit.* and n. 25, and *Sources¹*, pp. 40–2, 45.
4. *MSR*, ed. M. St Clare Byrne.

number of the leading features of the *Dream*. These precedents (if that is what they are) have been well summarized by Nevill Coghill:[1] Munday has:

Lovers in flight from parental opposition to their love.
Moonlit woods through which they flee to join their lovers.
A mischievous fairy imp, in service to a master of magic.
A crew of clowns who organise buffoonish entertainment in honour of their territorial overlord, on the occasion of a double wedding. Contention for the leading part. Malapropisms.
Young men led by an invisible voice until they fall exhausted.
A 'happy ending' with True Lovers properly paired and wedded.

These features are seen by Coghill as making 'in combination . . . a dramatic vehicle, a schema; . . . a main shape or formula for a stage-action'; the nearest thing, in fact, to the comprehensive source which beyond this the *Dream* does not have. As evidence of a relationship between the two plays these general resemblances are supported by three parallels in the dialogue, two of them verbally close.[2] As they sink down exhausted, 'Faintness constraineth me', says Demetrius, and Hermia, 'Never so weary . . . I can . . . no further go'. In like plight, Munday's Oswen exclaims 'I am grown so faint/That I must needes lye down on mere constraint,'[3] and Amery, 'I never was so wearie . . . I can goe no longer'. Coming upon the rehearsal, Puck cries 'What, a play toward! I'll be . . . an actor . . . if I see cause'. Shrimp, his equivalent in *John a Kent*, reports to his master, 'yonder's great preparation for a play', and their dialogue ends with the magician declaring 'in thy play I purpose to make one'. In Munday, the passages are connected: at the same time as this intervention is prepared for, so is that of Shrimp which leaves Oswen and Amery exhausted; hence if the one episode recurred to Shakespeare it would be likely to bring the other with it. There is no such

1. Coghill, pp. 50 f., 53. He also compares with Puck disrupting the rehearsal, his speed on Oberon's errands, and his pleasure in the resulting mischief, Shrimp's throwing the rustic's serenade into confusion (l. 580 S.D.s), his 'I fly Sir, and am there alreadie' (988), and his 'Why now is Shrimpe in the height of his bravery/That he may execute some part of his Master's knaverie (376 f.). The fool's coat thrust on Cumber (1378–84) compares with the ass-head clapped on Bottom; and with Theseus on the prospect of amateurish entertainment, Oswen and Pembrook on the like: 'How bad so ere, yet must ye needes accept it'; 'Else Oswen were we very much to blame', etc. (388–94).
2. III. ii. 428, 441, 443; m. i. 75 f. and nn.
3. The words in rhyme are the likelier to be the source.

juxtaposition at one point in the *Dream* to affect Munday, if he were the debtor, in the same way. The question of who influenced whom is complicated by uncertainty about the date of *John a Kent*. It is extant in Munday's autograph, signed by him; another hand has added a date, of which 'Decembris' and the year survive. Unfortunately, it is disputed how the final figure of the year should be read. In 1955, I. M. Shapiro published, with an enlarged facsimile, an article arguing that the MS. read, not '1596', but '1590':[1] if the play existed in 1590, it cannot have borrowed from the *Dream*. If the subscribed date tells us simply that it existed in December 1596,[2] that settles nothing; it does not tell us when, prior to that date, the autograph was written. It might have been at a time leaving Shakespeare ample opportunity to borrow from it. Alternatively, in 1596 after 19 February (the date of the latest occasion for which the *Dream* is likely to have been composed), and before December, there is an interval during which Munday might have been the borrower; if the *Dream* were in fact composed earlier the corresponding interval would be longer. Could we be certain, however, that Greg is correct in his reasonable guess that *John a Kent* is *The Wise Man of West Chester*, produced by the Admiral's Men on 3 December 1594 and remaining in their repertory up to 18 July 1597, we could be all but sure that it is a source of Shakespeare's play.[3] If so, it is, as Coghill's comparison shows, a very significant one.

Not all the antecedents of the *Dream* were written ones. Some were topical, like (probably) the Scottish affair of the lion (see p. xxxiv), or (without doubt) the behaviour of Elizabeth when on progress. At Warwick in 1572 the Recorder, Mr Aglionby, feared that in his speech of welcome he might, like the great clerks Theseus tells of, dumbly break off, throttling his accents in his fears. When he had finished, ' "Come hither, little Recorder", said Elizabeth . . . "It was told me that you would be afraid to

1. 'The Significance of a Date', *Sh.S.*, 8. The numeral was formed, as Shapiro proposes, in two strokes (which is unusual for a six); but the fact that it was made clockwise is unusual for a zero, and so is a zero with a tail and flourish such as this. Shapiro is incorrect when he says that no other six is to be found in which the 'loop' crosses the ascender: there is one on the same page, and examples do not seem hard to find. I owe these observations to Anthony Hammond, who kindly examined the original MS. on my behalf.

2. '. . . when I visited Greg for the last time in December 1958', wrote F. P. Wilson, 19 January 1961, to Harold Jenkins (by whose courtesy I quote the letter), 'I got him to look again at the date in the John a Kent MS. (Facsim.). He said after a minute or two "I still think it's 1596." '

3. Greg (ed.), *Henslowe's Diary*, II, 172; E. K. Chambers, *Elizabethan Stage*, Vol. III, p. 446.

look upon me or to speak boldly; but you were not so afraid of me as I was of you . . ." '. At Norwich in 1578, Stephen Limbert, the schoolmaster, 'having to make a Latin speech and seeming nervous, "Be not afraid" she said graciously; and at the end . . . declaring "It is the best that ever I heard" ', 'purchased a loyal heart at the cost of a small lie'.[1] Shakespeare's allusion[2] is no doubt to her habitual conduct rather than to any particular incident.

Whatever the topical allusion in the myth of the mermaid and the falling stars (II. i. 150 ff.), it cannot be, as Warburton and some of his successors asserted, to Mary Queen of Scots.[3] On the subject of her execution (1587), Elizabeth was far too sensitive for a dramatist to refer with safety to Mary and those who on her behalf and with her connivance in their treasons plunged to destruction. Even if Elizabeth were not present to hear it, such an allusion would quickly be reported to her. It is possible that attempts to interpret the allegory of Oberon's vision have been directed too much to the realm of high politics. Nashe, in *Pierce Penilesse* (1592), drawing, as I take it Shakespeare is, a contrast with the chaste virtue of the Virgin Queen, declares 'The Court I dare not touch, but surely there (as in the Heavens) be many falling starres, and but one true Diana.'[4] Perhaps the falling stars in Shakespeare and in Nashe are the same: the siren mermaid may personify the temptation of sexual desire. If individuals are concerned, as 'certain stars' suggests, maybe they should be looked for among those who pursued amorous affairs at court. The falls in Nashe are from sexual virtue: and royal favour was also a sphere from which it was easy to fall through an amour or even a disapproved marriage. During the period when the *Dream* must have been written, Raleigh, for his love-affair with Elizabeth Throckmorton (a maid of honour), was still forbidden the court. In 1592 both had been imprisoned in the Tower, Raleigh from July to September; it was not until after his Guiana voyage of

1. J. E. Neale, *Queen Elizabeth* (1934), p. 208; J. Nichol, *The Progresses and Public Processions of Queen Elizabeth* (1788), Vol. I, D2ᵛ; Vol. II, D3ᵛ–E1ᵛ.

2. v. i. 93 ff.

3. Furness, pp. 75–8, who quotes the best argument for the identification: Mary was caricatured in her own day as a mermaid, bearing a sceptre in the form of a hawk's lure (W. Pinkerton, *N. & Q.*, 1864). Dr Frances Yates (in conversation) maintained that the mermaid, as well as the imperial votaress, was Elizabeth; the one complimenting her virginity, the other her charms. Nashe's 'falling stars' image (see immediately below) seems to confirm the usual view that the mermaid (= siren) is to be looked on with disfavour; and though in *The Faerie Queene* Gloriana, Mercilla, and Belphoebe all symbolize Elizabeth, no two share a scene.

4. *Works*, ed. R. B. McKerrow, revised F. P. Wilson, (1966), Vol. I, p. 216.

1595 and his part in the triumph at Cadiz in the summer of 1596 that he was again allowed to exercise his court appointment of Captain of the Guard.[1]

Less elusive is the reflection in the vision of the mermaid of mythological water-pageantry and firework displays like those by which the Queen was entertained at Kenilworth in 1591 and at Elvetham in 1595. Dover Wilson, indeed, roundly asserts the Kenilworth entertainment as Shakespeare's original, while E. K. Chambers canvasses, without pressing, the claims of Elvetham.[2] At Kenilworth, Triton appeared upon a swimming mermaid; and upon a boat in the semblance of a dolphin there came and sang a personage variously identified as Proteus, or (which in view of the well-known legend is much more probable) Arion. At Elvetham, conducted by many 'sea-persons', Neæra the sea-nymph sang a ditty; the spectacle included what looked like a monster (having 'hornes of wild-fire continuously burning'). But as Chambers is careful to point out, at neither Elvetham nor Kenilworth did the main display of fireworks coincide with the water-pageant; nor did either actually have a mermaid on a dolphin's back. Reminiscence or report from Elvetham may have helped to associate a singing sea-maid with Oberon; among the items there, a dancing round of fairies was led by their queen, who named herself Auberon's consort. Yet while this may well be so, the very fact that what Oberon describes is comparable up to a point with each of the two entertainments confirms the conclusion that it has for antecedent not one occasion, but the kind of courtly diversion they both exemplify. It was a kind in which the pageantry frequently drew (as with Arion) from Ovid's mythology, or still better, created new myth in the Ovidian style, as Shakespeare does in Oberon's narrative.[3]

To recall such diversions was especially appropriate in a play which, unless we are much mistaken, was first and foremost a courtly diversion itself. Another is represented in the hunting-scene; and at night Theseus has three others offered him, besides

1. W. Stebbing, *Sir Walter Raleigh*, p. 133; M. C. Bradbrook, *The School of Night*, p. 5. Raleigh and his circle seem a target in *LLL*; in court affairs some continuity of censure would be far from surprising. Though sceptical of the 'school of night', Agnes Latham, the learned and judicious editor of Raleigh's poems, 'wouldn't say no' to his being the subject of Nashe's allusion and Shakespeare's here. The official story, she tells me, was of forced marriage after seduction; and his consequent fall from royal favour was spectacular.

2. Dover Wilson, pp. 194–9 (cf. in Furness, pp. 79–88, 91, Boaden, Halpin, and Furness himself); E. K. Chambers, *Gleanings*, pp. 63 f.

3. C. L. Barber, *Shakespeare's Festive Comedy*, p. 122.

the artisans' play he chooses. Courtly pastime is part of the festive tradition in which the *Dream* is strongly rooted, and of which we are so fortunate as to have C. L. Barber's admirable study.[1] In that tradition, even more important for the *Dream* are folk-customs and the folk-beliefs that went with them. Mumming was a popular custom; and the prologue and characters' self-announcements which take up almost half of 'Pyramus and Thisbe' are of the sort one gets, observes Barber, in the Mummers' Play. In that play the comic resuscitation episode is recognized by folklorists as a survival from the annual resurrection of the fertility god. There is something not altogether dissimilar about Bottom's comic alacrity in springing back to life after his stage-death, an effect prepared in the rehearsal-scene by his insistence that the audience must not think Pyramus 'killed indeed'. And (to claim no more) it is in keeping with the fertility theme in the fairy blessing which shortly follows. Wisely, Barber warns us that 'one can make too much of such analogies'. But, as he adds, they do illustrate the rich traditional meanings available in the materials 'Shakespeare was handling'.[2] The richest were in the May-game; even more than in the Mummers' Play it was in the May-game that the tradition of the ancient fertility cult lived on. The 'observaunce to May' was 'everybody's pastime': it was at least as much a popular custom as a courtly one. There is a correspondence in the *Dream*'s whole action with the movement of the May-game, from the town to the woods and back, bringing home the summer. The coming to court of the artisans, and even of the fairies with their blessing, has a certain kinship with the good-luck visit of a May King and May Queen to the great house of their neighbourhood. The May Queen presented the person of the Summer Lady, with whom Titania is associated when, identifying herself to Bottom as no common spirit, she declares

The summer still doth tend upon my state.

Oberon, traditional fairy ruler, has been given attributes of the May King, patron of new and renewed fertility, and vernal genius of the greenwood which is the seat of Oberon's magic

1. *Id.*; I am especially indebted to 'May Games and Metamorphoses on a Midsummer Night', his chapter (pp. 119-62) on the *Dream*. On courtly pastime, prominent but used differently in *LLL* and *MND*, see his pp. 119, 126, 144 f.

2. Chambers, *The English Folk Play*; Barber, pp. 138, 151 f., 154 n. 25 concluded; K. M. Briggs, *The Anatomy of Puck*, p. 77, adds the resemblance of Puck, on his final appearance, to the mummer who makes space for the rest by sweeping the floor with a broom.

power.[1] That power he employs to end the discord between himself and Titania (and so the blight it entailed); to further happy and prospectively fruitful marriages for the young lovers; and to bless both theirs and Theseus and Hippolyta's.

To go maying was not something people did only on May-day; and there were other similar customs; Shakespeare has Perdita speak of 'Whitsun pastorals', which might be among the festivities in his mind while composing the *Dream*: 'the middle summer's spring' to which Titania refers would aptly describe Whitsun. His title sends the reader's thoughts to St John's Eve and its associations with magic: yet it can be read as 'The Dream of a Midsummer Night' no less than as 'A Dream of Midsummer Night'. It would not be like Shakespeare to tie himself either to May-day or Midsummer Eve customs or beliefs. His fairy must gather dew, and Theseus' palace is to be asperged with the fairies' 'field-dew consecrate': it was to dew gathered on May-day morning that magic properties were attributed. But 'night-rule' in the woods was appropriated to Midsummer Eve: that was when in Puritan Stubbes's censorious phrase the young people ran 'gadding to the woods', and spent the night there.[2]

It was a time when both magic and madness were abroad. 'Midsummer madness' was proverbial; Olivia uses the expression in *Twelfth Night*. The lovers' follies in the wood doubly fit the season, both as folly, and as induced by magic. The fairy folklore fits with it too, and as Barber acknowledges, includes 'all the main characteristics of fairies in popular belief: they appear in the forest, at midnight, and leave at sunrise' (or sometimes shortly after); 'they take children, dance in ringlets'. For two excellent reasons, most of the popular folklore is about Puck as Robin Goodfellow.[3] It is by the Fairy's recognition of him, and his further identification of himself to her, that the audience is initiated into the fairies' part in the play, and Shakespeare is careful at that point to connect it with familiar beliefs:[4] in the action of the play it is Robin who has directly to do with mortals, just as in the folklore he was a household spirit, or out of doors plagued travellers with practical jokes.

How the size of Shakespeare's fairies relates to their ante-

---

1. Barber, pp. 119–21, 124, 132, 137 f.

2. *Id.*, pp. 119, 120 and n. 2, 123 n. 8, 127, 139. Plants with magic properties were also to be gathered then: see David P. Young, *Something of Great Constancy* (1966), p. 20, citing Brand's *Popular Antiquities*, ed. W. C. Hazlitt; R. W. Dent, 'Imagination in *A Midsummer Night's Dream*', *Sh.Q.* (1964), p. 119, n. 10.

3. Barber, pp. 122, 144; Dent, p. 118.   4. Cf. Dent, p. 118.

cedents is a question.[1] As depicted by Mercutio, Mab and her retinue are diminutive. In Oberon's and Titania's people, the audience is made to imagine elves with leathern coats made of bats' wings, who when frightened creep into acorn cups; or a fairy who is venturous in daring to raid a squirrel's hoard. The fairies' time-scale, too, enables them to accomplish important duties in 'the third part of a minute'. The hold Shakespeare trusts his dialogue to have on the imagination of the audience is apparent when Cobweb, though he is before their eyes at child-size, is commissioned to hunt the bumble-bee, taking care not to be 'overflown' with the honey bag. What precedent, if any, had Shakespeare for his diminutive fairies? Small fairies were the rule: but small meant the size of a three-year-old child, or the two-foot-tall goblins of Paracelsus, or in *Huon of Burdeux*, Oberon's stature as a three-foot dwarf. In Lyly's *Endimion*, like *Huon* a source of the *Dream*, the fairies are 'faire babies', and were no doubt impersonated by the smallest among Lyly's child actors from St Paul's choir-school.[2] In folk-belief, however, fairies of adult human size, though not the most frequent type, are not far to seek. Neither Titania nor Oberon—though Titania was played, presumably, by a boy rather than a man—is likely to have been (in performance) of small-child size. Titania winds Bottom in her arms.[3] But no mention of diminutive fairies before Shakespeare's was discovered by M. W. Latham, though in literature they subsequently became the norm and are found from time to time outside it. Latham concluded that Shakespeare invented them, and that all their later appearances derive ultimately from him.[4] Neither conclusion commends itself to our foremost living authority on fairy lore, Dr Katharine M. Briggs;[5]

1. *Id.*, pp. 144 f. and n. 20. The principal studies on this and on the question of antecedents for their benevolence are those of M. W. Latham in *The Elizabethan Fairies* (1930) Chs v and vi (see below, n. 4, pp. lxxii n. 1, lxxv n. 1), and Katharine M. Briggs in *The Anatomy of Puck* (1959). See further her later publications, cited below, and the 'Tiny Fairies' motif, no. F. 239.4.3. in Stith Thompson, *The Motif Index of Folk Literature* (1955), and Ernest Baughman, *Type and Motif Index of the Folk Tales of England and N. America* (1966), citing instances from Cornwall, Derbyshire, Northumberland and Scotland.

2. *Works*, ed. R. W. Bond, Vol. III, pp. 59 f.

3. Cf. Thompson, and Baughman, index nos. F.239.4.1 and (childsize) 2; Briggs, *Puck*, p. 78; and p. 25 and n. 7, quoting Richard Bovet, *Pandaimonium* (1684) on fairies 'generally nearer the smaller size of men'. *Pace* E. Schanzer, this was not the most prevalent belief: but his arguments hold good against a child-sized Titania ('*A Midsummer Night's Dream*' in *Shakespeare: The Comedies*, ed. K. Muir, p. 30; cf. Barber, p. 45).   4. Pp. 178–80; cf. 181–5, 188–90.

5. *Puck*, p. 13; cf. her *Fairies in Tradition and Literature* (1967) p. 3.

and both are inherently improbable. No doubt there is a literary tradition of such fairies which Shakespeare has inspired: it includes, most probably, Drayton's 'Nimphidia' and perhaps Ben Jonson's 'span-long fairies' in *The Sad Shepherd*;[1] with many other examples from that day to this. But a considerable number of stories of diminutive fairies have been collected from the lips of quite unliterary people,[2] and it is not credible that these are generally of literary and ultimately of Shakespearean origin. As with traditional ballads, the beliefs to which they testify are likely to have existed for generations before they attracted the attention of collectors and were recorded. Fairies of far less than child-size were conceived of before Shakespeare's time: Dr Briggs adduces the Portunes, described in the MS. of *Otia Imperialia*, by Gervase of Tilbury (*fl. c.* 1211), as half-an-inch in height, though the context suggests this is a scribal error for six inches.[3] Giraldus Cambrensis relates how Elidorus was taken to a fairy kingdom with inhabitants of the smallest stature, their horses being the size of hares (*leporariis in quantitate conformes*).[4]

We can, however, come much nearer to Shakespeare; there are genuinely diminutive fairies he is likely to have known about.

1. Latham, pp. 202 f., 200, 212.
2. For truly diminutive fairies cf. Thomas Keightley, *The Fairy Mythology* (1900), Appendix I. 26 ('little midgets'), II. 30 (cakes pockmarked by their dancing in high heels), II. 24 (like a swarm of bees: raid barn through keyhole); p. 95 (Danish Ballad, 'Eline of Villenskor', troll ant-size), quoted Briggs, *Puck*, pp. 14, 231; cf. p. 218 (from Robert Hunt, *Popular Romances of the West of England* (1881), p. 102) fairies like a swarm of bees; and Appendix II. 27 (from Mrs Bray, *Borders of the Tamar and Tavy*) a tiny pixy; and no. 40 (from S. H. O'Grady, *Sylva Godelica* (1892), pp. 269–85) 'Fergus MacLeda and the Wee Folk' (cf. her *Fairies*, p. 22, from Hunt, *op. cit.*, pp. 98–101, 'Fergus O'Conla'). See her *Dictionary of British Folk Tales* (1971), Part B, I. 279: 'I weat, you weat' (grain carried off straw by straw through keyhole); p. 235 'The Fairy Midwife, I' ('like a cloud of wasps'); also J. Lewis Spence, *The Fairy Tradition in Britain* (1948), p. 171 (Berwickshire: take refuge in snail-shells), p. 191 (from Douglas Hyde, *Legends of Saints and Sinners*: some Irish fairies stable their horses under leaves of the dock-plant), p. 135 (tiny *courils* or *gories* of Brittany frequent megalithic monuments), p. 26 (the Spriggans of Cornwall usually diminutive). For fairies the size of mice, or sand-swallows; or a foot high when on horseback, or riding horses round the rim of a large dish; or of 6, 12, or 18 inches, see Briggs, *Dictionary*, I, pp. 186, 215, 227, 239, 263, 277, 355, and her *Fairies*, pp. 133–5.
3. BM. MS. Cott. Vesp. E iv. ed. F. Liebrecht (1826). They were accustomed to visit houses at night: Briggs, *Puck*, p. 189; *Fairies*, pp. 3, 6 f.
4. *Itinerarium Cambriae* (1191), I. cap. 8: the fairies were 'staturae minimae'. For Elidorus, Briggs, *Puck*, p. 18, cites Giraldus; and in her *Dictionary of British Fairies* (1976) (see pp. 366–70), Geoffrey of Monmouth, *Historia Regnum Britanniae* (*c.* 1135).

The Tylwyth Teg ('the Fair Tribe') are among the principal
fairies of Wales, and are commonly reputed to dance on the tops
of rushes, or in a ring, sometimes by the light of a glow-worm,
and to hide in the foxglove.[1] (Judging from the documentation,
belief in tiny sprites pertains especially, though not exclusively,
to Celtic areas: Brittany, Cornwall, the Highlands and Ireland,
as well as Wales.) Louis B. Wright suggested to C. L. Barber that
Warwickshire folklore might well have been influenced by
Welsh.[2] This may well have been so; but there is ample reason to
think that Shakespeare would know of the Welsh fairies themselves: it is plain that in 1595-9 he was interested in matters
Welsh. The Chamberlain's Men had a boy who could sing in
Welsh; he did so as Lady Mortimer in *1 Henry IV*.[3] In addition,
'Glendower speaks to her in Welsh, and she answers him in the
same'. Three times more she speaks in Welsh: her tongue, says
Mortimer,

> Makes Welsh as sweet as ditties highly penn'd
> Sung by a fair queen in a summer's bower
> With ravishing division on her lute.

The best because the simplest explanation of Jacques's 'Ducdame'
equates it with Cymric 'Dewch da mi' ('Come to me', matching
Amiens' 'Come hither'). Owen Glendower and his belief in his
supernatural powers are from the sources; but the schoolmaster
of *The Merry Wives* need not have been a Welshman. Sir Hugh
Evans masquerades as a fairy, and Falstaff, recognizing the

---

1. John Rhys, *Celtic Folklore, Welsh and Manx* (1901), pp. 60, 83; and *Y Gen-
hinen*, XIII, p. 290; cf. Thomas Gwynn Jones, *Welsh Lore and Folk Custom* (1930),
pp. 54 f. (I owe these references to David Jenkins, Librarian of the National
Library of Wales.) In Glamorgan (Rhys, p. 671) they were known as Bendith
y Mamau (Mothers' Blessing) which may designate them tutelary spirits of
fertility (like Shakespeare's), though (Dr Briggs warns me) it may be a pro-
pitiatory euphemism for fairies given to stealing children. These are, however,
reported 'good towards mortals' (Rhys, p. 837). Another tribe, the Ellyllon
(Charlotte Guest (ed.), *Mabinogion*, old Everyman edn, p. 309; W. Wirt Sikes,
British Goblins (1880), pp. 13-17) are small enough to have for gloves the bells of
foxgloves. Sikes would derive from them Shakespeare's Queen Mab, 'Mab'
being Cymric for a little child. The only testimony to Mab as extant outside
Rom. seems to be in J. Brand's *Observations on Popular Antiquities* (1900 edn,
p. 799) where 'Mab-led' (= pixie-led) is said to have been a current phrase, in
older times, in Warwickshire.

2. Barber, p. 144, n. 20.

3. For this and the references following, see *1H4*, III. i. 238 S.D., 191 S.D.
and n., 193, 197, 205 S.D.s; *Wiv.*, v. v. 82; *AYL*, II. v. 51 n. (and Agnes Latham's
conclusion); *R2*, II. iv. 8-11. In *1H4*, III. i. 112, 188, 205, 259, Glendower's
verse may take some account of his accent; so Humphreys's nn.

accent, prays to be defended from 'that Welsh fairy'—'Welsh' and 'fairy' may have had closer associations for Shakespeare than we have realized. He was able to give Sir Hugh and Fluellen a genuine Welsh lilt and turn of phrase. He must have written their parts, and Glendower's, for one of his fellows who was either a Welshman, or well acquainted with Welshmen. His interest culminated in the creation of Fluellen, so finely comic and so sympathetic a Welsh character, and there may be a sign of it as early as *Richard II*. The desertion of Richard's Welsh troops is certainly crucial, and the short scene devoted to it is germane to the action. Yet it is not, perhaps, an obligatory scene: and Shakespeare makes the most of the Welshmen's belief in omens as a main motive of their defection. 'Ducdame', again, has its connection with the supernatural: it is a mock 'invocation to call [the subjects of the spell] into a circle'. It looks as though Shakespeare was apt to link the Welsh with their traditions of the supernatural.

In the period from *Richard II* (1595) to *Henry V* (1599), with the *Dream* near the beginning of it, it is safe to infer that he had Welsh contacts, among the players of his company if not also through the entourage of Henry Herbert, second Earl of Pembroke, President of the Council of Wales, who resided often at Ludlow. The Earl's son William[1] was addressed by Heminge and Condell in 1623 as having been (with his younger brother) a leading patron of Shakespeare's; and it is very possible that the Herbert patronage dated from before the *Dream*. In the early 1590s Pembroke's Men had *Titus Andronicus* and *2, 3 Henry VI* in their repertory, which makes it probable that before their collapse in 1593 Shakespeare was one of them, under the aegis of the second Earl.[2] Moreover, in E. K. Chambers's persuasive judgement,[3] 'William is the strongest candidate for identification with Mr W. H.', 'onlie begetter' of the Sonnets, of which 1 to 17, persuading the young man to marry, may have had a motive in the negotiations around October 1595 for a match between him (aged fifteen) and Elizabeth Carey. It was when these fell through, by early December, that the marriage between her and Thomas Berkeley was arranged, the likeliest occasion (I have argued) for the *Dream*'s original performance.

Shakespeare's contact with the Welsh through the Herberts remains of course conjectural; but through Welsh-speaking

---

1. For both, see *D.N.B.*
2. *Tit.*, ed. Maxwell, pp. xi, xxiv f. and n. 2.; *3H6*, ed. Cairncross, pp. xiii, xlv.   3. *Shakespeare*, Vol. 1, pp. 565–7.

members of the company it is not, and since Welsh fairies would have provided him with a perfect antecedent for Mercutio's, and for the smallest elves in the *Dream*, we are in no way obliged to believe that he invented them. On the contrary, what one would expect turns out to be most probably true; that all his fairies have tradition behind them—the full-sized king and queen; their child-sized and diminutive followers; and Robin Goodfellow.

Latham concluded that Shakespeare was an innovator also in the benevolence of his fairies; but on Latham's own showing, in this he was merely choosing to ignore one traditional characteristic of fairies in favour of another. Latham has no difficulty in demonstrating the fear in which they were often held, as malicious creatures to be associated with witches and devils; and that this view of them was perfectly well known to Shakespeare: one need go no further than the line in *Hamlet* which reports the belief that during Advent

> No fairy takes, nor witch hath power to charm.

There was every reason why Shakespeare should have Puck speak of ghosts and damnèd spirits, in order that Oberon might say explicitly:

> But we are spirits of another sort,

not obliged to shun the light of day.[1] Latham regards the tradition of fairy malevolence as by far the dominant one in popular belief, but quotes enough evidence of the benevolent traits attributed to some fairies to make one suspect him of exaggerating the dominance of the sinister view.[2] Furthermore, the fairies' punitive or kindly actions were frequently not capricious: nothing was better attested than their punishing sluttishness and rewarding the diligent and cleanly.[3] Corbett's 'Farewell rewards and fairies' is post-Shakespearean, but refers its fairy-lore to popular authority: the noddle of William Chourne of Staffordshire. He could tell of 'A hundred of these merry pranks', and assuredly did not derive his happy view of these from Shakespeare.[4] In the drama, they are addressed in *Locrine* (1591 or earlier) as 'You gracious Fairies'.[5]

---

1. Cf. Young, pp. 28 f.; Latham, pp. 34 f., 177 ff. Besides *Hamlet*, I. i. 86, 88, his citation of *Rom.*, I. iv. 88–91 is apposite.

2. He admits Spenser as Shakespeare's forerunner; and cf. pp. 26, 34–6 and nn., 51, 85, 132; 134 n. 90; and Briggs, *Puck*, p. 46.

3. Cf. *Wiv.*, v. v. 45 ff.

4. Richard Corbett, *Poems*, ed. J. A. W. Bennett and H. R. Trevor-Roper, pp. 49–52; on Chourne, further, pp. xxxi and 41 f. (*Iter Boreale*, ll. 299–316).

5. Briggs, *Puck*, p. 92.

Oberon, as a character in the perfunctory framework of Greene's *James IV* (*c.* 1591), is so far a sympathetic one that he ensures favourable fortune to Bohun's sons, Nano and Slipper, deprecates the King's evil designs, and intervenes to save Slipper from the gallows, gratifying at least his father, and the audience in their liking for a comic rascal. In Lyly's *Endimion* (1588) Corsites earns the pinching the fairies inflict; by contrast, they kiss the sleeping hero.[1] *Endimion* is one of Shakespeare's minor sources; and comparison of the *Dream* with its sources puts it beyond all doubt that in respect of fairy benevolence he is not innovating. Even Scot, a hostile witness, does not omit from the popular notions of Robin his good turns alongside his bad ones. In *Huon of Burdeux*, fairy godmothers give the baby Oberon splendid gifts; even the one who stunts his growth repents, and to comfort his mother makes him the fairest creature of the world.[2] Two marks of his own beneficence have been mentioned already: like his Shakespearean counterpart, he differentiates himself from damned and evil spirits; and (another parallel) his intervention is necessary to the happy solution. Spenser's Oberon, in the 'rolls of Elfin Emperours', possessed 'power and glorie' beyond all who before him 'that sacred seat did fill'; and he was, moreover, the father of *the* Faerie Queene, Gloriana, allegorical representative of Elizabeth herself.[3] In *The Shepheardes Calender*, in a passage to which we have found Shakespeare paying attention, Spenser writes of 'Friendly fairies', whose favoured dales he contrasts with the haunts of night-ravens, ghastly owls and elvish ghosts.[4] The phrase is the more prominent because E.K. quotes it as the lemma of a long gloss—which, along with the prologue to Lyly's *Woman in the Moon*, may have given Shakespeare the word 'shadows', applied by Puck in his epilogue to himself and the other fairies: 'we shadows', as fairies, and as creations, in the play, of the dramatist's art.[5]

One more kind of source is Shakespeare's own earlier plays:[6] he seems specially aware of what he had done in *The Comedy of Errors*, *Two Gentlemen of Verona*, and *Love's Labour's Lost*, as well as, if we are right in thinking it earlier, *Romeo and Juliet*. In important respects, the *Dream* is a successor of *Love's Labour's Lost*. As a play-within-the-play, an incompetent amateur performance for the entertainment of a court audience, 'Pyramus

---

1. Bullough, Vol. 1, p. 376.   2. Appendix 1. 6; *Huon, ed. cit.*, p. 265.
3. 11. x. 75 f.   4. 'June', ll. 23–7.   5. v. i. 419 and n.
6. Cf. Harold Jenkins, 'Shakespeare's *Twelfth Night*' (reprinted from *Rice Institute Pamphlet*, XLV, 1959) in *Shakespeare: The Comedies*, ed. K. Muir, p. 74.

and Thisbe' is the more developed successor of the show of the Nine Worthies. It is received, as that was, with mocking commentary; but the heckling is genial by comparison, and the performers 'are allowed to play out their play to the end'.[1] Games translated, as here, into drama, are characteristic of both plays, but in the *Dream*, as C. L. Barber observes, the fictions are not disabled as they are in *Love's Labour's Lost*. It is in these two comedies, he demonstrates, that Shakespeare begins to concentrate on constructive ideas drawn from festival.[2] Once more in similarity with difference, they are shown as a pair in G. K. Hunter's illuminating comparison of them with Lyly's drama. Unlike *The Comedy of Errors*, the *Shrew*, and *Two Gentlemen*, each derives its construction in part from Lyly's plan of relating to a central subject, such as might form a theme for disputation, a succession of episodes enacted by self-contained groups. These features of the structure are combined with others not Lylian, and are treated in ways not Lylian either. Yet both plays reflect a response to Lyly's court drama which it would be reasonable to attribute to their occasions being 'aristocratic rather than popular'.[3] A detail which confirms that in the *Dream* Shakespeare recalled *Love's Labour's Lost* is Puck's affirmation of the proverb, 'Jack shall have Jill', surely not without recollection, on Shakespeare's part, of Berowne's 'Jack hath not Jill' (v. ii. 865).

There will be sufficient opportunity to take account of inheritance from the other preceding plays we have mentioned, in the course of a new approach to our topic. So far we have been enquiring what sources Shakespeare drew upon in a *A Midsummer Night's Dream*, and what sort of antecedents it had from which we might learn about traditions and assumptions that might have influenced him as he composed it. Reversing this approach, I propose now (and even at the cost of occasional repetition) to look in the play for some of the features to which sources and antecedents appear to have contributed.

For Theseus and Hippolyta, Shakespeare's sources are North and Chaucer's *Knight's Tale*. Both told him of the Amazon queen won at sword's point; but in North she is Antiopa, except that one 'historiographer' makes her Hippolyta. Shakespeare follows Chaucer not only in her name but in his opening situation. The plan for wedding festivities reflects the 'feest' that was at Ipolita's wedding, each occasion an earnest of the 'blisse and melodye'

1. Alexander Leggatt, *Shakespeare's Comedy of Love* (1974), p. 113.
2. Barber, pp. 11, 126.
3. Hunter, pp. 318–23, 326–32.

when Theseus presides over wedding festivities at the conclusion: then, after this promise of joy, comes trouble[1]—the
distressful interruption by outcry, demanding justice: in Shakespeare, that of Egeus; in Chaucer, of the widows whose husbands
fell at Thebes, and who 'perturben Theseus's feet with crying'.[2]
As is usual in Shakespeare, the romance in the comedy springs
partly from threat: here, the initial threat is brought by Egeus.
As a 'heavy father', thwarting his daughter's choice in love, he
is the successor of the Duke in *Two Gentlemen of Verona*, and
perhaps of Capulet.[3] North mentions Theseus' responsibility
for 'preservation of the laws'; and like Duke Solinus at the start of
The Comedy of Errors, in the *Dream* he affirms his inability to
extenuate or mitigate them: like him, despite reluctance, he can
do no better than pass a suspended and conditional sentence.
Still like Solinus, eventually he does what he had declared
impossible, but in changed circumstances when no sensible and
magnanimous ruler could have done otherwise.[4]

In that episode, the *Dream* is again indebted to *The Knight's
Tale*. Out hunting, in both, Theseus stumbles upon the rival
lovers: the prison-breaker Palamon and the eloping Lysander
each convicts himself and his companion out of his own mouth.
The first reaction of Chaucer's Theseus is transferred by Shakespeare to Egeus, whose 'you have enough . . . I beg the law . . .
upon his head' corresponds in Chaucer to Theseus' 'Ye shal be
deed', there being no need, he declares, to extort more confession
than Palamon has supplied. His magnanimity in Shakespeare is
parallel with his second thoughts in Chaucer, in whose narrative
it is at this point that Theseus sees the comic side of the lovers'
behaviour. That view of romantic love is given him in the *Dream*
in his speech on the lunatic and the lover; as a direct comment
on the lovers' 'fond pageant' while it is taking place, it is Puck
who voices it:

> Lord, what fools these mortals be!

---

1. Cf. Nevill Coghill, 'The Basis of Shakespearian Comedy', *E. & S.* (1950),
p. 4, quoting Vincent of Beauvais (*fl. c.* 1250), and William Webbe, *A Discourse
of English Poetrie* (1588).

2. Appendix 1. 1.

3. A motif (but with fathers attempting to thwart sons) which goes back, as
Hunter (p. 322) reminds us, to classical New Comedy; cf. Leo Salingar, *Shakespeare and the Traditions of Comedy* (1974), p. 122.

4. The parallel with Solinus is noted (independently) by Leggatt, p. 102;
cf. Salingar, p. 312. In both instances 'it is the law itself, and not the prince's
will, which constitutes the threat'.

It is a perspective which has had full scope in *Two Gentlemen* and *Love's Labour's Lost*. Shakespeare had read *The Knight's Tale* with full appreciation of Theseus' role in it,[1] which has him become patron of the lovers without elevating him into a complete Providence, in control of their story: if it had gone according to Theseus' arrangements, Arcite, not Palamon, would have wedded Emelye; but supernatural power intervened. In the *Dream*, it is only after supernatural intervention that Theseus's reason and goodwill can decide the outcome and assure the lovers' happiness. Judging from what Shakespeare makes of Theseus, he evidently saw the value, in Chaucer, of his maturity, contrasted with the lovers' youth; and of his statesmanship, which helps Chaucer to place their love in a world where there are other claims. North reinforces the idea of Theseus as the good ruler, mentioning his foundation of the ordered community in Athens.[2] After the long series, in Shakespeare's earlier plays, of bad, inadequate, or disqualified sovereigns or potential sovereigns, in Theseus he sketches (as Una Ellis-Fermor observed) a ruler who is truly kinglike.[3] Theseus the Maytime hunter is straight from Chaucer; though North too makes him a hunter (of the Calydonian boar). From North (and Ovid) comes his relationship with Hercules, and, as we have seen, both Oberon's reference to his old amours and the doubt cast on them by Titania's denial. These amours show North's Theseus as the reverse of a patron of marriage, such as he is in Chaucer; in the companion life in North, however, Romulus has that role.[4]

Jealous conflict between the rival lovers in Chaucer has its climax when they start their duel in the wood, which Theseus interrupts. The climax of jealous discord in the *Dream* is reached when, likewise in the wood, Lysander and Demetrius 'seek a place to fight'—a purpose Puck interrupts as Oberon directs him. The girls' quarrel is brought to a parallel if milder climax, Helena running away from a Hermia intent on assaulting her. This climax (the *Summa epitasis* in narrowly-frustrated combats) recalls *The Knight's Tale*; but the lovers and their grouping inherit chiefly from *Two Gentlemen*. Both there and in Chaucer the claims of love conflict with the claims of friendship, and one of the rivals,

1. 'Theseus' is 'the only character Shakespeare [ever] took over whole from Chaucer' (Coghill).

2. Appendix 1. 2.

3. *The Frontiers of Drama* (2nd edn, 1964), p. 40.

4. Cf. Bullough, 1, 369, 388. To Romulus' credit stand 'all matrimoniall offices that he established betwixt man and wife'.

as a lover, has more merit.[1] In *Two Gentlemen*, to start with two girls have each a lover, as Helena and Hermia have before the *Dream* begins, then Proteus deserts Julia to pay unwelcome court to Silvia, as Demetrius transfers his love from Helena to Hermia. Hermia and Lysander, like Silvia and Valentine, return each other's love. The pattern is of a contrast, in the girls, between a more conventionally feminine character, and a bolder, more assertive one,[2] and in the men, between the traditional types of the faithless and the faithful lover. That, despite Lysander's aberration as a result of Puck's mistake with the love-juice, this is the basic conception of him and Demetrius, is confirmed by Oberon's comment on the inevitable sequel of the mistake:

> Some true love turn'd, and not a false turn'd true.

But Lysander's lapse is one difference which makes the pattern less diagrammatic than in the earlier play. Demetrius, besides, is no Proteus, who bears the double stigma of falsehood in friendship as well as in love. The conflicting claims of love and friendship are transferred from the faithless man to his victim—it is Helena whose passion makes her play her friend false, and blab the plan of elopement. As Hermia's unwanted suitor, Demetrius is both like Proteus, a truant from his former lady, and like Thurio, the heavy father's choice of son-in-law. From both besiegers, Silvia takes flight to the greenwood, as Hermia (but with her lover) does from forced marriage with Demetrius. As a dark lady, Hermia has a predecessor in Rosaline of *Love's Labour's Lost*; her want of inches she owes presumably to the boy-player for whom her part was written, though the use made of it in the quarrel-scene comes from Lyly's *Endimion*.[3] The desperation with which Helena 'fondly dotes', and her self-abasement, are much indebted to Seneca's Phaedra; and Demetrius' change towards her under supernatural influence in the moonlit wood parallels the conversion prayed for in Hippolytus, the object of Phaedra's infatuation.[4]

With Demetrius, Lysander, Bottom, and the empurpled flower, metamorphosis is back on the supernatural plane where Shakespeare and Lyly before him had found it in Ovid, and where it is

1. Arcite prays to Mars for the victory he is sure will give him Emelye; Palamon to Venus, leaving to her the means, so long as his love is rewarded. Emelye prays, if she must have one or other, to have the one who loves her best.

2. Most marked in them, in Kate and Bianca, and in Beatrice and Hero; but seen also in Adriana and Luciana, Julia and Silvia, Portia and Jessica, Rosalind and Celia.

3. See III. ii. 288–98, n.   4. Appendix I. 4.

essential to the plots of two of Lyly's comedies.[1] The imaginative Antipholus of Syracuse in *The Comedy of Errors* fancied himself exposed to it by Ephesian sorcery; none the less it was humanized in love's creation of him new, and in Egeon's dread that time had altered him out of all recognition.[2] As each of the 'Two gentlemen of Verona' in succession was 'metamorphosed with a mistress', it was a wholly human motif, with Proteus striving in vain to probe the psychology of his change.[3] Kate the Shrew's is realized as a psychological process;[4] Sly's translation, its counterpart in the induction, so far foreshadows Bottom's that it is a trick put upon him, and one which translates a clown into an alien courtly setting. Prior to the *Dream*, then, Shakespeare had explored a variety of developments from Ovidian metamorphosis as he knew it in Lyly's drama and in the narratives of Ovid himself. (That the pansy was white before it was purple is a piece of myth-making directly derived, no doubt, from Ovid's similar myth of the mulberry in his story of Pyramus.)

The metamorphoses of allegiance wrought by the flower's magic are always referred to those which Felicia effects in *Diana*, especially as in *Diana Enamorada* she reverses the spell on one lover, partly by means of herbs, of like power it seems to Dian's bud (and she is priestess of Diana's Temple).[5] But her magic liquid is in the form of philtres, requiring (what will not do in the *Dream*) the conscious co-operation of those on whom it is to work. And to induce love at sight is no part of its operation. For that, Shakespeare had a source at hand in his well-thumbed *Euphues and his England*: the herb Anacamforitis--whoever touches it falls in love 'with the person she next seeth'.[6] Its effect through sight, and the traditional operation of fancy ('it is engender'd in

---

1. *Gallathea* and *Love's Metamorphosis*. The 'magic changes of the lovers . . . are [Shakespeare's] nearest approach' to Lyly's use of physical metamorphosis 'In Katharine the Shrew and still more in the King of Navarre and his followers', he had 'evolved a new and subtler form of metamorphosis—an interior one' (M. C. Bradbrook, *The Growth and Structure of Elizabethan Comedy* (1955), p. 79; cf. pp. 222 f., n. 5). For parallels (not all equally convincing) between the *Dream* and *Gallathea*, see Leah Scragg in *Sh.S.*, 30 (1977). Her singling out of *Gallathea* as a decisive influence is unacceptable.

2. Cf. Hunter, *John Lyly*, pp. 305 f.; and my 'Themes and Structure in *The Comedy of Errors*', *Early Shakespeare* (1967: slightly revised from 1961 edn), pp. 58, 60, 65 f.

3. *Gent.*, I. i. 66; II. i. 29, II. iv. 188 ff.

4. See M. C. Bradbrook, 'Dramatic Role as Social Image: A Study of *The Taming of the Shrew*', *Sh.J.* (1958).

5. *Diana*, pp. 186–9, 375, and e.g. 242.

6. John Lyly, *Works*, ed. R. W. Bond, Vol. II, p. 115.

the eyes')[1] would be enough to suggest the anointing of the eyelids. It is worth noting, however, that in Book II of *The Faerie Queene* Phaedria's spell to prevent Cymochles awaking is administered like the juice of Love-in-idleness: while he sleeps,

> she with liquors strong his eyes did steep.

She is an erotic character, and lady of the Idle lake.[2] In *The Taming of the Shrew*, Lucentio confesses

> while I stood idly looking on,
> I found the effect of love in idleness.   (I. i. 145 f.)

That idleness and Cupid go together is affirmed from Ovid by Sir Thomas Elyot in *The Governour*, where Shakespeare will have read, 'If thou flee idleness Cupid hath no myghte'.[3] There is an association-link between Phaedria's spell and Felicia's: each puts the subject of it beyond awakening by ordinary means. Shakespeare may have remembered them in the call for music to 'strike more dead / Than common sleep' the slumbering lovers and Bottom (IV. i. 80 f.).

The shape-shift in which Bottom's metamorphosis consists has multiple sources and antecedents, including Reginald Scot's treatise and Apuleius' romance. In other places known to Shakespeare, changers of men into animal form were Spenser's Acrasia, and the model for her, Circe, depicted in Ovid (and originally in the *Odyssey*).[4] The transformation only of the head combines Scot's recipes,[5] folk-rituals with animal-headed performers, and playhouse practicability: Bottom wears 'the asshead' from the stock of 'properties'.[6] His role is evidently the latest of a series of vehicles for Will Kempe; a development from Launce and Costard. Kempe will shortly be playing Dogberry, with Cowley as his 'feed', Verges.[7] In the like double act in the *Dream*, Quince would offer Cowley more scope. Starveling, as his name shows, is a thin-man part for Sincklo, like the other (nameless) tailor in *The Shrew*, the apothecary in *Romeo* and Robert Falconbridge in *King*

---

1. *Mer.V.*, III. ii. 67.
2. II. vi. 18; of. 10, 14, 34.
3. Ed. Foster Watson (Everyman), p. 108; from Ovid, *Remedia Amoris*, l. 139.
4. *Faerie Queene*, II. xii. 85; Golding XIV. 319 ff.
5. And perhaps an episode in the Faust Book (1592), cited by Steevens: see III. i. 97 S.D. n., below.
6. Furness, p. xv.; Greg, p. 244.
7. In *Ado*, Q1, IV. ii their names appear (instead of those of the characters) as speech-prefixes.

John.[1] Flute belongs to a type not uncommon among groups of plebeian cronies in times gone by, the defective who is a comic butt yet amiably regarded—a type more familiar as the village half-wit: Flute, like Thomas Hardy's Christian Cantle, is 'no man'.[2] As Lion, Snug's part originates (we presume) in the Scottish incident: hence, since it is 'nothing but roaring', Quince's reassurance that he 'may do it extempore': hence the cue for the reassurance, that he is 'slow of study'. Behind the supposedly necessary impersonation of Wall, notably discharged by Snout, may stand such practicable stage walls as those in *Romeo* and *Susanna*.[3] The central idea of the artisan-plot, the organization of a boorish entertainment for their patron at aristocratic wedding celebrations, came, unless *John a Kent* is later than the *Dream*, from Munday.

Bottom's shape is shifted by Puck, from whom we hear about his shifting his own. This is one of the regular pranks, in popular belief, of Robin Goodfellow; the others Puck, or Robin, describes are likewise the sort attributed to him in folklore. The fairy's sketch of him, and his final appearance with his broom, are indebted also to Scot. He is related, but whether as offspring or prototype is uncertain, to Munday's Shrimp; and so is his master Oberon to John a Kent, in commanding events by means of magic. Oberon may owe something to his namesake in Greene's *James IV*, like him an onlooker at human action in which (though much more slightly) he intervenes. But the Oberon of the *Dream* has his principal origins in *Huon of Burdeux*, and, with Titania (who owes her name, we have seen, directly to Ovid), in the May-game, courtly pageants, and Chaucer's *Merchant's Tale*. They share, in their love to Theseus and Hippolyta, the pageant fairies' predilection for royal persons who are or represent the patrons of the entertainment.[4] They resemble Pluto and Proserpina, the king and queen of fairy in *The Merchant's Tale*,[5] in being at odds over a mortal. Chaucer's pair, like Oberon, intervene (the king by restoring eyesight) to settle the outcome of the human story. The *Tale* is one of Chaucer's 'marriage group', and it offered a hint for combining a fairy action with the theme of love and marriage, dramatized and examined. Shakespeare associates Oberon and Titania with India: Oberon

---

1. See Alison Gaw, 'John Sincklo as one of Shakespeare's Actors', *Anglia* (1926); Greg, pp. 114–15 and nn.
2. See I. ii. 43–4 n., below.
3. See above, p. xliv and n. 5; below, III. i. 61, n.
4. Barber, p. 121.   5. See above, p. lxi and n. 2.

has come thence, and Titania's changeling boy is child of her Indian votaress and an Indian king. In *The Faerie Queene*, Book II, the founder of Oberon's royal line

> Was Elfin: him all India obayd.[1]

The contrast in the *Dream* between fairies and evil creatures of the nocturnal and supernatural world is Spenserian—notably in the 'friendly faeries' of *The Shepheardes Calender* (and Oberon's ancestors in *The Faerie Queene* are a noble race). The contrast is warranted also by *Huon of Burdeux*. Even in folklore, though fairy malevolence may be the more prominent, fairy benevolence figures too. Presuming that the *Dream* was a wedding play, it is natural that, except for Puck's practical jokes, Shakespeare should have omitted, as ill-omened, what caused fairies to be feared.[2] That does not put his fairies out of line with tradition; nor does the tiny size of his elves. Their immediate ancestry, if *Romeo* precedes the *Dream*, is in Mercutio's fancies about Queen Mab: but behind both, it appears, we have reason to postulate Welsh folklore, if not Warwickshire folklore akin to it.[3]

In the *Dream*, the fairies' haunt is the moonlit wood. The wood corresponds to Oberon's in *Huon of Burdeux*; and in Lyly's *Endimion*, the fairies, small-child-size and acted by children (like Peaseblossom and his companions), are in the service of Cynthia, the moon-goddess. The greenwood is the route of escape for lovers in flight from parental oppression in *Two Gentlemen* and *John a Kent*; in the latter it is moonlit. In Ovid, the stolen meeting of Pyramus and Thisbe, as Quince reminds his cast, was to be by moonlight. The wood under the moonlight is the setting, in the *Dream*, for transformations; and in Seneca's *Hippolytus*, Diana, both as moon-goddess and as huntress all-powerful in the woods, is besought to work a transformation in the hero there. A wood near Athens is the scene in *The Knight's Tale* of Theseus' hunting,

---

1. II. x. 72. In *Huon*, Oberon's fairy kingdom is somewhere east of Jerusalem; his wood is fifteen days' journey from Babylon (*ed. cit.*, pp. 59 f., 62).

2. Cf. (but qualify) E. Schanzer, p. 31.

3. Yet, as Barber concludes, 'Shakespeare was not *simply* writing out folklore which he had heard in his youth: . . . his fairies are . . . a fusion of pageantry and popular game, as well as popular fancy' (p. 125). The spheres of the court and of folklore were not remote from each other: on progress in 1592, for example, Elizabeth was presented with a poem by Thomas Churchyard which alludes to one of Robin Goodfellow's traditional pranks (see K. M. Briggs, *Puck*, pp. 84 f., and below, II. i. 36 n.). At Norwich in 1578, Churchyard had seven boys dance before her '(as neare as could be ymagined) like the Phayries' (Nichols, Vol. II, M3ᵛ). See further references to Nichols in Young, p. 57, n. 71.

Arcite's 'observaunce' to May, and the duel of the rival lovers—each with its counterpart in the *Dream*. *Endimion* has Cynthia as its reigning sovereign (its audience was not likely to forget that that was one of the poetical names for Queen Elizabeth). Somewhat similarly, the Moon is the planetary regent of the *Dream*, and with the other aspects of 'the triple Hecate', its mythological regent; as such it draws in other source-material. Shining as Phoebe (the name and accompanying image are from *The Shepheardes Calender*) she will favour the eloping lovers. The blessing of the bride-beds accords with her predominance, in her aspects of fertility-goddess and Lucina, perhaps with recollection of *Epithalamion*.[1] She is a link with Shakespeare's source for much of *Two Gentlemen*, Montemayor's *Diana*, and with its sequel *Diana Enamorada*; not only through the titles, which refer to the heroine, but also through Diana's Temple, and its priestess Felicia who brings the lovers' tribulations to an end. In her sylvan aspect as Diana, the goddess, in Ovid, avenges herself on Actaeon; the description of his hounds, in Golding's version, contributes to Shakespeare's hunting-scene. The account of cosmic chaos in Titania's set speech is indebted to Medea's invocation of Hecate in Seneca, and so is Oberon's vision of the stars dislodged from their spheres by magic song. The title 'triple Hecate' is Golding's translation of Ovid's 'Hecate triformis', which is Senecan also.[2]

The first of the myths in which Oberon clothes topicalities—that of the stars and the mermaid—combines inspirations from Seneca and from court pageants. The seascape with Cupid, which begins the second, is derived from Seneca's *Hippolytus*. Two other set pieces, and 'Pyramus and Thisbe', are striking examples of how Shakespeare weaves or fuses together material from a whole series of sources. The hunting-scene recalls from *The Knight's Tale* Theseus' Maytime hunting at daybreak; and adds a reference to his having hunted in Thessaly, which comes from hints in Golding and North's Plutarch: North and Elyot in *The Governour* also associate him, as Shakespeare does, with

1. For *Epithalamion*, see above, pp. xxxv f. Lucina, though more usually a manifestation of Juno, is sometimes identified with Diana. Shakespeare will have read in the *Knight's Tale*, ll. 2083–5, of the 'womman travaillynge' pictured in Diana's temple: 'Ful pitously Lucina gan she calle.' (Cf. Seneca, *Agamemnon*, l. 7.) Diana of the Ephesians (Acts xix. 27–8), many-breasted, was a fertility-goddess (J. G. Frazer, *The Golden Bough*, one-volume edn, 1922, pp. 4, 184–6).

2. Golding, vii. 136 (cf. 242, 'three-formed goddess'); Seneca, *Hippolytus*, 412, *Medea*, 7.

Hercules.[1] Dawn hunts in Seneca and Sidney are echoed too: that which opens the *Hippolytus*, and Kalander's in the *Arcadia*. The description of the hounds owes a debt or two to Golding's description of Actaeon's. Titania's tale of devastation and dislocation is indebted not only to Seneca's *Medea*, but also, it seems, to the plague of Thebes in his *Oedipus*, though this last is a minor source compared with three appropriate episodes in Golding: the plague of Aegina, Ceres' curse, and Deucalion's flood.[2] The personification of Winter, fourth in the cycle of the seasons, is indebted to two further widely-separated passages in Golding, and to *The Shepheardes Calender*, from which (naturally, from the November and December eclogues) there are other borrowings. In calling the moon 'governess of floods', Shakespeare echoes Marlowe's *Hero and Leander*.[3]

On the sources of 'Pyramus and Thisbe' Kenneth Muir's study has left little or nothing more to do.[4] His findings are utilized to the full in the Commentary of this edition: here no more than a brief general account is needed. As a play-within-the-play, an incompetent amateur performance for the entertainment of the aristocrats, 'Pyramus and Thisbe' is the more developed successor of the show of the Nine Worthies in *Love's Labour's Lost*. It is received, as that was, with mocking commentary, which, however, is not ill-natured, so that without incongruity, the magnanimous key of Theseus' anticipatory comment can be recovered in his congratulation at the end. In choosing Pyramus and Thisbe as the subject, Shakespeare may have been influenced by the resemblance of their story to Romeo and Juliet's (which had not gone unobserved)[5] and by the reference to it in *The Merchant's Tale*, linking up with the fairy monarchs and other seminal features there. But the principal attraction, no doubt, was the specially good opportunity for burlesque, to which a number of extant versions were wide open. Shakespeare dramatized the story from Golding's narrative, with an occasional detail from Chaucer's in *The Legend of Good Women*: the only version, observes Muir, 'which was not in some way ludicrous'. Shakespeare can scarcely have despised Golding's translation of the *Metamorphoses*;

1. Below, IV. i. 102–26, n.; cf. *Governour*, pp. 81 f.

2. Cf. II. i. 88–114 nn. Warburton recognized the debt to Ceres' curse.

3. Below, II. i. 103 n.; cf. Scot, *Witchcraft*, xv, p. 513: 'The moone having dominion over all moist things'.

4. *Sources*[2], pp. 68–77 and nn. (I quote, below, from pp. 72, 77); *Sources*[1], pp. 31–47; and the earlier treatment, 'Pyramus and Thisbe: A study in Shakespeare's Method', *Sh.Q.* (1954).

5. See above, p. xlv n. 1.

phrases from it stuck in his head, and to good purpose; nor is its telling of the Pyramus story by any means despicable, but as Muir illustrates, it has lapses into unconscious humour and weaknesses of style on which the dramatist can capitalize in composing the burlesque his play requires. The absurdities of at least two and in all probability three other versions give him plenty to parody: one, anonymous, in *A Gorgious Gallery of Gallant Inventions* (1578); a second, Thomson's, in another miscellany, *A Handful of Pleasant Delites* (1584), and the third, Mouffet's, in his poem *Of the Silkewormes, and their Flies*, published in 1599, which presumably Shakespeare read in manuscript. So Muir argues (and as I have said, in my view convincingly); he is able to adduce more than a dozen instances where Shakespeare apparently parodies Mouffet or picks up an expression from him. For the laments of the lovers, Shakespeare (as Muir points out) adopts Thomson's stanza. It is a variation, with internal rhyme, of the fourteener used by Golding, or the 'eight and six' proposed by Quince for his prologue, though not actually employed for it. But the bad poetry of these versions of 'Pyramus' is not Shakespeare's only source of farcical effect in his mock-tragedy. He burlesques likewise 'the theatrical heroics of an earlier age', exemplified in Thomas Preston's *Cambises* (*ante* 1569),[1] of which the full title seems to be parodied in that of Quince's play, read out by Theseus. *Cambises* indeed has the crude mingle of tragedy and mirth still persisting in the mid-1590s in the lower levels of popular drama. Shakespeare's mockery extends to these, and to their progenitors in general, a class of play (including *Cambises* and *Sir Clyomon and Clamydes*)[2] common well into the 1580s, performed by small groups of professional actors prior to the firm establishment of such companies as the one playing 'Pyramus' and the *Dream*.[3] A third subject of caricature in 'Pyramus' is 'the absurdities of amateur actors'. The burlesque created from these

1. Soon to be named ('King Cambyses' vein') as a target for burlesque in *1H4* (II. iv. 382).

2. *c.* 1570. Salingar, pp. 69 f., compares Thisbe's death-speech with *Clyomon*, ed. Greg, ll. 1582 ff., commenting: 'Either Shakespeare remembered this passage in some detail, or . . . he and his audience had heard a number of passages in the same strain'. Others, 'to illustrate the kind of conventions he was satirizing' are quoted from Edwardes's *Damon and Pithias* (1565) and R.B.'s *Apius and Virginia* (*ante* 1567–8) by Young, pp. 38–41.

3. Typical features burlesqued (see below, p. cxix) are pointed out by J. W. Robinson, 'Palpable Hot Ice: Dramatic Burlesque in *A Midsummer Night's Dream*', *S.Ph.* (1964). When he supposes characteristics of these troupes themselves to be burlesqued in Quince's amateurs, I dissent.

sources made just the right contrast with the lyrical beauty of Shakespeare's poetry, the skilled sophistication of his rhetoric, and the deft humour of his comic prose, in the main play; and drew the sting of love-tragedy, while acknowledging its potential existence alternative to the romantic comedy of love.

II. THE PLAY

That *A Midsummer Night's Dream* was designed to grace a wedding is a presumption as strong as it can be in default of the direct evidence which would make it certain. Grant the presumption, and it accounts for the inclusion and clarifies the relevance of everything in the play. Reject it,[1] and there can still be no doubt that love in relation to marriage is the dramatist's subject.[2] It is the theme stated, along with the goal—a wedding—of the dramatic action, in the opening speech. The 'nuptial hour' of Theseus and Hippolyta 'draws on apace'; yet the brief time of waiting 'lingers' Theseus' 'desires': he is an ardent lover, and in her reply Hippolyta reciprocates his love.[3] At once there falls across the prospect of this love-match the shadow of Egeus' demand for the enforcement of a marriage contrary to love. The action has begun which from his entry keeps step with an exposition, lucid and economical, that introduces not only the situation and characters, but other features of the play as well.[4] When Puck has departed to fetch the magic flower, and Oberon has declared what he means to do with it, the exposition is complete.

I. THE EXPOSITION

By then, we have been made acquainted with the situations of conflict in the fairy world and for the young lovers.[5] The lovers'

1. As Stanley Wells does, pp. 12–14; cf. T. W. Baldwin, *On the Literary Genetics of Shakespeare's Plays, 1592–1594* (1959), p. 480, whose remarks 'are not convincing' (Young, p. 14, n. 5).

2. 'Marriage is here [a] goal of such attractive power that all the plots are given direction and relationship by the impulse and social pressure that it involves' (Hunter, p. 323).

3. Cf. E. Schanzer, 'The Moon and the Fairies in *A Midsummer Night's Dream*', *UTQ* (1955), p. 242.

4. For appreciation of the exposition, cf. Schanzer, pp. 242–4; Kermode, 'The Mature Comedies', in Brown and Harris (eds), *Early Shakespeare* (1961) pp. 214 ff.; Watkins and Lemmon, *A Midsummer Night's Dream* (*In Shakespeare's Playhouse* series), 1974, pp. 33–61.

5. In a quarrel-scene and (virtually) a trial-scene: types that scarcely ever fail in the theatre.

initial roles as true or false in love and friendship have been established, with Helena further characteriz d, and Puck, and so far as is needful Oberon, Titania, and Theseus characterized too. The chief agents in the development of the plot have been given due prominence: Oberon, whose eavesdropping leads him to extend the action he purposed in his own conflict with Titania and to intervene also in the lovers' conflict; and Puck, his jester and minister, known for practical joking and shape-shifting, to whom he delegates that intervention. Familiar with plebeian mortals, as we have been reminded he is, Puck, in turn, will eavesdrop on the artisans and interfere with their project.[1] The agent of which he and Oberon make use, the flower Love-in-idleness, has been dignified by a legendary origin, a metamorphosis in Ovid's manner. The centrality of these agents in complicating and then unravelling the plot, and involving in it the fairies, the quartet of lovers, and the artisans, is one of the main means by which the play is unified. Another is the single occasion to which we have learned its four stories are moving: the ducal marriage. The fairies have come to Athens to give it blessing; the artisans are preparing their performance as a contribution to the accompanying revels which Philostrate was instructed to set on foot; and the wedding-day, finally, was the term fixed for Hermia to arrive at the decision expected to settle the outcome of the four lovers' story.[2]

As one anticipates in Shakespeare, yet another means to dramatic unity is the pattern of correspondences. A salient one in the exposition is between the Athenian and the fairy courts:[3] the fairy ruler at strife with his consort, planning to end her rebellion; the Athenian recently at strife with his consort-to-be, but having now made conquest of her: the love between their fairy counterparts interrupted; their own about to be consummated. In Bottom, the artisan world has its uncrowned king,[4] and he is cast for the part of a lover whose love never is to be consummated: as Quince tells him (and with him any in the audience who do not know the tale[5]), Pyramus 'kills himself most gallant for love'.

1. On the place of eavesdropping in the *Dream*, see Bertrand Evans, *Shakespeare's Comedies* (1960), pp. 34 f., 38, 40; cf. Hunter, p. 321.

2. Cf. Hunter, pp. 322 f.; Schanzer, p. 242; Siegel, p. 139.

3. Cf. Young, p. 99; Leggatt, p. 105; Olson, pp. 96, 102 f., 107.

4. Wilson Knight, *The Shakespearian Tempest* (1932), p. 166.

5. It was known to the Elizabethan ballad-public. Sir Charles Firth quotes Elderton's stanza on it in *The Panges and Fits of Love*; and regards Thomson's narration in Clement Robinson's *Handefull of Pleasant Delites* (1584) as a ballad.

Each set of characters plays its part under the auspices of the moon, the measure, in Theseus' and Hippolyta's opening speeches, of the interval of time which is the only remaining impediment to their union. It is the interval occupied by the action of the comedy, of which the moon in its various aspects may be regarded as the regent. Before the exposition ends, it has been given significant roles for the young lovers, the artisans, and the fairies, as well as the ducal pair. When Hippolyta compares the new crescent to a silver bow the image is not only characteristic of herself, the Amazon huntress, accoutred probably as such, and to appear in that guise in the dawn scene; it is a reminder that the moon-goddess is also Diana, the virgin huntress of the woods.[1] Moonlit woodland is to be the scene for the weaving of the plot entanglements and the preparations for their untangling. The move from Athens to the wood is made at the final stage of the exposition, introducing the fairies in their domain; and the audience knows that the four lovers and the artisans are bound thither. The Duke (as yet) is not; but the artisans' rendezvous is associated with him: 'at the Duke's oak we meet' is Quince's directive. Even before the wood is reached, Shakespeare has begun, by poetic reference and poetic imagery, to evoke the beauty of his natural setting. Hermia's voice, says Helena, is

> More tuneable than lark to shepherd's ear,
> When wheat is green, when hawthorn buds appear.

The assignation for the elopement is at the spot where Lysander once foregathered with the two girls

> To do observance to a morn of May;

the spot, Hermia tells her friend, where they two

> Upon faint primrose beds were wont to lie.

He comments, 'there was nothing absurd in supposing that Elizabethan artisans were familiar with the story of Pyramus' (*Essays Historical and Literary*, pp. 19 f., reprinted from *Shakespeare's England*). His point remains pertinent, even though none of the artisans but Quince is supposed to have this familiarity; and though, however Elizabethan he and the rest may be, as Athenians they inhabit the ancient world to which the story is native.

1. The four-night interim and the moon's phases are to do what the play needs at this point, not to lay down a scheme for the sequel, in which they are discarded. To focus all purposes, the nuptials must be at hand; yet a lesser interval would make Theseus' impatience unreasonable, instead of acceptable proof that he is genuinely in love. The moon's phases link it with the theme of change. Once the action is launched, Shakespeare, as usual, makes one episode follow another with all dramatic speed. Cf. Kittredge, quoted in Young, pp. 86 f.; W. H. Clemen (*MND*, Signet edn, pp. xxxi f.); Schanzer, p. 243.

The midsummer night's experiences in the wood are to be the 'Dream' of the play's title (unless the whole play is so). Hippolyta has prophesied that in the interim before 'the night of our solemnities', daytime will quickly steep itself in night, and night will 'dream away the time'.[1] Apparent experience as perhaps dream, or as governed by imagination, is a theme which comes to share the central focus in the final phases of the play, from the awakenings of Act IV to the epilogue; but it has been present all through as a subtext to the main theme of love and marriage.[2] Love-sight, true and false, a principal motif in that main theme, belongs to the wide-ranging subject of appearance and reality, seldom far from Shakespeare's thought; a subject which includes the genuine though not rational insights of imagination, and its irrational aberrations.[3] The importance of these themes right from the beginning of the play is well brought out by Frank Kermode's account of their place in the opening scene.[4] Lysander is accused of having stamped himself upon Hermia's imagination by the customary specious methods of counterfeit love. She maintains that her vision of him is true love-sight, no induced fantasy, but valid: why can her father not see him so?

> I would my father look'd but with my eyes.

'Rather', her judge admonishes her,

> Rather your eyes must with his judgement look.

Love-sight, imaginative, impressionable, and deceivable, must yield to paternal judgement, supposedly rational. Lysander makes it plain that Egeus can have no rational grounds for preferring Demetrius as his son-in-law. Rational or not, however, the paternal choice carries authority, and Hermia is required to 'fit your fancies to your father's will'. Lysander has put his own claim (and hers) on its true foundation:

> I am belov'd of beauteous Hermia.

Accepting his plea, as they rightly will, the play's audience will be accepting the trustworthiness of Hermia's intuitive love-sight. Yet the eyes, traditional initiators of love, are liable to see false

1. Cf. Hunter, p. 322.
2. Cf. Kermode, pp. 314–20; and R. W. Dent's admirable 'Imagination in *A Midsummer Night's Dream*', *Sh.Q.* (1964), p. 115.
3. See J. R. Brown, *Shakespeare and his Comedies* (1957), pp. 83, 106.
4. Pp. 214 f.

under its irrational power: a fact typified by the love-juice, whose compulsive effect is to

> make or man or woman madly dote
> Upon the next live creature that it sees.

Love, Helena generalizes,[1] 'looks not with the eyes'—eyes which but for love would report the object as it really is—'but with the mind'—a mind which has not 'of any judgement taste'. So, she complains, Demetrius who once could see her as all Athens does, a woman no less attractive than Hermia, and at that time made love to her, now having 'look'd on Hermia's eyne' cannot or will not see 'what all but he do know', and is infatuated with her friend. She herself, she confesses, cannot discard her own infatuation and, unworthy as Demetrius now is, still adores his qualities. Shakespeare's word for such infatuation is 'doting'.[2] In *Romeo* and the *Dream*, it is applied especially (but not exclusively) to love persisted in even when met with indifference or aversion. While Romeo sighed for Rosaline, Friar Lawrence rebuked him 'for doting, not for loving'. As Demetrius 'errs, doting on Hermia's eyes, / So I' says Helena; to whom Lysander's adieu (prophetic of the sequel) has been

> As you on him, Demetrius dote on you.

Indeed, the first we heard of her (Lysander again the speaker) was of how

> she, sweet lady, dotes,
> Devoutly dotes, dotes in idolatry

upon Demetrius. These dotings would nowadays be called fixations; a term which may make clearer to us the first parallel with them in the fairy plot: the fixation Titania has developed on the Indian boy. That was originally, like Helena's for Demetrius, a love entirely admirable: it merited all the sympathy won for it by her story of the boy's mother. But now she 'makes him all her joy', arousing Oberon's jealousy, and disrupting the vital alliance between him, as her husband and consort, and herself: she no longer sees him as she ought. Her aberration is maternal, not sexual: but its importance, as with the others, lies in the sphere of love and marriage. Until the play nears its end, the theme of love and marriage holds without a rival the centre of

1. Kermode, p. 215; Stephen Fender, *Shakespeare: A Midsummer Night's Dream* (1968), pp. 20 f.; Dent, pp. 118 f.
2. Kermode, pp. 216 f.; Dent, p. 117. Cf. *Rom.*, cited immediately below.

attention: the imaginative disorders in the vision of reality are contributory to it. The profoundest source of the play's unity is thematic: the dominance of that theme, firmly established in the exposition.

2. DESIGN AND PLOT

This masterly exposition contains in embryo virtually the whole play, including the principles of its structure. The design presents a sequence of woodland scenes developing and resolving the dramatic conflicts, and framed within scenes laid in Athens. As part of the exposition, the transition has been made from Theseus and the Athenian polity to Oberon and the realm of magic in the wood; the transition is matched subsequently in reverse. Within Athens, the play has moved from Theseus to Quince and the artisans, who are among his citizens; again, a move to be repeated in reverse. Hence Theseus and with him Hippolyta, immune, so far as their own personalities are concerned, from the troubles in which the others are involved, stand at the start and conclusion of the dramatic conflict as a principal part of the frame in which it is set. The design depends, too, upon the chiaroscuro of night and day: daylight for opening scenes in Athens; moonlight followed by fog and then dawn, in the wood; day, presumably, for Bottom's return to his comrades; night (and torchlight, no doubt) for the married couples in the palace, with 'moonshine' (and 'starlight') in 'Pyramus and Thisbe'.[2] Finally, the fairies enter to

> give glimmering light
> By the dead and drowsy fire.

Without their coming, the design would be impoverished by reduction to the more obvious formula of an action sandwiched between two episodes under the aegis of Theseus. As it is, the play ends with variation upon the beginning. Having begun with Theseus, one of the two mentor-characters who effect the dénouement, it returns to him in the conclusion, but actually concludes with the other mentor, Oberon.[3] The fairies, naturally, must come at 'fairy time', and perform their ritual when the wedded couples are abed. For this reason among others, the final court scene is at night, so that again the obvious sandwich

1. Cf. Clemen, p. xxvi; Salingar, p. 299.
2. Cf. Hunter, p. 322; Welsford, pp. 326–8.
3. Cf. Welsford, p. 329; Young, p. 93.

pattern—day, night, day—is turned by an addition into something more aesthetically satisfying.[1] As a further feature of the design, there is a reverse parallel between the coming of the fairy court from the wood to the Athenian palace, and the expeditions the Athenian court characters made to the wood.[2]

The wood itself, as an otherworld, creates the largest-scale pattern of the play.[3] As a place of transformations it stages the central scenes of the drama; and it gives to the young lovers' adventure the archetypal form, frequent in romance and in Shakespeare, and well recognized in psychological and spiritual experience, of withdrawal from and return to the autonomous self.[4] Indeed Titania, without leaving the wood, is subjected to an equivalent process.

Enid Welsford went so far as to say 'the plot is a pattern, rather than a series of events occasioned by human character and action'.[5] Yet, though a pattern, it is also a sequence of cause and effect. It is conducted 'by balancing a number of self-contained groups, one against the other'.[6] Each group—Theseus and Hippolyta, the quartet of lovers, the artisans, and the fairies —has its own progressive story. In the wood, the lovers are unaware of the presence of the artisans or the fairies. They themselves are not known, even in Athens, to the artisans: when the wedding has become a triple one, Snug's report is that 'there is two or three lords and ladies more married'.[7] Introduced successively, the groups are 'manipulated in clearly symmetrical patterns';[8] and finally the artisans, like the fairies, make their purposed contribution to the marriage celebrations at court. The fairies' visit is necessarily unknown to the rest; but at 'Pyramus and Thisbe', Theseus and Hippolyta (with Philostrate), the young lovers, and the artisans unite in an ensemble scene, in which

1. Cf. Young, pp. 88 f.

2. Coghill, p. 59. He adds (p. 69): 'there is still the audience-world to have their participation in the experience acknowledged—so Puck speaks the epilogue'.

3. The contrast is misdescribed when (cf. Olson, pp. 106 f.; Fender, pp. 20, 25, 32 f., 41) associations are brought in which the play does not activate. It does not remind us that Athens was Minerva's city, a city of philosophers. Though people go astray in the wood, it is not in the least like Spenser's Wood of Error, a place of evil. What it resembles is the wood in *Huon*, where everyone who enters is bound to meet with alarming experiences, and with their author *and his indispensable help*. The contrast of wood and Athens is discriminatingly treated by Leggatt (p. 106).

4. Cf. *Gent.*, *AYL* (forests); *Ado* (tomb); *Cym.* (cave); *Tp.* (island).

5. P. 331.   6. Hunter, p. 318.   7. Evans, p. 45.

8. Young, p. 50; a Lylian method (Hunter, pp. 300, 317 f.).

Theseus and Bottom converse. It is a culminating ensemble such as Shakespeare is fond of, and with the fairy ritual that follows makes the *Dream* a version of his favourite comic form, which presents 'several groups of characters in relation and contrast', and concludes with 'some stable relationship' arrived at between them.[1]

Although until the four stories are brought together in the fifth act each group has its own, they are interlocked in the course of the plot. The lovers' story, the artisans' story, and the story of the fairies share a common factor, the enchantments wielded by Oberon and Puck. The love-juice, the magic agent the pair employ in the lovers' conflict, is decisive too, along with Puck's shifting of Bottom's shape, in the conflict between Titania and Oberon.[2] Each story contains something which is essential also to one or more of the others. In the main branch of the fairies' story, Puck provides from among the artisans a monster for Titania to dote on; in the artisans' story his intervention means the assification of Bottom, the disruption of their rehearsal, the dislocation of their plan, and for Bottom himself, the endearments of the fairy queen. In the other branch of the fairies' story, Oberon and Puck have to bestir themselves in order to rectify the consequences in the lovers' embroilment of the mistakes they have made in their attempt to end it. The lovers are unconscious victims and then beneficiaries of their magic. Theseus completes its work. He does more than sanction the lovers' unions; he associates them with his and Hippolyta's. His verdict was responsible for the lovers' resort to the wood in the first place; lifting from Hermia and Lysander the threat which that verdict represented, he lifts, in the story of himself and his bride, the threat of an ill-omened accompaniment to their happy marriage.

Together with the course of true love, threat posed and averted is what provides, generally speaking, the plot-interest in Shakespearean comedy.[3] In the *Dream* it begins with Egeus' invoking the law against his daughter. Theseus can mitigate the stark alternative of forced marriage or death, but the briefly-suspended sentence he pronounces must still deprive Hermia of Lysander

---

1. Brown, p. 43, cf. 34 f.; Hunter, pp. 317 f., 349.

2. Cf. e.g. Evans, p. 34.

3. Cf. Nevill Coghill, 'The Basis of Shakespearian Comedy', *E. & S.* (1950), p. 4, quoting Vincent de Beauvais (*fl. c.* 1250), and William Webbe, *A Discourse of English Poetrie* (1588); M. C. Bradbrook, *Elizabethan Comedy*, quoting *Mucedorus* (? 1580–92, acted by Pembroke's Men) on the 'triple joy' of comedy's dénouements.

and all experience of fulfilled love. Hippolyta is downcast at a prospect so out of keeping with the happiness Theseus has been promising in the celebration of their own marriage, and he has to offer comfort with 'What cheer, my love?'[1] The conflict, with the Athenian constitution on Egeus' side, and Hermia resolute, is beyond Theseus' solving if Egeus and Demetrius persist. Demetrius' perverse transfer of his love to Hermia threatens Helena with incurable wretchedness, and has already turned her love to dotage. Soon the play presents yet another unsolved conflict in the quarrel between Oberon and Titania. The gravity of the threat if it continues is made clear by Titania's picture of the blight and subversion it is causing throughout the natural world. What will be the consequence, moreover, for Oberon's purpose of blessing the ducal marriage, when the breach in his own and his fairy consort's is thwarting all fertility and overthrowing all order?

Once these conflicts and threats have been dramatized, everything is ready for the elaboration of the comic distresses; the play has reached what was technically known as the *epitasis*,[2] the threshold of the main complications. One further threat emerges in the course of them: caught by Puck, Bottom is detained in the wood 'whether [he] will or no', and until he is released the artisans' play cannot go forward, nor Theseus' revels be enlivened by it. However, Oberon has told us that Titania's infatuation is to be temporary, so we can presume that Bottom's detention will be temporary, too. None of the threats and distresses, in fact, is allowed to perturb us in anything like the same way as those in *The Merchant of Venice* or even *Much Ado About Nothing*.

Theseus' verdict on the lovers' conflict was a false solution; and early in the entanglement Lysander's countermove, the attempt at runaway marriage, proves a false solution likewise. Similarly Oberon's first attempt to intervene (though it is rightly conceived) fails in the execution. Because he knows only of one Athenian in the wood, he gives Puck inadequate instructions. Finding Hermia and Lysander, Puck attributes to the man's churlishness the chaste distance between them which Hermia has insisted upon, and so, mistaking his identity, anoints the eyes of Lysander instead of Demetrius. It is the misjudgement of relationship which leads to the mistake of identity: the two are closely

1. Cf. Leggatt, p. 102; Salingar, p. 10.
2. The *protasis* being complete, the plot thickens. See F. P. Wilson (ed. G. K. Hunter), *The English Drama 1485–1585* (1969), pp. 108–9.

connected in Shakespeare.[1] As a result of Puck's error in identification, the lovers' conflict, instead of being healed, is made
worse. Even his and Oberon's second intervention for the time
being makes matters worse still, though the action taken, the
anointing of Demetrius' eyes, is the one needed to bring about
the dénouement, as eventually it does. The episodes between the
lovers themselves, a series of cross-purposes partly dependent on
Puck's mistake of identity, are referred by Leo Salingar to the
model of 'the Italianate double plot with its confusions of identity
and crossed complications'.[2] They are in line with that tradition;
but as a master of comedy where it joins hands with farce, Shakespeare could not fail to take the cross-purposes through the
complete range of permutations:[3] each is an obligatory episode,
a *scène à faire*. They are compared by Enid Welsford to the figures
of a dance, and with some amplification one can adopt her
account.[4] As the situation stands at the start, 'there are two men
to one woman, and the other woman', Helena, is alone. The
entanglement begins with Helena vainly besieging Demetrius,
who is seeking Hermia and Lysander no less vainly. His fierce
rejection of Helena has the gentlest of parallels in Hermia's
refusal to let Lysander pillow his head beside hers. Their goodnight as faithful lovers prepares his spellbound desertion. That
brings the next figure: 'a circular movement, each one pursuing
and pursued'. Lysander importunes Helena, who takes his vows
for flouts and speaks of her fruitless love of Demetrius; Demetrius
urges his upon Hermia who cares only to find Lysander—
Lysander, whom we have heard declare he hates her. Next,
Demetrius, his imagination now also redirected by the love-juice,
begins to pay passionate court, like Lysander, to Helena, so that
'there is a return to the first figure, with the position of the
women reversed'. But whereas then Hermia, beloved of both
men, was in loving partnership with one of them, Helena, now,
can believe in Demetrius' love no more than in Lysander's. Since
the men are once again rivals, and Hermia supposes Helena
deliberately to have stolen Lysander's devotion, the entanglement,
so far as it concerns the young people, culminates in 'a cross
movement, man quarrelling with man, and woman with woman'.

Meanwhile, in three scenes interleaved with these, Titania's
part in the entanglement has been taken through its comparatively simple stages. Lulled asleep, she was vulnerable to

---

1. Cf. my 'Themes and Structure in *The Comedy of Errors*', *Early Shakespeare*,
pp. 66 f.

2. P. 190; cf. 172 f.   3. Coghill, p. 58.   4. P. 331.

Oberon and the love-juice. Awakened by Bottom in his ass-head, she succumbs to the magic: Oberon's plan to dislodge her fixation by fitting her with an absurd one instead is destined to succeed. Finally, the absurdity reaches its climax in the spectacle of her winding ass-headed Bottom in her arms. This spectacle, with her accompanying exclamation

O how I love thee! How I dote on thee!

and the exits of the young men, intent on violence, and of a bewildered Hermia, constitute the climax of the entanglement, at once in passion and in comic folly: the *summa epitasis*, characterized by Bertrand Evans as the point where 'the exploitation of discrepant awarenesses is at its peak'; where *'the greatest number of participants are ignorant of the greatest number of facts in a situation that has attained its greatest complexity'*.[1] The dénouement follows. A dotage so ridiculous as Titania's upon Bottom is easily cured—

O how mine eyes do loathe his visage now!—

when (Oberon reports) it has done its work of eclipsing and freeing her from the one which mattered, upon the Indian boy. 'New in amity', Oberon and she, dancing together as formerly they refused to do, will join in blessing the forthcoming union of Theseus and Hippolyta and the other lovers. Thanks to the re-orienting by the love-juice of Demetrius' fancy, his imagination as a lover,[2] the young people are no longer in conflict. Egeus' parental bullying, now that the suitor he chose has withdrawn, loses all semblance of reason: Theseus is put in a position to over-bear his will,[3] and makes his own requisite contribution to the dénouement by rescinding the sentence upon Hermia. Bottom, released, rejoins his fellows, bringing news (coloured by his characteristic euphoria, but we are sure it will prove justified) that 'our play is preferred'.

Thus the plot is completed (except for Theseus' decision to 'hear that play') before the start of Act v. The romantic comedy of threat is over; the human and fairy couples are each at one in reciprocated love; and the comedy that mocks absurdities has ceased to touch any of them, though it continues, hilariously, in 'Pyramus and Thisbe'. Act v is devoted to mirth and benediction,

1. P. 37.
2. On 'fancy', signifying love, as sometimes a straightforward synonym, sometimes a slanted term, see below, p. cxxxiii n. 5.
3. In six lines, his style has portrayed him: cf. his 'Thou, thou, Lysander. thou' in i. i.

befitting the theme (and in all likelihood the actual celebration) of marriage; to the extension and deepening of the thematic development; and to the final uniting of all the stories.

In the previous Acts, besides being interlocked from time to time in the plot, the groups and their stories are linked also by parallels, constituting a second kind of structure which depends not on sequence but on cross-reference.[1] The parallelism by which Shakespeare brings out the inner relationship between scenes belonging to different lines of plot has often been admired:[2] Paul Olson instances the onset of Titania's passion for Bottom placed next to the onset of Lysander's for Helena.[3] Shakespeare's genius creates in resemblances and contrasts. Puck and Bottom as the two leading comics are counterparts:[4] the jester is conscious of every joke, while the clown sees none, except a non-existent one he believes his comrades are trying to play on him. To name every feature that consciously or unconsciously we refer to a counterpart would be impossible, even if we could make ourselves aware of them all; yet some, like the comparison of the fairy court with the Duke's,[5] can hardly be passed over. Long before a stage-audience as such watches Quince's play, scenes are turned into the near semblance of plays-within-the-play by the 'invisible' stage-audience of Oberon, Puck or both.[6] The two conflicts in which Titania and the young lovers are involved each requires for its cure a period of worse aberration still, imposed on her deliberately, but on them by mishap.[7] Motifs span the groups. A clash of love and authority is recalled at the first entry of Theseus and Hippolyta, takes place at Egeus and Hermia's, Oberon and Titania's, and is implicit in Pyramus and Thisbe's.

1. On 'spatial structure', Wilson Knight and Una Ellis-Fermor were anticipated by Hazlitt: instancing from *Cymbeline*, he observed that 'the use [Shakespeare] makes of the principle of analogy' had not been 'sufficiently attended to' (*Works*, ed. P. P. Howe, IV, pp. 183 f.).

2. Cf., e.g., Hunter, p. 316.   3. P. 116.

4. Leggatt, pp. 97, 115.   5. Cf., e.g., Olson, p. 95.

6. Hunter, p. 321; cf. James L. Calderwood, '*A Midsummer Night's Dream*: The Illusion of Drama', *MLQ* (1965), p. 513.

7. 'Shakespeare's central characters are led through a passage of illusion, as in a rite of initiation' (Salingar, p. 283). Variations on the cure of aberration by inducing a greater are favourites with him: Benedick and Beatrice's fixed idea of their sparring partnership is broken thus; cf. the nonsense Kate has to embrace, and the gulling of Malvolio and Parolles. Dare one add Gloucester on Dover Cliff? Regarding the present instances, Hunter (p. 333) speaks of 'a . . . movement . . . to excess, and so to purgation'; and Calderwood (p. 514) of 'a disintegration' leading to 'a reformation' of relationships. Cf. Salingar, pp. 13, 282.

On the second and on the last occasion it has to do with the relationship of parent and child; on the others, with that of husband and wife. As George Hunter continues by reminding us, the theme of imagination at odds with reason is sounded out by all the groups in turn.[1] Lysander's imagination is divorced from reason by Puck's grand mistake of identity; correspondingly, the false focus of his imagination, and of Demetrius' imagination when he left Helena for Hermia, endangers personal identity. For the loss of identity, Shakespeare's recurrent image is that of melting;[2] Helena uses it of Demetrius, speaking not only of his oaths—'showr's of oaths did melt'—but of himself: 'So he dissolv'd'. And when Lysander has repudiated his relationship with Hermia, she too feels the outrage to identity, both his and hers:

> Am not I Hermia? Are not you Lysander?[3]

These shifts of identity are metamorphoses of inner attitude, the one which Demetrius has allowed to come over him, and the one which Lysander suffers. Ovid's *Metamorphoses* was apt to be regarded as 'a repertory of the deformations to which human nature was liable'.[4] Titania, who like Lysander suffers a compulsive deformation of the fancy (or imaginative love), like him has this annulled by an antidote. For him, this means simply a return to the normal attitude in which he began. But she and Demetrius began in perverse attitudes. They 'have been put beside themselves in order to take them beyond themselves'[5] as they were then, and back to a prior normality. Demetrius, however, owes his recovery of this true self not to the annulment of a metamorphosis, but to a metamorphosis itself, his second and magic one: it is his metamorphosed self which is in the end his former self restored. The change in him is the one thing brought back (for there will never be a ballad of Bottom's Dream), as in romance, by the mortals from the fairy otherworld;[6] and it makes him what Helena calls him, her jewel mysteriously found; his love, for right placing, the 'treasure hard to obtain'.[7] Against all the other metamorphoses, Bottom's is in strong contrast. They are of the mind, his of the body; and through the body, so far as

1. P. 319.
2. Cf., e.g., *Err.*, I. ii. 35–8 and Foakes's n.; Barber, p. 133.
3. Cf. Barber, p. 129; Calderwood, p. 513.
4. Hunter, p. 306; M. C. Bradbrook, *Elizabethan Comedy*, p. 79.
5. Barber, *loc cit.*
6. Cf. Evans, p. 42, and e.g. the green lace in *Sir Gawain and the Green Knight*.
7. C. G. Jung, *The Integration of the Personality*, pp. 139 f.

we can tell at the time, it makes its only impression upon his mind: he feels itchy, and desires hay. On waking he half-recollects a 'rare vision'; but except physically he has no need of being restored to a self he has never lost. Four characters, two of the lovers, an artisan, and the fairy queen, have experienced metamorphoses, yet no two of them have been taken through them by the dramatist along precisely the same path. The motif of metamorphosis further links Bottom in the ass-head with Bottom the actor, who transforms himself into tyrant, condoling lover, and heroine, who is ready to be lion in alternative voices, and who as fairy consort fills to admiration a part he never bargained for.[1] As Thisbe, Wall, Lion, and Moonshine, four of his fellows appear strangely transmogrified. And the focal hand-property in the *Dream* represents a metamorphosed flower.[2]

Yet while in the first four Acts there is no lack of connections, supplied whether by the progress of the plot, or by the interwoven resemblances and contrasts between one group and another, the groups are not brought to participate in one action until the artisans and fairies come to court. Then the richly patterned and rhythmic design is complete.

3. CHARACTERS AND COMEDY

Theseus is a sketch of the noble ruler, from the Chaucerian and the Renaissance humanist model. At the end of Peele's *Arraignment of Paris*, the golden apple is awarded to the nymph Eliza— the Queen in the audience (i.e. outside the play); Lyly in *Endimion* has his Cynthia preside within the action; but Shakespeare's sovereign does not simply preside, he is dramatized, and his own princely activities and qualities are depicted.[3] He has returned conqueror from war against Thebes as well as against the Amazons, and celebrated victory. He tries a cause in the light of the Athenian constitution, and eventually exercises his prerogative in the interests of equity. He is accustomed to go on progress to receive the addresses of his subjects, and as the Renaissance prince educated in humanistic disciplines, expects to appreciate loyal orations from learned men. He goes hunting, accompanied by his no less keen and expert lady, with his well-chosen pack of hounds. Being (like Hamlet) devoted to artistic

---

1. Young, pp. 101 f., 104; Leggatt, p. 109; Fender, p. 34.

2. Cf. Barber, pp. 122 f.; for the many changes with affinity to the metamorphosis-motif, cf. Young, pp. 155–8.

3. Cf. Hunter, p. 349. See above, pp. lv, lxvi f.

as well as active physical recreation, he is a patron of music, drama, and poetry[1] (whatever tone he may take about the poet's fine frenzy). These activities help to give his realm a degree of this-world actuality to contrast with dream characteristics and magic in the fairy otherworld, as does the association still made between him and the veritable sovereign, Queen Elizabeth—made briefly when he affirms himself a constitutional ruler,[2] as she like all the Tudors was at pains to do, but principally when he speaks of his behaviour on progress. The significance of that speech and its corollaries lies primarily, however, in what they show of his stature as a true statesman and a man, wise-hearted and wise-minded. He resembles Elizabeth in his genuine feeling for his people, and the high value he sets on their feeling for him. The artisans are not to him 'that barren sort'. For the present purpose, he sets no difference between their ignorance and inexperience, and the scholarship and 'practis'd accents' of the 'great clerks'. Whenever, in learned or in common men, the love and duty in their hearts fails of proper expression, it is for the prince to recognize it there, and respond magnanimously to it. For on that exchange rests the alliance of prince and subject, the political counterpart of wedlock (Theseus does not make the comparison, but it was a commonplace, and is drawn in *The Shrew*).[3]

Alike in his hunting-pack and his wedding celebrations, he cultivates what is harmonious and in keeping:[4] his hounds are matched in mouths like bells; the place of melancholy is at funerals; of satire keen and critical, not at a nuptial ceremony. He stands for rational order; even in his poetics for what cool reason comprehends. As lovers, he and Hippolyta are mature, not subject to the follies and tribulations which beset the young people.[5] His former delinquencies in love, at least his desertion of Ariadne,[6] were notorious outside the play. Shakespeare treats them according to the precepts of panegyric: if a defect is too well known to be ignored, it must be brought in as favourably as possible. Theseus' amours are touched upon only once; if they did occur, it was perhaps under Titania's fairy influence; alternatively, they can be disbelieved, accepting her disavowal, as 'the forgeries of jealousy'.[7] The maturity of the love between

---

1. Cf. Young, p. 17.   2. I. i. 120.   3. v. ii. 155 f., 159 f.
4. Young, p. 63; cf. Calderwood, p. 514.
5. Siegel, p. 40; Coghill, p. 53.
6. Whom Julia (*Gent.*, IV. iv. 165 f.) purports to have enacted.
7. Cf. Dent, p. 118; Fender, p. 11.

him and Hippolyta is apparent in the terms on which they converse. It does not lack warmth: they await their marriage with controlled impatience. Her enthusiastic recollection of an occasion in which he had no part, when she went hunting with Hercules and Cadmus, even piques him a little: he insists that his own hounds will give her at least equal pleasure. His generous admiration for Hercules, whom he is proud to call his kinsman, is, however, something in which he has wanted her to join with him: one of his reminiscences gave them that opportunity. A particularly sympathetic trait in his love is his concern at her disquiet over the course and outcome of Hermia's trial, a disquiet of which he is sensitively aware—the more, no doubt, because he is himself unhappy at the verdict he has had to deliver.

By at least one critic it is held to his discredit. In every situation, we are told, he can appreciate only the political bearing. He is the prisoner of his rational and therefore generalizing cast of mind: 'the really complete response' to Hermia's predicament 'would . . . take account of the particular as well as the general'.[2] By immediately recollecting the milder alternative to the sanction Egeus demands, and by imposing delay, Theseus does take account of it so far as he can: clearly in endorsing 'the ancient privilege of Athens' he acts reluctantly.[3] But the general principle at stake, the rule of law, is a great matter: he is not, as things stand, at liberty to contravene it. When a new and more favourable set of particular circumstances has arisen, he takes them into account immediately. At present, to alter the existing set by persuasion is all he can attempt—hence the 'private schooling' to which he summons Egeus and Demetrius. If that fails, the deadlock is inaccessible to reason. To dramatize the inability of unaided reason to ensure a tolerable outcome is the thematic function of the episode and of Theseus' dilemma in it.

The impasse is part of the context which acts as a control on the exaltation of reason at the expense of imagination in his homily on the lunatic, the lover and the poet.[4] His assessment is further put in perspective by his equivocal status as its spokesman. Are we meant to reflect that this disbeliever in antique fables is something of an antique fable himself,[5] despite his credentials from historical biography (Plutarch's *Lives*)? At all events it is one of those suspect fellows the poets who has given him his local habitation in the *Dream*, and the very sentiments he is expressing.

1. v. i. 44–7.   2. Fender, p. 51.   3. Cf. Leggatt, p. 102.
4. Cf. *id.*, p. 101; Dent, p. 124; Salingar, pp. 278 f.
5. So Dent, *loc. cit.*; Leggatt, p. 101; Hunter, p. 328.

As for the young lovers' experience, Hippolyta in her reply judges its authenticity better than he, and gives good ground for her opinion. Shakespeare keeps them in balance with each other: she is the wiser here, he about the artisans and their play.[1]

Reason has his allegiance, but this sceptical speech is his narrowest application of it. He appreciates the indispensable place of imagination in the reception of drama. On the lovers' and artisans' behalf, he does not desert reason, but applies it in a liberal spirit: to take a loyal tribute in the right way is something the highest kind of reason requires; and the lovers being now agreed, it would be against reason not to shield them from the letter of the law. The gently ironic humour with which he greets their awakening—

> Saint Valentine is past:
> Begin these wood-birds but to couple now?—

unites the sympathy and the rational detachment of the mature man. On 'Pyramus and Thisbe' he does not abdicate his judgement, but turns it into another playfully ironic jest: 'Marry, if he that writ it had played Pyramus, and hanged himself in Thisbe's garter, it would have been a fine tragedy'. 'And so it is', he immediately continues, 'and notably discharged'; words spoken not only to safeguard the terms he is on with these performers, the advantage which as a statesman he promised himself from welcoming them, but because without some such generous commendation he would have been false to his feeling for them. That feeling would not have been appropriate to a mere stereotype of the statesman and rational man; nor would his compunction while trying Hermia, his happy alacrity in joining the young lovers' weddings with his own, and the manifestations of his love for Hippolyta. Reason and statesmanship are his leading traits: but they are not the whole of him.

He and Hippolyta are 'principals without being protagonists'.[2] Their story moves, escaping an ill omen, and not deprived of a matchless entertainment, to their marriage-night; but 'it is without suspense, intrigue [or] continuity'.[3] Theseus is a mentor, ensuring a happy conclusion for the artisans and the young people. Yet though a necessary mentor, in the love-conflict he is not by himself a sufficient one: and this is a limitation calculated to make him a more sympathetic figure.[4]

1. Cf. Leggatt, p. 103.   2. Barber, p. 125.   3. Hunter, pp. 319–20.
4. Cf. Salingar, p. 16: 'no one character in Shakespeare's comedi introduces

Oberon is the lovers' other mentor: his sorting out of their tangle is essential before Theseus can bring their troubles to an end. What he does is benevolent from the first in intention, and eventually in result. Yet he is no less capable of making a mistake than Theseus of reaching an impasse. His magic does not tell him Lysander is in the wood, and so he fails to brief Puck against the error into which he falls.[1] Towards Titania he is again from one point of view a mentor: he takes charge of her experience in order to guide her into a change of attitude. But the typical mentor-character has nothing of his own at stake in the action in which he plays a decisive part: this is true of Oberon with the lovers. With Titania, he is in conflict: this is his own drama. His move against her is designed to reunite her with him; on his own terms, certainly, but it is of course she who is principally at fault.[2] Her attachment to her dead friend's child has become an obsession. It is perhaps (Puck may imply this) high time the boy was weaned from maternal dandling to be bred a knight and huntsman.[3] However that may be, in preferring him above her husband Titania has got her priorities wrong;[4] the worse when she has the responsibility of royal consort in the fairy world. Oberon and she being elementals, their discord, as she is too well aware, means discord throughout nature. Their reconciliation is

the festive movement in the play alone or controls it throughout'. See above, pp. xcvii, civ.

1. Cf. Evans, p. 36; Leggatt, p. 105.

2. That she is to be judged as a rebel wife, the parallel with Hippolyta directs (cf. Calderwood, p. 511). In *Two Noble Kinsmen* (i. i. 83 ff.; quoted Olson, pp. 102 f.) Shakespeare was to describe the Amazon's conquest by Theseus, applying to her his recurrent image for order gone by the board (cf. *MND*, ii. i. 91 f.): she was 'near to make the male/To thy sex captive; but that this thy lord/ . . . shrunk thee into/*The bound thou wast o'erflowing*' (italics mine). Titania is offending wifehood, as Hippolyta, formerly, did womanhood. For the criterion, cf. Olson, pp. 99 f. (citing *Err.*, ii. i. 15–25, and La Primaudaye, *The French Academie* (1536) sig. [Hh 8ᵛ]); Juliet Dusinberre, *Shakespeare and the Nature of Women* (1975), pp. 78–80; and next two nn.

3. 'The point seems to be that Titania is violating natural order in two ways: by making the changeling child "all her joy" at the expense of . . . Oberon, and by refusing to let the boy pass from a feminine into a masculine world where, if natural growth is to have its way, he belongs.' (Calderwood, p. 511; cf. Barber, p. 137.)

4. The relationship Oberon requires does not contravene what even progressive thinkers recommended. 'The Puritans' (to whom on this subject, Dr Dusinberre contends, the dramatists were responsive) 'did not repudiate the authority of the husband, but they qualified it . . . marriage worked best if a wife offered her husband voluntary submission out of, and in return for, love' (pp. 82, 83) (cf. 'Why should Titania cross her Oberon?').

imperative, and since she will not or cannot renounce the obsession which stands in the way, he must compel her. His action is again benevolent in result, and indeed, in ultimate aim, but not in temper:[1] he is jealous of her devotion to Theseus as well as to the changeling, and is resolved to 'torment her' for her slighting of him, and for this latest rebuff.

This Oberon is obviously not a perfect being, though he is capable, when he has obtained his end, of pitying Titania in her delusion, before freeing her from it. Just as obviously, he is not a creature of gauzy charm.[2] The fairies of the *Dream* are not the wisps of gossamer who stream through Reinhardt's film version. Partly perhaps in reaction to such notions of them, some recent critics have read into the play a subtext hinting at dark potentialities in their natures and their power: sinister, even malevolent.[3] Those romantics who on the contrary conceived them as ethereal and delightful were not without justification. In proposing to make Bottom 'like an airy spirit go', Titania implies that she herself is one. The first speech we hear from a fairy pictures her in beautiful and miniature attendance on grass and flowers. She is a vigorously active spirit, hastening, her very first quatrain announces,

> Over park, over pale,
> Thorough flood, thorough fire.[4]

What evidence is there of anything potentially sinister about this

---

1. Cf. Fender, p. 29.

2. So far one agrees with Fender, *loc. cit.*; and Benjamin Britten, who said 'I have always been struck by a kind of sharpness in Shakespeare's fairies' (quoted by W. Moelwyn Merchant, 'A *Midsummer Night's Dream*: A Visual Re-creation' in *Early Shakespeare*, p. 182).

3. Cf. especially, Jan Kott, *Shakespeare Our Contemporary* (1967); but even Merchant, *op. cit.*, concedes (I believe) too much to one of the pictorial traditions he fascinatingly describes; and other critics virtually re-import from folklore what Shakespeare has kept out, or fail to allow for his control of the darker features by their contexts: e.g. Wilson Knight, *The Shakespearian Tempest*, pp. 142 ff. (to demonstrate his postulated movement from a 'Macbeth-like atmosphere' to harmony); Young, pp. 26, 29; Fender, pp. 9, 30 f., 60. All three of course recognize (cf. Young, p. 23) the operation of fairy benevolence, to which proper justice is done by Leggatt (who is full on the darker features), pp. 104–6, 110, Schanzer, pp. 236 f., Evans, pp. 34 f., 40, and Dent, p. 120.

4. 'The fairies', wrote Granville Barker, 'are the producer's test' (see his *Prefaces to Shakespeare*, Vol. VI, ed. Edward M. Moore (1974), p. 35). To the eye, how are they to be differentiated from the mortals? Those of his unrivalled Savoy production, February 1914, in golden costumes with gold hair and gilded faces, showed that fairy beauty was compatible with strangeness, and need not be vapid or sentimental.

fairyland? There is a scene, and one or two further glimpses, of Oberon 'passing fell and wrath', the frame of mind in which he consigns Titania, for her new love-object, to 'some vile thing', some ugly or hostile beast, such as the woods evidently harbour. Even while he does, however, we have in mind that her obstinacy has to be overcome: his ill-feeling does not grate so much as it would without that context. As a rule, the context is a complete control when anything at all sinister is introduced. The wood, besides 'wild beasts', has other unpleasing inhabitants: the 'clamorous owl', 'spotted snakes', 'spiders' and the like, which are depicted in the lullaby scene; but only in order to be banished. It is the same with evils of the night or of the supernatural. Puck's description of them acknowledges their existence, but the acknowledgement prepares their exclusion. At the hour when lions roar, wolves howl, and death-boding screech-owls screech,

> Not a mouse
> Shall disturb this hallow'd house.

Damnèd spirits and other ghosts may walk, but the fairies are 'spirits of another sort' explicitly contrasted with that sinister company. They run

> By the triple Hecate's team,

but she is the triple Hecate—Diana, and Luna or Phoebe, as well as the goddess of the underworld: her team is identical with 'night's dragons', and no more evil than they. Other evils do not come from the fairies, or when they do it is not by their intention. The 'blots' foreseen as dangers to the offspring of the married couples would be from 'nature's hand': the fairies' ritual is a charm against them. The chaos in nature which Titania describes is indeed her fault and Oberon's; but she deplores it, and he takes steps which put a stop to it. It is contrary to their goodwill; not malice aforethought. Order in nature is shown as dependent on the amity which is normal between them: since their feud is abnormal and temporary,[1] the dependence is not potentially sinister. When Lysander, quite unintentionally, is taken from Hermia by fairy magic, Hermia has a symbolic nightmare; and for Lysander and Demetrius, led up and down by Puck, their frustration in the magic fog has nightmare characteristics. By these episodes a touch of nightmare is perhaps given to the resemblances the lovers' woodland adventure has to a dream.[2]

1. Cf. Leggatt, p. 106.
2. Cf. W. H. Clemen, pp. xxiv, xxx f. (dreamlikeness); Schanzer, p. 245

Yet so far as the fog-scene is concerned, what is nightmare for the would-be duellists is on Oberon's part prevention of bloodshed, and to the audience a capital piece of farcical stage-business. Puck's enjoyment has a spice of malice about it, but it is the malice of the practical joker, not of a spirit capable of serious malevolence.

All practical joking inflicts discomfiture; sometimes it inflicts pain as well. Puck's, when he claps the ass's nole on Bottom, or drives the other mechanicals in panic rout and sends one of them sprawling, is no exception. Yet the worst that can be said of him is that he is proud of his reputation as a parlous goblin, 'feared in field and town', and laughs at the harm of the night-wanderers he misleads. No harm we hear of him doing seems to be permanent: the mechanicals, when we next see them, are quite recovered from his harrying. It is not in harm that (like a sadist) he takes pleasure, but in the triumphs of his genius for mischief, and the absurd figure cut by his victims. He relishes topsy-turvydom itself:

> those things do best please me
> That befall prepost'rously.

Usually he makes no account of the distresses inseparable from the comic confusion. His mistake over Lysander was not committed wilfully or maliciously, but none the less he enjoys its effect upon the lovers:

> so far am I glad it so did sort
> That this their jangling I esteem a sport.[1]

Yet he has a moment, half-humorous, half-pitying, when the girls' suffering gets a response from him along with their folly:

> Cupid is a knavish lad
> Thus to make poor females mad.

He 'jests to Oberon', whether in beguiling a bean-fed horse, or narrating his discomfiture of the mechanicals. Jester-like, he enjoys his mischief most when it entertains an audience. The wiseacre beldame's tumble may have been uncomfortable as well as comical; but what delights Puck as much as the prank itself is the uproarious laughter of the rest. Besides the jester, he

---

(nightmarishness of fog-scene). And all supernatural power not attributed to God or his ministers has something of the uncanny.

1. Cf. Barber, pp. 130–1; Dent, p. 120; Evans, p. 38.

is a good deal of the small boy, as when he demands attention
and approval with his exit-line:

> I go, I go, look how I go![1]

As jester again, he draws Oberon's attention to the comic aspect
of what is going on:

> Shall we their fond pageant see?
> Lord, what fools these mortals be!

and more specifically,

> Then will two at once woo one:
> That must needs be sport alone.

We too are being made to see the lovers in a comic light, sharing
with Puck and Oberon the advantage—to adopt Bertrand
Evans's helpful term[2]—which those two invisible watchers hold
over them, knowing the situation which they misapprehend.
Only when he mistakes Lysander for Demetrius do we hold a
similar advantage over Puck, so that there he is himself a comic
victim, the more comic because of the false reasoning with which
he confirms the identification.

In addition to his characteristics of the jester and the mischievous small boy, Puck is close to the animal world.[3] Not only
is it an ass-head he fixes on Bottom; he tells of his shifting his own
shape into those of various animals. He is a 'lob of spirits' and
frequents the villagery and its habitations. In his dramatic
functions, too, he is a go-between, one of those characters who,
like Ariel and Menenius, have to do with each of the groups in
their plays; right-hand man to the fairy king, he works magic at
his bidding among the lovers in the wood, and on his own
initiative among the artisans; finally he leads the way for the
fairies into Theseus' palace.

Demetrius and Lysander, who at Puck's and Oberon's hands
undergo such metamorphosis of personality, are very properly
not endowed with much distinctive character: strong individuality
might have made the manipulations hard to accept.[4] They begin

1. I owe this comment to Dr Lillie Johnson.
2. 'We hold advantage over some person or persons during seven of the nine
scenes' (p. 34; cf. p. 1).
3. Trevor Ray (in Regent's Park, 1975) admirably combined a faun-like
physique with stance and movement studied from a three-year-old. For
Reinhardt in Headington Park, Oxford (1933) Leslie French emerged from
the earth by a turf trapdoor.
4. Cf. Dent, p. 115. It is by 'deliberate intention', W. H. Clemen recognizes

as embodiments of the truelove and the deserter, exchange roles, and when Lysander is himself again end as trueloves both. The final pairing of the lovers accords with the original choice made by the girls, in which they remain constant: Orsino's words to 'Cesario' are anticipated:

> For boy, however we do praise ourselves,
> Our fancies are more giddy and unfirm,
> More longing, wavering, sooner lost and won,
> Than women's are.[1]

Lysander's lapse is not, I think, portraiture of him individually, representative of latent inconstancy in his character: we make full allowance for his being under compulsion. The magic corresponds in human terms to something beyond the personal. In the girls, that something never changes direction. They are not subjected to the love-juice and, unlike the men, do not need to be malleable in order to fulfil their dramatic roles. Critics (R. W. Dent is an honourable exception[2]) commonly overlook the difference in characterization, and say of 'the lovers' what can rightly be said only of the men, that they are little characterized. The physical differentiation between Helena and Hermia, one tall and fair, the other short and dark, is of course almost always observed, though one critic, who thinks it hard to remember which is which, can scarcely be trusting us to visualize them (as we should even while we read) speaking their lines upon the stage. But the differentiation goes much beyond their looks, as even pictorial art can show: witness Arthur Rackham's portrayals, sufficiently true to the impression made by the text.[3] They are strongly contrasted in temperament. Hermia is spirited and warm-blooded, tender in happy love, hot and militant in anger. Helena is much more the lady: very feminine, and very much aware of it. Though she cannot forbear to pursue Demetrius, the pursuit offends her womanhood:

> We should be woo'd, and were not made to woo,

she reproaches him,

> Your wrongs do set a scandal on my sex.

(p. xxx), that there is not more differentiation of character; 'the characters are easily malleable', notes Enid Welsford (p. 345): comments which fit the young men, though not the girls.

1. Cf. *Gent.*, where, according to the serenade, through Silvia's eyes Love sees straight.   2. Pp. 115 f. He quotes Orsino's lines.

3. Heinemann edn of the *Dream* (1908), facing pp. 6, 10, 74, 82.

Men are almost an alien species: it is another scandal that Hermia (as Helena thinks) should 'join with men' against a bosom friend since girlhood. Until in a speech of dignity and pathos Helena renounces her doting chase, the contrast between the two is of a kind to generate a preference: 'would any of us', wrote R. W. Chambers, 'go hiking through the Athenian forest with Helena, if we could get Hermia?'[1]—and that despite Hermia's readiness, being provoked, with her nails. Helena betrays her friends' confidence: and she demeans herself, spaniel-fashion, to Demetrius.[2] Both aberrations have the same psychological origin, loss of self-respect as a result of being jilted. The key is given on her first appearance:

> Call you me fair? That fair again unsay,

is her opening line. Attractions she has none, since 'Demetrius thinks not so'.[3] All trust in herself has deserted her: she would give up her own identity if she could have Hermia's. Her third great aberration has the same cause. She cannot believe that Lysander's or even Demetrius' addresses are anything but mockery. Just before Lysander starts up with his avowal, her monologue reminds us of her self-depreciation.

> I am as ugly as a bear . . .
> What wicked and dissembling glass of mine
> Made me compare with Hermia's sphery eyne?

Naturally she cannot suppose the young men are in earnest: she is not a girl for whom men become rivals: she is a girl who gets jilted. That is her fixation. Psychologically, the character is consistently conceived.

Though none of the lovers' characters develop, Helena's and Hermia's are unfolded. Lysander and Demetrius simply return to the normality which was originally theirs. Lysander's 'wonted sight' is restored to him, and lest there should be any doubt that as Demetrius declares in the wood his heart 'to Helen . . . is home return'd', the declaration is repeated to Theseus: he is 'come to my natural taste'. But before Hermia and Helena too recover

---

1. *Man's Unconquerable Mind* (1954), p. 293.

2. Her pursuit of him is not brazen (the impression I received from Peter Brook's production), the coarse comedy of the man-eating female. Its comedy is coloured with the pathos of her desperation: her forwardness, the paradoxical result of the collapse of all self-confidence: ' I did never, no, nor never can/ Deserve a sweet look from Demetrius' eye' (ii. ii. 125 f.); she begs leave (ii. i. 206 f.), 'Unworthy as I am', to follow him.

3. Cf. Brown, p. 84.

their normal balance, they display in the great quarrel-scene traits which are not new developments but which the events of the play have not led them to display before. Aggression with Helena takes the form of cattiness. She knows where Hermia is vulnerable. Hermia is conscious of what in unsympathetic eyes may be considered her 'bad points' despite her beauty, and Lysander has attacked one of them, her unfashionable dark complexion. Taking the hint, Helena attacks the other, her lack of inches. Finding the attack reaches its mark (though Hermia, with 'thou painted maypole', retorts woundingly in kind) she keeps returning to it. Hermia's hot temper can be reckoned on for an outburst which will enable her to be characterized as curst and shrewish: a type of female personality particularly obnoxious to men. The masterstroke is

> She was a vixen when she went to school,

making the men visualize, in place of the grown-up lady ripe for admiration and love, an undignified demon of a small child under tutelage. Probably Hermia's fury is a bit more than Helena bargained for, and genuinely frightens her: but not so much that she fails to capitalize on her feminine need for male protection. As for Hermia, we have seen her fierce before—

> There is no following her in this fierce vein,

admitted Demetrius—but could not have anticipated what a vixen she indeed here shows herself, so ready with her nails, and clamouring to be 'let get at' her tormentor.[1]

This exhibition is comedy of character, the only instance (I think) in the lovers' story, since Lysander's rationalization of his switch from Hermia to Helena is rather comedy of human nature. As the climax, with the frustrated duel, of the lovers' troubles and of their follies, the quarrel brings out the relationship in the audience's response between amusement at the one and commiseration of the other. Even in a comic situation, distress is still distress, and arouses some sympathy. But we are free to laugh at the lovers much more than we pity them. They cannot, while Oberon watches over them, come to great harm. Puck encourages us to view their tribulations as a 'fond pageant'—

> Lord, what fools these mortals be!

What they experience as torturing disorder is dramatized for us in a highly patterned form. The lovers' griefs thus reach us under

---

1. I venture to give the modern English of 'Let me come *to* her!'

threefold control—'encapsulated', R. G. Collingwood might have said,[1] within this comedic structure, Puck's showmanship of them as comic, and (which removes the threat that would make their case too serious for such a comedy as this) Oberon's guardianship.[2] Yet if they did not touch our commiserating sympathy at all, the entanglement would yield farce, not comedy.

Bottom, too, might have been a figure of farce; but he again is no simple laughing-stock, though he needs no such sympathy. A laughing-stock he is: the clown of the play where Puck is the jester; but with our laughter there mingles admiration and affection. He belongs to the robust plebeian comedy of the artisans' story, and to Puck he is 'the shallowest thickskin' among them. Were that a fair assessment, he would be a mere butt; the satirized Dogberry is little more. At the other extreme is his fellows' affectionate admiration, naïve and unqualified, as ours is not. His part and personality have their motto in the words with which he awakes after his adventure in the wood: 'When my cue comes, I will answer it'. It is characteristic that he is sure his next cue is: 'Most fair Pyramus'. In his vanity he even takes up cues which are not there. He is sorry it is not his cue to play a tyrant; but he gives a sample of the Ercles vein nevertheless, and applauds his own performance: 'This was lofty'. He hopes that it might be his cue to play the lady too, or the lion. One of his devices to reassure the ladies happens to include a revelation of who is playing the hero's part. His malapropisms are in character: full of self-confidence, he uses a more ambitious vocabulary than he is master of. Comedy of absurd language is not confined to him, but his speech is the richest in it.[3] Much of the best comedy of situation comes in his role, too: the finest of all when, grotesquely 'translated', he is made the adored consort of the fairy queen. His being chosen for Pyramus is itself ludicrous: it means the clown of the *Dream* is cast for the romantic lover and tragic hero of the play-within-the-play.[4] When Puck procures him as the

1. *Autobiography* (Pelican edn, 1944), p. 78.

2. Cf. Evans, p. 40; Dent, p. 120; Olson, p. 117; Young, p. 151; Leggatt, pp. 96 f.; Barber, p. 131; Brown, p. 84.

3. Cf. Fender, pp. 19, 35; L. Borinski, 'Shakespeare's Comic Prose', *Sh.S.*, 8 (1955), p. 64, notes the differentiation of Bottom's style from Quince's: 'Quince is the pedant, whose talk abounds in redundancies: Bottom is no fool and has real wit, and accordingly he alone has sufficient imagination for witty associations, as, for instance, when he talks to the fairies: these association are . . . half-funny, half-picturesque and quaint, in keeping with the atmosphere of the play'. Cf. also Milton Crane, *Shakespeare's Prose*, pp. 75 f., Brian Vickers, *The Artistry of Shakespeare's Prose*, pp. 66–8.

4. Cf. Hunter, p. 329.

monster for Titania to dote on, and be-monsters him with the ass-head, a sequence of ludicrous situations ensues. In his ass-head, he sings; given fairy grooms, he sets two of them to scratch his hairy ass-scalp; and around his ass-neck the fairy queen twines her arms. Yet there is no communication between them: their kinds of understanding are totally different, and 'each one comically dislocates the other'.[1] She offers him fairy music, and with the tastes of the weaver, he proposes the tongs and bones; hastily heading him off, she offers him fairy food, and with the tastes of the ass, he would like hay. He is quite unsusceptible to the romance of fairyland.[2]

But none of the things which make Bottom ridiculous deprives him of our liking or even of the admiration we have for him. His vanity 'is a pleasant vanity, and founded on a real superiority'.[3] Dogberry's vanity is pompous, as befits a jack-in-office: Bottom's is not. Dogberry is called an ass; an enormity to which he alludes again and again. Bottom repeatedly says things which we refer to his ass-hood; but Bottom could never, like Dogberry, in normal circumstances have made conscious allusion to himself as an ass without seeing the point. It is by buttering his vanity that Quince manages to keep him to the part of Pyramus; but it is the best butter: Quince is only making tactful use of his real opinion of Bottom. Bottom's weft of absurdity is woven on a warp of practical ability and common sense. He has an urge to be doing: 'in every difficulty he sets to work at once',[4] and his counsel is by no means always to be despised. He gets the preparations for 'Pyramus' off to a good start: 'First, good Peter Quince, say what the play treats on; then read the names of the actors; and so grow to a point'; and, bringing the news that 'The Duke has dined', directs them to as good a conclusion. He makes one of the most sensible speeches in the play, epitomizing half its critique of love: 'To say the truth, reason and love keep little company together nowadays. The more the pity, that some honest neighbours will not make them friends'. There his cue indeed came and he answered it. He always does: he is equal to all occasions.[5] In all

1. Vickers, p. 69; Leggatt, pp. 89, 110. Yet though the humour resides partly in the contrast between his animal form and her 'airy spirit', even a controlled suggestion of carnal bestiality is surely impossible: jealous Oberon will not have cast his spell to cuckold himself. Her dotage is imaginative and emotional.
2. Cf. Barber, p. 157; W. H. Clemen, p. xxxv.
3. Stopford A. Brooke, *On Ten Plays of Shakespeare* (1930), p. 28.   4. *Ibid.*
5. Cf. Schanzer, p. 235; Bradbrook, *Shakespeare*, p. 157; Young, pp. 101, 104, 157.

his ludicrous situations, his bearing carries him triumphantly through. If he were simply their victim, that would be low comedy: what turns them to high comedy is his imperturbability. The contrast between the situation, which should discomfit him, and the fact that he is not discomfited, is comic; but it makes him admirable as well as comic. He has courage: he catches no panic from his terrified companions. He is at home everywhere.[1] With his fairy grooms, he is admirably courteous, and not without humour.[2] At Theseus' court, Quince, all nerves, mangles the delivery of his prologue, and Moonshine, put out by mocking comments, falls back on a prose summary of his lines; but Bottom, when Demetrius comments, sets him right with ready aplomb. Even if it is the Duke who raises an objection, Bottom will take it as his cue to answer, and will clear the difficulty with patient courtesy. Among the craftsmen, as an expert in drama he is fond of 'explaining . . . to the lesser intellects' about him:[3] and so, during the command performance, when he thinks Theseus is getting things wrong he is perfectly prepared to help him out, and to step out of his part to do it. In his part or out of it, everywhere he is comically at ease, even where he should not be; and yet—shouldn't he? His manners at court are conventionally wrong; yet they are right enough, because they are easy and natural. The object of good manners is to establish relationships that work smoothly. Bottom's do (though at the Athenian court, it has to be admitted, part of the credit must go to the urbanity of Theseus' response).

This imperturbability of Bottom's is a regular gambit for high-class clown humour. It is used by Shaw;[4] and to perfection by Shakespeare in Falstaff. Like Falstaff until his downfall, Bottom is rather more than equal to any situation. But Bottom's triumphs, in contrast with Falstaff's, are unselfconscious: he does not see the difficulty and walks through it, his boundless self-confidence and genuine qualities taking him through. Falstaff sees with perfect clearness the difficulties in which he is placed by his flight from Gadshill, his encountering Douglas or the Lord Chief Justice, or Mrs Quickly's attempt to have him arrested. But the difficulties give him enjoyable occasion for what Dr Johnson calls 'the wit of

1. Cf. Evans, p. 44; Fender, p. 20, observes how remarkably, when his face is hidden by the ass-head, the rest of him remains the same; cf. Bradbrook, *Shakespeare*, p. 158.

2. Young, p. 103.   3. Brooke, p. 29; Vickers, p. 66.

4. See *Three Plays for Puritans*, preface, pp. xxii f. (1901), on his *Plays Pleasant* and the tradition of *Cool as a Cucumber*.

escape'. To adapt what Johnson said of Foote the comedian, Falstaff is driven into a corner and we think his adversaries have got him: 'but he's gone, sir, like an animal that jumps over your head'.[1] That is even finer comedy than we have in Bottom, whose imperturbability is not mastery of the situation, but a species of invincible ignorance,[2] coupled, however, with a gift of rapport despite misunderstanding.

The finest passage in Bottom's part is his monologue when he wakens without the ass-head, and the finest thing in that is its conclusion. The ballad Quince is to write 'shall be called "Bottom's Dream", because it hath no bottom'. That combines the old academic joke of non-sequitur nomenclature, *lucus a non lucendo*, with the two opposites implied: no bottom because no foundation, and no bottom because unfathomably profound.[3] Then 'Pyramus and Thisbe' returns to his mind—but not as the play which he and his fellows are almost due to present. The memory of it comes back to him in a sort of luminous mist, with clouds of glory trailing from the experience, the 'dream', he has had. He envisages himself on a grand occasion, which somehow the future holds for him, having a great triumph with the ballad which shall express his 'most rare vision': 'I will sing it in the latter end of a play, before the Duke'—*a* play, not *the* play. The ballad as he conceives it will have all the pathos and poetry appropriate to the man who has had the love of a high and noble lady, and lost her. He has forgotten Titania, and does not yet remember Thisbe; but something deep in his mind transfigures the rising image of the one with the emotion proper to the lost image of the other: 'Peradventure, to make it the more gracious, I shall sing it at her death'.

Comedy of language, of stage-spectacle (including costume, and mime and other 'business'), and of situation, all contribute to make Bottom's a great comic role. Furthermore, not forgetting Puck, he is the foremost comic personality of the play. 'There is a definite conception of some particular sort of man at the back of all Shakespeare's characters', wrote Bernard Shaw. 'The quantity of fun to be got out of Bottom . . . [and, for instance] Autolycus . . .

1. Boswell, *Life of Johnson*, ed. Birkbeck Hill, Vol. III, p. 69: the application is Dover Wilson's in *The Fortunes of Falstaff*, p. 56.

2. Cf. Evans, pp. 43 f.; Young, p. 161.

3. 'No bottom', for a weaver, is also no skein to weave from. Profundity is suggested by St Paul's continuation from the verse Bottom garbles: Dent, p. 121, quotes Tyndale's tr. of I. Cor. ii. 9–10 from the Genevan N.T., 1557, which has 'the Spirite searcheth . . . the botome of Goddes secretes'. Cf. Olson, pp. 98 f., 114.

is about the same; but underneath the fun there are two widely different persons'.[1] The comedy of character in Bottom is individually his.

'Pyramus and Thisbe' brings into the *Dream* yet another type of comedy, burlesque. As part of the whole play the performance is organic not only because it is the achieved goal of the artisan-plot, but also by its relevance to the main themes: love, and the relation between imagination, illusion, and reality.[2] The burlesque is laughable, first of all, by its contrast with the original story (though even Ovid's version skirts the preposterous at times). It satirizes the ineptitude of amateur actors;[3] styles of drama which are or should be now outmoded; and the absurdities of poetasters. Kenneth Muir has shown how, 'by a beautiful piece of artistic economy', Shakespeare culled 'his choice blooms' of bad poetry 'from all the best-known versions of the Pyramus and Thisbe story'. He notes the faults which Shakespeare comically exaggerates: the recourse to archaism for rhyme in 'certain'; the trite comparison of the heroine's beauties to flowers, which are transferred to the hero, applied to the wrong features and reduced to bathos when they are extended to the vegetable 'leeks'; the lines padded out with expletives ('eke', and Golding's overworked 'did') or redundancies such as

> Did scare away, or rather did affright,

and 'there, there to woo'; the multiplied alliteration, as in

> Quail, crush, conclude, and quell;

and the fustian apostrophes to the Furies and Fates, to Night, to Nature—and to Wall.[4]

The bad rhetoric, categorized by R. W. Dent as 'mind-offending tropes' and 'ear-offending schemes',[5] is typical also of the

---

1. *Our Theatres in the Nineties*, Vol. I, p. 181.

2. See above, pp. xcii f.; below, pp. cxxxvii ff.

3. And no doubt (though Quince and Co. envisage only this performance) the 'ingenious tradesmen' who, says Strype, 'would sometimes gather a Company of themselves, and learn Interludes . . . And then they played at certain Festival Times, and in private Houses at Weddings or other splendid Fntertainments'. Some became semi-professionals (see F. P. Wilson, *The English Drama 1485–1585*, pp. 50 f.). The cap fits these much better than J. W. Robinson's candidates, the full professionals of an earlier generation who, in default of a livery, for legal purposes described themselves as tradesmen ('Palpable Hot Ice', pp. 195–7).

4. Muir, *Sources*[2], pp. 69–76 (the purposes of the burlesque are summarized on p. 77). Cf. Barber, p. 153; Young, pp. 37, 43–5.   5. P. 125.

drama Shakespeare is making fun of. To the kinds burlesqued from the poetasters, W. H. Clemen adds the overdone hyperbole and rhetorical questions from English Senecan tragedies, which offered targets also in their 'stereotyped phrases for expressing grief', their 'ponderous conventions', and their melodrama.[1] Some lines of the *Hercules Furens* in Jasper Heywood's translation are thought by D. P. Young to be parodied in Bottom's specimen of 'Ercles' vein'.[2] Certainly English Seneca seems to be one sort of drama burlesqued in 'Pyramus', along with the Tudor interludes like *Apius and Virginia* and especially those like *Cambises* performed to popular audiences by small troupes of professionals. Since 'comedy' could mean merely 'play', the title of *Apius*, 'A new Tragicall Comedie', was not absurd unless unfairly interpreted; but that of *Cambises*, 'A Lamentable Tragedie mixed full of pleasant mirth', though an accurate description, invited mockery. It is burlesqued, and probably the *Apius* title too, or some resembling it, when 'Pyramus' is announced as 'The most Lamentable Comedy', and, still worse, as 'very tragical mirth'.[3] In 'Pyramus' itself, the burlesque of interlude-dramaturgy has been demonstrated by J. W. Robinson.[4] He dwells on the direct informing of the audience, as in the prologue and the over-explicit presenter's review of the actors' dumb-show, and, for example, Wall's departure-speech. Wall justifies his exit with crass naïvety; Moonshine's is unmotivated. Their very presence in the cast burlesques the personifying characters who appear in the interludes. In those, personification stops at collective persons, types generalized into abstractions, and embodiments of mental factors, such as Commons Complaint, Proof, and Diligence in *Cambises*: Wall and Moonshine personify physical facts. Wall personified is especially ridiculous, since a wall 'is so concrete'. 'A riot of personifications' invades the dialogue: Thisbe's mantle is 'slain'; in her death-speech she addresses her tongue, her sword, and its blade; Pyramus in his, sword, tongue and tears.

The *Dream*'s comedy of language attains its peak of extravagance in 'Pyramus'. One favourite effect is continued from the play proper: the misassignment of sense-experience—Pyramus sees a voice, hopes to hear his Thisbe's face, and bids his tongue lose its light. In the rehearsal-scene he is supposed to have gone 'but to see a noise that he heard', and the effect has been taken to its highest point in Bottom's garbling of St Paul: 'The eye of

1. P. xxxvi.   2. Pp. 35 f.   3. J. W. Robinson, p. 194.
4. Pp. 200-3, with references to David M. Bevington, *From Mankind to Marlowe* (1962).

man hath not heard ...'. That parody would not have been possible in anything but comic prose; and prose, as is normal in Shakespeare, is the vehicle for the scenes of plebeian comedy. Bottom's adherence to it in fairyland, while Titania speaks verse, adds to the characterization and the comic effect, emphasizing how unshakeably he remains himself, and how out of touch, inhabiting still their disparate worlds, they are with each other. He departs from prose in his snatch of song about birds and cuckolds, and in the doggerel he spouts from a tyrant-rant supposed to belong to some play. That prepares for the doggerel of 'Pyramus and Thisbe', which he and Flute begin to rehearse, and which all the artisans speak when the play is performed. During the performance Shakespeare mingles prose and verse to wonderfully comic effect. With the plebeians speaking burlesque verse, the Duke and the other aristocrats for their bantering commentary are switched to prose; but furthermore, to answer them Starveling and Bottom drop their doggerel and revert to the prose—a different sort, simple and direct despite comic blunders—which elsewhere is the staple of the artisans' language.[1] Together with the verbal comedy, the comedy of spectacle, which has had its climaxes when Bottom appeared in the ass-head and later was enfolded in Titania's embrace, and when Demetrius chased blindly about the stage in pursuit of Puck's voice, continues in the burlesque 'business' of 'Pyramus', and is concluded by the Bergomask dance.

4. LYRICISM, MUSIC AND DANCE

Poetry has no less a place than comedy in the language and spectacle of the *Dream*;[2] and their poetry has a potent ally in the music. The grotesque Bergomask, with music to match, contrasts with the graceful dances and their music before and after: the dignified measure which Oberon and Titania tread, and the fairy ensemble which concludes the play. The verse and language are often in themselves exquisitely musical: to take no other examples, 'Over hill, over dale', and 'I know a bank where the wild thyme blows' are famous for their melody, as well as for

---

1. On what precedes in this paragraph, cf. Crane, pp. 75-7; Vickers, pp. 65-71. 'The clown-scenes are entirely dominated by "poetic" illine because the atmosphere of the whole play is purely lyrical and poetic' (Borinski, p. 64).

2. 'The spirit of comedy and the poetic imagina ion' together form (as Clemen says, p. xxiv) the power which unifies its disparate elements.

their imagery, which is no less lyrical.[1] Among English poets, we know from the echoes in *Comus* and the underlinings in Keats's Shakespeare of two in particular who were entranced by the lyrical magic of the *Dream*; and what more musical ear or finer taste for romance has there been than theirs?[2]

The verse of the play is of many forms.[3] The variations help to define the character of the different groups: Theseus and Hippolyta (except for their prose in Act v) speak always in blank verse; none but the fairies use the short couplet. Yet they also speak blank verse; and the young lovers, though never deviating from the pentameter (again, except in Act v), have it now with and now without rhyme. The changes of verse within a group are made for dramatic ends, including the modulation of emotion. Thus the passion to which the lovers' conflicts mount in their quarrel-scene is a climax in blank verse after the rhyme of their earlier, more formally treated, exchanges. Blank verse is wanted for the confrontation of Oberon and Titania, in keeping both with its emotion and with their royal dignity. Titania's blank verse in the scenes with Bottom maintains her as still the fairy queen, and makes the best contrast with his prose. The incantations are in short rhymed lines; all but one in the short couplet. The effect of that measure elsewhere is described by Granville Barker, who comments in the first place on the fairies' exit lines after the dance of reconciliation, with Oberon's summons:

> Then my queen, in silence sad,
> Trip we after night's shade:
> We the globe can compass soon,
> Swifter than the wandering moon.

'The lilt, no less than the meaning, helps to express them to us as beings other than mortals, treading the air'. The metre, he adds, carries its suggestion of the fairy kind of supernatural in 'its lightness, its strange simplicity' A student of the *Dream* could wish no better guide to the modulations of the play's lyricism than the analysis which runs through Granville Barker's 1924 preface.[4] Few critics approach him in appreciation of poetical

1. What more alien to the *Dream* than a charmless performance? Peter Brook's adaptation (rather than production), however effective as theatrical entertainment, realized none of the charm except in the speaking of the verse.

2. For Keats, see Caroline Spurgeon, *Shakespeare's Imagery*, p. 263, and her *Keats's Shakespeare*, pp. 87–104, cf. pp. 51 f., 62–5.

3. See above, pp. l, li; and for their functions, Crane, pp. 73–5; Doran, pp. 14–16.

4. Reprinted in the posthumous *Prefaces to Shakespeare*, Vol. vi. For what follows, see pp. 103 f., 112–15, 120–3.

nuances and the effects to be made with them in the theatre by actors who know how to speak. In illustration he analyses as dramatic poetry the movement of the opening scene; we can follow him no further than the end of the first episode. It begins with 'the formal serenity' of Theseus and Hippolyta, 'mellow-toned'.

> Impinging on this comes the shrill rattle of Egeus . . . Next, Hermia's meek obstinacy, rhythmical, distinct, low . . . Then Demetrius and Lysander strike each his note. Demetrius, slow, hard-bitten, positive, pleasantly surly—not much romance in this young man . . . And Lysander, . . . impertinent, melodious, light . . . Fine spirit in him, too, though; for he says his say to the Duke . . . rings it out confident and clear. The measured speech and mellow voice of Theseus now modulate the scene back to the tone it began upon.

(But, one would add, for his need to cheer a troubled Hippolyta.) The play abounds, Barker observes, in passages designed for sustained and often for varied art in their delivery: among them Titania on disorder and her speech beginning 'Be kind and cour-teous to this gentleman'; Oberon's visions of the mermaid and of Cupid; Puck's 'My fairy lord, this must be done with haste' and Oberon's reply; and both Theseus and Hippolyta on the hounds. In all these there is a lyrical note, and Barker rightly finds it even in the more conventional rhetoric so often spoken by the lovers. That comes off best when it is 'let depend on the charm' of the voice; its appeal lies most in 'the verse and in the fancy of the images'. The lyricism works as drama, given the kind of drama the *Dream* is. The set speeches have all of them their functions to perform: Barker points out how in the lovers' quarrel-scene, the poetry of Helena's appeal to 'schooldays' friendship' sustains, among the wrangling and comic misunderstandings, 'the play's beauty and romance', and 'our sentimental interest in the . . . fortunes of the four'.

When the spoken verse is so various in its forms, and so often lyrical in tone, the distance from dialogue to song is not great. And the songs and dances are no less an integral part of the drama than the set speeches.[1] The lullaby is part of the action. Titania must sleep in order that the love-juice spell may be cast upon her. The dance and song of her fairies is a ritual to protect her from molestation: but Oberon is not a party to it and (ironically) it

1. Cf. Welsford, pp. 331 f. Richmond Noble (*Shakespeare's Use of Song*, p. 53), claiming *MND* as the play where Shakespeare first achieves this, overlooks the serenade in *Gent.* But he well describ   the functions of the lullaby.

does not protect her from him. Yet, from another point of view, it has not failed in its purpose of keeping away what would harm her, since the spell is ultimately for her good. The lullaby is part of a dramatic pattern, too: Titania falls asleep to the lullaby and she is awakened by the singing of Bottom. This pattern of mortal music which awakens, fairy music which induces sleep, is repeated in the instrumental music at the dénouement.[1] It is dramatically necessary that while Oberon and Titania 'shake the ground' in their dance, the five still sleeping characters should remain so—the lovers until found by Theseus, and awakened by the hunting horns of his (offstage) attendants; and Bottom right through that scene also. Hence fairy music is summoned to cast them into a sleep beyond the natural.

Dance is again an essential part of the action and the symmetric structure. The dance of Oberon and Titania is the ritual which ratifies the reconciliation of the fairy rulers, and symbolizes the renewed dance in the realm of nature which depends upon them.[2] It corresponds inversely to the dance of Titania's fairies from which Oberon was absent, and to his earlier refusal to dance with her on her terms. And as they move in harmony, he announces the further ritual which will crown the fairy action: they

> will tomorrow midnight, solemnly,
> Dance in Duke Theseus' house triumphantly,
> And bless it to all fair prosperity.

When, as the last action of the play, that resolve is fulfilled, the blessing is spoken in lyrical short couplets, and sung as well as danced.[3]

1. Cf. Long, pp. 88, 95.
2. Cf. Olson, p. 115; Wilson Knight, p. 165.
3. Does the extant text preserve the words of the song, or are they missing? To Dr Johnson's mind, 'the series of the Scene' requires a song from Oberon and his fairies after v. i. 382, and one from Titania and hers after l. 386; so there are two songs missing. It is by no means certain that his straightforward reading is not correct. The Folio, however, heads as 'The Song' the lines (387 ff.) beginning

> Now, until the break of day

and italicizes them accordingly. It may have been guided by the prompt-book; but after two speeches calling for song, it would have been easy to suppose that what followed must be the song, none other appearing. Noble (pp. 55-7) concludes that F is right. A missing lyric, he contends (it is his least unpersuasive argument) could only have duplicated the blessing Oberon pronounce (but a sung blessing would hardly be felt to duplicate a spoken one: and although we may not be able to imagine a second set of words for it, that scarcely shows

For Shakespeare and in the thought of his time the harmony of music and of movement in the dance signified concord and was capable of promoting it in the body and the mind.[1] It is so in the *Dream*: the dance of Oberon and Titania expresses and confirms their recovered amity; the concluding ritual will foster the fertile union of the couples, and ward off from their offspring the physical disharmonies, the 'mole, hare-lip or scar' which random Nature sometimes inflicts. In the theatre, symbolic dance, and especially music, can transport us beyond the realm of actuality which more or less naturalistic action suggests, and in the *Dream* as elsewhere, Shakespeare uses them to prepare or accompany the supernatural.[2] The refrain of the lullaby is an apt illustration,

---

Shakespeare could not). Long would begin the song or at least the tune with Oberon's first line (377) upon the fairies' entrance, finding that the whole passage can then be seen (if ll. 389 f. are transferred from Oberon to Titania) as five six-line stanzas and 'a brisk concluding couplet'. Oberon and Titania would each sing, or intone to the tune, a stanza of instructions; the fairies would have two stanzas for their blessing, and Oberon would repeat his commands and conclude the song. This accepts neither F's indication for the song nor Q's non-indication. It emends a speech-prefix which shows no signs of being corrupt. It overrides the unlikelihood of instructions being sung, and to mitigate that introduces the unwarrantable notion of intoning. It treats as one of a set of five stanzas the first six lines, which have a different rhyme-scheme. Against both Long and Noble it is to be noted that all the fairies' other passages in short couplets are to be spoken (as is 'On a day' in *LLL*). Such couplets, except for Juno and Ceres' masque song in *Tp.*, are nowhere sung in Shakespeare. Granville Barker seems to me unanswerable: 'Dramatically, the context, Titania's

Will we sing, and bless this place,

and Oberon's

Now, until the break of day

suggest a gap that some song has filled. Why "Now", otherwise?' A 'ditty sung and danced', he adds, in which Oberon takes a communal, even if a leader's part, will deprive him of 'an ending commensurate with [his] importance'. And in the lines, Barker, with his ear for theatre-utterance, heard (as I with mine, not unpractised though ordinary by comparison) speech-rhythms. To supply the place of the missing song, Barker used the wedding-song from *Two Noble Kinsmen* (I. i, a scene of which the dialogue is clearly Shakespearean). See Barker, pp. 39, 108, 109 and n. 10 (the whole note, in answer to Noble, is worth reading).

On the dances, C. L. Barber (p. 138) suggests that in line with village festival tradition (for which he quotes E. K. Chambers, *The Mediaeval Stage*, Vol. I, pp. 165 f.) the fairies enter in a processional dance led by Oberon; then 'hand in hand', as Titania directs, are led by her in a round dance. This is attractive, though not altogether easy to match with Oberon's entry-speech.

1. Cf. Olson, p. 115; Brown, pp. 140 f.; Long, p. 93.

2. Cf. Long, p. 101; *Caes.*, IV. iii. 265; *Ant.*, IV. iv. 11; *Per.*, III. ii. 91, v. i. 225; *Cymb.*, v. iv. 29; *Tp.*, *passim*.

in brief, of this and other characteristics of the poetical in the play. It is danced and sung as a charm; it prepares for the magic of the love-juice; Philomel, whom it invokes, is the nightingale, the most melodious inhabitant of the natural world; and she is also the lyric voice of love. The lyrical feeling of the *Dream* springs always from romantic love, or the beauty of nature, or the marvel of fairyland and its enchantments. Beauty of spectacle, in the performances Shakespeare reckoned on, came from dance and costume; the setting was poetically beautiful not to outward sight, but to the eye of imagination; it was created by the poetry sung and spoken.

5. SETTING: WOODLAND AND FAIRYLAND; MOON

In bringing before the mind's eye more than the actual scene presents to bodily vision, and much that is not staged at all, allusion and imagery are the dramatist's resources. In the *Dream*, as D. P. Young points out, they frequently take the form of lists, vignettes, or panoramas. The 'lists are simple and concrete': he quotes Elizabeth Sewell's instance of 'the showers of apricocks and figs and dewberries, not to mention honey and butterflies and bees and glow-worms' which figure in Titania's commands to the attendants upon Bottom. The vignettes are vivid 'glimpses of single figures and activities': Lysander courting; the old dame made to spill the ale in 'her withered dewlap'; the sick man who hears the owl screech and is put 'in remembrance of a shroud'. The panoramas, such as Oberon's seascape with the siren and Cupid, and Titania's with herself and her Indian friend, are 'composed of sharp and realistic details'.[1]

The primary task of the appeals to the mind's eye and ear is to create the setting of the main action, the wood, both as woodland and as the haunt of the fairies.[2] Before it is reached we hear of localities in it: 'faint primrose beds' known to Helena and Hermia, and 'the Duke's oak'. The moment a fairy denizen appears she speaks of cowslips as the pensioners of the fairy queen: to her they are 'cowslips tall', which, despite her actual stature, suggests that some fairies, at least, are diminutive. Fairyland is made circumstantial in great measure by description of what the fairies do. It is the duty of the First Fairy to hang dew-drop pearls in the cowslips' ears, and to dew orbs upon the green, where the fairy rounds are danced. Others kill cankers in the musk-rose buds; for fans, pluck the wings from painted butterflies; war

1. Pp. 75, 76–80, 85.   2. Cf. Spurgeon, pp. 259–62.

with bats for their leathern ones to make the small elves coats; hunt the bees for their honey-bags and wax, and light beeswax candles at the fiery eyes of glow-worms. One, specially daring, is ready to raid the squirrel's hoard of nuts. The elves, terrified at their rulers' angry quarrel, take refuge in acorn cups. Such details of the fairies' dealings with nature thus poetically depict the setting.[1] Most likely there was a stage-property bank for Titania to sleep on; but it is Oberon's description which invests it with romantic beauty. Quince appreciates the 'green plot' and 'hawthorn brake' as 'marvellous convenient' for the rehearsal (the brake, too, may have been a 'property'). Further than this, there is little direct reference to the woodland scene—Theseus, in hunting costume, gives it contour: a western valley, and a mountain-top. Oberon, at dawn, can tread the groves 'like a forester', but there are few other specifically sylvan images; though the imagery of birds and flowers and trees[2] creates an irresistible impression of rural beauty which we carry into our imagination of the wood. In Helena's imagery the hawthorn buds belong to the wood, but the double cherry probably does not, and the lark that delights the shepherd must be the skylark not the wood lark. More than once the imagery is of the ocean: the shore, or with the leviathan, beyond it. Of the places where Oberon and Titania have wrangled, the 'pavèd fountain' and the 'rushy brook' might be part of the woodland scene; not so 'the beachèd margent of the sea'. The setting, for the audience's imagination, is widened beyond the wood, and becomes the world of nature itself. It does not matter whether 'the red rose on triumphant briar' (even 'Pyramus' has its truly poetical nature-image) belongs to the woodland or not. The image of 'high Taurus' snow', and the talk of hunting 'in Crete, in Sparta, or in Thessaly', take us outside the immediate scene. The 'lightning in the collied night' and the 'far-off mountains turnèd into clouds' are from the universal treasure-house of nature-imagery. The setting is extended to take in hostile features both of universal nature and of the wood: the evil season Titania describes, the wild beasts, the unpropitious and intrusive owl, and other possible intruders on Titania's sleep.[3] The wood is the more realistic for its briars and 'dank and dirty ground', not ignored amid its beauty. There are two especially vivid and

1. Cf. Bradbrook, *Elizabethan Comedy*, p. 158.

2. Cf. Barber, p. 135; Welsford, p. 325; and especially Wilson Knight, pp. 155–8.

3. On the beasts, cf. Wilson Knight, pp. 150 f., 154.

realistic glimpses of country activities, whether we refer them to
the inhabited countryside or to the environs of Athens (or
Stratford): the recreations obliterated by the atrocious weather:

> The nine-men's-morris is fill'd up with mud,
> And the quaint mazes in the wanton green
> For lack of tread are undistinguishable,

and Puck's image of the fowler and the wild geese eyeing him,
or the choughs

> Rising and cawing at the gun's report.

The world of the fairies, too, is extended. All nature suffers
when their rulers are at enmity. Their empire stretches to 'the
farthest step of India', and it was in the spiced Indian air that
their queen sat with her ill-fated friend:[1] following darkness, they
'the globe can compass soon': Puck can 'put a girdle round
about the earth / In forty minutes'. His second sphere of influence, where he plays pranks on the villagery, or sometimes
does them service, brings the fairy supernatural into the realm of
familiar life. What could make his magic easier to accept, and
with it everything else that pertains to fairyland, than the
humorous vignette of the old cronies' gathering?

As Robin Goodfellow, known to the villagery, Puck is the
closest of the links between fairyland and folklore. The natural
setting, at the more literary end of its range, would have some
affinities, for Elizabethans, with pastoral, and still more with
Ovidian mythology.[2] Shakespeare, as we have seen, borrows
from the pastoral *Shepheardes Calender*; and Oberon's lines on the
flowery bank where Titania sleeps might be compared with the
catalogues in the April eclogue of the flowers which on two
occasions deck Elisa; though characteristically, except perhaps
for the oxlips (where he should have the benefit of the doubt),
Shakespeare's flowers are all to be found in bloom at the same
season, while, true to pastoral tradition, Spenser's are not. As in
Venus and Adonis, Shakespeare combines the natural world with
the mythological world of the *Metamorphoses*.[3] The yellow sands
are Neptune's: the morning star is 'Aurora's harbinger'; Helena

1. Cf. Wilson Knight, pp. 142, 144 f. The jewel-imagery (pp. 158 f.), evoking
court-life, links the fairy court with the Athenian, and the Athenian court-
setting with that of dew-jewelled nature.

2. Cf. Barber, pp. 122 f., 145; Young, p. 147: 'the *Dream* takes up the topics
of pastoralism, while avoiding the . . . artificiality of the convention'.

3. Bradbrook, *Shakespeare*, p. 154.

inverts the legend of Apollo and Daphne. These are allusions the audience hears: if we start looking into sources, immediately we find Actaeon's hounds, the plague of Aegina, Deucalion's flood, and Ceres' curse; perhaps some of the audience were reminded of them or at least of the Ovidian region which the echoes come from.

In the wood, part of the setting is the night sky, with its stars and planets, 'yon fiery oes and eyes of light', particularly the appropriate Venus 'yonder . . . in her glimmering sphere'.[1] Above all, there is the moon: nature's great nocturnal luminary, and at the same time a goddess, Phoebe, Luna, one of the forms of the triple Hecate. The moon in her many aspects is regent of the *Dream*.[2] Prominence is given her from the first, in Theseus' opening speech and Hippolyta's reply, where the interim before their nuptials, which will set the scope of the dramatic action, is measured with reference to her. The play is framed between their dialogue and the concluding fairy ritual. Heralding that, Puck not only makes the moon a mark of the hour and its character: 'Now . . . the wolf behowls the moon', but leads us to imagine the fairies departing, their ritual performed, to 'run', as is their custom, 'By the triple Hecate's team'. Hecate herself, the underworld form of the triple goddess, associates them with the darkness they follow like a dream; Diana, her form on earth, with the woods she ranges as virgin huntress; and Luna, in the heavens, with moonlight. Luna, again, angry with them, as 'governess of floods' is responsible for the devastation of the land with her waters.[3] When Oberon has ended the feud which provoked her, he and Titania make their exit to start on a flight 'swifter than the wandering moon'. Allusions to the moon punctuate their relationship: their quarrel-scene, the previous dialogue between them, ended with Oberon rejecting Titania's invitation to 'see our moonlight revels', as it began with his challenge,

> Ill met by moonlight, proud Titania.

1. Cf. Wilson Knight, pp. 148 f.

2. Cf. Spurgeon, pp. 259–61 (The word 'moon' occurs twenty-eight times; the moon—with woodland beauty—supplies the dominant imagery). As iterative image, it has thematic significances which she ignores: see Young, p. 75 and n. 15.

3. Olson (pp. 109 f.) points out that in the *Knight's Tale* Diana is goddess in heaven, earth, and 'the regne of Pluto' (ll. 2297 ff.); and that Lyly's Luna in *The Woman in the Moon* (S.R., 22 September 1595) likewise is queen of the woods, and wife of Pluto: thus, as third in the triplicity, Hecate can = Proserpina, who, as Shakespeare knew, in the *Merchant's Tale* is Queen of Faery.

Those words are the first we hear at their initial entry. The exposition makes the moon significant also for the other three groups, and accordingly an important link between all four. As we have observed, Theseus vents upon her his impatience; and it is his impatience which shows him genuinely in love. Hippolyta's image of the crescent as a silver bow connects with Diana the huntress not only the moon but herself, the Amazon, and touches her with poetry. Hermia and Lysander resolve to elope, and the artisans to rehearse, by moonlight.

The artisans' trouble with the moonlight in the story of Pyramus is itself all moonshine. They think it a hard thing to bring moonlight into the great chamber: at the private performance of the *Dream*, the audience would scarcely fail to reflect that Shakespeare, being a poet, was managing the feat without difficulty. The adoption of Quince's proposal, so that Starveling appears as Moonshine in the performance, makes the moon-motif one of the connections between the comicality of the burlesque and the romance of the main play.

Starveling's impersonation of the Man in the Moon is one of the shifts of identity which carry the theme of metamorphosis through the play. For Hippolyta, this moon lacks an attribute of the real one: 'would he would change'. In the opening lines of the play, the phases of the moon introduce at once not only the theme of metamorphosis but, appropriately to the marriage theme (including the resumption of married amity between Oberon and Titania), the discarding of old for new. In keeping with metamorphosis, too, are the three forms of Hecate.[1] The lunatics of whom Theseus speaks were regarded as being under the influence of Luna: the moonlight in the wood is not only a part of its poetry, but suits with the follies enacted there. Like Diana, Luna or Phoebe is a virgin goddess of chastity: 'Cupid's fiery shaft' is

Quench'd in the chaste beams of the wat'ry moon;

and when the moon weeps, flowers in sympathy mourn the rapes they have suffered. Yet she and Diana are goddesses of fertility as well. Without due measure of the moisture she controls, vegetation could not grow, and she rules the monthly rhythm of fertility in women. As we have had occasion to note, Lucina, guardian of procreation and childbirth, was sometimes identified

---

1. Cf., on some of their attributes, Young, p. 25, Fender, p. 30.

with Diana, and Diana of the Ephesians was many-breasted.[1]
The regency of the moon bridges the contrast between the ideal
virginity of the imperial votaress, and the ideal of fertile marriage
celebrated in the conclusion toward which the play has moved
from the beginning.

6. THE PRINCIPAL THEMES

Love and marriage is the central theme: love aspiring to and
consummated in marriage, or to a harmonious partnership within
it. Three phases of this love are depicted: its renewal, after a
breach, in the long-standing marriage of Oberon and Titania;
adult love between mature people in Theseus and Hippolyta;
and youthful love with its conflicts and their resolution, so that
stability is reached, in the group of two young men and two
girls.[2] The affirmation of its value is the work of the whole
dramatic action, from the opening line spoken by Theseus, to
Oberon's final benediction: there is no one expression of it so
intense and profound as Juliet's

> My bounty is as boundless as the sea,
> My love as deep: the more I give to thee,
> The more I have, for both are infinite.[3]

Its note is sustained, however, in the terms on which Theseus and
Hippolyta converse. It breathes in Lysander and Hermia's
antiphonal duet,[4] and in her teasing of him with her playful
contrast of women's constancy with men's oath-breaking; it is
heard again in Lysander's plea to sleep close beside her, attesting
the union of their hearts and troths, which he waives with good
grace at her insistence (no disparagement of their love) on what
is right before marriage, between 'a virtuous bachelor and a
maid': the mild disagreement ends with their quietly loving
good-nights. The quality of true love is clearly and firmly established in the early scenes, not least by Hermia's hearing before
the Duke. It is reaffirmed at the dénouement in the characters
who lacked it at the start. Oberon and Titania are 'new in
amity'. To love Helena, Demetrius recognizes, is to recover his
natural taste; her dotage gives place to the joy and wonder of

1. Proserpina (see p. cxxviii n. 3 above), daughter of Ceres, who returns to
earth each spring, is also a fertility goddess.
2. On 'true love once stabilised', cf. Dent, p. 120.
3. II. ii. 133–5.
4. Cf. Bernard Shaw (quoted I. i. 136–40 n., below); Leggatt, p. 95.

finding him, as though she had found a jewel, her lover once again. And for Hermia and Lysander there is a better endorsement of true love than the success of their elopement would have been. In the initial situation, our sympathy is of course all on their side. But according to received ideas, while right-minded parents should not 'force unpleasant matches upon their offspring but . . . "have respect . . . to the [duly] ordinate consent of the parties" ', right-minded children should accept 'that marriage must be undertaken only with the consent of their parents'.[1] By those principles, Egeus is a tyrannous father: Hermia is justified in resisting his command to take as her lord and husband one 'to whose unwishèd yoke' her

> soul consents not to give sovereignty.

(Theseus's verdict, be it noted, avoids imposing that upon her with no alternative but death.) But the same principles accord her no right to choose for herself and marry Lysander (Theseus's verdict will not permit that).[2] At the dénouement, the two partial rights are reconciled in the complete rightness of the love-match endorsed by lawful authority: the parent's, which it lacks, being superseded by a higher, the sovereign's.

The celebration of true love ancillary to marriage is central to a whole number of related themes. It is supported by the inclusion of other sorts of love. Female friendship is one: between Titania and her Indian votaress, and between Helena and Hermia from girlhood days. Another is the love between prince and subject. Shakespeare's Chaucerian source would remind him (though he would scarcely need reminding) of the place of marriage in 'the fayre cheyne of love' which bound

> The fyr, the eyr, the water and the lond
> In certeyn bonds.[3]

Oberon and Titania being elementals, with the hiatus in their marriage this cosmic love fails too, and there figures in the description of consequences Shakespeare's favourite image for anarchic rebellion: the waters that overbear the bounds which should contain them.[4]

The honouring of marriage is worth more from a dramatist

---

1. Olson, p. 101, quoting and paraphrasing Heinrich Bullinger, *The Christian State of Matrimony*, tr. Coverdale, 1546, Sigs D4^r, E3^r.
2. Cf. Olson, pp. 116, 118.
3. *Knight's Tale*, ll. 2988, 2991 f., quoted Olson.
4. See II. i. 92 n.

who is aware of an alternative ideal, and pays it no less honour.[1] The myth of the imperial votaress is not solely a compliment to the Virgin Queen, and a means of giving importance to the 'little western flower': it is an organic part of the marriage theme. The freely chosen virginity it exalts is, moreover, in contrast with the virginity to be enforced, if Theseus' sentence stands, upon Hermia. To find place for a noble virginity in his marriage-play must have been deeply satisfying to Shakespeare's 'comprehensive soul'.[2]

These themes clearly enhance the valuation of love. But much of the *Dream* presents not only the foes of love and the obstacles standing in its way, but also the aberrations of love itself. The foes and obstacles are essential to the romantic and the aberrations to the comic aspects of the play. But they are no less essential to its theme of love and marriage. To have excluded these negative possibilities would have been a cheap and shallow way of dramatizing it, if drama the result, shorn of conflict, could have been called. They are displayed, but so as to be exorcized.[3] There are two actual exorcisms in the play: the lullaby, and the one incorporated in the fairy blessing, and as C. L. Barber says, 'The exorcism represented as magically accomplished at the conclusion is accomplished in another sense, by the whole dramatic action'.[4] A love-tragedy, the artisans' choice of entertainment for Theseus, might seem 'not sorting with a nuptial ceremony', but in preparation and performance it exorcizes by burlesque the alternative tragic outcome of such love and such a rendezvous as Hermia and Lysander's.[5] The woman's risk in childbirth is acknowledged in the fate of the Indian mother, but that is distanced by report, by lapse of time, and by having happened

1. In 'Henry James's term, a "possible other case" ' (Salingar, p. 277, on 'Pyramus' as 'a conceivably tragic outcome' for the elopement). Taken as a whole, *MND* has the 'recognition implicit in the expression of every experience, of other kinds of experience which are possible' (T. S. Eliot, in praise of Marvell, *Selected Essays*, p. 289).

2. John Dryden, *Essays*, ed. W. P. Ker, Vol. I, p. 79.

3. 'Throughout the play, we seem to be witnessing a constant process of exorcism, as forces which could threaten the safety of the comic world [add, and of the celebration of love and marriage] are called up, only to be driven away' (Leggatt, p. 111).

4. Barber, p. 139; cf. Calderwood: 'one aspect of the play's blessing is its providing for the containment of irrationality and chaos' (p. 521).

5. 'Only their ineptitude and Shakespeare's skill' makes 'Pyramus' 'fit pastime for a wedding night' (Dent, p. 123). 'The dangers that threaten love are systematically destroyed by the way they are presented' (Leggatt, p. 100). For present purposes, they are made 'farcically irrelevant' (Kermode, p. 219).

in a far country. Besides the mother's risk, the child's of being
born blemished is acknowledged; but in the charm being woven
against it. At the same point in Shakespeare's epithalamium as
in Spenser's, evils of the night are evoked: by Spenser, in an
explicit exorcism; in the *Dream*, to build up to the assurance Puck
goes on to give, that

> Not a mouse
> Shall disturb this hallow'd house.

His broom, it has been observed, is an implement symbolically
apt for sweeping the evils away.[1] Lysander's catalogue of the
traditional causes whereby

> The course of true love never did run smooth

has part of its sting drawn even at the time he enumerates them:
Hermia, and we, find comfort in their being traditional.

> Then let us teach our trial patience
> Because it is a customary cross.[2]

The 'customary cross' which is germane to her predicament, compulsion 'to choose love by another's eyes', she is eventually freed
from. None of the rest applies to the lovers in the *Dream* itself. Only
within the farce of 'Pyramus and Thisbe' does one of them, the
last and worst, come true: love quickly cut short by death.[3]
Oberon's prognosis for the young people of 'a league whose date
till death shall never end' envisages death as remote; and by the
weddings in the temple, declares Theseus, all three couples 'shall
eternally be knit'.

The aberrations of love are even more prominently displayed
than the threats which can menace it, and of course many of the
threats arise from the aberrations, including the persecution of
Hermia; the breach between Oberon and Titania; and the lovers'
quarrel, in which jealous rivalries mount to the pitch of violence.
Some of the aberrations are induced by the spells laid upon
Titania's and the young men's sight; but even those we take as
'deft parody' of the follies to which lovers' imaginations are
prone in real life:[4] fancy 'is engendered in the eyes', and is 'full
of shapes' and 'high-fantastical'.[5] It can go astray without magic:

---

1. Cf. Barber, pp. 138 f.   2. *Id.*, p. 123; Fender, pp. 38 f.
3. Dent, p. 123; Olson, p. 118.   4. Bradbrook, *Shakespeare*, p. 157.
5. *Mer. V.*, III. ii. 63 ff.; *Tw.N.*, I. i. 14 f. 'Fancy' can range in meaning from
'fantasy', unconnected with love (cf. Nashe, *Works*, I. 355. 10) to a straightforward synonym for 'love' (often in Shakespeare). Usages in *Euphues and his
England*, familiar to Shakespeare, include each man's wilful choice in love (Lyly,

Demetrius' abandonment of Helena for Hermia, and Titania's rejection of Oberon in her obsession with the changeling, are spontaneous. Like the sudden reversals of the men's allegiances in the wood, they exhibit love's mutability. The new obsessions (barring Demetrius' return to Helena) are dotages, like the dotage Helena's passion for Demetrius has become. 'To love them that hate us', as Demetrius loves Hermia, 'to follow them that fly from us', as Helena follows Demetrius, 'must be confessed', wrote Barnaby Rich in 'Apollonius and Silla', 'an erroneous love, grounded neither in wit nor reason'.[1] Dotage may not only persist where it can expect no return, but like Titania's upon Bottom, may light on an object totally unsuitable in itself. It is no less irrational in its mutability than in these fixations. Not only is it subject to fascination through the eyes: that is, with appearance; its response to appearance is incalculable. Demetrius jilts Helena for a woman no more than her equal in beauty. Lysander taunts Hermia with her dark complexion, which he had found no defect in her before: 'I am as fair now', she protests, 'as I was erewhile'. Titania, while her eye is enthralled to Bottom's shape, admires his 'fair large ears'. The magic power of the love-juice mirrors the compulsive nature, in real life, of such seizures of the imagination. The attempts of the victims to rationalize them render their irrationality the more obvious: Lysander's is particularly laughable. The girls, too, offer themselves rational explanations: bewildered by the young men's behaviour, each accounts for it in her own way, but since they are ignorant of its real and irrational cause, their explanations are altogether mistaken.[2] It is these false rationalizations which precipitate their ultimate aberration, their quarrel.

The abuse of parental authority by Egeus, Helena's treachery to friendship, and the murderous hatred in which the young men's rivalry culminates, are all prevented from doing lasting damage; similarly, the follies of which love is capable are

---

Works, II. 57), love that responds to sensuous appeal (II. 87); and 'disordinate fancy' contrasted with 'honest affection' (II. 181); but see p. cxxxvi n. 3 below. Cf. the discussion by Felicity A. Hughes (*RES*, May 1978, pp. 140 f.) of Fancy personified in *The Faerie Queene*, III. xii. 7: 'English writers', she observes, 'throughout the sixteenth century retained awareness that . . . "fancy" was a contraction of . . . "fantasy" '. In Shakespeare's mind, as the passages in *Mer.V.* and *Tw.N.* show, it could signify love prompted by fantasy, or under the sway of imagination: such it seems is the love induced by 'Cupid's flower'.

1. *Riche his Farewell to Militarie Profession* (1581), quoted Salingar, p. 227.
2. Cf. Evans, p. 39.

exorcized partly by not being allowed to persist. Lysander's fidelity to Hermia is restored by the help of Dian's bud, which also frees Titania from her second dotage when that has done its work of breaking her fixation on the Indian boy. Helena is persuaded—by the bewilderment and suffering it has brought upon her—to relinquish the folly of pursuing Demetrius (III. ii. 315 f.). She does not renounce her love: she would leave behind with him her 'foolish heart'. Her love is not folly in itself, but only so long as Demetrius is incapable of returning it. When his imagination is directed back from Hermia to her, what was her dotage recovers the nature and status of true love. These rectifications all result from the intervention of Oberon, whose mentorship, as we have seen, is one of the means by which the love-troubles are kept within the key of comedy. Each of those means contributes to the exorcism: principally the position of vantage from which we understand aright what the characters do not, and the sense of vagaries controlled which comes from the ordered pattern of the play.[1] In retrospect, the follies—'all this derision'—are to 'seem a dream and fruitless vision'.

Since the follies illustrate, one and all, the phenomena of irrationality in love, reflect Helena's generalization, near the beginning of the play, that love's mind has not 'of any judgement taste', and have for epilogue Theseus' comparison of lovers and lunatics, it is not surprising that critics have often been tempted to see love itself, in the *Dream*, as censured for its unreason, and reason prescribed as the remedy.[2] That interpretation is not borne out by the play. The final pairings accord with the choice the girls have faithfully adhered to, but the choice and the fidelity are not dictated by reason. On that ground, it is plain from Lysander's comparison of himself and Demetrius, Helena could have found little to choose between them: she warmed to Demetrius' courtship, as Hermia did to Lysander's, which consisted of the regular tokens of a lover's devotion. Hermia knows not by what power she is made bold to plead her cause before the Duke, any more than Demetrius knows by what power —'But by some power it is'—his love is 'home returned' to Helena. In each it is a power other than reason's: in Demetrius we know it is that of the love-juice; in Hermia it is the mysterious power of true love, which in her needs no new prompting. When

1. Cf. Barber, p. 31; Leggatt, p. 96.
2. Cf. *Diana* (Kennedy, pp. 156–8) on love and reason. Helena (I. i. 235, 237) echoes 'And this is the cause why they paint him blind and void of all reason. . . . They paint him with wings because [of his swiftness].'

the young men return to their right lovers, that means for Lysander, no less than for Demetrius, a recovery of the emotion which originally possessed him but not a return to reason as such.[1] Among the four, none of the love-relationships is any longer at odds with reason:[2] they fulfil Bottom's wise wish, which was not that love be subjected to reason, but that the two be made friends. The generalizations of Theseus and Helena are half-truths: his, characteristic of him; hers, drawn from her situation. The inescapable fact about love and reason in the *Dream* is that when the human love-conflict is first presented for judgement, reason has its chance to solve it, if unaided reason can; and it cannot, even to the satisfaction of the judge himself. Not until the imagination of Demetrius has been reoriented (for love waits upon the prompting of imagination)[3] does the love-conflict become amenable to reason.[4] It is for the power beyond reason which works that change that the compulsive magic of the love-juice stands. Far from the irrational in love being a source only of aberrations, it has an essential part in love's true order.[5] For harmony in love between man and woman, the irrational in them must be in tune. Similarly, the love which keeps Nature in her courses requires the attunement of elementals, the fairy king and queen in their realm beyond the rational.

Lovers are irrational, according to Theseus, because they are at the mercy of imagination. Questions about the role of imagination (not only in love) and related but yet wider questions about illusion, appearance, the actual and the real, combine to form the other major theme of the play. Guided by Kermode, we have seen their recurrence, in relation to love, from the very start. During the entanglement, their scope is widened. Through the rehearsal scene, we begin to recognize how crucial they are to the art of drama.[6] As more and more is heard and seen of the operations

1. For these points cf. Dent, pp. 116 f., 120.

2. Stabilized, and 'properly terminated in marriage', they 'are part of the natural—and in that sense rational—order' (Dent, p. 118; cf. p. 117).

3. Cf. Dent, p. 117: 'in *A Midsummer Night's Dream* the origin of love never lies in reason', though love 'may be consistent with reason' (as scarcely in Lyly: Bradbrook, *Elizabethan Comedy*, p. 63). 'Fancie', an Elizabethan critic of it could concede, 'is Vox aequivoca, which either may be taken for honest love or fond affection' (Robert Greene, *Tritameron*, quoted Hughes, p. 141).

4. A fact fatal to Kermode's categorization (p. 219) of the lovers' dream as 'phantasma', contrasting with Bottom's 'somnium' of high import. Demetrius' 'dream', however imposed, is valid, coinciding with true sight.

5. The 'realignments of love wrought by the dream-drama of the night simply do not disappear at dawn' (Calderwood, p. 515).

6. For the relation between 'the illusions foisted upon and generated by the

of sight and of transformations under magical compulsion, we become increasingly responsive to contributory themes already introduced: the relativity of perception, and the doubt that may attach to the self-consistency and self-determination of personal identity. These themes and questions reach their full development after the dénouement,[1] in the lovers' dialogue as they prepare to follow Theseus to Athens, in his dismissal of what they have told of their experiences and in Hippolyta's dissent from it, in the episode of the play-within-the-play, and in Puck's epilogue. In this final movement of the *Dream*, the theme of imagination, illusion, appearance and reality is given explicit expression, ensuring that we shall be consciously aware of it.

Only as Shakespeare has dramatized it can the theme be apprehended in the interrelationship of all its facets, and the subtleties of meaning they reflect in the light of the action, the comedy, and the poetry. Yet within the limitations of critical discourse, some exploration of it is possible.

The way perception is dwelt upon is illustrated by the fact that 'eyes' are mentioned far more frequently than in any other play of Shakespeare's.[2] With five anointings of eyelids, and the planning for them, this is hardly surprising: but the importance of eyes in the action is itself a contribution to the theme. Hermia, finding Lysander by the sense of hearing, generalizes on the sharpening of that sense when the eye cannot see. But in Puck's fog, hearing serves only to lead Lysander and Demetrius astray: the emphasis on perception, naturally, is most often on its liability to error. Its confusions have their counterpart in the most striking among the confusions of language: misassignment of the senses,[3] as in 'he goes but to see a noise that he heard'.

Identity in turn rests in great measure upon perception, upon how we appear to others and to ourselves. 'If we imagine no worse of them than they of themselves', says Theseus of Quince and his troupe, 'they may pass for excellent men'. In the eyes of his fellows, Bottom is translated; but he is oblivious of the reason they have to see him so: he does not find himself so, and in essential character is not. In Lysander and Demetrius, abrupt

---

characters within the play' and 'the master illusion which is the whole play', see Calderwood, p. 507 and *passim*.

1. Cf. Dent, p. 124; Young, p. 167.

2. Dent, p. 118.

3. See above, p. cxix; the same joke is exemplified by Leggatt (p. 91 n. 1) from *Mucedorus*: he notes its thematic aptness in the *Dream*. Cf. Fender, p. 35; Young, p. 101.

unmotivated reversals bring about flat contradictions of former attitudes. These have begun in Athens with Demetrius' switch from Helena to Hermia: the rest, with Titania's, are closer to Ovidian metamorphoses, being involuntary and supernatural. They raise doubts about the self-consistency, even the continuous existence, of personal identity,[1] and whether we are not, in Auden's words, 'lived by powers we pretend to understand'. They raise these doubts: they do not endorse them, as in an absurdist frame of mind a modern sceptic might. They are counterpointed against the constancy of the two girls, and the unassailable persistence of Bottom's personality. With Titania, Lysander and Demetrius, however, a former true identity has to be recovered, and so a usurping pseudo-identity has to be banished. Shakespeare's favourite image of liquefaction, which he used for the dissolution of identity in Demetrius' desertion of Helena, is repeated when he returns to her, his 'love for Hermia . . . melted as the snow'.

Imagination is liable to impose, upon the object as it really is, an identity and a value answering to its desire. Lovers are prone to such falsifications, especially when their love most deserves the name of fancy. Imagination-ridden, the lover 'sees Helen's beauty in a brow of Egypt'. In this accusation, Theseus picks up, as it were, Helena's against love which is able 'to transpose to form and dignity' things in themselves base and worthless. It is not only in love that imagination 'looks . . . with the mind': a mind moved by desire or terror is always colouring its vision. It is given to wish-fulfilment: envisaging some joy, it fabricates the notion of some means by which the joy will arrive. It is given no less to groundless or grossly exaggerated fear, as in the madman's of phantom devils; or in the panic of the mechanicals fleeing before Puck, which endows inanimate obstacles with seemingly active enmity; or simply when in the night a bush is taken for a bear.

Like this last, many of the errors of imagination are mistakes of appearance for reality. In the *Dream*, appearance and reality are presented on a series of different planes: at the climax of the entanglement, in the lovers' quarrel-scene, these are to be seen disposed one behind another.[2] The young men's rivalry in courtship and Hermia's suffering are supposed by Helena to be an appearance, staged in order to mock her. Hermia's suffering is real enough, though occasioned by a desertion which is not, as she thinks, wilful, but forced on Lysander by magic, and so

1. Cf. Hunter, p. 306.   2. I amplify Hunter's analysis (p. 329).

lacking normal reality. Unaware that they are under enchantment, the young men regard their rivalry as spontaneous; that is
how it appears to them, but in reality it is induced. By a further
complication, Demetrius' induced love of Helena corresponds
to his original love, which was and now again is real. To Puck
and Oberon, who know the true causes, the whole imbroglio is a
'fond pageant'. It is a pageant, the audience are aware, which is
being performed by actors, two of them in appearance women
but actually boys. Yet the performance, like the whole play, is
designed as a commentary upon real human experience. Throughout the *Dream* there is comparable interplay between appearance
and reality: this episode is just a specially elaborate instance of it.

Drama itself creates an illusion which may point past the
superficial or seemingly structureless actual to a meaningful
reality.[1] Quince and his actors quite misconceive the relationship
between dramatic illusion, realism, and the imagination of the
audience.[2] With their swords and lion, they are afraid of produc-
ing an effect which will be mistaken for reality, and so they take
measures to destroy the dramatic illusion—the little illusion they
were likely to achieve. On the other hand, they cannot see how to
introduce moonlight *except* realistically, by courtesy of the actual
moon; unless by bringing an actor on stage to impersonate the
moon. Yet when they might have gone in for realism, with a comparatively realistic property wall, the wall too must be personified.[3] They do not credit the audience with the power either to
imagine, or to discriminate between the imaginary and the real.
The terms on which drama relies for reception by its audience,
and on which dramatic art itself exists, are implied in the words
of Theseus and Hippolyta. 'The best in this kind are but shadows,
and the worst are no worse', he declares, 'if imagination amend
them': all are shadows, including the best, so all need the help of
imagination (and need to be designed, like the *Dream* itself, with
a view to enlisting it). Hippolyta's reply, 'It must be your
imagination then, and not theirs', applies in its entirety only to
the ridiculous play before her, where the audience has been left,
with every discouragement, to do such imagining as may be

1. For the corresponding concept in Elizabethan poetics, see Dent's quotation
(p. 128) from William Rossky, 'Imagination in the English Renaissance:
Psychology and Poetic', *Studies in the Renaissance* (1958). Cf. Siegel, p. 143;
Salingar, p. 23; Young, p. 48; Calderwood, p. 520.

2. Cf. Dent, pp. 125 ff.; Brown, pp. 87 f.; Leggatt, pp. 99 f.; Fender, p. 34;
Young, p. 150.

3. See above, pp. xliv n. 3, lxxxiii n. 3.

possible;[1] but it reminds us that there is always work for the audience's imagination to do.

Before giving his judgement on imagination and drama, Theseus has done the same on imagination and poetry, in his famous lines attacking the irrationality of imagination. T. S. Eliot draws attention to the occurrence from time to time in drama of

> the voices of the author and the character in unison, saying something appropriate to the character, but something which the author could say for himself also, though the words may not have quite the same meaning for both.[2]

In the present instance they actually have opposite meanings.[3] Theseus intends them as censure; but his eloquence, summoned like Balaam to curse, blesses altogether. The clue is given at once: the 'fine frenzy' with which he charges the poet, is the 'furor poeticus' so much honoured in the Renaissance, following Plato and Aristotle, as the mark of true poetic inspiration.[4] In the line of his argument, his stress is on the 'airy nothing' which is all that the poet's fabric is made of: but to make a world out of nothing is a godlike attribute. For the audience, what Theseus says is a tribute to the power of the poet: the power of which Shelley was to write

create he can
Forms more real than living man,

the power that enables him to find 'objective correlatives' for perceptions otherwise inexpressible and incommunicable.

Theseus' general attack on imaginative folly is nevertheless a persuasive contribution on one side of the debate between imagination and reason.[5] It has behind it Shakespeare's interest in the pathology of imagination, seen about this time in Romeo's hysteria when he learns of the sentence of banishment, and in Richard II as a full-length study of the weaknesses of the imaginative temperament.[6] Are we to heed Theseus' scepticism about

---

1. Cf. Dent, p. 127; Calderwood, p. 520.
2. *On Poetry and Poets*, p. 100.
3. Cf. Fender, pp. 49 f.
4. '[S]ome divine instinct, the Platonicks call it *furor*' (George Puttenham, *The Arte of English Poesie* (1589), ed. G. D. Willcock and A. Walker (1970), p. 3); Plato, *Phaedrus*, 245, 249 (madness or inspiration in poets and lovers): *Ion*, 533, 534; Aristotle, *Poetics*, c. 17.
5. Cf. Hunter, pp. 319, 326–9; Young, p. 108.
6. Cf. Barber, pp. 157, 161.

the lovers' experiences to the extent of regarding the fairy-haunted wood as a dreamland? They themselves, leaving it for Athens, mean to 'recount our dreams'. Bottom has had, he believes, 'a most rare vision': 'Bottom's dream'. It is traditional, however, for otherworld experience to be recalled only in this way: it is a condition often imposed by the supernatural powers themselves, as it evidently is by Oberon: the five are to

> think no more of this night's accidents
> But as the fierce vexation of a dream;

all they have been through is to 'seem a dream and fruitless vision'. If it is to *seem* so, it was not so. Like Bottom, Titania on first reawakening exclaims on 'What visions' she has seen: but, pointing to the object of her love still in his ass-head, Oberon gives her ocular proof that her experience was real. It again accords with tradition that one such proof, a fact or object, should subsist after the lifting of a spell or a return from the otherworld.[1] In the lovers' story, that proof is the permanent change in Demetrius: their seeming vision is not 'fruitless'.

Theseus' scepticism is immediately countered by Hippolyta. She will not cease to wonder at what the young people report, nor agree that he has convincingly explained it away as the sort of fantasy one can expect from lovers. Its coherence, with 'all their minds transfigur'd so together', testifies to more than that.[2]

Shakespeare is interrelating his planes of appearance and reality,[3] the imagined and the actual, illusion and kinds of truth, neither equating them, nor discounting any. On one level Athens is the 'real' world, a world to which one returns from the fairy otherworld in the wood, distinguished as on another plane of actuality. Yet after Theseus has attempted to relegate the fairies to the realm of fantasy, they conclude the play with an action of the highest moment, performed in his own palace, a place which indubitably belongs to the Athenian plane of actuality. In every sense, they have the last word.[4]

---

1. E.g., besides the green lace in *Sir Gawain and the Green Knight*, the golden candlestick stolen, and the mortal wound suffered by Chaus in the *Perlesvaus*; and the receipt in Wandering Willie's tale in *Redgauntlet*.

2. In their 'resonance . . . beyond the play' (Howard Nemerov, 'The Marriage of Theseus and Hippolyta', *Kenyon Review* (1956), p. 639) the lines suggest that 'where the imagined facts hang together with inner logic and consistency, as of a world that could be lived in, then the imagination may have some claim to truth' (Hunter, p. 328).

3. Cf. Hunter, p. 308.

4. Cf. Fender, p. 9.

Rejecting the lovers' story, Theseus (critics point out) is denying what the audience has seen with its own eyes.[1] We have as much evidence for the reality of their ordeal as for the existence of Theseus himself and his Athenians. We can think of the woodland drama as a dream, but only, in fairness, by embracing Puck's invitation to think that the whole play, in our actual experience of it as an audience, has been a dream likewise.[2] Yet it is only if we have disliked it that we are invited to suppose we dreamed it.

If it be permissible for us to imagine that while we sat broad awake at the play we were dreamers, what of the rest of our waking life? On what plane of reality does that take place? In terms of the dramatic action the lovers' sense of awe and uncertainty as they prepare to return from the scene of their mystifying experiences to Athens and ordinary life is a skilful and natural transition,[3] which leaves them in the end free of doubt: 'Why then we are awake'. Yet before this conclusion is reached, the poetic power of their dialogue generates reflections beyond the dramatic situation.

> These things seem small and undistinguishable,
> Like far-off mountains turned into clouds.
>   . . . Are you sure
> That we are awake? It seems to me
> That yet we sleep, we dream.

In some sense, one is inclined to comment, they do and will, even when no longer aware of it. In the proximity of a dimension beyond the normal, such as the play's otherworld represents, one hears in Demetrius' words a distant anticipation of Prospero's in *The Tempest*:

> We are such stuff
> As dreams are made on,

part of his sublime denial to 'the great globe itself' and 'all which it inherit' more than a temporal and relative reality.

A significance beyond the immediate occasion is even more plainly heard in Hippolyta's lines on the lovers' story. Directly, they answer Theseus' disbelief in it. Indirectly, they answer his

---

1. Cf. Fender, p. 53; Siegel, p. 140; Young, p. 139.

2. On Lyly's interest 'in the idea that his plays were "unreal"' (of. the prologues to *Endimion*, *Sapho and Phao*, and *The Woman in the Moon*), and on Shakespeare's in the relation between play and reality, which he 'never uses . . . in the same way as Lyly', see Hunter, pp. 306 f. Cf. Young, pp. 117–20, 122 f.

3. Cf. Welsford, pp. 325 f.; Leggatt, p. 108.

too-sweeping attack on imagination. 'All the story of the night' is not only what the lovers have told: it is what the poet has dramatized.[1] His story of the night, his *Midsummer Night's Dream*, is a work of imagination whose comprehensiveness, balance, and coherence entitle it to be accepted as a vision of truth, far more authentic than fancy's images. What fitter praise can be found for it than the words of Hippolyta? Strange and to be wondered at, it

> grows to something of great constancy.

1. 'Shakespeare was deeply concerned with the ways in which actors and audience accept the 'truth' of dramatic illusion, and as a poet, he saw in these relationships an image of man's recognition of imagined truths' (Brown, p. 91). Cf. Clemen, pp. xxiv f., xxxi, xxxv; Calderwood, p. 520.

A MIDSUMMER NIGHT'S DREAM

DRAMATIS PERSONÆ[1]

THESEUS, *Duke of Athens.*
HIPPOLYTA, *Queen of the Amazons, betrothed to Theseus.*
LYSANDER ⎱ [2] *young courtiers*
DEMETRIUS ⎰   *in love with Hermia.*
HERMIA,[3] *in love with Lysander.*
HELENA, *in love with Demetrius.*
EGEUS,[4] *Hermia's father.*
PHILOSTRATE,[5] *Theseus' Master of the Revels.*

OBERON, *King of the Fairies.*
TITANIA,[6] *Queen of the Fairies.*
A Fairy, *in Titania's service.*
PUCK, *or Robin Goodfellow, Oberon's jester and lieutenant.*
PEASEBLOSSOM[7] ⎫
COBWEB   ⎪
MOTH[8]   ⎬ *Fairies, in Titania's service.*
MUSTARDSEED[9]   ⎭

PETER QUINCE,[10] *a carpenter; Prologue in the Interlude.*
NICK BOTTOM,[11] *a weaver; Pyramus in the Interlude.*
FRANCIS FLUTE, *a bellows-mender; Thisbe in the Interlude.*
TOM SNOUT, *a tinker; Wall in the Interlude.*
SNUG,[12] *a joiner; Lion in the Interlude.*
ROBIN STARVELING,[13] *a tailor; Moonshine in the Interlude.*

Other Fairies attending on Oberon and Titania.
Lords and Attendants to Theseus and Hippolyta.

1. This edn, after Kittredge. A character-list was first given by Rowe.

2. Needing classical names, Shakespeare probably recollected these from North's Plutarch. A 'M[aster] Demetrius' is mentioned in the Nashe/Harvey controversy (Nashe, *Have with you to Saffron-Walden*, 1596: *Works*, III. 125). It has been suggested that 'Demetrius' had associations lending point to Lysander calling it, vituperatively (II. ii. 105 f.), a 'vile name', a 'fit word' to perish on his sword. Terence Spencer (*MLR*, 1954) refers it to the infamous Demetrius Poliorcetes in North (Life of Marcus Antoninus); Stanley Wells (*Cahiers Elisabéthains*, Oct. 1976) to Shakespeare's own villainous Demetrius in *Tit*.

3. The name of Aristotle's mistress (Nashe, *op. cit.*, III. 111). Shakespeare ignored or forgot the disreputable association.

4. Named from Theseus' father, *Knight's Tale*, l. 1980; cf. Golding, VII. 510: 'Aegeus'.

5. From Arcite's alias, *Knight's Tale*, l. 1428.

6. Since Shakespeare took the name directly from Ovid, he probably followed the Elizabethan pronunciation of the Latin: Tietainia (so Wells).

7. Peaseblossom, Cobweb, and Mustardseed have a common factor, being all used in folk-medicine. Moths were used too, but boiled (L. A. Reynolds and P. Sawyer, 'Folk Medicine and the Four Fairies of *A Midsummer Night's Dream*', *Sh.Q.*, 1959).

8. Almost certainly Shakespeare had in mind not 'moth' but 'mote', of which 'moth' is a regular Elizabethan and Shakespearean spelling: see Kökeritz, *Shakespeare's Pronunciation*, p. 320; Grant White and A. J. Ellis (Furness, III. i. 168 n.). Cf. *MND*, v. i. 306, Q1; *LLL*, IV. iii. 159 f. and David's n. Mote matches Cobweb for insubstantiality, and has a virtually decisive link with Mustardseed through Scripture, minuteness being the point of the Gospel references to each. In *LLL*, *loc. cit.*, the reference is explicit to the contrast in Matthew vii. 3-5, Luke vi. 41 f., between the tiny mote and the huge beam.

9. A 'grain of mustard seed . . . indeed is the least of all seeds' (Matthew xiii. 31-2); cf. Mark iv. 31.

10. From 'quines' or 'quoins': wooden wedges used by carpenters.

11. From 'bottom', the core on which the weaver's skein of yarn was wound.

12. On Snug, Snout, and Flute cf. N.C.S., p. 102: '*Snout* means nozzle or spout . . . which suggests the tinker's trade in mending kettles; *Snug* means compact, close-fitting, tight, a good name for a joiner; and *Flute*, the bellows-mender, would . . . repair fluted church-organs'. He is, moreover, a lackbeard with a fluty treble: see p. lxxxiii; II. i. 43-4 n.

13. Proverbially, tailors were thin and feeble; cf. Francis Feeble in *2H4* (III. iv, especially ll. 260-2), and Tilley, T23: 'Nine (or three) tailors make a man'. Starveling is a 'thin-man' role: cf. above, p. lxxxii.

A MIDSUMMER NIGHT'S DREAM

ACT I

[SCENE I]

Enter THESEUS, HIPPOLYTA, [PHILOSTRATE,] *with* Attendants.

The. Now, fair Hippolyta, our nuptial hour
　　Draws on apace; four happy days bring in
　　Another moon: but O, methinks, how slow

ACT I

Scene 1

ACT I] F (*Actus Primus*); *not in Qq*.　　SCENE 1] *Rowe; not in Qq,F.*　　[*Location*]
the Duke's Palace in Athens. Theobald; not in Qq,F.　　S.D. *Philostrate . . . Atten-*
dants.] Theobald; with others. Qq,F.

Act 1 Scene 1] On the F division into
Acts, for which it is patent the play was
not originally designed, see Introduction, pp. xxxii f. There are no Act
divisions in Qq, and no scene divisions
in Qq,F. As is normal in Elizabethan
drama, a scene ends when none of the
participants is left on stage: another
begins with a fresh entrance. But in
order that consultation of works of
reference, and other editions, may not
be impeded, the customary divisions
are here retained.

Location] The scene is unlocalized,
though Hermia's trial will benefit if
there is a judgement-seat Theseus can
take after l. 23 and rise from at l. 114.

1. *Hippolyta . . . nuptial*] In beginning
with the nuptial, and Hippolyta as
the Amazon bride, Shakespeare
follows Chaucer; whether she were
Hippolyta or Antiopa is undecided in
North: see below, pp. 135–6, 129, at
nn. 59–64 (especially 63, 4).

2. *four . . . days*] In the action of the
play, the nuptials follow a single night
of woodland scenes. The longer
interval is wanted at this point to
justify Theseus' impatience. The discrepancy, which does not trouble an
audience and so did not trouble
Shakespeare, is a minor instance of
his 'double time': he seems often to
have conceived his stories both in the
more leisurely terms of a narrative,
and in the rapid progression proper
to drama. What the playwright must
avoid is 'dramatically empty time,
imaginary gaps without service to the
action' (Salingar, p. 82).

3. *Another moon*] Presiding planet of
the *Dream* (see Introduction, pp.
cxxviii ff.), the moon is given prominence at once. To object that between
the old and the new moon there would
be moonless nights is an inappropriate
demand for consistent naturalism.

5

This old moon wanes! She lingers my desires,
Like to a step-dame or a dowager   5
Long withering out a young man's revenue.

Hip. Four days will quickly steep themselves in night;
Four nights will quickly dream away the time;
And then the moon, like to a silver bow
New bent in heaven, shall behold the night   10
Of our solemnities.

The.   Go, Philostrate,
Stir up the Athenian youth to merriments;
Awake the pert and nimble spirit of mirth;
Turn melancholy forth to funerals;
The pale companion is not for our pomp.   15

[*Exit Philostrate.*]

---

4. wanes] *Q2,F;* waves *Q1.*   7. night] *Q1;* nights *Q2,F.*   8. nights] *Q1,F;*
daies *Q2.*   10. New bent] *Rowe;* Now bent *Qq,F;* New-bent *Dyce.*   13.
pert] *Qq* (peart), *F.*   15. S.D. *Exit Philostrate.*] *Theobald; not in Qq,F.*

4–6.] The old moon keeps Theseus waiting for her demise, as a young heir is kept waiting by the stepmother interposed between him and his inheritance, or by the dowager, the widow with proprietary rights in it (*OED*, sense a, citing l. 157 below). While she lives his revenue (income) is withheld or diminished. Cf. *Wiv.*, I. i. 251 f.

6. *withering out*] Steevens compared Chapman's *Iliad*, IV. 528: 'the goodly plant lies withering out his grace'.

revenue] exceptionally, rèvenue, as today: contrast l. 158 below.

7. *steep*] bathe (in slumber), *OED* v.¹3a, like the sun setting in the sea; cf. Spenser, *Shepheardes Calender*, March, l. 116: 'stouping Phoebus steepes his face'.

10. *New*] afresh (*OED* 5); and newly (*OED* 3) in which sense it is frequent from 1530 (twenty times in Shakespeare). 'Now' could only be defended as proleptic: 'then the moon' will be 'now bent in heaven'. But an audience would hear 'Now' as in contrast with 'then'. Rowe's emendation assumes the misreading

of 'e' as 'o': common in secretary hand.

bent] A bow bent is ready either to be strung, or to let fly the arrow. In a context like the present, it is an archetype of fruitful union: the woman draws the man but follows him; together they project the child (cf. 'quiverful' for a family with many children).

11. *solemnities*] from Chaucer's 'solempnyte' (below, p. 129, at n. 5); it signifies celebration (often of nuptials) in a festive spirit, not an unsmiling solemn one. Cf. Latin *solennis*, and *OED* 1a.

13. *pert*] brisk; quick to see and act: *OED* II †3b.

15. *companion*] fellow (contemptuous): *OED* sb. ¹†4; cf. *2H4*, II. iv. 132: scurvy companion.

not . . . pomp] inadmissible in our grand procession, opposite to that of funerals. In ancient Greek festivals, the 'pomp' was the spectacular procession (Warton, quoted W. A. Wright). On a victorious return by Theseus in Golding, VII. 575 ff., 'Ther was not to be found / In all the Citie

Hippolyta, I woo'd thee with my sword,
And won thy love doing thee injuries;
But I will wed thee in another key,
With pomp, with triumph, and with revelling.

Enter EGEUS *and his daughter* HERMIA, *and*
LYSANDER *and* DEMETRIUS.

Ege. Happy be Theseus, our renowned Duke!   20
The. Thanks, good Egeus. What's the news with thee?
Ege. Full of vexation come I, with complaint
    Against my child, my daughter Hermia.
    Stand forth Demetrius. My noble lord,
    This man hath my consent to marry her.   25
    Stand forth Lysander. And, my gracious Duke,
    This hath bewitch'd the bosom of my child.
    Thou, thou, Lysander, thou hast given her rhymes,
    And interchang'd love-tokens with my child:
    Thou hast by moonlight at her window sung   30

19. S.D. *and Lysander*] Q*1* (*subst.*); Lysander *Q2,F* (*subst.*).   *and Demetrius.*] *F;*
and Helena, *and* Demetrius *Q1;* Helena *and* Demetrius *Q2.*   24. Stand . . .
Demetrius.] *As Rowe; as S.D.* (*italic*), *Qq,F.*   26. Stand . . . Lysander.] *As*
Rowe; as S.D. (*italic*), *Qq,F.*   27. This] *F2;* This man *Qq,F.*   bewitch'd] *Qq,F;*
witch'd *Theobald.*

any place of sadness'. But, as here by
Egeus, the joy is broken in upon: '(So
hard it is of perfect joy to find so great
excesse, / But that some sorrow there
withall is medled more or lesse), / . . .
there followed in the necke a piece of
fortunes spite.'
    S.D.] Qq,F give no exit for Philo-
strate. It seems unlikely that an actor
doubled as Philostrate and Egeus: he
would have only four lines to exit,
assume Egeus' wig, beard, and outer
garb, and on re-entry, reach Theseus.
See v. i. 35–6 n.
    16–17.] Cf. North (below, p. 135,
at nn. 60, 62).
    16–22.] The sequence parallels
Chaucer's: Hippolyta taken by force;
wedding festivities anticipated; interruption by clients in trouble. See
below, p. 129-30, at nn. 3, 6–9. Shakespeare was to dramatize Chaucer's
episode of the interruption in *Two*

Noble Kinsmen, I. i.
    19. *triumph*] public rejoicing; festive
show, cf. Bacon's essay, 'Of Masques
and Triumphs'.
    S.D.] Helena's premature inclusion
(Qq) comes no doubt from Shakespeare's foul papers. Sometimes he
seems to have noted (in a 'massed
entry') everyone he expects to need
in a scene, anticipating actual points
of entrance.
    24, 26.] The two curt summons,
to Demetrius and Lysander, were
taken in Q1 for imperative stage-
directions; Q2 and F followed suit.
    27. *This*] Metre (more regular in
Shakespeare's blank verse at the time
of the *Dream* than later) suggests that
in Q1 'This' was wrongly assimilated
to 'This man' in l. 25. So Sisson[2], I.
125, commenting that 'the antithesis
is more marked and dramatic' with
'this' alone.

With faining voice verses of feigning love,
And stol'n the impression of her fantasy
With bracelets of thy hair, rings, gauds, conceits,
Knacks, trifles, nosegays, sweetmeats (messengers
Of strong prevailment in unharden'd youth):   35
With cunning hast thou filch'd my daughter's heart,
Turn'd her obedience (which is due to me)
To stubborn harshness. And, my gracious Duke,
Be it so she will not here, before your Grace,
Consent to marry with Demetrius,   40
I beg the ancient privilege of Athens:
As she is mine, I may dispose of her;
Which shall be either to this gentleman,
Or to her death, according to our law
Immediately provided in that case.   45

---

31. faining voice] *Qq,F;* feigning voice *Rowe.* feigning love] *Qq,F* (faining), *Rowe.*   32. fantasy] *Q2,F* (fantasy,); fantasy: *Q1.*

31. *faining voice . . . feigning*] (1) with veiled voice, singing softly; (2) deceitful; two distinct words, spelled alike in Q1: modernizing the spelling, one can mark the difference. See *OED v.* 12, *ppl.* a. †4, 2 quoting *MND.*

32.] captured her imagination by making a clandestine impression on it (Martin Wright, subst.).

33. *gauds*] showy toys; *OED* quotes H. Smith, *Triumph of Saul,* 1591: 'Solomon maketh us fooles and giveth us gauds to play withal.' Cf. *Cor.,* II. i. 236.

conceits] fancy articles; *OED sb.* III†9, quoting *MND,* and Holinshed: 'Ouches, or ear-rings and other conceits made of amber' (*Chron.,* I. 33/1).

34. *Knacks*] knick-knacks (cf. 'knack' used in contempt, *Shrew,* IV. iii. 67). Such gifts for one's 'she', Florizel dismisses as 'trifles'; yet if they resembled those in Autolycus' pack, they will have been very acceptable, though, as in Dowland's song 'Fine Knacks for Ladies', true love will have conferred the real value (see *Wint.,* IV. iv. 220 ff., 350, 358–60; N.

Ault (ed.), *Elizabethan Lyrics,* p. 303).

35. *prevailment*] power to gain decisive influence; 'rare', notes *OED:* the present is its earliest example.

39. *Be it so*] Supposing.

41–5.] Cf. Old Capulet when Juliet would reject Paris: '*An you be mine,* I'll give you to my friend'; and (quoted by Salingar, pp. 313 f.) what he says in Painter's and Arthur Brooke's versions. In Painter (*Palace of Pleasure,* 1567) he invokes 'the authority our *ancient* Roman Fathers had over their children'; in Brooke (*Romeus,* 1562, Shakespeare's chief source for *Rom.*) he details this *patria potestas:* 'if children did rebell', '*by lawe*', 'the parentes had the power, of . . . *sodayn dcth*' (italics mine).

45. *Immediately provided*] as provided, without respite or reprieve (cf. *OED,* 'with nothing intervening': here, between sentence and execution). Onions, after Steevens, glosses as 'apparently a legal term = expressly'; but the only support is the legal terminology of the next phrase: *OED* lends none.

provided . . . case] Indictments of

The. What say you, Hermia? Be advis'd, fair maid.
    To you your father should be as a god:
    One that compos'd your beauties, yea, and one
    To whom you are but as a form in wax
    By him imprinted, and within his power   50
    To leave the figure, or disfigure it.
    Demetrius is a worthy gentleman.
Her. So is Lysander.
The.   In himself he is;
    But in this kind, wanting your father's voice,
    The other must be held the worthier.   55
Her. I would my father look'd but with my eyes.
The. Rather your eyes must with his judgement look.
Her. I do entreat your Grace to pardon me.
    I know not by what power I am made bold,
    Nor how it may concern my modesty   60
    In such a presence here to plead my thoughts,
    But I beseech your Grace that I may know
    The worst that may befall me in this case,
    If I refuse to wed Demetrius.
The. Either to die the death, or to abjure   65
    For ever the society of men.
    Therefore, fair Hermia, question your desires,
    Know of your youth, examine well your blood,
    Whether, if you yield not to your father's choice,

---

offenders against statute law ended with the formula: 'Contrary to . . . the statute in that case . . . provided' (Cuningham, quoting Rushton, *Shakespeare a Lawyer*, 1858, p. 38.)

48. *compos'd*] framed (in begetting); cf. *OED* v. 1†b; *All's W.*, I. iii. 21.

54. *in this kind*] in a matter of this nature.

voice] vote; a father's conclusive say. Cf. *All's W.*, II. iii. 54 f., and the plebeians' voice in *Cor.*, especially II. iii *passim*.

56–7.] 'The play is to be much concerned with troubles caused by . . . dislocation between the evidence of the senses and the reasoning power' (Wells). Yet Egeus' judgement is

found less trustworthy than Hermia's eyes—and heart.

60. *concern*] suit with, well or ill (cf. Schmidt).

61. *plead . . . thoughts*] submit them as a plea; no exact equivalent in *OED*; earlier than its first example (1601) of 'urge as a plea'.

62–3. *know The worst*] proverbial: Tilley, W915, cf. 912, quoting *John*, IV. ii. 135, *Caes.*, v. i. 95, and Udall, *Ralph Roister Doister*: 'It is good to cast [reckon] the worst' (II. iii. 10).

65. *die the death*] be put to death: *OED* v¹I.2.c, quoting *MND*.

68. *Know of*] ascertain from.

69. *Whether*] perhaps contracted to

You can endure the livery of a nun,   70
For aye to be in shady cloister mew'd,
To live a barren sister all your life,
Chanting faint hymns to the cold fruitless moon.
Thrice blessed they that master so their blood
To undergo such maiden pilgrimage;   75
But earthlier happy is the rose distill'd
Than that which, withering on the virgin thorn,
Grows, lives, and dies, in single blessedness.

Her. So will I grow, so live, so die, my lord,
Ere I will yield my virgin patent up   80
Unto his lordship whose unwished yoke
My soul consents not to give sovereignty.

The. Take time to pause; and by the next new moon,
The sealing-day betwixt my love and me
For everlasting bond of fellowship,   85

76. earthlier happy] *Qq,F;* earthly happier *Capell.*

'Wh'er'; it was not infrequently so spoken.

70. *livery . . . nun*] nun's habit, her distinctive garb; cf. *OED sb.* 2b, quoting *MND.* Nuns were first instituted in the Middle Ages; but orders of celibate women in antiquity might be termed nuns by Shakespeare's contemporaries; North, to help his readers' understanding, calls the Vestal Virgins nuns.

71. *mew'd*] cooped up (term applied to hawks or poultry).

73. *cold . . . moon*] identified with Diana, patroness of chastity: cold = sexless, devoid of sensual heat (earlier than *OED*'s first instance, 1597, of this figurative sense); fruitless = barren, without offspring. With l. 72, cf. Seneca, *Hippolytus,* ll. 478–80.

76–7. *the rose . . . thorn*] Cf. Lyly, *Euphues,* 1578 (I. 234. 16): 'the Damaske Rose which is sweeter in the still than on the stalke' and *Sapho and Phao, c.* 1582: 'Roses that lose their colours, keepe their savours, and pluckt from the stalke, are put to the

still' (to distil their scent, for perfumes). Walker and Halliwell (see Furness) cite Erasmus, 'Colloquium Proci et Puellae', where Pamphilus, persuading to matrimony, declares: 'rosam existimo feliciorem [cf. 'happy'] quae marescit in hominis manu, delectans interim et oculos et nares, quamquae senescit [cf. 'withering'] in frutice'. See further, on wedlock *v.* virginity (from Erasmus) in Thomas Wilson's *Arte of Rhetorike,* 1553, J. W. Lever, *The Elizabethan Love Sonnet,* pp. 190 f.

78. *single blessedness*] celibacy, with the divine blessing it carries; but 'single' had also the sense of 'feeble', 'attenuated'. Cf. Marlowe, *Hero and Leander,* I. 262–4: 'Virginitie, albeit some highly prize it, / Compared with marriage . . . differs as much as wine and water doth'.

80. *virgin patent*] entitlement to virginity: *OED* patent *sb.* 5 (its earliest example).

81. *his . . . whose*] the dominion (as a husband) of a man whose . . .; 'his' takes a metrical stress (Wells).

Upon that day either prepare to die
For disobedience to your father's will,
Or else to wed Demetrius, as he would,
Or on Diana's altar to protest,
For aye, austerity and single life.   90
Dem. Relent, sweet Hermia; and Lysander, yield
Thy crazed title to my certain right.
Lys. You have her father's love, Demetrius:
Let me have Hermia's; do you marry him.
Ege. Scornful Lysander, true, he hath my love;   95
And what is mine my love shall render him;
And she is mine, and all my right of her
I do estate unto Demetrius.
Lys. I am, my lord, as well deriv'd as he,
As well possess'd; my love is more than his;   100
My fortunes every way as fairly rank'd,
If not with vantage, as Demetrius';
And, which is more than all these boasts can be,
I am belov'd of beauteous Hermia.
Why should not I then prosecute my right?   105
Demetrius, I'll avouch it to his head,
Made love to Nedar's daughter, Helena,
And won her soul: and she, sweet lady, dotes,
Devoutly dotes, dotes in idolatry,

---

101. fortunes] *Qq,F;* Fortune's *Rowe.*   102. Demetrius'] *Qq,F* (Demetrius),
Hanmer.

89. *protest*] vow.
92. *crazed*] flawed; and cf. Pres. E.,
'a crazy structure'.
98. *estate unto*] settle upon.
99. *as well deriv'd*] of as good
descent, good family. *OED*'s earliest
example is Shakespearean: *Gent.,* v.
iv. 146.
99 ff.] Bernard Shaw (*Our Theatres
in the Nineties,* I. 179) for once mis-
judges a stage-effect, insisting that
Lysander address these representa-
tions to the Duke apart. They are his
public self-justification and counter-
charge against Demetrius in what is a
form of trial-scene.

102. *vantage*] the advantage on my
side; cf. *OED* sense †4.
106. *head*] to one's head = to one's
face (earlier than *OED*'s first example,
Meas., IV. iii. 147).
108–9. *dotes . . . idolatry*] Cf. *Rom.,*
II. iii. 81 f.: '*Romeo.* Thou chidst me
oft for loving Rosaline. / *Fr. Laurence.*
For doting, not for loving, pupil
mine.' In Lyly, *Endimion* (III. iv. 60–2),
Eumenides, declaring himself 'the
most fond' lover of a woman 'the
most froward', is told 'You doted
then, not loved'. 'Thou that com-
mittest idolatry' is the reproach
earned (I. i. 66) by Endimion for his

Upon this spotted and inconstant man.   110

The. I must confess that I have heard so much,
And with Demetrius thought to have spoke thereof;
But, being over-full of self-affairs,
My mind did lose it. But, Demetrius, come,
And come, Egeus; you shall go with me: 115
I have some private schooling for you both.
For you, fair Hermia, look you arm yourself
To fit your fancies to your father's will;
Or else the law of Athens yields you up
(Which by no means we may extenuate)   120
To death, or to a vow of single life.
Come, my Hippolyta; what cheer, my love?
Demetrius and Egeus, go along;
I must employ you in some business
Against our nuptial, and confer with you   125
Of something nearly that concerns yourselves.

Ege. With duty and desire we follow you.

Exeunt all but Lysander and Hermia.

127. S.D.] F (*Exeunt*/*Manet Lysander and Hermia*); *Exeunt. Qq.*

rhapsody on Cynthia. Portraying
Helena's love, Shakespeare takes
hints from Phaedra's compulsive
passion in Seneca, *Hippolytus*; see
above, p. lxiii n. 2 (Latin); below, pp.
140–2 (translations). For being jilted
as the key to Helena's behaviour, see
Introduction, p. cxii.

113. *self-affairs*] my own concerns.
OED self- 5. quotes *MND*.

114. *lose*] lose sight of.

114–16, 119–22, 125 f.] The 'preservation of the lawes' was an especial
care of Theseus' (North, below, p. 135,
at n. 56). Using the ducal 'we', he
pronounces sentence accordingly; but
suspends it. Personally, he is dissatisfied with it, he sees it troubling
Hippolyta, and by private suasion
will try to talk Egeus and Demetrius
out of their insistence. Comparison
with Solinus in *Err.*, I. i (see Salingar,
cited above, p. lxxxviii), helps to confirm this interpretation, and as with
Solinus, in the rift between the Duke's

constitutional and his humane personal judgement, Shakespeare is preparing for his part in the dénouement.

116. *schooling*] admonition: *OED*
vb. *sb* ¹†2, quoting *MND*.

120. *extenuate*] mitigate: *OED* I. 4†b,
quoting *MND*.

122. *what . . . love?*] She is downcast
at the ill-omen, intruding upon the
joyous preparations for her wedding,
of love threatened with death or a
compelled celibacy. And cf. the
compunction of Chaucer's Hippolyta
at Theseus' harsh sentence (thereupon rescinded) on the lovers in the
Knights Tale (ll. 1748 ff.).

124. *business*] three syllables.

127. S.D.] Naturalistic-minded critics exclaim at Egeus leaving Hermia
with Lysander. But dramatic art is
the true criterion: Shakespeare fur-
thers the exposition, while varying
the scene from full stage to intimate
dialogue (and then to triologue). He
regularly employs similar technique:

Lys. How now, my love? Why is your cheek so pale?
　　How chance the roses there do fade so fast?
Her. Belike for want of rain, which I could well   130
　　Beteem them from the tempest of my eyes.
Lys. Ay me! For aught that I could ever read,
　　Could ever hear by tale or history,
　　The course of true love never did run smooth;
　　But either it was different in blood—   135
Her. O cross! too high to be enthrall'd to low.
Lys. Or else misgraffed in respect of years—
Her. O spite! too old to be engag'd to young.
Lys. Or else it stood upon the choice of friends—
Her. O hell! to choose love by another's eyes.   140
Lys. Or, if there were a sympathy in choice,

131. my] *Qq*; mine *F.*   132. Ay me! For] *Qq* (Eigh *Q1*); For *F.*   I could ever]
Qq; ever I could *F.*   136. low] *Theobald;* love *Qq,F.*   139. friends] *Qq*;
merit *F.*   140. eyes] *Qq*; eye *F.*

e.g. *Othello,* I. iii, II. i, II. iii: Iago left
in dialogue with Roderigo or Cassio,
and then in soliloquy.

　131. *Beteem*] grant: *OED* v¹1; 'perhaps with secondary reference to
"teem" = pour' (still in N. and W.
dialects)' Onions.

　136–40.] 'Shakespeare makes the
two star crossed lovers speak in alternate lines with an effect which sets
the whole scene throbbing with their
absorption in one another: . . . with a
Hermia who [knows] how to breathe
out these parentheses the duet [is] an
exquisite one' (Bernard Shaw, *Our
Theatres in the Nineties,* I. 180 f.). To
see the potential for this effect in a
form, stichomythia, notably rigid in
English, in Seneca, and even in the
Greek tragedians, was a piece of
genius. Much closer to the riddling
style of classical stichomythia is the
keen trial of wits between Edward and
Lady Grey in *3H6,* III. iii. 36 ff.

　136.] Cf. the ballad of 'King
Cophetua and the beggar-maid', *Rom.,*
II. i. 54, *LLL,* I. ii. 103–4, IV. i. 66–7,
and R. David's n.

　low] confirmed by the passage
Shakespeare evidently had in mind

(see next note). The antithesis,
parallel to that in l. 138 (both proper
to the gnomic quality of stichomythia)
was destroyed in Q1 by a minim
misreading: 'lowe' as 'loue'.

　136, 139 f.] Cf. in Lyly, *Euphues and
his England,* Surius on 'the choyce of a
wife': 'my friends are unwilling I
should match so low, not knowing
that love thinketh the Juniper shrub
to be as high as the tal Oke' and
'Made mariages by friends, how
daungerous they have bene I know'
(II. 219: 24, 5, 14). 'Friends' here is
echoed in what I take for Shakespeare's final version of l. 139 (see
Appendix II. 1).

　137. *misgraffed*] ill-matched (grafted
amiss); *OED*'s sole example.

　139. *stood upon*] was dependent
upon.

　friends] On the Q1 and F readings,
see Appendix II. 1.

　141. *sympathy*] accord: 'the only
Shakespearean use': dictionaries down
to Bailey (1721) give first place to the
sense 'the natural agreement of
things, a conformity in nature, passions
etc.' (Onions).

War, death, or sickness did lay siege to it,
Making it momentany as a sound,
Swift as a shadow, short as any dream,
Brief as the lightning in the collied night,   145
That, in a spleen, unfolds both heaven and earth,
And, ere a man hath power to say 'Behold!',
The jaws of darkness do devour it up:
So quick bright things come to confusion.
Her. If then true lovers have been ever cross'd,   150
It stands as an edict in destiny.
Then let us teach our trial patience,
Because it is a customary cross,
As due to love as thoughts and dreams and sighs,
Wishes and tears, poor fancy's followers.   155
Lys. A good persuasion; therefore hear me, Hermia.
I have a widow aunt, a dowager
Of great revenue, and she hath no child—
From Athens is her house remote seven leagues—
And she respects me as her only son.   160

---

143. momentany] *Qq;* momentarie *F.*   159–160.] *As Qq,F;* And . . .
son/From . . . leagues, *conj. Johnson.*   159. remote] *Qq;* remov'd *F.*

143. *momentany*] momentary—which
is found seven times in Shakespeare,
'momentany' (cf. instant*an*eous) only
here; but, says *OED*, common in
16th and 17th centuries.

144. *Swift . . . shadow*] Cf. *Rom.*, II. v.
4 f., where 'thoughts', as 'love's
heralds', 'ten times faster glide than
the sun's beams driving back shadows'
(Furness).

145–9.] Cf. *Rom.*, II. ii. 117–20,
where the love-contract is 'Too like
the lightning, which doth cease to
be / Ere one can say "It lightens"';
and Lyly, *Euphues*, 1578 (I. 209. 13);
'ther is nothing which is permanent
that is violent . . . the ratling thunder-
bolte hath but his clappe, the
lyghteninge but his flash, and as they
both come in a moment, so doe they
both ende in a minute'.

145. *collied*] blackened (*OED*, quoting *MND.*). Cf. *Oth.*, II. iii. 208, and

'collier' (from 'colly', to blacken with
coal-dust).

146. *spleen*] fit of anger or passion:
the spleen was the bodily organ believed responsible.

155. *fancy's*] love's. But on 'fancy'
and its shades of meaning, see Introduction, p. cxxxiii, n. 5.

156. *A good persuasion*] well urged;
a good way to look at it (persuasion =
conviction).

158. *revenue*] revènue.

159–60.] The Q1 order of the lines
is illogical, but that is not enough to
justify Johnson's belief that it is
corrupt. It neither obscures the
sense, nor contravenes the way people
speak.

159, 165.] The distance to be
traversed (through Oberon's wood)
is given, in leagues, in *Huon* (below, p.
145, at n. 148).

160. *respects*] regards.

There, gentle Hermia, may I marry thee,
And to that place the sharp Athenian law
Cannot pursue us. If thou lov'st me then,
Steal forth thy father's house tomorrow night;
And in the wood, a league without the town   165
(Where I did meet thee once with Helena
To do observance to a morn of May),
There will I stay for thee.

Her.   My good Lysander,
I swear to thee by Cupid's strongest bow,
By his best arrow with the golden head,   170
By the simplicity of Venus' doves,
By that which knitteth souls and prospers loves,
And by that fire which burn'd the Carthage queen
When the false Trojan under sail was seen;
By all the vows that ever men have broke   175
(In number more than ever women spoke),
In that same place thou hast appointed me,
Tomorrow truly will I meet with thee.

167. to a] *Qq;* for a *F.*   172. loves] *Q1;* love *Q2,F.*

167.] Chaucer's Arcite rode wood-ward 'to doon his observaunces to Maie'; below, p. 131, at n. 24; for Emelye, 'in a morwe of May,' prompted to the like 'observaunce', cf. p. 130, at n. 10. Cf. IV. i. 103 below.

170.] echoing Marlowe, *Hero and Leander*, I. 161: 'Love's arrow with the golden head' (Bullen, cited Cuning-ham); 'best' in contrast with Cupid's other arrow: 'tone causeth Love, the other doth it slake; / That causeth love, is all of golde with point full sharpe and bright, / That chaseth love is blunt, whose steele with leaden head is dight' (Golding, I. 565 ff.).

171. *simplicity*] harmlessness. From Matthew x. 16, 'harmlesse as the . . . Doves' (Bishops' Bible), this was proverbial: Tilley, D572; he quotes *2H6*, III. i. 171. In love, simplicity is the contrary of duplicity: mating for life, doves typified fidelity.

Venus' doves] sacred to Venus. In *Ven.* (final stanza) she 'yokes her silver doves' to 'her light chariot'.

171–251.] On the rhyming couplets, here and elsewhere, see Introduction, pp. l, li, cxxi.

172.] Possibly the cestus, Venus' girdle, which endows with irresistible beauty anyone to whom she lends it (Keightley, *Expositor* (1867), cited Cuningham).

knitteth souls] probably a traditional expression; cf. 'body and soule togyder knit', Hampole, *Prikke of Conscience (OED)*.

173–4.] It is in Virgil (IV. 584 ff.) that before she immolates herself on the pyre Dido actually sees Aeneas sailing away, and not in Marlowe and Nashe, *Dido Queen of Carthage*, or Chaucer's *Legend of Good Women*, which last Shakespeare follows (see J. R. Brown's n.) in *Mer.V.*, v. i. 9–12.

175–6.] tender teasing, like Jessica's accusing Lorenzo of 'many vows of faith, / And ne'er a true one' (*Mer.V.*, v. i. 19 f.).

Lys. Keep promise, love. Look, here comes Helena.

Enter HELENA.

Her. God speed fair Helena! Whither away?   180
Hel. Call you me fair? That fair again unsay!
Demetrius loves your fair: O happy fair!
Your eyes are lode-stars, and your tongue's sweet air
More tuneable than lark to shepherd's ear,
When wheat is green, when hawthorn buds appear. 185
Sickness is catching; O were favour so,
Yours would I catch, fair Hermia, ere I go:
My ear should catch your voice, my eye your eye,
My tongue should catch your tongue's sweet melody.
Were the world mine, Demetrius being bated,   190
The rest I'd give to be to you translated.
O, teach me how you look, and with what art
You sway the motion of Demetrius' heart.

187. Yours would I] *Hanmer;* Your words I *Qq,F;* Your words I de *F2.*
191. I'd] *Hanmer* (I'ld) *;* Ile *Qq,F.*

179. *Keep promise*] *Hero and Leander,* in Shakespeare's mind at l. 170 above, furnishes a slight echo here. At parting (II. 96) Hero bids 'let your . . . promises be kept'.

182. *your . . . fair*] your beauty (the fairness which is yours), O fortunate beauty: (1) fairness; (2) fair one: for 'fair' = fairness (beauty), cf. 'that fair thou owest' *Sonn.,* XVIII. 10; for word-play with 'fair', *ibid.,* l. 7, *Sonn.,* XXI. 4. And see Introduction, p. xxxvi.

183. *lode-stars*] guiding-stars: they fix lovers' attention as those fix the navigators'. By association with lodestone, magnetic quality may also be implied. Cf. Peele, *Old Wives Tale,* 1595, ll. 433 f.: 'When shall I Delia see? / When shall I see the loadstar of my life?'

air] tune.

184. *tuneable*] melodious; cf. IV. i. 123 below.

185.] with an echo from Spenser, *Shepheardes Calender,* 1579, the eclogue for May, 'thilke . . . season when' the woods are clad 'With green leaves, the bushes with bloosming Buds', and the church pillars decked 'With Hawthorne buds, and swete Eglantine' (ll. 6, 8, 12 f.; for 'sweet . . . eglantine' and 'sweet honeysuckle' cf. below, II. i. 251 and IV. i. 41).

186–9. *catching . . . catch*] infectious . . . catch by infection: *OED v.* 34, its earliest example of the figurative sense.

186. *favour*] (1) appearance, good looks; (2) the charm these can exert, the favour they can win (see Onions, senses 2, 3, 4).

187. *Yours would I*] Q1's error originated, no doubt, in misreading 'woud' as 'word' ('u' as two-stemmed 'r').

190. *bated*] excepted.

192. *art*] address, studied conduct: *OED* III. 13; *Sonn.,* CXXXIX, 'slay me not by art.'

Her. I frown upon him; yet he loves me still.

Hel. O that your frowns would teach my smiles such skill!

Her. I give him curses; yet he gives me love.   196

Hel. O that my prayers could such affection move!

Her. The more I hate, the more he follows me.

Hel. The more I love, the more he hateth me.

Her. His folly, Helena, is no fault of mine.   200

Hel. None but your beauty; would that fault were mine!

Her. Take comfort: he no more shall see my face;

Lysander and myself will fly this place.

Before the time I did Lysander see,

Seem'd Athens as a paradise to me.   205

O then what graces in my love do dwell,

That he hath turn'd a heaven unto a hell!

Lys. Helen, to you our minds we will unfold:

Tomorrow night, when Phoebe doth behold

Her silver visage in the wat'ry glass,   210

Decking with liquid pearl the bladed grass

(A time that lovers' flights doth still conceal),

Through Athens' gates have we devis'd to steal.

Her. And in the wood, where often you and I

Upon faint primrose beds were wont to lie,   215

---

200. no fault] *Q1;* none *Q2,F.*   201. beauty] *Qq,F;* beauty's *Daniel.*
205. as] *Q1;* like *Q2,F.*   207. unto a] *Q1;* into *Q2,F.*

194–201.] stichomythia: see ll. 136–140 n.

194, 196, 198.] 'But so extreame are the passions of love, that the more thou seekest to quench them by disdayne, the greater flame thou encreasest by desire'; Lyly, *Euphues and his England,* 1580, II. 132. 4; Tilley, S150 (quoting only Lyly, *id.,* elsewhere, and *Love's Metamorphosis, c.* 1589; and *Gent.,* III. i. 95).

209–10. *when . . . glass*] For reminiscences here of Spenser, *Shepheardes Calender,* August, ll. 89, 81, June, 29 f., see Introduction, p. lxii. Cf. nn. to III. ii. 388, IV. i. 95, v. i. 362–72.

Phoebe] 'in heaven she is called *Luna*' (the moon goddess), 'in the woods *Diana,* under the earth *Hecate* or *Proserpina*' (Abraham Fraunce, *The Third Part of the Countesse of Pembroke's Yvychurch,* 1592, L4ᵛ–M1ʳ).

209–14.] Diana (Phoebe) is regent of moonlit woods in Seneca, *Hippolytus* (below, p. 140, at n. 109).

211. *bladed*] many-bladed; cf. *OED* ppl. a. 2, quoting *MND.*

214–16.] preparing for Helena's reproachful appeal to this friendship (III. ii. 198–216), during the two girls' quarrel.

215. *faint*] probably 'pale' (cf. *Cym.,* IV. ii. 221, *Wint.,* IV. iv. 122), not 'faint-scented' (N.C.S.); cf. *OED* a. 5, 'dim'.

Emptying our bosoms of their counsel sweet,
There my Lysander and myself shall meet;
And thence from Athens turn away our eyes,
To seek new friends, and stranger companies.
Farewell, sweet playfellow; pray thou for us,   220
And good luck grant thee thy Demetrius!
Keep word, Lysander; we must starve our sight
From lovers' food, till morrow deep midnight.
                                                    Exit Hermia.

Lys. I will, my Hermia. Helena, adieu;
As you on him, Demetrius dote on you!   *Exit Lysander.*
Hel. How happy some o'er other some can be!   226
Through Athens I am thought as fair as she.
But what of that? Demetrius thinks not so;
He will not know what all but he do know;
And as he errs, doting on Hermia's eyes,   230
So I, admiring of his qualities.
Things base and vile, holding no quantity,
Love can transpose to form and dignity:
Love looks not with the eyes, but with the mind,
And therefore is wing'd Cupid painted blind;   235
Nor hath Love's mind of any judgement taste:
Wings, and no eyes, figure unheedy haste.
And therefore is Love said to be a child,
Because in choice he is so oft beguil'd.
As waggish boys, in game, themselves forswear,   240

216. sweet] *Theobald;* sweld *Qq,F.*   219. stranger companies] *Theobald;*
strange companions *Qq,F.*   225. dote] *Qq;* dotes *F.*   229. do] *Qq;* doth *F.*
239. is so oft] *Q1;* is oft *Q2;* is often *F;* often is *F2.*

216. *sweet*] Q1 'sweld' is an easy
misreading, 'ld' for 'te', of 'swete'.
219. *stranger companies*] the com-
panionship of strangers (*OED* company *sb.* 1.). To misread 'companies'
(or 'cōpāies') as 'companiōs' (or
cōpāiōs) was easy; and as a metrical
corollary, 'stranger' would naturally
be misread 'strange'. The emendation
is confirmed by the rhyme.
232. *holding no quantity*] bearing no
proportion (to what they are estimated
at by love): Schmidt.

234.] 'Love is prompted not by the
objective evidence of the senses, but
by the fancies of the mind' (Wells).
Usually it is love 'engendered in the
eyes' (*Mer.V.*, III. ii. 67) which, if it
lacks further insight, is judged un-
reliable.
235.] For *Diana* on love and reason,
verbally echoed here, see Introduction, p. cxxxv, n. 2.
237. *figure*] symbolize.
240. *waggish*] roguish ('game' is
'sport').

So the boy Love is perjur'd everywhere;
For, ere Demetrius look'd on Hermia's eyne,
He hail'd down oaths that he was only mine;
And when this hail some heat from Hermia felt,
So he dissolv'd and show'rs of oaths did melt.   245
I will go tell him of fair Hermia's flight:
Then to the wood will he, tomorrow night,
Pursue her; and for this intelligence
If I have thanks, it is a dear expense.
But herein mean I to enrich my pain,   250
To have his sight thither and back again.   *Exit.*

[SCENE II]

Enter QUINCE, *the Carpenter; and* SNUG, *the Joiner; and* BOTTOM,
the Weaver; and FLUTE, *the Bellows-mender; and* SNOUT, *the
Tinker; and* STARVELING, *the Tailor.*

Quin. Is all our company here?

244. this] *Q1,F;* his *Q2.*   248. this] *Qq;* his *F.*

Scene II

SCENE II] *Capell; not in Qq,F.*   [*Location*] *Scene changes to a Cottage. Theobald;
A Room in Quince's House. Capell; not in Qq,F.*   S.D. *Enter . . . Tailor.*] *Q1;
Enter . . . Carpenter, Snug . . . Joyner, Bottome . . . Weaver, Flute . . . bellowes-mender,
Snout . . . Taylor. Q2,F.*

242. *eyne*] eyes; from M.E. eyen:
archaic in Shakespeare's day, and
rare except for rhyme (N.C.S.); cf.
v. i. 175 below and *Ant.,* II. vii. 113.
245. *dissolv'd*] broke faith (with
play on 'melted'), N.C.S.
247–51.] In *Hippolytus,* Seneca's
Phaedra resolves to follow at all costs
the man she hopelessly loves. See
above, p. lxiii, n. 2; below, p. 141, at
n. 112.
249. *If . . . expense*] If she gets so
much as a 'thank-you' from Demetrius he will grudge it as a rare and
painful effort, as though parting with
something precious. Wryly ironic
about his likely reception of her, she

also (I think) reflects, with a touch of
self-pity, on how much she will do
for so little. To her his thanks *will* be
precious, though dear-bought at a
price rarely paid for mere thanks.
Dear = (1) precious, (2) grievous
(*OED adj.* ¹†4 and †4†b, and *adj.*²);
(3) rare (Onions compares *Rom.,* III.
iii. 28: 'This is dear mercy').

Scene II

S.D.] In North, the artificers are
the most numerous and least well off
of the three classes of Athenians
(below, p. 135, at nn. 57–8. Cf. v. i.
72 f.

Bot. You were best to call them generally, man by man,
        according to the scrip.

Quin. Here is the scroll of every man's name which is
        thought fit through all Athens to play in our inter-   5
        lude before the Duke and the Duchess, on his wed-
        ding-day at night.

Bot. First, good Peter Quince, say what the play treats
        on; then read the names of the actors; and so grow
        to a point.   10

Quin. Marry, our play is 'The most lamentable comedy,
        and most cruel death of Pyramus and Thisbe'.

Bot. A very good piece of work, I assure you, and a
        merry. Now, good Peter Quince, call forth your
        actors by the scroll. Masters, spread yourselves.   15

Quin. Answer as I call you. Nick Bottom, the weaver?

Bot. Ready. Name what part I am for, and proceed.

Quin. You, Nick Bottom, are set down for Pyramus.

Bot. What is Pyramus? A lover, or a tyrant?

3. according to] *Q1,F;* according *Q2.*   10. to] *Qq;* on to *F.*

2. *generally*] Bottom's malapropism
for 'severally'.

3. *scrip*] script (cf. Hulme, *Explorations,* p. 36). Cuningham exemplifies
the synonyms 'scrip or scroll' (l. 4), =
'written document', from Holland's
Pliny, 1601.

5. *interlude*] play; though a leading
professional company like Shakespeare's, or the 'tragedians of the city'
in *Hamlet,* would not ordinarily call
their plays 'interludes' (but cf. in *Ben
Jonson,* ed. Herford and Simpson, v.
20, the dedication to *Volpone*). The
term is reminiscent of such performances as are appreciatively discussed
in T. W. Craik, *The Tudor Interlude,*
1967, and Richard Southern, *The
Staging of Plays before Shakespeare,* 1973.

7. *at night*] normal idiom: Lyly's
Gallathea was played 'on New Yeere's
day at night' (Craig, *apud* Cuningham). But here the context of comic
language brings out a slight absurdity

in 'day at night'.

9–10. *grow . . . point*] draw to a conclusion; cf. 'grow to an end', *R3,*
III. vii. 20; *OED* point, *sb.* 29, citing
MND. Supporting the gloss 'come to
the point', N.C.S. quotes 'you would
fain be hidden in a net . . . I will grow
to a point with you' (*Epitome,*
Marprelate Tracts, ed. Pierce, p.
120); but what point more essential
than the rest would Quince have
come to?

11–12. *lamentable comedy . . . death*]
parodying such titles as that of
Thomas Preston's *Cambyses* (published
c. 1570): 'A lamentable tragedy
mixed full of pleasant mirth', and
perhaps, as Steevens thought, that
title specifically. Cf. v. i. 56–7 below.

12. *Pyramus and Thisbe*] already
known in a popular ballad; on which
and on other versions before Shakespeare's see Introduction, pp. xc, n. 5,
lxxxviii.

Quin. A lover, that kills himself most gallant for love.   20
Bot. That will ask some tears in the true performing of it.
If I do it, let the audience look to their eyes: I will
move storms, I will condole in some measure. To the
rest—yet my chief humour is for a tyrant. I could
play Ercles rarely, or a part to tear a cat in, to make   25
all split.

> The raging rocks,
> And shivering shocks,
> Shall break the locks
>   Of prison-gates;   30
> And Phibbus' car

---

20. gallant] *Qq;* gallantly *F.*   24. rest—yet] *Theobald* (rest;—yet,)*;* rest yet,
Qq,F.   25–6. in, to . . . split./The] *Theobald, subst.* (split/"the)*;* in, to . . .
split the *Qq,F;* in./To . . . split the *Pope.*   27–34.] *As Johnson; prose, Qq,F.*
31. Phibbus'] *Theobald²;* Phibbus *Qq,F.*

23, 37. *condole . . . measure . . . condoling*] He will portray grief to some
purpose, in accord with a lover's
lamenting style. Cf. *OED* condole
v. 1† 1 condoling *ppl. a.,* quoting *MND.*
23–4. *To . . . —yet*] Though in
Elizabethan idiom 'To the rest yet'
could mean simply 'to the rest now'
(so Staunton and Aldis Wright), the
Qq,F punctuation deprives Bottom
of the 'yet' ('all the same') needed to
introduce his renewed hankering after
a display in a different hero-role.
24. *humour*] inclination (fitting my
disposition); cf. *OED sb.* II. 6. b
(earliest instance).
25. *Ercles*] See below, l. 36 n.; and
Sidney, *Arcadia,* 1590, whose Dametas
spoke 'with the voice of one that
plaieth *Hercules* in a play, but never
had his fancie in his head' (ed.
Feuillerat, p. 87): cited Halliwell.
tear a cat] rant and swagger; cf.
OED tear B.I.1†d phr.: earliest
instance; N.C.S. compares Day, *Ile
of Guls,* 1606: 'a whole play of such
tear-cat thunderclaps'. Cf. Hamlet
on not tearing a passion to tatters
(III. ii. 10).
26. *all split*] everything go to pieces,

'as the Mariners say': Greene, *Never
too late,* 1590 (Dyce).
27–34.] 'probably . . . Shakespeare's burlesque of the kind of
writing found in two . . . passages of
John Studley's translation (1581) of
Seneca's *Hercules Oetaeus*' (Wells).
Less cautiously, Rolfe, who first drew
attention to them, claimed them as
clearly Shakespeare's target. They
run (italics mine): 'O Lord of
ghosts, whose *fiery flash* / That forth
thy hand doth shake / Doth cause the
trembling lodges twain / Of *Phoebus car*
to *quake* . . . / The *roaring rocks* have
quaking stirred, / And none thereat
have pushed; / *Hell gloomy gates I
have brast ope* / Where grisly ghosts all
hushed / Have stood'.
31–4.] In Huanebango's mock-
heroics, Peele too burlesques ranting
classical allusion: 'Now, by Mars and
Mercury, Jupiter and Janus, Sol and
Saturnus, Venus and Vesta, Pallas
and Proserpina . . .', (*Old Wives
Tale,* 1595, ll. 257 f.).
31. *Phibbus' car*] the chariot of
Phoebus Apollo; cf. Studley, above,
ll. 27–34 n., and 'Phoebus fierie carre'
(Spenser, *Faerie Queene,* I. ii. 1)

Shall shine from far
And make and mar
The foolish fates.

This was lofty. Now name the rest of the players.   35
This is Ercles' vein, a tyrant's vein: a lover is more
condoling.

Quin. Francis Flute, the bellows-mender?

Flu. Here, Peter Quince.

Quin. Flute, you must take Thisbe on you.   40

Flu. What is Thisbe? A wandering knight?

Quin. It is the lady that Pyramus must love.

Flu. Nay, faith, let not me play a woman: I have a beard
coming.

Quin. That's all one: you shall play it in a mask; and you   45
may speak as small as you will.

Bot. And I may hide my face, let me play Thisbe too.
I'll speak in a monstrous little voice: 'Thisne,

---

36. Ercles'] *Theobald;* Ercles *Qq,F.*   40. Flute, you] *Q1;* you *Q2,F.*   47. too]
Qq (to), *F.*   48-9. Thisne, Thisne] *Qq,F* (*Thisne, Thisne*)*;* Thisby, Thisby
Hanmer.

---

echoed in *R3,* v. iii. 20: the sun's 'fiery car'.

36. *Ercles' vein*] the style of Hercules; for the possible reference to *2 Hercules,* 1595, see Introduction, p. xl. Cf. the strolling player in *Greenes Grots-worth of Witte,* 1592 (ed. Harrison, p. 34): 'The twelve labors of Hercules have I terribly thundred on the stage'. Cf. 'Cambyses' vein' (*1H4,* iv. 382 n.), Herod's rant (*Ham.,* III. ii. 14), and 'Pilates voys' (Chaucer, *Canterbury Tales,* I (A), 3124), the traditional style (especially in their introductory gabs) of mediaeval and early Elizabethan stage-tyrants.

41. *wandering knight*] knight-errant. Flute (unmanly treble and all) hopes for a hero's part like those in *Sir Clyomon, Knight of the Golden Shield . . . and Clamydes the White Knight* (*c.* 1570). For this old-fashioned genre, see Introduction, p. lxxxvii.

43-4. *a beard coming*] wishful

thinking (though tactfully met by Quince); the absent beard and fluty tones proclaim him, like Chaucer's Pardoner, 'no man'. As late as Hardy, Christian Cantle, a sexual defective not unsympathetically laughed at, was in place in a group like this.

45. *mask*] not, for Thisbe, disguise; normal outdoor wear for women careful of their complexions; cf. *Gent.,* IV. iv. 151 and Leech's n.

46. *as small*] in as thin tones: not, *pace OED,* 'low', but 'the opposite of deep' (Oliver, on *Wiv.,* I. i. 43, comparing Viola's 'small pipe', 'the maiden's organ, shrill and sound'). Chaucer's effeminate Pardoner has a 'smal' bleating voice, but sings loud.

48. *monstrous*] extraordinarily; *OED*'s earliest instance of use as a colloquial intensive (a. †8b).

48-9. '*Thisne, Thisne*'] pet-name for Thisbe (cf. 'a wench . . . my sweet pretty pigsnie': Peele, *Old Wives Tale,*

Thisne!'—'Ah, Pyramus, my lover dear! thy Thisbe
dear, and lady dear!'   50

Quin. No, no, you must play Pyramus; and Flute, you
Thisbe.

Bot. Well, proceed.

Quin. Robin Starveling, the tailor?

Star. Here, Peter Quince.   55

Quin. Robin Starveling, you must play Thisbe's mother.
Tom Snout, the tinker?

Snout. Here, Peter Quince.

Quin. You, Pyramus' father; myself, Thisbe's father;
Snug the joiner, you the lion's part. And I hope here   60
is a play fitted.

Snug. Have you the lion's part written? Pray you, if it
be, give it me; for I am slow of study.

Quin. You may do it extempore, for it is nothing but
roaring.   65

Bot. Let me play the lion too. I will roar, that I will do
any man's heart good to hear me. I will roar, that I
will make the Duke say: 'Let him roar again; let
him roar again!'

Quin. And you should do it too terribly, you would fright 70
the Duchess and the ladies, that they would shriek:
and that were enough to hang us all.

All. That would hang us, every mother's son.

60. here] *Qq;* there *F.*   62. if it] *Qq;* if *F.*   70. And] *Q1;* If *Q2,F.*

l. 648): Bottom first gives himself his
cue in his 'condoling' voice as
Pyramus; then, as Thisbe, takes it up
in his 'monstrous little' one. 'No actor
could miss the opportunity' (Sisson[2],
i. 125, refuting W. A. Wright's
interpretation, 'Thisne' = 'thissen'
(dialect), 'in this manner', approved
by Furness and entertained by Cuningham). To show off his aptitude
for either role by playing both is just
like Bottom.

49–50. *thy Thisbe dear*] Thisbe
addresses the identical phrase to
Pyramus in Mouffet (Muir[1], p.
44).

59.] Shakespeare had evidently not
yet planned the play's scenario: in
the performance, the fathers, and
Thisbe's mother (l. 56), do not appear.
It was not worth his while to turn
back and remove the discrepancy: at
this point, there is none for the
audience; and when finally the play
is put on, they will not recall this
allotment of minor parts.

63. *of study*] at learning a part: 'to
study a part' is still theatre-termin-
ology.

70–2.] See III. i. 29–30 and n.
below.

70. *And*] If. Cf. 47 above.

73. *every . . . son*] proverbial: Tilley,
M1202.

Bot. I grant you, friends, if you should fright the ladies
out of their wits, they would have no more discre-   75
tion but to hang us. But I will aggravate my voice
so, that I will roar you as gently as any sucking
dove; I will roar you and 'twere any nightingale.

Quin. You can play no part but Pyramus: for Pyramus
is a sweet-faced man; a proper man as one shall see   80
in a summer's day; a most lovely, gentleman-like
man: therefore you must needs play Pyramus.

Bot. Well, I will undertake it. What beard were I best to
play it in?

Quin. Why, what you will.   85

Bot. I will discharge it in either your straw-colour beard,
your orange-tawny beard, your purple-in-grain
beard, or your French-crown-colour beard, your
perfect yellow.

Quin. Some of your French crowns have no hair at all,   90
and then you will play bare-faced. But, masters,

74. if] *Qq;* if that *F.*   77. roar you] *Qq;* roare *F.*   86. colour] *Qq;* colour'd *F.*

76. *aggravate*] intensify (*OED* II†5) Bottom's malapropism for 'mitigate', tone down.

77–8. *sucking dove*] Bottom confuses the sitting dove ('Columbae . . . cum sedent', Erasmus, *Adagia*) and the sucking lamb (1 Samuel, vii. 9: quoted Cairncross on *2H6*, III. i. 71, 'the sucking lamb or harmless dove'). See Tilley, D572, 573; L33, 34.

80. *sweet-faced man*] Marlowe (*Jew of Malta*, l. 1758) has 'a sweet-fac'd youth' (Craig, *apud* Cuningham).

80–1. *proper . . . day*] proverbial; cf. 'as fine a man as a wench can see in a summer's day' (*Wily Beguiled*, 1606) and Lyly, *Mother Bombie*, 1594, I. iii. 44, quoted Tilley, S967.

83–9.] 'Bottom . . . discovers a true genius for the stage by . . . his deliberation which beard to choose among many beards, all unnatural' (Johnson's n., calculated to tease his friend Garrick).

86. *discharge*] perform.

86–9.] To know dyes perhaps belongs to Bottom's trade as weaver (Martin Wright, Wells). In Stratford records of 1596, Hulme found 'orange tawnye brode cloth' and 'violet in grayne', side by side (*Explorations*, p. 334).

87. *orange-tawny*] tan-coloured; at III. i. 121 below, the colour of a blackbird's bill, but here distinguished from 'perfect yellow'. Mouffet, notes Muir (p. 73), has 'orange' and 'tawny' in consecutive lines.

purple-in-grain] red (scarlet or crimson!); for 'in grain' (fast-dyed, originally with cochineal from the *coccus* insect) and its history, see Cuningham's extensive n.

88. *French-crown*] a gold coin, the *écu.*

90. *Some . . . all*] being bald from the 'French disease' (syphilis).

91. *bare-faced*] (1) beardless; (2) exposed without disguise: cf. 'barefaced [= undisguised] power', *Mac.*, II. i. 118.

here are your parts; and I am to entreat you, request you, and desire you, to con them by tomorrow night; and meet me in the palace wood, a mile without the town, by moonlight; there will we rehearse,   95
for if we meet in the city, we shall be dogged with company, and our devices known. In the meantime I will draw a bill of properties, such as our play wants. I pray you fail me not.

Bot. We will meet, and there we may rehearse most ob-   100
scenely and courageously. Take pains, be perfect: adieu!

Quin. At the Duke's oak we meet.

Bot. Enough: hold, or cut bow-strings.   *Exeunt.*

95. will we] *Q1;* we will *Q2,F.*   100. most] *Q1;* more *Q2,F.*   101. Take]
Qq,F; Quince. Take *Collier².*

98–9. *I . . . wants*] Quince's duty as
bookholder. One such list is extant,
appended by a playhouse scribe
(probably the bookholder) to Massinger's autograph *Believe as you list*
(Fol. 29b). See the M.S.R. edn, and
W. W. Greg, *Dramatic Documents from
the Elizabethan Playhouses*, I. 234, 293 f.

100. *obscenely*] The malapropism is
probably for 'seemly'. The obscene is
*un*seemly: the reversal gives the intended sense of the same malapropism
in *LLL*, IV. i, 142: 'so obscenely as
it were, so fit' (Deighton). Bottom
may have felt an appropriateness in
'obscenely': the obscene is that which
should not be done unless in private,
and the rendezvous is to ensure that
the rehearsal *will* be in private.

101. *perfect*] word-perfect without
book: still the theatre-term.

104. *hold . . . bow-strings*] The precise
meaning is uncertain. The phrasing
may be, as Capell assumed, 'hold' (to
the agreement)—'or cut bowstrings'
(to cut them will be the penalty).
Alternatively 'hold or cut' may go
closely together; Malone's view: 'To

meet, *whether bowstrings hold or are cut*,
is to meet in all events'. (Cuningham
approves; and cf. *Shakespeare's England*,
II. 380 n.) That requires the 'cut' to
be a fortuitous possibility which is
accepted; is it not more naturally a
positive act? In *Ado* (III. ii. 10), where
Malone sought support, 'Cupid's
bowstring' has been 'twice or thrice
cut' to inhibit his mischievous
archery; a quasi-penalty which seems
rather to favour Capell. Capell prejudiced his interpretation by the
claim, never verified, that archers
making appointments actually used
the present formula. But his interpretation itself, that the cut is a forfeit
the archer invokes should he fail the
assignation, is in line with the variant
'Hold or cut codpiece point' (the
codpiece-lace which kept it respectable) recorded by Ray in 1678 as
proverbial (Tilley, C502): like bowstrings, a lace may *break*, but does
not *cut*, spontaneously. The general
sense of both expressions, as Wells
takes Shakespeare's, may be 'keep
promise, or suffer disgrace'.

ACT II

[SCENE I]

Enter a Fairy *at one door, and* PUCK *at another.*

Puck. How now, spirit! Whither wander you?

Fai.   Over hill, over dale,
                      Thorough bush, thorough briar,
                 Over park, over pale,
                      Thorough flood, thorough fire,   5
                 I do wander everywhere,
                 Swifter than the moon's sphere;

ACT II

Scene ɪ

Act II] *F; not in Qq.*   Scene ɪ] *Rowe; not in Qq,F.*   [*Location*] A Wood near Athens. *Capell.*   S.D. *Enter . . . Puck . . . another.*] *Enter . . . Robin goodfellow . . . another. Qq,F.*   1. *Puck*] *Rowe; Robin Qq,F.*   Whither] *Q1;* Whether *Q2,F.* 2–9.] *Divided, Pope;* over . . . briar,/ . . . fire;/ . . . sphere:/ . . . greene. *Qq,F* (*subst.*).   3. Thorough] *Q1;* Through *Q2,F.*   5. Thorough] *Q1;* Through *Q2,F.*   7. moon's] *Qq,F* (Moons); moones *Steevens.*

Scene . . . another] the first scene in the wood: the 'doors' are those of the tiring-house or a hall-screen, giving access to the acting area.

1–58.] Cf. *Gallathea*, ɪ. ii, a dialogue where, to further the exposition, Lyly has Cupid (a mischief-maker, like Puck) interrogate a 'Nimph of Diana' about herself and her mistress, who, she indicates, is at odds with his mother Venus: cf. Puck on Titania and Oberon. Cupid begins (cf. Puck's 'Whither wander you?') 'Faire Nimphe, are you strayed from your companie by chance, or love you to wander solitarily on purpose?'

1.] Pedantic prosodists have boggled over this freely rhythmical line. Yet it scans as three trochees and a dactyl.

2–3.] Cf. Spenser, *Faerie Queene*, vɪ. viii. 32 (published 1596): 'Through hills and dales, through bushes and through briars' (Halliwell).

3. *Thorough*] alternative Elizabethan spelling of 'through': here (but not invariably) distinguishing the pronunciation.

4.] 'All land is common to the fairies' (N.C.S.); 'park', ground enclosed (by royal grant) for game; 'pale', ground simply fenced in by palings.

7. *moon's sphere*] the transparent hollow globe which according to the Ptolemaic astronomy carried it round the earth. Each planet was attached to such a sphere, and so were the fixed stars collectively. In 'moons'

And I serve the Fairy Queen,
To dew her orbs upon the green.
The cowslips tall her pensioners be,   10
In their gold coats spots you see;
Those be rubies, fairy favours,
In those freckles live their savours.
I must go seek some dew-drops here,
And hang a pearl in every cowslip's ear.   15
Farewell, thou lob of spirits; I'll be gone;
Our Queen and all her elves come here anon.
Puck. The King doth keep his revels here tonight;
Take heed the Queen come not within his sight;
For Oberon is passing fell and wrath,   20
Because that she as her attendant hath
A lovely boy, stol'n from an Indian king—
She never had so sweet a changeling;

22. stol'n] *F;* stolen *Qq.*

the long 'oo' and liquid 'n' suffice the
verse, which does not need the archaic
'moon'es.

9. *orbs*] circles (*OED*'s earliest instance): fairy rings; see Brand,
Popular Antiquities of Great Britain, III.
20 ff. (Kittredge). The grass is richer
in them, actually because nourished
by extra nitrogen from fungi of the
year before (Sidney Turner, in
Furness).

10. *pensioners*] fairy counterparts to
Elizabeth's, her gentlemen of the
royal bodyguard within the palace
(founded 1509), who were chosen for
birth, height, and good looks, and
wore uniforms adorned with gold
lace and jewels (cf. ll. 11 f.).

11–13. *spots . . . freckles*] Cf. 'the
freckled cowslip', *H5*, v. ii. 49
(Cuningham), 'the crimson drops /
I'th'bottom of a cowslip', *Cym.*, II. ii.
38 f. (Percy, in Furness).

12. *favours*] marks of (royal) favour.

14.] metrically, a transition: in four
beats, like ll. 6–13; iambic, like ll.
15 ff.

14–15. *dew-drops . . . ear*] Fashion-
able Elizabethans, men as well as

women, often wore jewels in the ear.
Pearls were associated with dew-drops
the more readily because according
to Pliny (Holland's tr., book IX, cap.
35) and others they might begin as
dew-drops (Halliwell).

16. *lob of*] country lout among.

20. *passing . . . wrath*] exceedingly
fierce and wrathful: 'wroth' is not
found in Shakespeare.

22. *stol'n . . . king*] not incompatible
with the story of his mother, below,
ll. 123 ff.; Shakespeare may or may
not already have conceived that.

23. *changeling*] Cf. Scot, *Witchcraft*
(below, pp. 147, at n. 170). Here,
trisyllabic, and (sole instance in *OED*)
the mortal child stolen by fairies;
normally, the fairy brat left in exchange. So Spenser, *Faerie Queene*, I.
ix. 65, no doubt intends; but in his
account of Red-Cross 'reft' in 'swad-
ling band' by a Faery who 'her base
Elfin brood there for [him] left: / Such
men do Chaungelings call, so
chaung'd by Faeries theft', Shakespeare might have understood 'such'
as applying the term to both the
exchanged children.

And jealous Oberon would have the child
Knight of his train, to trace the forests wild: 25
But she perforce withholds the loved boy,
Crowns him with flowers, and makes him all
    her joy.
And now they never meet in grove or green,
By fountain clear, or spangled starlight sheen,
But they do square; that all their elves for fear   30
Creep into acorn-cups, and hide them there.

Fai. Either I mistake your shape and making quite,
Or else you are that shrewd and knavish sprite
Call'd Robin Goodfellow. Are not you he
That frights the maidens of the villagery,   35
Skim milk, and sometimes labour in the quern,
And bootless make the breathless housewife churn,
And sometime make the drink to bear no barm,
Mislead night-wanderers, laughing at their harm?

33. sprite] *Q1;* spirit *Q2,F.*   34. not you] *Q1;* you not *Q2,F.*   35. villagery]
Q1 (Villageree), *Hanmer;* Villagree *Q2,F.*

25. *trace*] range.

30. *square*] quarrel, take up a hostile
posture; cf. 'square up to one another'.

32. *making*] build.

33–4, 40.] Scot (*Witchcraft*) speaks
of the 'knaverie of Robin goodfellow', and of 'the puckle' and 'hob
gobblin' (below, pp. 146–7, at nn. 164,
158, 171–2).

33. *shrewd*] malign; but the sense is
weakening toward 'mischievous': in
M.E., the Shrew could mean the Devil.

35–6. *frights . . . Skim*] 'frights' looks
back to 'he', 'skim' to 'you'. The
inconsistency is not unShakespearean
(Abbott, § 415).

35. *villagery*] village population,
villagers collectively; cf. peasantry,
tenantry.

36.] mischievous pranks like those
enumerated in ll. 35, 37–9 (Ritson).
Puck deprives the milk of its cream. If
'labour in' = 'labour at', and the
quern is the hand-mill used for grinding corn, mustard, etc., he grinds

what is not due to be ground (Cuningham). But 'quern' is also a variant
of 'churn' (*OED*) and the sense is
clearer if Puck works within ('labours
in') the churn, frustrating (l. 37) the
housewife's efforts (so Delius).

37. *bootless*] all in vain: the butter
will not 'come'.

38.] Puck arrests the fermentation.
'Barm' can mean either 'yeast' (in
1847 Halliwell 'observed a card
advertising "fresh barm" . . . within
a few yards of the poet's birthplace':
cf. Lancs. and Yorks. dialect today),
or the 'head' of froth which should
top a pot of ale. Wells opts for this
'head', which 'drink' supports;
Schmidt, Onions, and N.C.S. for
'yeast': as the cream yields no butter,
the liquor yields no yeast. Shakespeare may not have decided for either
meaning against the other.

39.] Cf. Tyndale (1531), quoted
Tilley, R147: '(as we say) led by
Robin Goodfellow . . . they cannot
come to the right way'.

Those that Hobgoblin call you, and sweet Puck,   40
You do their work, and they shall have good luck.
Are not you he?
Puck.   Thou speak'st aright;
I am that merry wanderer of the night.
I jest to Oberon, and make him smile
When I a fat and bean-fed horse beguile,   45
Neighing in likeness of a filly foal;
And sometime lurk I in a gossip's bowl
In very likeness of a roasted crab,
And when she drinks, against her lips I bob,
And on her wither'd dewlap pour the ale.   50
The wisest aunt, telling the saddest tale,
Sometime for three-foot stool mistaketh me;
Then slip I from her bum, down topples she,
And 'tailor' cries, and falls into a cough;
And then the whole quire hold their hips and loffe   55

42. Puck.] *Rowe; Robin. Qq,F.*   42-3. Thou . . . night] *As F; one line, Qq.*
46. filly] *Q1;* silly *Q2,F.*   54. tailor] *Qq,F* (tailour); rails, or *Hanmer;* tailer
conj. Furness.

night-wanderers] This compound (and cf. Puck as 'wanderer of the night', l. 43, and the Fairy's wandering, swifter than the moon's sphere, ll. 6 f.) is from Marlowe, *Hero and Leander*, I. 107: 'that night-wandering pale and watery starre', and Seneca, *Oedipus*, l. 254: 'noctivagans Phoebe'.

40. *Puck*] See Introduction, p. lx.

41. *do their work*] as Scot relates (*Witchcraft*, below, p. 146, at nn. 159–60). The 'grinding' in Scot may have suggested 'quern', l. 36 above (but see n.).

46. *filly foal*] female foal.

47. *gossip's*] here, a gossip has the modern sense: a tattling woman.

48. *crab*] crab apple; cf. *LLL*, v. ii. 915 and R. David's n. He quotes Peele, *Old Wives Tale*, 1595, 'Lay a crab in the fire to roast for lamb's wool', the spiced drink here meant.

49. *bob*] knock, as he bobs up and down in the liquid; see *OED* v²†2, v ³¹.

50. *dewlap*] from cattle, humorously

transferred to 'pendulous folds of flesh about the human throat' (*OED*'s earliest instance).

51. *wisest aunt*] aunt = old woman (*OED*'s sole instance): the greatest wiseacre among the cronies.

the saddest tale] Cf. Lyly, *Endimion*, III. iv. 8: 'welcomest is that guest . . . that can rehearse the saddest Tale, or the bloodiest tragedie'.

54. *tailor*] 'The custom of crying *tailor* at a sudden fall backwards I think I remember to have observed. He that slips beside his chair falls as a tailor squats upon his board' (Johnson). Agreeing that the cry may have become associated with the tailor's posture, Hulme (pp. 99–102) finds it primarily an indelicate reference to the posterior (tail). 'Oh, my bum!' might be some sort of equivalent.

55. *quire*] company: perhaps 'vocal group', like a choir, of which 'quire' was a regular spelling.

55–6.] The out-of-the-way forms,

And waxen in their mirth, and neeze, and swear
A merrier hour was never wasted there.
But room, fairy! Here comes Oberon.
Fai. And here my mistress. Would that he were gone!

Enter OBERON, *the King of Fairies, at one door, with his* Train;
and TITANIA, *the Queen, at another, with hers.*

Obe. Ill met by moonlight, proud Titania.   60
Tita. What, jealous Oberon? Fairies, skip hence;
  I have forsworn his bed and company.
Obe. Tarry, rash wanton; am not I thy lord?
Tita. Then I must be thy lady; but I know
  When thou hast stol'n away from fairy land,   65
  And in the shape of Corin, sat all day
  Playing on pipes of corn, and versing love
  To amorous Phillida. Why art thou here,
  Come from the farthest step of India,

---

59. S.D. *Enter Oberon, the King . . . Titania, the Queen . . . hers.*] *Qq,F (Enter . . .
the King . . . the Queene . . . hers).*   61. *Tita.*] *Capell (Tit.); Qu./Qq,F (so
throughout scene).*   Fairies] Theobald *(subst.)*; Fairy *Qq,F.*   65. hast]
Qq; wast *F.*   69. step] *Q1* (steppe), *Capell;* steepe *Q2,F.*

'loffe' for 'laugh' (*OED* cites *MND*,
and *Townley Mystery Plays*, XXIV. 90),
'waxen' for 'wax', increase (archaic
inflexion), and 'neeze' for 'sneeze'
(unique in Shakespeare), have evidently been chosen to suit the episode
described.
  58. *room, fairy*] make room: stand
back! (Kittredge). Neither faëry
(Johnson, N.C.S.) nor any emendation for metre (Dyce, etc.) is wanted:
the marshal-like cry of 'room!' fills
the place of a beat and a light
syllable.
  61. *Fairies*] Titania summons her
whole train to sweep out with her.
Editors determined to remain faithful
to Q1 can defend 'Fairy' as addressed
to her 'gentleman-usher, whose mov-
ing-off would be a signal' for the
rest (Capell), or to the Fairy who
talked with Puck (Wells), while she
only beckons the others. But mistakes
of number are frequent with com-

positors. Here, carrying 'Fairies skip'
as sounds in his head, the compositor
would be liable to lose the 's' of
'Fairies' in the 's' of skip' (Cuningham).
  63. *wanton*] skittish, wilful creature.
  63-4. *lord? . . . lady*] husband, with
his authority; wife, with her claim to
his devotion.
  66, 68. *Corin, Phillida*] traditional
names, in pastoral, for a shepherd
and shepherdess.
  67. *pipes of corn*] shepherds 'pipe on
oaten straws', *LLL*, v. ii. 893; Virgil's
'avena'.
  69. *farthest step*] 'utmost limit of
travel or exploration' (Onions, who
compares *Ado*, II. i. 277, 'the furthest
inch of Arabia'; so Wells); 'step' is a
modernization, not an emendation:
it assumes Q1's 'steppe' is the variant
spelling then common. But 'steppe'
may be a corruption of Shakespeare's
intended 'steep', perhaps written

But that, forsooth, the bouncing Amazon,   70
Your buskin'd mistress and your warrior love,
To Theseus must be wedded, and you come
To give their bed joy and prosperity?
Obe. How canst thou thus, for shame, Titania,
Glance at my credit with Hippolyta,   75
Knowing I know thy love to Theseus?
Didst not thou lead him through the glimmering night
From Perigouna, whom he ravished;
And make him with fair Aegles break his faith,
With Ariadne and Antiopa?   80
Tita. These are the forgeries of jealousy:
And never, since the middle summer's spring,
Met we on hill, in dale, forest or mead,
By paved fountain, or by rushy brook,
Or in the beached margent of the sea,   85
To dance our ringlets to the whistling wind,

---

77. not thou] *Qq;* thou not *F.*   78. Perigouna] *Theobald* (Perigune), *Grant White; Perigenia Qq,F.*   79. Aegles] *Chambers;* Eagles *Qq,F;* Ægle *Rowe.*

'step' in the MS. (a spelling for which N.C.S. cites F *Ham.,* I. iii. 48; I know no indication that it is Shakespearean). The sense proposed by Onions for 'step' has no exact parallel in Shakespeare; nor does he elsewhere use 'steep' as a noun (= 'mountain'), proposed here by *OED* (steep *sb.* B1.) which may nevertheless be right (so N.C.S., Alexander). The modern sense of 'steppe', as in 'the Russian steppes', is ruled out, not having been found to exist in Shakespeare's time.

71. *buskin'd*] in high hunting-boots.

75. *Glance at*] obliquely cast aspersions on.

78–80.] On these amours see North (below, pp. 134, 135, 136, at nn. 49, 52, 59, 61, 65–6, 69–70.

78. *Perigouna*] so North (below, p. 134, at n. 49). 'Perigenia' (Q1) is perhaps more probably the compositor's error (e and three minims for o and four), as assumed by editors who emend (e.g. *Camb.,* N.C.S., Alexander) than Shakespeare's, or

than his assimilation to names like 'Iphigenia' as is argued in Sisson[2], I. 126.

79. *Aegles*] North (below, p. 135, at n. 52) and no doubt Shakespeare: the true classical form is Aegle. 'Eagles' (Q1) is the compositor's vulgarization.

81.] Of the stories about Theseus' desertion of Ariadne 'there is no truth or certaintie' (North, p. 134, at n. 51).

82. *the . . . spring*] the time midsummer springs from: the beginning of midsummer (Steevens).

84. *paved fountain*] 'a clear fountain with a pebbly bottom' (E. K. Chambers, quoted N.C.S.); cf. Marlowe's 'pebble-paved channel' in lines preserved in *England's Parnassus,* 1600 (Knight). See *Marlowe's Poems,* ed. L. C. Martin, p. 301.

85. *margent*] 'Margin' is seldom found in Shakespeare's time, and never in him.

86. *ringlets*] circular dances (*OED's* earliest instance), in a fairy ring.

But with thy brawls thou has disturb'd our sport.
Therefore the winds, piping to us in vain,
As in revenge have suck'd up from the sea
Contagious fogs; which, falling in the land,   90
Hath every pelting river made so proud
That they have overborne their continents.
The ox hath therefore stretch'd his yoke in vain,
The ploughman lost his sweat, and the green corn
Hath rotted ere his youth attain'd a beard;   95
The fold stands empty in the drowned field,
And crows are fatted with the murrion flock;

91. pelting] *Qq;* petty *F.*

87. *brawls*] The transition from 'dance' may be deliberately ironic: 'brawls' = dances in the form of French bransles having given place to 'brawls' = shindies. Cf. *LLL*, II. i. 9 and R. David's n.

88–114.] Cf. Ulysses on the overthrow of order when 'degree is shak'd', *Troil.,* I. iii. 85 ff. On sources in Seneca's *Medea* and *Oedipus*, Ovid (especially Ceres' curse, the plague of Aegina, and Deucalion's flood) and Spenser, *Shepheardes Calender*, see Introduction, pp. lxiii, lxxxvi.

88–90. *the winds . . . fogs*] indebted to Ovid (see Golding, below, pp. 137, 138, at nn. 72, 81–2, 84) and Seneca, *Oedipus* (below, p. 139, at n. 100).

88. *piping . . . vain*] Matthew, xi. 17, Luke, vii. 31: 'We have piped unto you and ye have not danced.' Cf. Spenser, *Shepheardes Calender*, June, ll. 30 f.: 'Pan . . . will pype and dance, when Phoebe shineth bright'.

91–2.] In Golding, Deucalion's flood is fed by tributaries which have 'yswolne above their bankes' (below, p. 137, at n. 77). Waters rising over their 'continents', the bounds which should contain them, are Shakespeare's recurrent image for anarchical insubordination. See R. W. Chambers in A. W. Pollard (ed.) *Shakespeare's Hand in Sir Thomas More,* pp. 159–61, citing it from the 'Three Pages' al-

most certainly in Shakespeare's holograph; from *Ham.*, IV. v. 99, and from *Cor.*, III. i. 246–8. In the tenth Homily appointed to be read in Churches, 'the comely . . . order' of 'fountains, springs, yea the seas themselves' is an instance of 'the goodly order of God, without the which no House, no City, no Commonwealth can continue' (quoted Harbage, p. 31).

91. *pelting*] paltry; cf. *R2,* II. i. 60 and Ure's n.

93. *ox*] Plough oxen are smitten in Golding (below, p. 138, at n. 79); cf. *id.* and Seneca, *Oedipus* (pp. 138, 139, at nn. 79, 103).

94. *ploughman . . . sweat*] In Golding, the 'Tilman' loses what he 'toyled' for; and the 'wretched Plowman' suffers (below, pp. 137, 138, at nn. 74, 85).

94–5. *green corn . . . beard*] indebted to the *Shepheardes Calender*, December, ll. 99, 106 f.: 'The eare that budded faire, is burnt and blasted', 'The . . . fruite is . . . rotted, ere they were halfe mellow ripe'; *Oedipus* and Golding (below, pp. 139, 138, at nn. 101, 80); and Golding XV. 224, 'greene . . . and foggy is the blade'.

96–7.] Cf. *Oedipus* and Golding (below, pp. 139, 137, 138 at nn. 102, 78, 86); in Golding (plague of Aegina, VII. 703, 786) 'ravening foules' and 'murren'. The 'murrion flock' are 'murrained': victims of sheep-plague.

The nine-men's-morris is fill'd up with mud,
And the quaint mazes in the wanton green
For lack of tread are undistinguishable.   100
The human mortals want their winter cheer:
No night is now with hymn or carol blest.

101. want their . . . cheer] *Hanmer, conj. Theobald* (chear) *withdrawn;* want
their . . . heere *Qq,F;* want their . . . heere *Q2,F;* want their . . . gear *conj.
Bruce apud Camb.;* want; their . . . here *Knight;* want, their . . . here *Grant
White*[2]; wail their . . . here *Kinnear.*

98. *nine-men's-morris*] The diagram
cut in the turf when this game was
played out-of-doors with nine 'men'
(pegs or pebbles) a side; usually two,
or three concentric squares one within another. The positions for the
'men' were the corners and mid-points
of the sides: the opponents alternately
placed a man, and when all were
placed, moved them along the lines
of the diagram. The aim was to
reduce the opposing 'men' to two:
you removed one every time you
formed a line of three with your own:
pace N.C.S., the game resembled an
elaborate noughts and crosses, not
hopscotch. Cf. the accounts in
Furness, especially W. A. Wright's
who saw it in Sussex; *Shakespeare's
England,* II. 467, and *The Week-End
Book,* ed. Mendel, Meynell, and Goss,
revised 1925, p. 269 (rules) and end-
papers (diagram).

99. *quaint*] ingeniously elaborated.

wanton] luxuriant, rank (*OED*'s
earliest instance of this sense).

100. *undistinguishable*] impossible to
pick out (*OED*'s earliest instance).

101. *mortals . . . cheer*] suffering an
untimely winter, they lack the cheer
which that season normally brings
them (e.g. at Yuletide). Theobald's
withdrawn conjecture is adopted because: (1) Q1 seems corrupt, 'here'
being (as Dyce observed) defensible
only by straining; (2) 'h' for 'ch' is an
easy misreading; (3) 'cheer' fits the
context, (4) introducing expressions
('hymns and carols') of the 'cheer' in
question; (5) it postulates for 'want'

the sense ('be without') most frequent
in Shakespeare; (6) it was probably
suggested to him from the November
eclogue of *The Shepheardes Calender,*
present to his mind in this speech; cf.
ll. 103, 106: 'happy cheere is turn'd
to heavie chaunce . . . / And shepherds
wonted solace is extinct' (cf. 'wonted',
l. 113 below). This seems decisive,
confirming the cogent support for
'cheer' by Cuningham, Wells, and
N.C.S., yet N.C.S. obelizes the line
as perhaps beyond cure; and 'here'
remains worth consideration: it is
retained (silently) by Alexander and
Clemen, and is best defended by
Capell (*Notes,* II. 104): the mortals,
he explains, 'in a country so afflicted'
lack 'their accustomed winter', enlivened (l. 102) with mirth. (But
would the reason why winter would
have been welcome be left a puzzle
until the succeeding line?) Of alternative emendations 'gear' may attract
as assuming one of the easiest mis-
readings in secretary hand, and the
re-punctuation adopted by Knight
as a minimal change. Ostensibly
minimal, it is, however, in its violent
check to the rhythm, and the con-
structions it imposes ('are in a state of
deprivation' and 'their winter being
here') foreign to Shakespeare's style
at this period and in this speech;
while 'gear' does not lead into the
next line, besides requiring the slightly
less likely sense 'need' for 'want'.

102-3. *carol . . . Therefore*] 'Therefore' picks up the argument, here as
at l. 93, from l. 88: the cause is the

Therefore the moon, the governess of floods,
Pale in her anger, washes all the air,
That rheumatic diseases do abound.   105
And thorough this distemperature we see
The seasons alter: hoary-headed frosts
Fall in the fresh lap of the crimson rose;
And on old Hiems' thin and icy crown,

106. thorough] *Q1;* through *Q2,F.*   107. hoary-headed] *Q1 (unhyphenated),*
F3; hoared headed *Q2,F.*   109. thin] *Halliwell, conj. Tyrwhitt;* chin *Qq,F;*
chill *conj. Theobald.*

fairy feud, prior to the absence of 'hymn or carol', not offence taken at that absence (Malone). Hence 'carol', originally a ring-dance with song, can mean any joyous song, religious or not, 'sung at times of festival' (N.C.S.).]

103–4.] Cf. the paling moon, and air made pestilent, in Seneca's *Oedipus* (below, p. 139 and n. 99); and previous n.

103. *governess of floods*] by extension from causing tides and (supposedly) the menstrual flow. In *Hero and Leander,* I. 107, 111, in a passage Shakespeare recalled at II. i. 39 and III. ii. 379, that 'pale and watrie' planet 'over-rules the flood'.

105. *rheumatic*] characterized by rheum: peccant fluid from eyes or nose; or within the body where it was believed to be the cause of rheumatism. Accented 'rhèumatic'.

106. *distemperature*] (1) loss of temper, discomposure; (2) upset in the weather (Onions).

107. *The seasons alter*] as, in Seneca, by Medea's sorceries on Hecate's behalf: see below, p. 144, at nn. 140–1, and Introduction, p. lxiii, n. 4. In *Sonn.,* xcvii, an autumn is experienced as like a winter.

hoary-headed frosts] echoing *Shepheardes Calender,* December, l. 135, 'My head besprent with hoary frost', emphasized by E.K.'s gloss: 'Hoary frost, a metaphor of hoary heares scattered lyke to a gray frost';

Spenser's phrases link with 'heade', 'hoarie' and 'frozen' in Golding (below, p. 139, at nn. 92, 94–5).

109. *old Hiems*] Ovid's 'senilis hiems' (*Metamorphoses,* xv. 212); '*Hiems,* Winter', *LLL,* v. ii. 888. Cf. Ovid's personifications, in Golding's versions (below, pp. 138–9), xv. 233–235, II. 36–9. Three lines before II. 36 comes a phrase which Shakespeare borrows word for word from Golding, at IV. i. 51 below.

thin] Q1's 'chinne', introducing a sudden oddity into the visual portrait, is almost certainly an error; no doubt, as Tyrwhitt's conjecture (generally adopted) assumes, the misreading of 'th' as 'ch', one of the easiest in secretary hand. Golding's 'Winter' has 'shirle thinne heare as whyght as snowe' (cf. 'thin and icy'); E.K.'s gloss on Colin's frosty hairs calls them 'scattered': see l. 107, second n., above, and below, p. 138, at nn. 87–8. Aged, bare-headed Lear's 'thin helm' (IV. viii. 36) and the 'white-beards' with 'thin and hairless scalps' in *R2* (III. ii. 112) further support the emendation (Steevens); cf. *Tim.,* IV. iii. 137 (W. A. Wright). For 'chin' Malone adduced Winter's 'bearde' laden with icycles (cf. 'icy') in Golding (*loc. cit.,* at nn. 93–4): but they equally load his 'crowne'. The association they prompted need not have extended beyond the crown, to which chaplets are 'almost restricted' (Furness). Retaining 'chin', Theobald

An odorous chaplet of sweet summer buds   110
Is, as in mockery, set; the spring, the summer,
The childing autumn, angry winter, change
Their wonted liveries; and the mazed world,
By their increase, now knows not which is which.
And this same progeny of evils comes   115
From our debate, from our dissension;
We are their parents and original.
Obe. Do you amend it then: it lies in you.
Why should Titania cross her Oberon?
I do but beg a little changeling boy   120
To be my henchman.
Tita.   Set your heart at rest:
The fairy land buys not the child of me.
His mother was a votress of my order;
And in the spiced Indian air, by night,
Full often hath she gossip'd by my side;   125
And sat with me on Neptune's yellow sands,

---

115. evils comes] *F2; evils,/ Comes Qq,F.*

and Capell have to equate 'chaplet' with 'garland'. Halliwell thought that the grotesque effect might be intentional, part of the 'mockery' Hiems is suffering.

icy crown] from Golding's 'isycles' on Winter's 'snowie frozen crowne'; cf. 'My head besprent with hoary frost', *Shepheardes Calender*, December, l. 135, forming one of the associative links between the two sources, see n. 109, first, and 107, second n., above.

110.] Cf. 'coloured chaplets', *Shepheardes Calender*, November, l. 115. Another reminiscence of that eclogue.

112. *childing*] 'teeming Autumn, big with rich increase', *Sonn.*, XCVIII (Knight).

113. *wonted*] accustomed; cf. *Shepheardes Calender*, November, l. 68: 'The earth now lacks her wonted light', and l. 106 quoted above, l. 101 n.

mazed] bewildered, by terror (cf. *OED*).

114. *increase*] aggrandizement.

115–16. *progeny . . . dissension*] Cf. Seneca, *Oedipus*: 'omnia nostrum sensire malum' (below, p. 139, at n. 103; Oedipus acknowledges himself the source of the plague, *ibid.*, at n. 99).

116. *debate*] contention, quarrel.

117. *original*] origin.

121. *henchman*] page of honour (*OED* 16).

Set . . . rest] proverbial: Tilley, H327.

123. *votress*] vowed woman member.

125. *gossip'd*] been my gossip, woman friend (strictly, 'gossips' were godfathers and godmothers, relatives as god-sibs).

126. *Neptune's yellow sands*] echoed from Marlowe, *Hero and Leander*, I. 347: that the passage stuck in Shakespeare's mind is shown by Ariel's first song in *Tp.* where 'whist' and 'these yellow sands' recall 'when all is whist . . . save . . . the sea playing on yellow sand'.

Marking th'embarked traders on the flood:
When we have laugh'd to see the sails conceive
And grow big-bellied with the wanton wind;
Which she, with pretty and with swimming gait   130
Following (her womb then rich with my young squire),
Would imitate, and sail upon the land
To fetch me trifles, and return again
As from a voyage rich with merchandise.
But she, being mortal, of that boy did die;   135
And for her sake do I rear up her boy;
And for her sake I will not part with him.
Obe. How long within this wood intend you stay?
Tita. Perchance till after Theseus' wedding-day.
If you will patiently dance in our round,   140
And see our moonlight revels, go with us;
If not, shun me, and I will spare your haunts.
Obe. Give me that boy, and I will go with thee.
Tita. Not for thy fairy kingdom. Fairies, away!
We shall chide downright if I longer stay.   145
Exeunt Titania and her Train.
Obe. Well, go thy way; thou shalt not from this grove
Till I torment thee for this injury.
My gentle Puck, come hither. Thou rememb'rest
Since once I sat upon a promontory,

130. gait] *Qq,F* (gate), *Capell.*   136. do I] *Qq;* I do *F.*   139. Theseus']
Qq,F (Theseus), *Rowe³.*   145. S.D.] *Exeunt. Qq,F; Exeunt Queen and her
train./Theobald.*

127. *embarked traders*] merchant-men.
130. *swimming*] as though gliding through the waves; and with a glide as in dancing: Jonson's Philautia (*Cynthia's Revels*, II. iv. 55), accused of lacking 'the *swim* i'the turn', claims that 'the *swimme* and the *trip* are properly mine' (Furness).
131. *Following*] copying.
140. *round*] 'The simplest form of country dance is that in which the dancers form a circle; this was called a Round or Roundel' (*Shakespeare's England*, II. 440).

142.] 'shun' = avoid; 'spare' = not trouble (with my presence).
147. *injury*] affront; cf. III. ii. 148 and n.
149. *Since*] the time when: *OED's* earliest instance.
149–57.] Dangerous Cupid, all armed, and taking aim as he flies above the shore in a moonlit and starry sky and a seascape including sea-dwellers, is evidently indebted to Seneca's similar picture in *Hippolytus*. In Seneca, there is no moon; instead of the dolphin and mermaid there are monsters and Nereids; and the

And heard a mermaid on a dolphin's back   150
Uttering such dulcet and harmonious breath
That the rude sea grew civil at her song
And certain stars shot madly from their spheres
To hear the sea-maid's music?
Puck.   I remember.
Obe. That very time I saw (but thou couldst not),   155
Flying between the cold moon and the earth,
Cupid all arm'd: a certain aim he took
At a fair vestal, throned by the west,
And loos'd his love-shaft smartly from his bow
As it should pierce a hundred thousand hearts.   160
But I might see young Cupid's fiery shaft
Quench'd in the chaste beams of the watery moon;
And the imperial votress passed on,

150. mermaid] *Qq,F* (mearemaid *subst.*), *Rowe.*   155. saw] *Q1;* say *Q2,F.*
158. the west] *F;* west *Qq.*   163. votress passed] *Qq,F;* votaress passed
Knight; votaress pass'd *Keightley.*

august targets, *not* immune, are
Apollo and other gods. See above, p.
lxiii, n. 1; below, p. 142, at nn. 124, 125.
'Cupid all arm'd' is rebuked in
Golding (1. 548 ff.) by Apollo who
'the God of love espide / With bowe,
in hand already bent and letting
arrows go: / To whome he sayd, And
what hast thou thou wanton baby so /
With warlike weapons for to toy?'
    150-4. *a mermaid . . . music*] On the
unsolved problem of this topical
allusion, see Introduction, pp. lxvii f.
    153. *stars . . . spheres*] spheres =
orbits: cf. l. 7 n.; *Ham.*, I. v. 17. When
in 1591 Elizabeth was entertained at
Elvetham, the pageant Fairy Queen
told how 'amorous starres / Fall
nightly in my lap' (Nichol, II. 21).
Cf. *Lucr.* l. 1525.
    154. *To . . . music*] So in Seneca's
Medea, l. 769, the enchantress has
made the constellation Hyades fall
by her incantations ('cantibus', also
meaning 'by songs'). Another borrow-
ing from the same passage is noted at
l. 107 above; and a famous one is at
Tp., v. i. 41 ff. (Prospero's 'rough

magic'). 'Sea-maid', mermaid; cf.
Marlowe, *Hero and Leander*, I. 105
(for echoes of ll. 107 f., 111, see above,
l. 103 n.).
    155. *but . . . not*] The mythology to
be created about Elizabeth is thus
placed 'on a level more sublime and
occult than that about the mermaid'
(Barber, p. 148).
    158, 163-4.] For the compliment
to Elizabeth, and Lyly on the same
topic, see Introduction, p. cii.
    158. *vestal*] vowed to virginity, like
the Vestal Virgins, Roman priestesses
of Vesta.
    159. *lous'd*] 'th'Archers' term, who
is not said to finish the feate of his
shot before he give the loose, and
deliver his arrow from his bow'
(Puttenham, *Arte of Poesie*, 1589, p.
145, quoted Dyce).
    smartly] Cuningham refers us to
Rushton, *Shakespeare an Archer*, 1897,
p. 47.
    163-4.] For thoughts free of concern
with love, in a devotee of the moon-
goddess, cf. Golding, I. 568 ff., on
Daphne (Peneis): 'unwedded Phoebe

In maiden meditation, fancy-free.
Yet mark'd I where the bolt of Cupid fell: 165
It fell upon a little western flower,
Before milk-white, now purple with love's wound:
And maidens call it 'love-in-idleness'.
Fetch me that flower; the herb I show'd thee once.
The juice of it, on sleeping eyelids laid,   170
Will make or man or woman madly dote
Upon the next live creature that it sees.
Fetch me this herb, and be thou here again
Ere the leviathan can swim a league.

Puck.   I'll put a girdle round about the earth   175
         In forty minutes.   [*Exit.*]

Obe.   Having once this juice,

175-6.] *As Pope; one line Qq,F.*   175. round about] *Q1; about Q2,F.*
176. S.D.] *F2; not in Qq,F.*

---

doth she haunt and follow as her guide. / And as for *Hymen* or for love, and wedlocke often sought / She tooke no care, they were the furthest end of all her thought'. Cf. also Emilye's prayer to Diana, Chaucer, *Knight's Tale*, 2304 ff., and *Rom.*, I. ii. 206-9: with 'Dian's wit', Rosaline 'lives unharm'd' of 'Cupid's arrow'.

164, 168.] Immunity from Cupid's bow, and idleness giving scope to his power, are juxtaposed in Shakespeare's favourite *Boke of the Gouernour*, (I. xxvi. 108), where Sir Thomas Elyot cites 'Ovidius the poet': 'If thou flee Idlenesse, Cupid hath no myghte / His bow lyeth broken, his fire [cf. l. 161] hath no lyghte'.

165. *bolt*] arrow (not here a quarrel, the blunt square-headed kind).

167.] The metamorphosis is transferred from the once-white mulberry in Ovid, stained 'darke purple' by Pyramus' blood: below, p. 151, at n. 206 (so Joseph Hunter, quoted Furness). Cf. the purple violet in *Sonn.*, xcix. 1, 3 ff.

168. '*love-in-idleness*'] 'called . . . in English Pances [*sc.* Pansies] *Love in idleness* and *Hartes ease*' (Lyte,

Dodoens, 1578, quoted *OED*: viola tricolor). See further, H. N. Ellacombe, *Plant Lore . . . of Shakespeare*, p. 151 (Furness).

169-72.] That the effects of Felicia's magic in Montemayor's *Diana* helped to suggest those of the love-juice is well-recognized. It directs love; but not to the next creature seen: that idea Shakespeare owes to Lyly's *Euphues and his England*. On both sources, see Introduction, p. lxxxi.

170-2.] a variant of the traditional vulnerability to love on the instant through the eye: for the tradition (familiar in 'love at first sight') see C. S. Lewis, *The Allegory of Love*, pp. 128 f. Cf. Chaucer's Palamon, (below, p. 130, at n. 13), and *Mer.V.*, III. ii. 63-9, characterizing 'fancy'.

174. *leviathan*] Cf. Psalms, civ. 26: 'There go the ships, and there is that Leviathan'; and Job, xli, especially 31 f., suggestive of speed: 'He maketh the deep to boil like a pot; . . . He maketh a path to shine after him, one would think the deep to be hoary.' The Bishops' and Genevan Bibles identify him as the whale (Noble, *Shakespeare's Biblical Knowledge*, p. 274).

I'll watch Titania when she is asleep,
And drop the liquor of it in her eyes:
The next thing then she waking looks upon
(Be it on lion, bear, or wolf, or bull,   180
On meddling monkey, or on busy ape)
She shall pursue it with the soul of love.
And ere I take this charm from off her sight
(As I can take it with another herb)
I'll make her render up her page to me.   185
But who comes here? I am invisible;
And I will overhear their conference.

    Enter DEMETRIUS, HELENA *following him.*

Dem. I love thee not, therefore pursue me not.
  Where is Lysander and fair Hermia?
  The one I'll slay, the other slayeth me.   190
  Thou told'st me they were stol'n unto this wood;
  And here am I, and wood within this wood
  Because I cannot meet my Hermia.
  Hence, get thee gone, and follow me no more.
Hel. You draw me, you hard-hearted adamant—   195
  But yet you draw not iron, for my heart

177. when] *Q1,F*; whence *Q2*.   179. then] *Q1*; when *Q2,F*; which *Rowe*.
183. from off] *Q1*; off from *Q2,F*.   190. slay . . . slayeth] *Theobald, conj.*
Thirlby; stay . . . stayeth *Qq,F*.   191. unto] *Qq*; into *F*.   194. thee] *Q1*
(the), *Q2,F*.

175. *girdle . . . earth*] Among
Whitney's *Emblems*, 1586, one on
Drake's circumnavigation depicts the
globe encircled by a girdle, of which
one end is fastened to the prow of the
Golden Hind, the other held in the
hand of God (H. Green, *Shakespeare
and the Emblem Writers*, p. 413; quoted
Furness).

182. *soul*] animating principle; cf.
1H4, IV. i. 50, *OED*'s earliest instance.

184. *another herb*] See IV. i. 70–3
and n.

186. *I am invisible*] He may fold
about him a cloak like the 'robe for to
goo invisibell' in Henslowe's list of
props and costumes belonging to the
Admiral's Men (*Diary*, ed. R. A.
Foakes and R. T. Rickert, pp. 319 ff.);

cf. Greg, p. 123, comparing S.D.s for
Prospero and Ariel 'invisible'.

190. *slay . . . slayeth*] I: t misreading
in Q1.

192. *and wood*] mad: frantic with
anger.

195.] Throughout the following
episode, Helena's self-abandonment
in obsessive love owes a good deal to
Phaedra's in *Hippolytus*. Here she
shares with her the sense of not being
her own mistress (below, p. 141, at
n. 115).

adamant] (1) loadstone (magnet);
(2) metal of supreme hardness: for
the confluence of meanings see *OED*
2, quoting *MND*.

196. *draw . . . iron*] Susceptible to
magnetism, her heart is not ironhard.

    Is true as steel. Leave you your power to draw,
    And I shall have no power to follow you.
Dem. Do I entice you? Do I speak you fair?
    Or rather do I not in plainest truth   200
    Tell you I do not, nor I cannot love you?
Hel. And even for that do I love you the more.
    I am your spaniel; and, Demetrius,
    The more you beat me, I will fawn on you.
    Use me but as your spaniel, spurn me, strike me,   205
    Neglect me, lose me; only give me leave,
    Unworthy as I am, to follow you.
    What worser place can I beg in your love—
    And yet a place of high respect with me—
    Than to be used as you use your dog?   210
Dem. Tempt not too much the hatred of my spirit;
    For I am sick when I do look on thee.
Hel. And I am sick when I look not on you.
Dem. You do impeach your modesty too much

201. not, nor] *F*; not, not *Qq.*   202. you] *Q1*; thee *Q2,F.*   210. use] *Qq*; doe *F*; do use *Var. '21.*

197. *true as steel*] proverbial (Tilley, S840); not to be discounted as cliché here, though in *Troil.*, III. ii. 172, quoted as 'tir'd with iteration'.

197–8. *Leave . . . follow you*] Cf. Lyly, *Euphues and his England* (*Works*, II. 167 f.): 'I cannot think you will say that the virtue attractive is in the yron which is drawn by force, but in the Adamant that searcheth it by force'.

203–4.] proverbial (Tilley, S705); verbally close to Lyly, *Euphues*, 1578 (I. 249. 7): 'Wilt thou resemble the kinde Spaniell, which the more he is beaten the fonder he is?' With a reversal of sex, Helena's comparison illustrates Lyly's in *Euphues and His England*, 1580 (II. 155): 'The Spaniel that fawneth when he is beaten, will never forsake his master, the man that doateth when he is disdained will never forgoe his mistresse'. Cf. *Gent.*, IV. ii. 14, and on Shakespeare and fawning dogs, Spurgeon, pp. 195–8, but also J. L. Jackson, *Sh.Q.* (1950), pp. 260 ff.

204, 207.] So Phaedra grovels before Hippolytus, and declares she will follow him at all hazards (below, p. 141, at nn. 115–17).

211.] Hippolytus is unlikely to give up his hatred of Phaedra, the Nurse warns her (below, p. 141 and n. 113).

212. *sick*] nauseated.

214.] Cf. *Gent.*, I. vii. 61, and its source, *Diana*. Julia, planning to follow Proteus in men's clothes, fears 'so unstaid a journey' will make her 'scandaliz'd' (at V. iv. 103–8 she reproaches him for her excusable immodesty, a 'lesser blot' than his desertion). Felismena similarly follows Don Felix: 'love blinding my eies and minde with an inconsiderate regard of mine owne estate and condition, I went . . . out of my dear reputation (which (I thinke) I shall never recover againe') (Kennedy, p. 87).

impeach] call in question: *OED*'s earliest instance.

> To leave the city and commit yourself   215
> Into the hands of one that loves you not,
> To trust the opportunity of night
> And the ill counsel of a desert place
> With the rich worth of your virginity.
>
> *Hel.* Your virtue is my privilege: for that   220
> It is not night when I do see your face,
> Therefore I think I am not in the night;
> Nor doth this wood lack worlds of company,
> For you, in my respect, are all the world;
> Then how can it be said I am alone,   225
> When all the world is here to look on me?
>
> *Dem.* I'll run from thee and hide me in the brakes,
> And leave thee to the mercy of wild beasts.
>
> *Hel.* The wildest hath not such a heart as you.
> Run when you will; the story shall be chang'd: 230
> Apollo flies, and Daphne holds the chase;
> The dove pursues the griffin, the mild hind

220. privilege: for that] *Qq,F;* privilege. For that *Sisson;* privilege for that. *Var.* '78, conj. *Tyrwhitt;* privilege for that: *N.C.S.*   221. face,] *Rowe* (face); face. *Qq,F.*

218. *desert place*] In pursuit of Hippolytus, Phaedra tells him, she will brave the wilds (below, p. 141, at n. 116).

220–6.] From the premise 'Your virtue is my privilege', Helena's argument shows that by the 'virtue' which privileges or exempts her from what Demetrius has threatened, she means the especial quality, like that of a herb or precious stone (cf. *Rom.,* II. iii. 13–16), which is his. It is two-fold: 'for that' (= because) (1) by the light of his countenance he has the virtue of banishing the night, the night presents no risk to her virginity; nor does the 'desert place', since (2) he populates it, having the virtue of being (for her) 'all the world'. As Cuningham observes, she rebuts his several reproaches, in reverse order.

220. *privilege: for that*] From the meaning of 'virtue' and its place in the argument as explained in the previous n., it follows that Q1's

punctuation is right. Emenders take 'virtue' as aversion from (sexual) wrongdoing.

224. *in my respect*] in my eyes.

227–30.] Cf. the Nurse's warning that Hippolytus will 'runne away' (Studley's tr.), and Phaedra's retort (below, p. 141, at nn. 114, 119).

231. *Daphne*] the nymph who, fleeing from Apollo's importunities, was metamorphosed into the laurel-tree: Ovid, *Met.,* 1. 584 ff., Golding, 1. 569–700.

232. *griffin*] a fabulous beast, 'the body upward as an Eagle, And benethe as a Lyoune' (part of the account in *Mandeville's Travels,* ed. P. Hamelius, E.E.T.S., o.s. 153, 1. 178 f.). In *Huon* (II. 425), a source for *MND,* Huon slays a griffin which has carried him off (Craig, quoted Cuningham, who refers us to Phipson, *Animal Lore of Shakespeare's Time,* 1883, p. 460).

hind] female deer: especially, doe of the red deer.

Makes speed to catch the tiger—bootless speed,
When cowardice pursues and valour flies!

Dem. I will not stay thy questions; let me go,   235
Or if thou follow me, do not believe
But I shall do thee mischief in the wood.

Hel. Ay, in the temple, in the town, the field,
You do me mischief. Fie, Demetrius!
Your wrongs do set a scandal on my sex.   240
We cannot fight for love, as men may do;
We should be woo'd, and were not made to woo.

                                                        [Exit Demetrius.]

I'll follow thee, and make a heaven of hell,
To die upon the hand I love so well.   *Exit.*

Obe. Fare thee well, nymph; ere he do leave this grove   245
Thou shalt fly him, and he shall seek thy love.

Enter PUCK.

Hast thou the flower there? Welcome, wanderer.

Puck. Ay, there it is.

Obe.   I pray thee give it me.
I know a bank where the wild thyme blows,
Where oxlips and the nodding violet grows,   250
Quite over-canopied with luscious woodbine,
With sweet musk-roses, and with eglantine.
There sleeps Titania sometime of the night,
Lull'd in these flowers with dances and delight;
And there the snake throws her enamell'd skin,   255

---

238. the field] *Q1;* and field *Q2,F.*   242 S.D.] *After Capell (Demetrius breaks
from her, and Exit.); not in Qq,F; Exeunt./Rowe (following 244).*   243. I'll]
Qq; I *F.* 244.   S.D.] *Q2,F; not in Q1.*   246. S.D.] *Qq,F (following 247).*

243–4.] Phaedra's sentiment when
Hippolytus draws sword upon her
(below, p. 141, at n. 118); a scene
Shakespeare recalled in *R3*, I. ii. 174
ff.

245–6, 260–6.] For Oberon's
benevolent intervention cf. *Huon*
(below, p. 146, at n. 156): see
Introduction, pp. lxix f., lxxv f.

250. *oxlips*] 'the small . . . white
Mulleyn' (Lyte, *Niewe Herball*, 1578,
quoted Furness): it unites features of

cowslip and primrose (*OED*).

251. *woodbine*] honeysuckle; but cf.
IV. i. 41–2 n.

252. *musk-roses*] large, rambling
white roses, so called from their
fragrance (*OED*).

255. *throws*] casts: *OED*'s earliest
instance, v¹22.

enamell'd] For this figurative use
cf. *Gent.*, II. vii. 28, *OED*'s earliest
instance.

Weed wide enough to wrap a fairy in;
And with the juice of this I'll streak her eyes,
And make her full of hateful fantasies.
Take thou some of it, and seek through this grove:
A sweet Athenian lady is in love   260
With a disdainful youth; anoint his eyes;
But do it when the next thing he espies
May be the lady. Thou shalt know the man
By the Athenian garments he hath on.
Effect it with some care, that he may prove   265
More fond on her than she upon her love:
And look thou meet me ere the first cock crow.

Puck. Fear not, my lord, your servant shall do so.   *Exeunt.*

[SCENE II]

Enter TITANIA, *Queen of Fairies, with her* Train.

Tita. Come, now a roundel and a fairy song;
Then for the third part of a minute, hence:
Some to kill cankers in the musk-rose buds;
Some war with reremice for their leathern wings,

268. S.D.] *Qq; Exit. F.*

Scene II

SCENE II] *Capell; not in Qq,F.*   [*Location*] Another Part of the Wood. *Capell; not in Qq,F.*   S.D. *Enter Titania, Queen . . . Train.*] *Q1; Enter Queene . . . train. Q2,F.*

256. *Weed*] garment: the word survived in 'widow's weeds'.

257. *streak*] smear.

258. *fantasies*] figments of imagination.

266. *fond on*] enamoured of, with compulsive but not (as often) foolish passion. Viola says of Orsino's love for Olivia and her own for him: 'My master loves her dearly, / And I, poor monster, fond as much on him', *Tw.N.*, II. ii. 32 f.).

267. *ere . . . crow*] See III. ii. 388 n.

Scene II

1. *roundel*] round dance; cf. II. i. 140 n., and ll. 9–23 below.

2. *third . . . minute*] 'This quaint subdivision of time exactly suits the character of the speaker and her diminutive world' (Halliwell).

3. *cankers*] 'canker-worms': caterpillars or other grubs.

4. *reremice*] bats: 'And we in English language . . . Reremice call the same' (Golding, IV. 513).

To make my small elves coats; and some keep back   5
The clamorous owl, that nightly hoots and wonders
At our quaint spirits. Sing me now asleep;
Then to your offices, and let me rest.

The Fairies sing.

First Fairy. *You spotted snakes with double tongue,*
            Thorny hedgehogs, be not seen;   10
            Newts and blind-worms, do no wrong,
            Come not near our fairy queen.
Chorus.   *Philomel, with melody,*
            Sing in our sweet lullaby;
            Lulla, lulla, lullaby; lulla, lulla, lullaby;   15
            Never harm, nor spell, nor charm,
            Come our lovely lady nigh;
            So goodnight, with lullaby.
First Fairy. *Weaving spiders, come not here;*

8. S.D. *The . . . sing.] Qq,F (Fairies sing).*   9. *First Fairy.] Capell; not in Qq F.*
13. *Chorus.] Capell; not in Qq,F.*   14. *our] Qq; your/ F.*   19. *First Fairy.]*
Qq (1. Fai./subst.); 2. Fairy. F.

6. *clamorous owl*] Cf. *Mac.*, II. iii.
60 f. (Cuningham).

nightly] either 'every night' (*LLL*,
v. ii. 916: but that was in winter) or
'at night' (*Rom.*, IV. i. 81).

7. *quaint*] dainty, fine, spruce, brisk
are among Cotgrave's synonyms
(translating 'coint').

Sing . . . asleep] She lies down, no
doubt on a moss bank such as Henslowe lists among the stage-properties
of the Admiral's Men. If it were set
in a discovery-space, Oberon could
draw its curtain at his exit (l. 33) to
hide it: but probably, with the action
continuing unbroken till she awakens
at Bottom's song (III. i. 124), the boy
acting Titania lies 'asleep' through
some 300 lines (Wells). In the production reflected by the F S.D.s, the
lovers so lie for 160 lines and an Act
interval (III. ii. 463 S.D. n.).

8. *to . . . offices*] omitting, as often,
the vb of motion; cf. modern Ulster:
'I want out'.

9–23.] The song is divided as Capell
makes clear. For the roundel to be

danced to the chorus would fulfil
Titania's commands in l. 1 (Furness).

9.] Cf., in reverse, the Pages' song
to awake Sir Tophas in Lyly, *Endimion*, III. iii. 120, 122 f. 'Let Adders hiss
in's eare, / Else Eare-wigs wriggle
there'.

double] forked.

11. *Newts . . . blind-worms*] Both
are harmless (blind-worm = slow-
worm, a non-poisonous snake): but
Topsell (1608), attributing venom to
both, gives the belief 'not only of the
common folk, but of the naturalists
of the time' (Furness). Both contribute 'poison'd entrails' to the
witches' cauldron in *Mac.*, IV. i. 14,
16.

13. *Philomel*] the nightingale (into
which violated, tongue-cut Philomela,
victim of her sister Progne's husband
Tereus, was metamorphosed: Ovid,
Met., VI. 440–668, Golding, VI. 542
ff.).

19. *spiders*] among 'creeping,
venom'd' things in *R3*, I. ii. 19. No
English spider has venom able to

>   *Hence, you long-legg'd spinners, hence!* 20
>   *Beetles black, approach not near;*
>   *Worm nor snail, do no offence.*
> *Chorus.*   *Philomel, with melody, &c.*   *Titania sleeps.*
> *Second Fairy.* Hence, away! Now all is well;
>   One aloof stand sentinel.   [*Exeunt Fairies.*] 25

Enter OBERON [*, and squeezes the juice on Titania's eyelids*].

Obe.   What thou seest when thou dost wake,
>   Do it for thy true love take;
>   Love and languish for his sake.
>   Be it ounce, or cat, or bear,
>   Pard, or boar with bristled hair,   30
>   In thy eye that shall appear
>   When thou wak'st, it is thy dear.
>   Wake when some vile thing is near.   [*Exit.*]

Enter LYSANDER *and* HERMIA.

Lys. Fair love, you faint with wand'ring in the wood,

20. *spinners*] *Q1,F; Spinders Q2.*   23. *Chorus.*] *Capell; not in Qq,F.*
23. S.D.] *F (She sleepes./following 25); not in Qq.*   23–4. *with melody, &c./. . .
Hence . . . well;*] *As Capell; both lines roman, Qq; both italic, F.*   24. *Second
Fairy.*] *Qq; (2. Fai./subst.); 1. Fairy. F.*   25. *Exeunt Fairies.*] *Rowe; not in
Qq,F.*   S.D. *Enter . . . eyelids.*] *After Capell (Enter Oberon to Tit. squeezing
the flower upon her eyelids.); Enter Oberon. Qq,F.*   33. *Exit.*] *Rowe (Exit Oberon);
not in Qq,F.*   34. *wood*] *Q1; woods Q2,F.*

harm a man. Topsell conceded that
some 'neyther doe nor can doe much
harme': though 'All spyders are
venomous, . . . yet some more, and
some lesse' (Furness).

20. long-legg'd spinners] most likely
a second apostrophe to the 'Weaving
spiders'; cf. Cotgrave: 'Araigne: A
spider, a spinner', and Latimer in
Foxe, using 'spinner' in the proverbial
antithesis of spider and bee (Cuningham). In 'long spinner's legs' (*Rom.*,
I. iv. 60, the Queen Mab speech) and
here, Cairncross argued (*N. & Q.*,
April 1975) for 'spinner' as 'crane-
fly, daddy-long-legs', still current in
Scotland. Conceding that its legs
suit Mab's wheel-spokes better than
spiders' do, and that they and the
'spider's webs' (l. 58) would belong

more satisfactorily to different creatures, in *MND* the association of
spinning and weaving seems to point
to *the* spinning-and-weaving species.
Whichever Shakespeare had in mind,
however, can one suppose it was not
the same in both places?

22. offence] harm; cf. *Caes.*, IV.
iii. 199.

25.] One has seen the sentinel
kidnapped by attendants upon Oberon. Wells, who notes this as sometimes
stage-practice, hazards the suggestion
that in Elizabethan performance
perhaps he was stationed 'above'.

29. *ounce*] lynx.

34–5.] In *Huon* (below, p. 145, at
n. 149) all who attempt the route
through Oberon's wood are bound to
lose themselves.

And, to speak troth, I have forgot our way.   35
We'll rest us, Hermia, if you think it good,
And tarry for the comfort of the day.

Her. Be it so, Lysander: find you out a bed,
For I upon this bank will rest my head.

Lys. One turf shall serve as pillow for us both;   40
One heart, one bed, two bosoms, and one troth.

Her. Nay, good Lysander; for my sake, my dear,
Lie further off yet; do not lie so near.

Lys. O take the sense, sweet, of my innocence!
Love takes the meaning in love's conference.   45
I mean that my heart unto yours is knit,
So that but one heart we can make of it:
Two bosoms interchained with an oath,
So then, two bosoms and a single troth.
Then by your side no bed-room me deny;   50
For lying so, Hermia, I do not lie.

Her. Lysander riddles very prettily.
Now much beshrew my manners and my pride,
If Hermia meant to say Lysander lied!
But, gentle friend, for love and courtesy,   55
Lie further off, in human modesty;
Such separation as may well be said
Becomes a virtuous bachelor and a maid,
So far be distant; and good night, sweet friend:
Thy love ne'er alter till thy sweet life end!   60

37–8. comfort . . . / . . . Be it] *Q2,F.* comfor . . . / . . . Bet it *Q1*; comfort . . . /
. . . Be't *Pope.*   42. good] *Q2,F;* god *Q1.*   44–5. innocence . . . / . . . con-
ference] *Qq,F;* conference . . . / . . . innocence *Theobald, conj. Warburton.*   46.
is] *Q2,F;* it *Q1.*   47. we can] *Qq;* can you *F.*   48. interchained] *Qq;*
interchanged *F.*   56. off, . . . modesty;] *Q1* (off . . . modesty;)*;* off, . . .
modesty, *Q2,F;* off; . . . modesty, *Theobald.*

35. *troth*] truth.

38. *Be it*] Q1's intrusive 't' came
from comfor(t) in l. 37; not, *pace*
N.C.S., from a compositor who 'set
up the contracted form and then
expanded it'.

44. *take the sense*] Cf. *Rom.,* I. iv. 46:
'Take our good meaning' (Kittredge).

45.] It is love (which thinks no
evil) that lays hold of the meaning

in what is said ('conference' = conversation) between people assured of
each other's love: it is taken as it is
meant (Johnson's interpretation).

48. *interchained*] *OED*'s earliest
instance: rare.

52. *prettily*] with charming in-
genuity.

53. *much beshrew*] a proper curse
on.

Lys. Amen, amen, to that fair prayer say I;
    And then end life when I end loyalty!
    Here is my bed; sleep give thee all his rest.
Her. With half that wish the wisher's eyes be press'd.

                                                    They sleep.

                      Enter PUCK.

Puck.   Through the forest have I gone;   65
            But Athenian found I none
            On whose eyes I might approve
            This flower's force in stirring love.
            Night and silence—Who is here?
            Weeds of Athens he doth wear: 70
            This is he my master said
            Despised the Athenian maid;
            And here the maiden, sleeping sound,
            On the dank and dirty ground.
            Pretty soul, she durst not lie   75
            Near this lack-love, this kill-courtesy.
            Churl, upon thy eyes I throw
            All the power this charm doth owe:
            When thou wak'st, let love forbid
            Sleep his seat on thy eyelid.   80
            So awake when I am gone;
            For I must now to Oberon.   *Exit.*

           Enter DEMETRIUS *and* HELENA, *running.*

Hel. Stay, though thou kill me, sweet Demetrius!
Dem. I charge thee, hence, and do not haunt me thus.
Hel. O wilt thou darkling leave me? Do not so.   85

64. S.D. *They sleep.*] *F; not in Qq.*   66. found] *Q1;* find *Q2,F.*

67. *approve*] test.
76.] Some edd. from Theobald onward are troubled by the variation of
this line from the four-beat measure.
But the rhythm keeps its tripping
step: and the longer line concludes the
first part of Puck's speech, before the
spell; carries his misdirected indignation to a climax; and highlights his
mistake.

lack-love] Cf. *1H4*, II. iii. 16 (lack-
brain), *Ado*, v. i. 184 (lackbeard).
78. *owe*] own, possess.
79–80. *let . . . eyelid*] May love
thenceforward so obsess him as to
banish sleep from his eyes.
84. *haunt me*] hang about me.
85. *darkling*] in the dark.

Dem. Stay, on thy peril; I alone will go.   *Exit.*
Hel. O, I am out of breath in this fond chase!
     The more my prayer, the lesser is my grace.
     Happy is Hermia, wheresoe'er she lies,
     For she hath blessed and attractive eyes.   90
     How came her eyes so bright? Not with salt tears;
     If so, my eyes are oftener wash'd than hers.
     No, no; I am as ugly as a bear,
     For beasts that meet me run away for fear:
     Therefore no marvel though Demetrius   95
     Do, as a monster, fly my presence thus.
     What wicked and dissembling glass of mine
     Made me compare with Hermia's sphery eyne?
     But who is here? Lysander, on the ground?
     Dead, or asleep? I see no blood, no wound.   100
     Lysander, if you live, good sir, awake!
Lys. [*Waking.*] And run through fire I will for thy sweet sake!
     Transparent Helena! Nature shows art,
     That through thy bosom makes me see thy heart.
     Where is Demetrius? O how fit a word   105
     Is that vile name to perish on my sword!
Hel. Do not say so, Lysander, say not so.
     What though he love your Hermia? Lord, what though?

86. S.D.] *F* (*Exit Demetrius.*); *not in Qq.*   102. S.D.] *Rowe; not in Qq,F.*
103. Nature shows] *Qq;* Nature her showes *F;* Nature here showes *F2;*
Nature shows her *Var. '21, conj. Malone.*

87. *fond*] foolish; with the overtone
'foolishly *loving*'. This, suggested by
W. A. Wright, is supported by *Tw.N.*,
II. ii. 32 f.: quoted above, II. i. 266 n.
88. *the . . . grace*] 'the less favour do
I win' (Kittredge).
95–6. *no . . . Do*] no wonder
Demetrius should.
96. *as*] as if I were.
98. *compare*] vie; cf. Spenser, *Faerie
Queene*, II. v. 29: 'Art, stryving to
compare / With Nature' (*OED, vb*
46).
     sphery] native to the spheres, like
the stars they are.
     eyne] See I. i. 242 n.
102.] In abruptness, the exclama-

tion resembles Palamon's when he
falls in love at sight: Chaucer, below
p. 130, at n. 11.
     103. *Nature . . . art*] Ordinarily
Nature produces opaque bodies; she
exhibits art like a magician's (Wells)
in creating Helen's, so exquisitely
textured as to be transparent, enabling
Lysander (l. 104) through her bosom
to see her heart. As at ll. 110 ff.,
114 f., 117, 131, Shakespeare recalls
Diana; Arsileus sang to Belisa;
'Nature in framing thee . . . / . . .
shew'd so . . . suttle art' (Kennedy,
p. 121).
     108. *What . . . though?*] What if he
does? what matter?

Yet Hermia still loves you; then be content.
Lys. Content with Hermia? No. I do repent   110
The tedious minutes I with her have spent.
Not Hermia, but Helena I love:
Who will not change a raven for a dove?
The will of man is by his reason sway'd,
And reason says you are the worthier maid.   115
Things growing are not ripe until their season:
So I, being young, till now ripe not to reason;
And, touching now the point of human skill,
Reason becomes the marshal to my will,
And leads me to your eyes, where I o'erlook   120
Love's stories, written in love's richest book.
Hel. Wherefore was I to this keen mockery born?
When at your hands did I deserve this scorn?
Is't not enough, is't not enough, young man,
That I did never, no, nor never can   125
Deserve a sweet look from Demetrius' eye,
But you must flout my insufficiency?

112. I] *Q1;* now I *Q2,F.*

110–13.] In *Diana*, Sylvanus, transferring, thanks to the philtre, his love from Diana, exclaims: 'O faire *Selvagia*, what a great . . . folly have I committed, by imploying my thoughtes upon another, after that mine eyes did once behold thy rare beautie?' (Kennedy, p. 187).

113. *raven . . . dove*] So in *Rom.*, I. v. 46, Juliet, newly beloved by the hero, appears to him in comparison with possible rivals, 'like a snowy dove trooping with crows'. Dove and raven are contrasted again in *Tw.N.*, v. i. 129 (Craik).

114–15.] Shakespeare had not the psychologist's term 'rationalization', but he knows the propensity and laughs at it. The comedy of lovers' belief in their own wisdom amuses Theseus in Chaucer: below, p. 133, at n. 40. For love and reason in *MND* and *Diana*, see Introduction, pp. lxi, civ f., cxxxv f.

117. *being young*] Repentant Don Felix, in *Diana*, disclaims 'the yong age that I was then in' as an excuse for his desertion of Felismena for Celia (Kennedy, p. 240).

ripe . . . reason] have not (lit. 'am not') matured so as to be capable of rational judgement. 'Ripe' is a verb: Steevens compares *AYL*, II. vii. 26; 'We ripe and ripe'.

118. *touching . . . skill*] attaining the height of human discernment (Cuningham).

point] summit.

119. *marshal*] the officer who led the guest to his proper place (*OED*'s sole instance of the figurative use in this metaphor). Cf. *Mac.*, II. i. 42; and Chaucer's Host, literally fit to be a marshal in a hall.

121.] 'stories' = true histories (Kittredge). In *Rom.*, I. iii. 82 ff., Paris as lover is a 'fair volume' containing a 'golden story'. For Berowne

Good troth, you do me wrong, good sooth, you do,
In such disdainful manner me to woo.
But fare you well; perforce I must confess   130
I thought you lord of more true gentleness.
O that a lady, of one man refus'd,
Should of another therefore be abus'd!   *Exit.*
Lys. She sees not Hermia. Hermia, sleep thou there,
And never mayst thou come Lysander near!   135
For, as a surfeit of the sweetest things
The deepest loathing to the stomach brings;
Or as the heresies that men do leave
Are hated most of those they did deceive;
So thou, my surfeit and my heresy,   140
Of all be hated, but the most of me!
And, all my powers, address your love and might
To honour Helen, and to be her knight!   *Exit.*
Her. [*Starting.*] Help me, Lysander, help me! Do thy best
To pluck this crawling serpent from my breast!   145
Ay me, for pity! What a dream was here!
Lysander, look how I do quake with fear.
Methought a serpent ate my heart away,
And you sat smiling at his cruel prey.
Lysander! What, remov'd? Lysander! lord!   150
What, out of hearing? Gone? No sound, no word?
Alack, where are you? Speak, and if you hear;

139. they] *Qq;* that *F.*   144. S.D.] *Capell, not in Qq,F.*   149. you] *Qq;*
yet *F.*   151. hearing? Gone?] *Capell;* hearing, gone? *Qq,F.*

'women's eyes' are the 'books' which
'contain . . . all the world' (*LLL,*
IV. iii. 349 f.).
   128. *Good troth . . . good sooth*] really
and truly.
   131. *lord . . . gentleness*] a better
master of what becomes a true gentleman. In *Diana*, Felismena, pretending
to think Don Felix's protestations
insincere, replies: 'Consider . . . how
seldome, things, commenced under
suttletie and dissimulation, have good
successe; and that it is not the part of
a Gentleman, to meane them one
way, and speak them another'
(Kennedy, p. 86).

   136-7.] *Rom.,* II. vi. 11 f., employs
the same adage: 'The sweetest honey /
Is loathsome'. It is from Proverbs,
xxv. 27; cf. Lyly, *Campaspe* (1584),
II. ii. 73: 'There is no surfet so
dangerous as that of honney'. Both
are quoted, with Lyly, *Euphues
and his England,* II. 191, in Tilley,
H560.
   138-9. *the . . . deceive*] Heresies
renounced are detested especially by
the men formerly duped by them.
The aphorism sounds proverbial: but
is not in Tilley.
   149. *prey*] preying (upon me).

Speak, of all loves! I swoon almost with fear.
No? Then I well perceive you are not nigh.
Either death or you I'll find immediately.   *Exit.*

[*Titania remains lying asleep.*]

153. *of all loves*] by all the love that
lovers ever felt (Kittredge); cf. *Wiv.*,
II. ii. 109.

ACT III

[SCENE I]

[Titania still lying asleep.]

Enter QUINCE, BOTTOM, SNUG, FLUTE, SNOUT, *and* STARVELING.

Bot. Are we all met?

Quin. Pat, pat; and here's a marvellous convenient place for our rehearsal. This green plot shall be our stage, this hawthorn-brake our tiring-house; and we will do it in action, as we will do it before the Duke.　　5

Bot. Peter Quince!

Quin. What sayest thou, bully Bottom?

Bot. There are things in this comedy of Pyramus and Thisbe that will never please. First, Pyramus must draw a sword to kill himself; which the ladies can-　　10

ACT III

Scene 1

ACT III] F (*Actus Tertius.*); not in Qq.　　SCENE 1] Rowe; not in Qq,F.　　[Location] *The same part of the wood. (after Capell: The Same.)*; not in Qq,F.　　S.D.] Rowe (*Starveling. The Queen of Fairies lying asleep.*); *Enter the Clownes.* Qq,F.　　7. *Quin.*] Q1; *Peter.* Q2,F.

2. *Pat*] on the dot (Kittredge).

convenient] suitable (*OED*†4).

4. *hawthorn-brake*] evoked perhaps by the mere gesture towards a stage-door; or the door might be masked by a property-thicket. Cf. in a court-disguising of 1515, 'a place like a wood'; probably, thinks T. W. Craik (*The Tudor Interlude*, pp. 14, 17), a 'construction painted to look like a clump of trees': he refers also to *Common Conditions* (published 1576). Cf.

also the 'grove', in the 'staging at court' (French), 1581, plate 39, C. Walter Hodges, *The Globe Restored*; and the arbour in *Ado* or *The Spanish Tragedy.*

tiring-house] attiring-house; green room (*OED*'s earliest instance).

7. *bully*] a prefix of hearty appreciation. Vulgarly overdone, it is the Garter innkeeper's catch-phrase in *Wiv.*

52

not abide. How answer you that?

Snout. Byrlakin, a parlous fear.

Star. I believe we must leave the killing out, when all is done.

Bot. Not a whit; I have a device to make all well. Write   15
me a prologue, and let the prologue seem to say we
will do no harm with our swords, and that Pyramus
is not killed indeed; and for the more better assurance, tell them that I, Pyramus, am not Pyramus,
but Bottom the weaver. This will put them out of   20
fear.

Quin. Well, we will have such a prologue; and it shall be
written in eight and six.

Bot. No, make it two more; let it be written in eight and
eight.   25

Snout. Will not the ladies be afeard of the lion?

Star. I fear it, I promise you.

Bot. Masters, you ought to consider with yourself; to
bring in (God shield us!) a lion among ladies is a
most dreadful thing; for there is not a more fearful   30
wild-fowl than your lion living; and we ought to
look to't.

Snout. Therefore another prologue must tell he is not a
lion.

Bot. Nay, you must name his name, and half his face   35

---

12. Byrlakin] *Qq,F* (Berlakin *subst.*).   28. yourself] *Qq* (your selfe); yourselves *F.*   32. to't] *Q1* (toote); to it *Q2,F.*

20–1. *put . . . fear*] free them from
fear: cf. I am out of fear / Of death
(*1H4,* IV. i. 135 f.).

23. *eight and six*] lines of eight
syllables alternating with lines of six
(properly, of four beats and three),
the commonest ballad-metre. It should
not trouble us that the performance
in v. i. does not tally with the plans
and the rehearsal, either in the metre
of the prologue, or in the *dramatis
personae* (I. ii. 56–9), or in the dialogue
tried over at ll. 78–98 below, which
finds no place in it: see I. ii. 59 n.

29. *lion among ladies*] alluding,

probably, to the plan at a royal
christening in 1594 at the Scottish
court to have a chariot drawn in by a
lion—given up as too frightening,
and perhaps dangerous, see Introduction, p. xxxiv.

30–1. *fearful wild-fowl*] In *Huon,* the
griffin, half lion, half eagle (above II.
i. 232 n.), is 'a crewell fowle', 'ferful
. . . to beholde' (Cuningham).

35. *name his name*] The story to
which Malone thought this might
allude, of a man who, at a water-
spectacle for Queen Elizabeth, while
impersonating Arion on a dolphin's

must be seen through the lion's neck; and he himself must speak through, saying thus, or to the same
defect: 'Ladies,' or 'Fair ladies, I would wish you,'
or 'I would request you,' or 'I would entreat you,
not to fear, not to tremble: my life for yours! If you   40
think I come hither as a lion, it were pity of my life.
No, I am no such thing; I am a man, as other men
are': and there, indeed, let him name his name, and
tell them plainly he is Snug the joiner.

Quin. Well, it shall be so. But there is two hard things: 45
that is, to bring the moonlight into a chamber; for
you know, Pyramus and Thisbe meet by moonlight.

Snout. Doth the moon shine that night we play our play?

Bot. A calendar, a calendar! Look in the almanac; find
out moonshine, find out moonshine!   50

Quin. Yes, it doth shine that night.

Bot. Why, then may you leave a casement of the great
chamber window, where we play, open; and the
moon may shine in at the casement.

Quin. Ay; or else one must come in with a bush of thorns   55
and a lantern, and say he comes to disfigure or to

---

44. them] *Qq;* him *F.*   48. *Snout.*] *F2; Sn. Qq,F.*   50. moonshine!] *Qq*
(*subst.*); Moonshine.|*Enter Pucke.*|*F.*   52. *Bot.*] *Q2,F; Cet. Q1.*

---

back announced himself as 'honest
Har. Goldingham', rests on the
dubious authority of a jest book,
much after Elizabeth's time (BM.
MS. Harl. 6395: see fol. 36b),
and sounds reminiscent of *MND*
itself.

38. *defect*] Bottom means 'effect'—
Polonius plays on these words (*Ham.,*
II. ii. 101–3).

47. *Pyramus . . . moonlight*] Cf.
Golding, below, p. 151, at n. 202.

48. Snout] *Sn.* (Q1) has by some
editors been expanded *Snug,* because
otherwise, alone of the mechanicals,
he is mute in the scene (Flute, silent
in the discussion, speaks as Thisbe).
But the bibliographical facts strongly
favour *Snout.* The ambiguous abbreviation is not the author's, but the
compositor's, who resorts to it to get

the speech into the line, and into the
page, the line being the final one. On
the same page, ll. 12, 26, he set *Snout*
in full; at l. 33, to get the speech into
the line, he used the unambiguous *Sno.*
This, for the same reason, he used
again at l. 61. After l. 108 S.D.,
'*Enter* Snowte', he used *Sn.,* which
there can only mean *Snout* (N.C.S.).
If at l. 48 Shakespeare wrote *Snug,*
that would likewise have been
abbreviated *Sn.,* but the supposition
is gratuitous. The presumption is that,
each time, we have the compositor's
treatment of the same speech-prefix,
and that if he had had room for
another letter, *Sn.* would have been
Sno.

55. *bush of thorns*] See v. i. 134,
below.

56. *disfigure*] Quince means 'figure'.

present the person of Moonshine. Then there is
another thing: we must have a wall in the great
chamber; for Pyramus and Thisbe, says the story,
did talk through the chink of a wall.   60

Snout. You can never bring in a wall. What say you,
Bottom?

Bot. Some man or other must present Wall; and let him
have some plaster, or some loam, or some rough-
cast about him, to signify wall; and let him hold his   65
fingers thus, and through that cranny shall Pyramus
and Thisbe whisper.

Quin. If that may be, then all is well. Come sit down,
every mother's son, and rehearse your parts. Pyramus, you begin: when you have spoken your speech,   70
enter into that brake; and so every one according to
his cue.

Enter PUCK [*behind*].

Puck. What hempen homespuns have we swaggering here,
So near the cradle of the Fairy Queen?
What, a play toward? I'll be an auditor;   75
An actor too perhaps, if I see cause.

Quin. Speak, Pyramus; Thisbe, stand forth.

61. *Snout.*] *Q1 (Sno.); Sn. Q2,F.*   65. and] *Dyce, conj. Collier MS.; or Qq,F.*
72. S.D. *Enter Puck*] *After Qq,F (Robin), Rowe.   behind*] *Theobald; not in Qq,F.*
76. too] *Q1 (to), Q2,F.*

57. *present*] personate; cf. *LLL,*
v. i. 120–130.
  61. *You . . . wall*] 'The comedy . . .
depends . . . upon the artisans'
fantastic circumvention of what they
ought to have been able to do'; the
'action of Thomas Garter's *Susanna*',
1578, 'is intelligible only if we imagine
an acting area bisected by a partition
which runs from the front to the back.
This is the orchard wall' (Craik, pp.
18, 17.). Probably therefore the
orchard wall in *Rom.*, II. i was a
structure on stage.
  65. *and let*] Q1 assimilates 'and' to
the preceding 'or's'.
  69. *every . . . son*] Cf. I. ii. 73 and n.

73.] 'What have we here?' is
Robin's phrase in Scot, *Witchcraft,*
below, p. 147, at n. 161. 'Hemton',
his next word, may have suggested
'hempen'.
  hempen homespuns] rustics, clad in
homespun cloth made of hemp.
  74. *cradle*] place of repose: *OED's*
earliest instance, *sb.* 4, of this poetical
use.
  75–6.]Cf. Munday, *John a Kent,* ll.
1014, 1030: 'Shrimp. Sir, yonder's
great preparations for a play . . .
Iohn. . . . for in the play I purpose to
make one.'
  75. *toward*] impending, in preparation.

Bot. Thisbe, the flowers of odious savours sweet—
Quin. '*Odorous*'! '*odorous*'!
Bot.   Odorous savours sweet;
    So hath thy breath, my dearest Thisbe dear.   80
    But hark, a voice! Stay thou but here awhile,
    And by and by I will to thee appear.   *Exit.*
Puck. A stranger Pyramus than e'er played here!   [*Exit.*]
Flu. Must I speak now?
Quin. Ay, marry, must you; for you must understand   85
    he goes but to see a noise that he heard, and is to
    come again.
Flu. Most radiant Pyramus, most lily-white of hue,
    Of colour like the red rose on triumphant briar,
    Most brisky juvenal, and eke most lovely Jew,   90
    As true as truest horse that yet would never tire;
    I'll meet thee, Pyramus, at Ninny's tomb.

---

78. *Bot.*] *Camb.; Pir./Qq,F.*   *flowers . . . savours*] *Qq,F;* flowers . . . savour's
Rowe; flower . . . savour's *Pope;* flowers . . . savour *Halliwell.*   *of*] *Qq,F;* have
conj. Collier, Collier MS.; ha' *N.C.S.*   79. 'Odorous'! 'odorous'!] *Cuningham*
(*subst.*), *conj. Collier;* Odours, odorous. *Qq;* Odours, odours, *F;* 'Odious'—
odorous. *Alexander, N.C.S.*[2] (*subst.* Odious?/*conj. M.*).   79. *Bot.*] *Camb.; Pir.*
Qq,F.   *Odorous*] *This edn, conj. Jenkins (privately);* Odours *Qq,F.*   80. *hath*]
Qq,F; that *Rowe;* doth *Rowe*[3].   83. *Puck.*] *F;* Quin. *Qq.*   *Exit.*] *Capell; not*
in Qq,F.   84. *Flu.*] *Camb.; Thys. Qq,F. (subst.).*   85. *Quin.*] *Q1; Pet. Q2,F.*
88. *Flu.*] *Camb.; Thys. Qq,F (subst.).*

78–9.] On this crux, see Appendix
ii. 2.

78. savours sweet] Scriptural 'sweet
savours': Genesis, viii. 21, 2 Corinthians, ii. 15.

79. odorous] 'a sweet smelling
savour', Ephesians, v. 2, tends to
support 'odorous' as the reading of
Quince's prompt-copy; and cf. 'odorous . . . sweet . . . buds', ii. i. 110
above.

82. by and by] in a moment.

83. Puck] Q1's wrong S.H. comes
from supposing Quince's dialogue
with Bottom continues.

90.] 'Juvenal' certainly, 'Jew' probably, are comic language for 'youth';
cf. the byplay with 'juvenal' in *LLL*,
i. ii. 8–15.

brisky] *OED*'s sole instance.

eke] here, burlesque (an idle filler-
out of the line); but, *pace* Halliwell,
not always so in Shakespeare.

91. truest . . . tire] the most un-
weariable and willing horse. According to Gervase Markham's ch. 'Of
Tyred Horses' (quoted, from his
Masterpeece, by R. David, *LLL*, iv. ii.
126 n.) a 'tired horse' is one that
'refuseth reasonable labour'. Even in
less technical usage, 'tired', 'tire' had
frequent application to horse or rider:
cf. *LLL*, ii. i. 220 f., *Err.*, iv. iii. 24,
Shr., iv. i. 1, 46, *R2*, ii. i. 36, v. v. 94,
1H4, iii. i. 154, none earlier than 1590
or later than 1597.

92. Ninny's] ninny = fool; cf.
Robert Armin, *A Nest of Ninnies*,
1608.

Quin. 'Ninus' tomb', man! Why, you must not speak that
    yet; that you answer to Pyramus. You speak all
    your part at once, cues and all.   95
    Pyramus, enter! Your cue is past; it is 'never tire'.
Flu. O—*As true as truest horse that yet would never tire.*

    Enter [PUCK, *and*] BOTTOM *with the ass-head* [*on*].

Bot. If I were fair, Thisbe, I were only thine.
Quin. O monstrous! O strange! We are haunted! Pray,
    masters! Fly, masters! Help!   100
        Exeunt Quince, Snug, Flute, Snout, and Starveling.
Puck. I'll follow you: I'll lead you about a round!
    Through bog, through bush, through brake, through
        briar;
    Sometime a horse I'll be, sometime a hound,

93. *Quin.*] *Q1; Pet. Q2,F.*   97. *Flu.*] *Camb.; Thys. Qq,F (subst.)*   97 S.D.
Enter . . . Bottom] *Theobald; Enter Bottom/F (following 106); not in Qq.   with
the ass-head*] F *(Asse head.); not in Qq.   on*] *This edn; not in Qq,F.   98. Bot.*]
Camb.; Py. Q1; Pir. Q2,F.   98. were fair,] *Qq,F; were, fair Collier, conj.
Malone; were fair, fair conj. anon. apud Camb.; were true, fair Cuningham., conj.
Hudson.   99. Quin.*] *Q1; Pet. Q2,F.   100.* S.D. *Exeunt. . . Starveling.*] *After F
(The Clownes all Exit); not in Qq.   101. Puck.*] *F; Rob. Qq.*

95–6.] An actor's written part consisted of his own speeches, with a brief
cue before each from the line it was
to follow. Alleyn's part, a long MS.
strip, as the hero of Greene's *Orlando
Furioso*, is among the Henslowe papers
and is reproduced and described in
Greg, *Dramatic Documents*, pp. 173–87.

97. S.D.] The literary sources for
setting 'an asses head on a man's
neck and shoulders' are Scot, *Witchcraft* (below, p. 148, at nn. 177–9),
and perhaps *The History of the Dam-
nable Life and Deserved Death of Dr
John Faustus*, 1592, ch. xliii: 'The
guests having sat, . . . Dr Faustus
made that everyone had an ass's head
on, with great and long ears.'
(Steevens, by whom Robin R. Reed
jr (*N. & Q.*, 1959) is unaware of
being anticipated.) For the property
ass-head, relevant folk-lore, beasts
(in *Huon*) that brayed in Oberon's
wood, and, in Scot and Apuleius,

change of the whole body from
human to ass, see Introduction, pp.
lix f., lxxxii.

98.] designed primarily for the
comic irony ('if I were fair' and the
ass-head); but also (so Malone) as a
possible reply to Thisbe, mis-
punctuated by Bottom: 'if I were
(even so supremely true as that), fair
Thisbe, I (and all my truth) would
be yours'. To these aims, the blank-
verse rhythm comes second; but with
'fair' as two syllables, the pentameter
is no worse than the alexandrine with
'fair, fair' proposed on the assumption
of inadvertent failure to repeat the
word (haplography).

101. *a round*] (1) (ironically) in a
ring-dance; (2) a way which turns in
a circle (*OED*'s earliest instance).

103–6.] For Puck in animal likeness
cf. II. i. 46; for non-human shape-
shifters as beasts, Scot, *Witchcraft*
(below, p. 148, at n. 175).

A hog, a headless bear, sometime a fire;
And neigh, and bark, and grunt, and roar, and burn, 105
Like horse, hound, hog, bear, fire, at every turn.   *Exit.*
Bot. Why do they run away? This is a knavery of them
to make me afeard.

Enter SNOUT.

Snout. O Bottom, thou art changed! What do I see on
thee?   110
Bot. What do you see? You see an ass-head of your own,
do you?   [*Exit Snout.*]

Enter QUINCE.

Quin. Bless thee, Bottom, bless thee! Thou art trans-
lated.   *Exit.*
Bot. I see their knavery: this is to make an ass of me, to 115
fright me, if they could. But I will not stir from this
place, do what they can; I will walk up and down
here, and I will sing, that they shall hear I am not
afraid.
[*Sings.*]   *The ousel cock, so black of hue,*   120

112. *Exit Snout.*] Dyce; *Exit. Capell (at 110)*; not in *Qq,F.*   112. S.D. *Quince*]
Q1; *Peter quince Q2,F (Quince)*.   113. *Quin.*] *Q1*; *Pet. Q2,F.*   118. I will]
F; will *Qq*.   120. *Sings.*] *Pope*; not in *Qq,F.*   120. *ousel*] *Qq,F (Woosell)*.

105-6.] For this rhetorical 'scheme' of. *Ham.*, III. i. 151: 'The courtier's, soldier's, scholar's eye, tongue, sword'; Spenser, *Faerie Queene*, I. xi. 28: 'Faynt, wearie, sore, emboyled, grieved, brent, / With heat, toyle, wounds, armes, smart, and inward fire'; Sidney, *Arcadia* (ed. Jean Robertson, 1973, p. 229), Philoclea's song, beginning 'Virtue (1), beauty (2) and speech (3), did strike (1), wound (2), charm (3) / My heart (1), eyes (2), ears (3), with wonder (1), love (2), delight (3)'; and *Enamoured Diana* (Kennedy, p. 401), where five verbs in l. 1, and five more in l. 3, are matched with nouns in ll. 2, 4.

109-16.] Cf. Scot, *Witchcraft* (below, pp. 148 f., at nn. 179 ('standers by'), 180, 182). Bottom's fellows, unlike those of Scot's hero, do not *call* him ass; comically, at unawares *he* supplies the designation. In Scot, the 'metamorphosis' is likewise 'of bodie but not of mind': on this, Bottom's preference for ass's provender (IV. i. 31-3), an invasion of the mind by an appetite of the changed body, is a subtle variation.

111-12.] a retort used also by Dekker and T. Heywood, no doubt (though they are writing later) from its colloquial currency; cf. *Wiv.*, I. iv. 121, Tilley, A388, F519.

113. *translated*] transformed.

118. *will sing*] Weavers were addicted to singing. Cf. *1H4*, II. iv. 130.

120. *ousel cock*] cock-blackbird: the hen's bill is not yellow. In so naming the blackbird, is Bottom (and is Shakespeare) wrongly identifying

> *With orange-tawny bill,*
> *The throstle, with his note so true,*
> *The wren with little quill—*
>> [*The singing awakens Titania.*]

Tita. What angel wakes me from my flowery bed?

Bot. [*Sings.*]   *The finch, the sparrow, and the lark,*   125
> *The plain-song cuckoo gray,*
> *Whose note full many a man doth mark,*
> *And dares not answer nay—*

for indeed, who would set his wit to so foolish a
bird? Who would give a bird the lie, though he cry   130
'cuckoo' never so?

Tita. I pray thee, gentle mortal, sing again:
> Mine ear is much enamour'd of thy note;
> So is mine eye enthralled to thy shape;
> And thy fair virtue's force perforce doth move me   135
> On the first view to say, to swear, I love thee.

Bot. Methinks, mistress, you should have little reason for
that. And yet, to say the truth, reason and love
keep little company together nowadays. The more
the pity that some honest neighbours will not make   140
them friends. Nay, I can gleek upon occasion.

Tita. Thou art as wise as thou art beautiful.

Bot. Not so neither; but if I had wit enough to get out of

---

123. *with*] *Qq*; *and F.*   S.D. *The singing awakens Titania*] *This edn; Waking/*
Rowe (at 124); not in Qq,F.   125. *Sings.*] *Theobald; not in Qq,F.*   134–6.] *As*
Q1; On . . . thee/So . . . shape./And . . . me. *Q2,F.*   135. virtue's force per-
force] *Rowe³;* vertues force (perforce) *Qq,F;* virtue, force perforce *conj. Collier.*

---

it with the ring-ousel? T. A. Coward
(*Birds of Britain*) complains of this as
a continuing confusion. I am indebted to Mrs Magdalen Pearce
for drawing my attention to this
point.

123. quill] pipe; her shrill note.

126. plain-song] with its simple
melody (term from church-music of
early type, in modes and free rhythm);
OED's earliest example of attributive
use.

129–30. *who . . . bird?*] Not to set
your wit against a fool's is proverbial:

Tilley, W547, quoting More, *Utopia*,
tr. Robinson, 1551.

131. '*cuckoo*'] supposed to be a cry
of 'cuckold', 'unpleasant to a married
ear'; cf. *LLL*, v. i. 888–92.

135. *thy fair virtue's*] of the beauteous
qualities which are yours.

138–41. *reason . . . friends*] See Introduction, pp. cxv, cxxxv f.

141. *gleek*] jest pointedly: *OED*'s
first instance of this intransitive use.

143–4. *wit . . . wood*] Tilley, W732,
implies an overtone from the proverbial 'in a wood' = befogged.

    this wood, I have enough to serve mine own turn.
Tita. Out of this wood do not desire to go: 145
    Thou shalt remain here, whether thou wilt or no.
    I am a spirit of no common rate;
    The summer still doth tend upon my state;
    And I do love thee: therefore go with me.
    I'll give thee fairies to attend on thee;   150
    And they shall fetch thee jewels from the deep,
    And sing, while thou on pressed flowers dost sleep:
    And I will purge thy mortal grossness so,
    That thou shalt like an airy spirit go.
    Peaseblossom! Cobweb! Moth! and Mustardseed!   155

Enter four Fairies:
PEASEBLOSSOM, COBWEB, MOTH, *and* MUSTARDSEED.

Peas. Ready.
Cob.   And I.
Moth.   And I.
Mus.   And I.
All.   Where shall we go?
Tita. Be kind and courteous to this gentleman;
    Hop in his walks, and gambol in his eyes;
    Feed him with apricocks and dewberries,

155. Peaseblossom! . . . Mustardseed!] *Q1 (Peaseblossom, Cobweb, Moth, and Mustard-seede?), Q2 (subst.); not in F.*   155. S.D. *Enter . . . Fairies:/Pease-blossom, . . . Mustardseed.] Enter foure Fairyes. Qq; Enter Pease-blossome, Cobweb, Moth, Mustard-seede, and four Fairies. F.*   156. Peas. . . . go?] *White; Fairies. Ready; and I, and I, and I, where shall we go? Qq,F; 1. Fair. Ready./2. Fair. And I./3. Fair. And I./4. Fair. And I. Where shall we go? Rowe.*

145–6.] Fairy power, the hero believes in *Huon* (below, p. 146, at n. 155), will never let them escape from the wood.

147. *rate*] value, estimation.

148.] Cf. Nashe's Queen Elizabeth, in *Summers Last Will and Testament*, 1600, 'On whom all seasons prosperously attend'. Shakespeare's 'tend' = attend (aphetic form).

153. *mortal grossness*] materiality as a mortal. Cf. *Mer.V.*, v. 1. 64 f. 'To bring the bodie of a man . . . into such a thin aerie nature . . . is verie impossible' (Scot, *Witchcraft*, bk v,

p. 98, on a corollary of the ass-story).

155. S.D.] Shakespeare did not include the names; F added them by a textual blunder (see Introduction, p. xxxi). We give them, not because F does, but to make the S.D. precise.

158. *in his eyes*] before him: lit. in his sight; cf *Ham.*, iv. iv. 6, *Ant.*, ii. ii. 107.

158–9.] With 'feed him' and 'in his walks', cf. Mouffet (just before his tale of Pyramus), 'Feede in her walkes' (Muir[2], p. 76): 'in his walks' = 'about him in the paths he takes'.

159. *dewberries*] normally, black-

With purple grapes, green figs, and mulberries;   160
The honey-bags steal from the humble-bees,
And for night-tapers crop their waxen thighs,
And light them at the fiery glow-worms' eyes,
To have my love to bed, and to arise;
And pluck the wings from painted butterflies   165
To fan the moonbeams from his sleeping eyes.
Nod to him, elves, and do him courtesies.

Peas. Hail, mortal!
Cob. Hail!
Moth. Hail!   170
Mus. Hail!
Bot. I cry your worships mercy, heartily. I beseech your
worship's name?
Cob. Cobweb.
Bot. I shall desire you of more acquaintance, good Mas-   175
ter Cobweb: if I cut my finger, I shall make bold
with you. Your name, honest gentleman?
Peas. Peaseblossom.
Bot. I pray you, commend me to Mistress Squash, your
mother, and to Master Peascod, your father. Good   180

168–71. *Peas.* Hail, mortal! . . . *Mus.* Hail!] *Dyce; 1. Fai.* Haile, mortall,
haile . . . *3. Fai.* Haile. *Qq,F; 1. F.* Hail mortal! . . . *4.* Hail!/*Capell.*

berries (so Lyte, *Dodoens*, 1578, VI. iv.
661) but the context has been thought
to require a cultivated fruit, like the
others. If so, the dwarf-mulberry,
strongly supported by Halliwell because 'still called . . . dewberry by
the Warwickshire peasantry', and
plentiful in lanes near Stratford, is
also ruled out. 'Gooseberries' has
found favour: Hanmer suggested
'raspberries'. See *OED*. With G. B.
Harrison and Martin Wright, I would
accept 'blackberries', with 'dwarf-
mulberries' distinctly possible.

163. *eyes*] Johnson wonders 'how
Shakespeare, who commonly derived
his knowledge of nature from his
own observation', came 'to place the
glow-worm's light in his eyes, which
is only in his tail'. Eye-like things are
often called 'eyes'; Shakespeare *might*

know quite well where the lights
shining like eyes were shining from:
actually from 'the further segments
of the abdomen' (Halliwell) in female
glow-worms.

164.] As royal paramour, Bottom
is to have the full honours of the
couchée and the levée.

175. *desire you of*] a normal usage:
Abbott, § 174; *OED* desire *vb.* 6†b.
Cf. ll. 121–2, 188 below.

176–7. *Cobweb . . . you*] A bit of
cobweb served as a homely adhesive
styptic to staunch the bleeding.

177. *honest gentleman*] my good sir;
cf. *OED* honest †1c.

179. *Squash*] Cf. 'as a squash is
before it is a peascod', *Tw.N.,* I. v.
159; viz. an unripe peascod. *MND*
is *OED*'s earliest instance.

Master Peaseblossom, I shall desire you of more
acquaintance too. Your name, I beseech you sir?

Mus. Mustardseed.

Bot. Good Master Mustardseed, I know your patience
well. That same cowardly giant-like ox-beef hath   185
devoured many a gentleman of your house: I promise you, your kindred hath made my eyes water
ere now. I desire you of more acquaintance, good
Master Mustardseed.

Tita. Come, wait upon him; lead him to my bower.   190
The moon, methinks, looks with a watery eye,
And when she weeps, weeps every little flower,
Lamenting some enforced chastity.
Tie up my love's tongue, bring him silently.   *Exeunt.*

[SCENE II]

Enter OBERON, *King of Fairies.*

Obe. I wonder if Titania be awak'd;
Then, what it was that next came in her eye,
Which she must dote on in extremity.

---

181. you of] *Qq;* of you *F.*   183. Mustardseed.] *Qq;* Mustard-seede./*Peas.*
Pease-blossome. *F.*   188. you of] *Dyce;* you *Qq,F;* your *F3.*   192. weeps,
weeps] *Q1;* weepes, weepe *Q2,F.*   194. love's] *Pope;* louers *Qq,F.*   *Exeunt*]
Rowe; Exit Qq,F.

Scene II

SCENE II] *Capell; not in Qq,F [Location] Another part of the Wood. Capell; not in Qq,F.*
S.D.] *Enter King of Pharies, solus. F; Enter King of Fairies, and Robin goodfellow. Qq.*

184. *your patience*] the patience
characteristic of the Mustardseeds
in their adversity, specified in ll.
185 f.

188. *of*] Though the construction
without 'of' is in itself possible, that
Bottom pointlessly varies his formula
is less likely than that the compositor
dropped a particle.

192.] because the moon was
thought 'the mother of dew'. 'She
printeth the vertue of her moysture

in the aire, . . . and gendreth deaw in
the utter part thereof', *Batman upon
Bartholome*, 1582, XI. 6, VIII. 29
(Kittredge).

193. *enforced*] violated by force. And
see Introduction, p. cxxix.

194.] As Bottom, Kempe would no
doubt (like many modern actors) give
the cue by 'involuntary' asinine
noises (Wells). Cf. the beasts braying
in Oberon's wood in *Huon* (below, p.
146, at n. 152).

Enter PUCK.

Here comes my messenger. How now, mad spirit?
What night-rule now about this haunted grove?   5
Puck. My mistress with a monster is in love.
Near to her close and consecrated bower,
While she was in her dull and sleeping hour,
A crew of patches, rude mechanicals,
That work for bread upon Athenian stalls,   10
Were met together to rehearse a play
Intended for great Theseus' nuptial day.
The shallowest thick-skin of that barren sort,
Who Pyramus presented in their sport,
Forsook his scene, and enter'd in a brake,   15
When I did him at this advantage take:
An ass's nole I fixed on his head.
Anon, his Thisbe must be answered,
And forth my mimic comes. When they him spy—
As wild geese that the creeping fowler eye,   20
Or russet-pated choughs, many in sort,
Rising and cawing at the gun's report,
Sever themselves, and madly sweep the sky
So, at his sight, away his fellows fly;

3. S.D.] *F; not in Qq.*   5. haunted] *Qq;* gaunted *F.*   6–7. love./Near . . .
bower,] *Rowe;* love,/Neere . . . bower, *Q2,F;* love,/Neere . . . bower. *Q1.*   19.
mimic] *F* (Mimmick); Minnick *Q1;* Minnock *Q2.*

Scene II

3. *extremity*] 'in what great ex-
tremities love has put me': *Diana*
(Kennedy, p. 82).

5. *night-rule*] affairs (or perhaps
'diversions') belonging to the night.

7. *close*] secluded.

9. *patches*] clowns, boors. On 'patch'
=fool, see IV. i. 208 n., and in
OED, T. Wilson, *Rhetoric*, 1580: a
foolishly-behaved person got called
'Patche'.

13. *thick-skin*] coarse-fibred fellow.
'Some . . . suppose creatures are
brutish more or lesse, according as
their skin is thicker or thinner'

(Holland's Pliny, quoted Furness).
barren sort] empty, unprofitable
crew.

14. *sport*] entertainment; disport
(aphetic form).

17. *nole*] head, noddle.

19. *mimic*] mime, burlesque actor;
OED's earliest instance. 'Minnick' is
a minim-misreading.

21.] not 'many different kinds' but
a 'numerous flock' of drab-headed
jackdaws: 'russet' covers a range of
neutral colours from reddish-brown
to almost black. Florio, *A World of
Wordes*, 1598, equates 'light-russet'
with 'gray', which fits the jackdaw's
poll.

And at our stamp, here o'er and o'er one falls;   25
He murder cries, and help from Athens calls.
Their sense thus weak, lost with their fears thus strong,
Made senseless things begin to do them wrong:
For briars and thorns at their apparel snatch;
Some sleeves, some hats, from yielders all things catch.
I led them on in this distracted fear,   31
And left sweet Pyramus translated there;
When in that moment, so it came to pass,
Titania wak'd, and straightway lov'd an ass.

Obe. This falls out better than I could devise.   35
But hast thou yet latch'd the Athenian's eyes
With the love-juice, as I did bid thee do?

Puck. I took him sleeping—that is finish'd too—
And the Athenian woman by his side,
That when he wak'd, of force she must be ey'd.   40

Enter DEMETRIUS *and* HERMIA.

Obe. Stand close: this is the same Athenian.
Puck. This is the woman, but not this the man.
[They stand apart.]

38. *Puck.*] *Rowe; Rob. Qq,F.*   42. *Puck.*] *Rowe; Rob. Qq,F.*   *They stand apart.*]
Collier MS.; not in Qq,F.

25. *our stamp*] That Robin had a potent stamp might be suggested by his customary exclamation when abandoning a house where he had been offended: 'Hemton hamton, here will I never more tread nor stampen' (Scot, *Witchcraft*, below, p. 147, at n. 162). By 'our stamp' he might mean 'the stamp we are both familiar with'. Or, since it launched his (magic) powers against those who fled, the stamp might seem to him like a signal given by a king, and hence he might jocularly use the royal 'our'. But Johnson's conjecture 'a stump' may be right: 'stump' could easily have been misread 'stamp'; and N.C.S. points out that the 'spurred a', found in what is believed to be Shakespeare's autograph contribution to *Sir Thomas More*, could have been mistaken for

'or', the abbreviation for 'our'. Johnson quoted the parallel in Drayton's 'Nimphidia', a poem apparently indebted to *MND*: 'Against a stubbed tree he reels, / And up went poor Hobgoblin's heels ... / A stump doth trip him in his pace, / Down fell poor Hob upon his face'. If this were derived from what Drayton heard in performance, it would be strong evidence.

30. *from . . . catch*] Everything is ready to despoil those who abandon themselves in rout and keep no hold of anything.

36. *latch'd*] moistened (*OED* leach v^2, O.E. leccan, to water; and Skeat, quoted Furness), with an overtone from 'latch' $v^1\dagger2$, capture (by the spell): 'caught' is E.K.'s gloss on 'latched', *Shepheardes Calender*, March, l. 93.

Dem. O why rebuke you him that loves you so?
    Lay breath so bitter on your bitter foe.
Her. Now I but chide, but I should use thee worse,   45
    For thou, I fear, hast given me cause to curse.
    If thou hast slain Lysander in his sleep,
    Being o'er shoes in blood, plunge in the deep,
    And kill me too.
    The sun was not so true unto the day   50
    As he to me. Would he have stol'n away
    From sleeping Hermia? I'll believe as soon
    This whole earth may be bor'd, and that the moon
    May through the centre creep, and so displease
    Her brother's noon-tide with th'Antipodes.   55
    It cannot be but thou hast murder'd him:
    So should a murderer look, so dead, so grim.
Dem. So should the murder'd look, and so should I,
    Pierc'd through the heart with your stern cruelty;
    Yet you, the murderer, look as bright, as clear,   60
    As yonder Venus in her glimmering sphere.
Her. What's this to my Lysander? Where is he?
    Ah, good Demetrius, wilt thou give him me?
Dem. I had rather give his carcase to my hounds.
Her. Out, dog! Out, cur! Thou driv'st me past the bounds
    Of maiden's patience. Hast thou slain him then?   66
    Henceforth be never number'd among men!
    O once tell true; tell true, even for my sake!

48–9. Being . . . too.] *As Rowe*[3]*; one line, Qq,F.* 58. murder'd] *Qq; murderer F.*
60. look] *Qq; looks F.*   64. I had] *Q1; I'de Q2,F (subst.)*   65. bounds]
Q1,F; bonds Q2.   68. tell true; tell true,] *Q1; tell true, Q2,F; tell true,
and F2.*

43–81.] 'Demetrius uses the respectful "you" . . . Hermia . . . the
contemptuous "thou" ' (Furness). Her
tone changes momentarily in l. 63.
    48.] Cf. the proverb 'over shoes,
over boots': waded in so far, wade in
further (Tilley, S379; see also S380).
    53. *whole*] entire and impenetrable;
cf. *Mac.*, III. iv. 21 (W. A. Wright).
    54. *centre*] earth's mid-point.
    displease] by bringing night with it
(Wells).

    55. *Antipodes*] dwellers on the
vertically opposite side of the earth.
    56. *but*] otherwise than that: *OED* 7.
    57. *dead*] like a death-dealer.
    59. *Pierc'd . . . heart*] Cf. Chaucer,
below, p. 130, at n. 12.
    61.] Venus the planet; for 'sphere',
see II. i. 7 n.
    62. *to*] to do with.
    68. *once . . . true*] tell the truth and
be done with it; 'once' = once for
all.

Durst thou have look'd upon him, being awake,
And hast thou kill'd him sleeping? O brave touch!   70
Could not a worm, an adder, do so much?
An adder did it; for with doubler tongue
Than thine, thou serpent, never adder stung!

Dem. You spend your passion on a mispris'd mood:
I am not guilty of Lysander's blood;   75
Nor is he dead, for aught that I can tell.

Her. I pray thee tell me then that he is well.

Dem. And if I could, what should I get therefor?

Her. A privilege, never to see me more.
And from thy hated presence part I so: 80
See me no more, whether he be dead or no.   *Exit.*

Dem. There is no following her in this fierce vein;
Here therefore for a while I will remain.
So sorrow's heaviness doth heavier grow
For debt that bankrupt sleep doth sorrow owe;   85
Which now in some slight measure it will pay,
If for his tender here I make some stay. *Lies down [and
sleeps]. [Oberon and Puck come forward.]*

Obe. What hast thou done? Thou hast mistaken quite,
And laid the love-juice on some true love's sight;
Of thy misprision must perforce ensue   90
Some true love turn'd, and not a false turn'd true.

---

69. have] *Qq;* a *F.*   80–1. And ... more,] *As Pope; one line, Qq,F.*   80. I so]
Pope; I *Qq,F.*   85. sleep] *Rowe;* slippe *Qq,F. (Q2,F* slip).   87. *Lies down*]
*Qq,F (Ly doune/subst.).   and sleeps.] Dyce; not in Qq,F.   Oberon . . . forward.]
After Collier*[2] *(coming forward with Puck.); not in Qq,F.*

70. *brave touch*] grand exploit (so
Johnson).
71. *worm*] serpent; cf. *Ant.,* v. ii.
242.
74. *spend*] expend; with overtone
from the hound which 'spends' (gives
tongue) inappropriately.
mispris'd] mistaken.
mood] anger; cf. *Gent.,* iv. i. 51;
Mirror for Magistrates, ed. L. B.
Campbell, p. 167 (Suffolk, l. 144).
78. *therefor*] for that: both syllables
stressed.
80. *so*] Rhyme makes Pope's
emendation certain.

81. *whether*] pronounced wh'er;
Abbott, § 466.
85. *sleep*] Q1 'slippe' may be a
pronunciation-spelling by the compositor; cf. Ship (for Sheep) Street in
inland towns.
87. Lies down] On Q1, 'Ly doune',
and other S.D.s in the imperative, see
Introduction, p. xxvii.
90. *misprision*] mistaking one thing
for another; with *LLL,* iv. iii. 96,
OED's two earliest instances.
91. *turn'd*] (1) changed; (2) faithless; cf. *Pilgr.,* vii. 16: 'she bad love
last and yet she fell a-turning'.

Puck. Then fate o'er-rules, that, one man holding troth,
        A million fail, confounding oath on oath.
Obe. About the wood go swifter than the wind,
       And Helena of Athens look thou find;   95
       All fancy-sick she is, and pale of cheer
       With sighs of love, that costs the fresh blood dear.
       By some illusion see thou bring her here;
       I'll charm his eyes against she do appear.
Puck.   I go, I go, look how I go!   100
            Swifter than arrow from the Tartar's bow.   *Exit.*
Obe. [*Squeezing the juice on Demetrius' eyelids.*]
            Flower of this purple dye,
            Hit with Cupid's archery,
            Sink in apple of his eye.
            When his love he doth espy,   105
            Let her shine as gloriously
            As the Venus of the sky.
            When thou wak'st, if she be by,
            Beg of her for remedy.

                    Enter PUCK.

Puck.   Captain of our fairy band,   110
                Helena is here at hand;

92. *Puck.*] *Rowe; Rob. Qq,F.*   99. do] *Qq;* doth *F.*   100. *Puck.*]*Rowe; Rob.*
Qq,F.   101. *Exit.*] *Q2,F; not in Q1.*   102. *Squeezing . . . eyelids.*] *After Dyce*
(*squeezes the flower on Demetrius' eyelids.*); not in Qq,F.

92–3.] If so, fate has taken charge,
so that while one man keeps faith, a
million fail and break oath after oath.
Has 'fail' two senses: 'default' and
(because of fate) 'cannot manage it'?
'To confound' was then 'to subvert
utterly'.
    94. *swifter . . . wind*] 'swift as the
wind' is proverbial: Tilley, W411.
    96.] 'fancy-sick': love-sick (cf. In-
troduction, p. cxxxiii, n. 5; 'cheer':
face, *OED*'s latest instance.
    97. *sighs . . . dear*] Each sigh was
believed to cost a drop of blood; cf.
2H6, III. ii. 60, 62; *3H6*, IV. iv. 22;
Rom., III. v. 59, 'Dry sorrow drinks
our blood'.

costs] sing., by attraction to 'love';
Abbott, § 247.
    99. *against*] ready for when (Wells).
    100.] Suited to the action and
emphasis, the line is lengthened in
effect.
    101.] an echo of Golding, x. 687:
Atalanta ran 'as swift as arrow from
a Turkye bowe'; cf. 'a Tartar's . . .
bow', *Rom.*, I. iv. 5; 'The Oriental
bow, of three ply construction, was
more powerful than the English bow',
N.C.S. citing *Shakespeare's England*,
II. 379.
    104. *apple . . . eye*] (1) pupil; (2)
seat of what he most cherishes: the
idiom still current.

> And the youth, mistook by me,
> Pleading for a lover's fee.
> Shall we their fond pageant see?
> Lord, what fools these mortals be!   115
> *Obe.*   Stand aside. The noise they make
> Will cause Demetrius to awake.
> *Puck.*   Then will two at once woo one:
> That must needs be sport alone;
> And those things do best please me   120
> That befall prepost'rously.   [*They stand aside.*]
>
> *Enter* LYSANDER *and* HELENA.
>
> *Lys.* Why should you think that I should woo in scorn?
> Scorn and derision never come in tears.
> Look when I vow, I weep; and vows so born,
> In their nativity all truth appears.   125
> How can these things in me seem scorn to you,
> Bearing the badge of faith to prove them true?
> *Hel.* You do advance your cunning more and more.
> When truth kills truth, O devilish-holy fray!

121. prepost'rously] *Q1;* preposterously *Q2,F.*   *They . . . aside.*] *Collier²; not in Qq,F.*   123. come] *Q1;* comes *Q2,F.*   129. devilish-holy] *hyphenated/Capell.*

114–15.] So comments Chaucer's Theseus on the spectacle of Palamon and Arcite: '. . . loketh, is not this a greate folie? / Who maie be a foole, but if he love?' (below, p. 133, at n. 39). Cf. Peele, *Old Wives Tale*: 'It is a wonder to see what this love will make silly fellows adventure' (ll. 259–60) continuing the sentence quoted above, I. ii. 31–4 n.).

114. *fond pageant*] foolish spectacle they present (Onions).

119. *alone*] (1) in itself; (2) alone of its kind, unrivalled; cf. *Gent.*, II. iv. 162 (*OED*).

121. *prepost'rously*] backside foremost, out of the natural course. In Shakespeare the word keeps much of its etymological meaning.

124. *Look when*] all the while (lit. whenever); see M. Eccles, 'Shakespeare's Use of "Look How" and similar Idioms', *JEGP*, xlii.

124–5. *vows . . . appears*] The simplest supposition is Abbott's, §§ 376, 417 (which Wells follows): 'vows so born' is an absolute construction, 'vows being so born'; then 'all truth appears in their nativity'. But Furness maintains (and N.C.S. accepts) that 'appears' is sing. by attraction to 'truth', and 'vows' is its grammatical subject. He paraphrases: 'vows, thus born, appear from their very nativity, to be all truth'; and he may be right.

127. *badge of faith*] denoting him servant to fidelity.

128. *advance*] carry further and increasingly exhibit; N.C.S. cites *OED* 6.

129. *truth kills truth*] The truth of your vows to one of us, Hermia or me, destroys the truth of your vows to the other.

devilish-holy] devilish because your truth to one of us is diabolically killed;

These vows are Hermia's: will you give her o'er?   130
Weigh oath with oath, and you will nothing weigh:
Your vows to her and me, put in two scales,
Will even weigh; and both as light as tales.

Lys. I had no judgement when to her I swore.

Hel. Nor none, in my mind, now you give her o'er.   135

Lys. Demetrius loves her, and he loves not you.

Dem. (*Waking.*) O Helen, goddess, nymph, perfect, divine!
To what, my love, shall I compare thine eyne?
Crystal is muddy. O how ripe in show
Thy lips, those kissing cherries, tempting grow!   140
That pure congealed white, high Taurus' snow,
Fann'd with the eastern wind, turns to a crow
When thou hold'st up thy hand. O let me kiss
This princess of pure white, this seal of bliss!

Hel. O spite! O hell! I see you all are bent   145
To set against me for your merriment.
If you were civil, and knew courtesy,
You would not do me thus much injury.
Can you not hate me, as I know you do,

---

137. *Waking.*] *F* (*Awa.*); *not in Qq.*   144. princess] *Qq,F;* pureness *Hanmer;*
impress *Staunton, conj. Collier* (*Collier MS.*).   145. all are] *Qq;* are all *F.*

---

holy because what kills it is the sanctity of your truth to the other (after Kittredge).

133. *tales*] idle rumours, tittle-tattle.

134.] Cf. III. i. 138–41 and n.

137.] At first sight of Emelye, Palamon starts, is uncertain whether she is a woman or goddess, but believes she must be Venus (below, p. 130, at nn. 11, 14).

138. *eyne*] See I. i. 242 n.

139. *ripe*] red and full.

141–2.] improving on the commonplace, a hand or 'arme whiter than driven snow' (*Diana*, Kennedy, p. 227).

141–2. *high . . . wind*] Taurus, a mountain range in Asia Minor, is mentioned twice in Seneca, *Hippolytus*

(ll. 168, 382 f.). Shakespeare needs the freezing east wind: the melting season in Seneca would not suit his comparison: 'qualiter Tauri jugis / tepido madescunt imbre percussae nives' (ll. 382 f.); tr. Studley: 'as on the toppe of Taurus hill / The watry snowes with lukewarme shoures to moisture turnd do drop.'

144. *princess . . . white*] 'i.e. of sovereign whiteness' (N.C.S.).

seal] When she gives it in troth-plight, it will set the seal on her lover's happiness.

146. *set . . . me*] set upon me.

147. *knew courtesy*] were acquainted with good manners.

148. *do . . . injury*] insult me so; cf. II. i. 147 and n.

But you must join in souls to mock me too?   150
If you were men, as men you are in show,
You would not use a gentle lady so:
To vow, and swear, and superpraise my parts,
When I am sure you hate me with your hearts.
You both are rivals, and love Hermia;   155
And now both rivals to mock Helena.
A trim exploit, a manly enterprise,
To conjure tears up in a poor maid's eyes
With your derision! None of noble sort
Would so offend a virgin, and extort   160
A poor soul's patience, all to make you sport.
Lys. You are unkind, Demetrius; be not so,
For you love Hermia; this you know I know:
And here, with all good will, with all my heart,
In Hermia's love I yield you up my part;   165
And yours of Helena to me bequeath,
Whom I do love, and will do till my death.
Hel. Never did mockers waste more idle breath.
Dem. Lysander, keep thy Hermia; I will none.
If ere I lov'd her, all that love is gone.   170
My heart to her but as guest-wise sojourn'd,
And now to Helen is it home return'd,
There to remain.

150. souls] *Qq,F;* flouts *Hanmer;* scorns *conj. Johnson (withdrawn);* scoffs *conj. Johnson (withdrawn).*   151. were] *Qq;* are *F.*   159. derision! None] *Theobald;* derision None *Q1;* derision, none *Q2;* derision; none *F.*   167. will do] *Qq,F;* will love *conj. Camb.*   till] *Q1;* to *Q2,F.*   171. to] *Qq,F;* with *Johnson.*   172. is it] *Q1;* it is *Q2,F.*

150. *join in souls*] 'Join heartily, unite in the same mind' (Steevens).

158. *conjure*] bring, as by an evil spell; cf. *OED v.,* its earliest instance of this figurative use.

159. *sort*] quality.

160–1. *extort . . . patience*] wrest her patience from her (N.C.S.).

166. *to me bequeath*] (in your turn) bequeath to me.

170.] Cf. in *Diana,* the effect of the philtre on Selvagia's love of Alanius: 'His memorie is now exited from my thoughts' (Kennedy, p. 188).

171. *sojourn'd*] (1) travelled to (N.C.S.), antedating *OED*'s sole instance, †4 Harington, 1608; (2) remained on a visit to.

172–3. *And . . . remain*] Demetrius has undergone what in Seneca it is prayed that Hippolytus may undergo: by a supernatural power dominant in moonlit woods, his mind has been captured so as to reclaim him for the fealty of love. Oberon's power corresponds to Diana's. See below, p. 140, at n. 111.

Lys.   Helen, it is not so.
Dem. Disparage not the faith thou dost not know,
   Lest to thy peril thou aby it dear.   175
   Look where thy love comes; yonder is thy dear.

Enter HERMIA.

Her. Dark night, that from the eye his function takes,
   The ear more quick of apprehension makes;
   Wherein it doth impair the seeing sense,
   It pays the hearing double recompense.   180
   Thou art not by mine eye, Lysander, found;
   Mine ear, I thank it, brought me to thy sound.
   But why unkindly didst thou leave me so?
Lys. Why should he stay whom love doth press to go?
Her. What love could press Lysander from my side?   185
Lys. Lysander's love, that would not let him bide—
   Fair Helena, who more engilds the night
   Than all yon fiery oes and eyes of light.
   Why seek'st thou me? Could not this make thee know
   The hate I bare thee made me leave thee so?   190
Her. You speak not as you think; it cannot be!
Hel. Lo, she is one of this confederacy!
   Now I perceive they have conjoin'd all three

173. Helen, it] *Q1;* It *Q2,F.*   175. aby] *Q1;* abide *Q2,F.*   182. thy] *Qq;* that *F.*

174–5.] Cf. Palamon reproving Arcite's trespass on his love: below, p. 131, at n. 17.
175. *aby it dear*] pay dearly for it.
178. *of apprehension*] in seizing with its physical sense; *OED*'s earliest instance.
179. *Wherein*] in that respect in which (*OED* II. 3b, its earliest instance). The 'respect' is its effect on each physical sense.
187–8.] The eulogy outgoes that in Montemayor on 'faire Diana more resplendant, than the Emerauld, or Diamond in the night' (Kennedy, p. 226); the nocturnal brilliants Diana outshines are only gems.
188. *oes and eyes*] stars; oes = orbs,

and spangles (for visual effect in a masque, says Bacon, '*Oes*; or *Spangs* . . . are of most glory': *Essays*, ed. Wright, xxxvii, quoted Halliwell). The phrase plays on the plurals of 'o' and 'i'; cf. *Ham.*, II. ii. 511.
190. *the hate . . . thee*] reiterated, ll. 264, 270–2, 281; in *Enamoured Diana*, Syrenus, under the philtre-spell, sings: 'I did never so much love thy name, / As from my heart I now abhor the same' (Kennedy, p. 362). Cf. II. ii. 136–7 and n.
191. *You . . . think*] Cf. Lyly, *Euphues and his England*, II. 83: 'that I speake as I thinke, thou never beleevst'; Tilley, S725, quoting Erasmus, *Adagia*, etc.

To fashion this false sport in spite of me.
Injurious Hermia! Most ungrateful maid!   195
Have you conspir'd, have you with these contriv'd,
To bait me with this foul derision?
Is all the counsel that we two have shar'd,
The sisters' vows, the hours that we have spent
When we have chid the hasty-footed time   200
For parting us—O, is all forgot?
All school-days' friendship, childhood innocence?
We, Hermia, like two artificial gods,
Have with our needles created both one flower,
Both on one sampler, sitting on one cushion,   205
Both warbling of one song, both in one key,
As if our hands, our sides, voices and minds,
Had been incorporate. So we grew together,
Like to a double cherry, seeming parted,
But yet an union in partition,   210
Two lovely berries moulded on one stem;
So, with two seeming bodies, but one heart;
Two of the first, like coats in heraldry,

204. needles] *Qq,F;* neelds *Rann.*   210. an] *Qq;* a *F.*   213. first, like]
Theobald, conj. Folks; first life *Qq,F;* first life, *F2.*

194. *in . . . me*] to spite me.
197, 370. *derision*] Especially at the
end of a line, the i in -ion is lightly
sounded before the final syllable.
203. *artificial*] skilled in art which
creates something; see *OED* 11†6†b.
204. *needles*] pronounced 'neelds', as
often.
206. *both . . . key*] both = both of
us. That the two *voices* must have
been in one key is obvious, but
Helena has gone on to say that the
two *girls* were (Wells, subst.).
213.] 'Coats' are heraldic coats of
arms, as borne upon the shield; 'of
the first' is herald's language in
blazoning a coat. In heraldry it
refers to the first colour or metal
mentioned, which will be that of the
field: e.g. 'Argent, on a chevron
azure, three mullets of the first'; the
mullets are silver, like the field.

Helena's reference back is not to
colour or metal, but to the 'two . . .
bodies'; Shakespeare makes her employ the heraldic method of reference
so that she can slide into the metaphor
in which the 'one heart' is the single
crest surmounting the shield. (So
Douce, endorsed Furness.) Shakespeare's mind may have begun to
move towards heraldry from the word
'partition', which Staunton showed
to have a technical sense: the way of
dividing the shield vertically into a
dexter and a sinister half is described
as 'the first . . . partition' of nine by
Gerard Leigh in *The Precedence of
Armorie*, 1597. A shield so divided is
clearly the image Shakespeare intends: but Staunton's view that by
'first' Helena means this 'first partition' is unconvincing; while 'the first'
might be thus explained, 'of the first'

Due but to one, and crowned with one crest.
And will you rent our ancient love asunder   215
To join with men in scorning your poor friend?
It is not friendly, 'tis not maidenly;
Our sex, as well as I, may chide you for it,
Though I alone do feel the injury.
Her. I am amazed at your passionate words: 220
I scorn you not; it seems that you scorn me.
Hel. Have you not set Lysander, as in scorn,
To follow me, and praise my eyes and face;
And made your other love, Demetrius,
Who even but now did spurn me with his foot,   225
To call me goddess, nymph, divine and rare,
Precious, celestial? Wherefore speaks he this
To her he hates? And wherefore doth Lysander
Deny your love, so rich within his soul,
And tender me, forsooth, affection,   230
But by your setting on, by your consent?
What though I be not so in grace as you,
So hung upon with love, so fortunate,
But miserable most, to love unlov'd?
This you should pity rather than despise.   235
Her. I understand not what you mean by this.

220. passionate] *F; not in Qq.*

cannot, but must be taken as Douce takes it. Similarly with Wells's idea that the reference is to two identical quarters of a coat divided in four: that would be blazoned: 'Quarterly, first and fourth . . .; second and third . . .'; 'of the first' would not be used of the quarterings.

like] Q1 has misread 'k' as 'f'; how excusably is clear from Plate v in A. W. Pollard (ed.), *Shakespeare's Hand in Sir Thomas Moore* (N.C.S.).

220.] A foot has been lost from Q1's line. F's 'passionate' may be only a felicitous guess, without authority; but it may be the true reading, recovered from the prompt-book. Its dialogue was not often consulted for F, but the examination (in Appendix II) of F's 'merit' at I. i. 139 gives some reason to believe that on occasion it was: cf. also v. i. 189 and n. The present expression is Shakespearean enough: for 'passionate words' found puzzling, or deprecated, cf. *2H6*, I. i. 103, 'what means this passionate discourse?'; *Ant.*, II. ii. 12, 'Your speech is passion'; and above, l. 74. N.C.S. adopts a suggestion made privately by J. W. Mackail: that the line began: '*Her. Helen*', with *Helen* being then mistakenly deleted as 'a duplication'. But could it have been taken for even a *wrong* speech prefix?

226–7. *goddess . . . celestial*] For the debt to Chaucer see above, l. 137 n.

Hel. Ay, do! Persever: counterfeit sad looks,
   Make mouths upon me when I turn my back,
   Wink each at other; hold the sweet jest up;
   This sport, well carried, shall be chronicled.   240
   If you have any pity, grace, or manners,
   You would not make me such an argument.
   But fare ye well; 'tis partly my own fault,
   Which death, or absence, soon shall remedy.
Lys. Stay, gentle Helena; hear my excuse;   245
   My love, my life, my soul, fair Helena!
Hel. O excellent!
Her.   Sweet, do not scorn her so
Dem. If she cannot entreat, I can compel.
Lys. Thou canst compel no more than she entreat;
   Thy threats have no more strength than her weak
      prayers.   250
   Helen, I love thee, by my life I do;
   I swear by that which I will lose for thee
   To prove him false that says I love thee not.
Dem. I say I love thee more than he can do.
Lys. If thou say so, withdraw and prove it too.   255
Dem. Quick, come!
Her.   Lysander, whereto tends all this?
Lys. Away, you Ethiope!
Dem.   No, no; he'll

243. my] *Q1;* mine *Q2,F.*   250. prayers] *Theobald;* praise *Qq,F;* prays
Capell, conj. Theobald.   257–8.] *Divided as Q1;* No, ... hee'l seem ... loose;/
Take ... follow, *Q2,F* (*F reading* Sir, *for* heele).   *Dem.* No, no; he'll/Seem] *Q1;*
Dem. No, no, hee'l seem *Q2; Dem.* No, no, Sir, seem *F; Dem.* No, no; he will/
Seem *Alexander; Dem.* No, no, he'll but/Seem *conj. Nicholson, apud Camb.; Dem.*
No, no; he'll only/Seem *conj. this edn; Her.* No, no; he'll—/*Dem.* Seem *Chambers;*
Her. No, no, he'll kill thee!/*Dem.* Seem *Cuningham; Hermia.* No, no!/*Demetrius*
[*scoffs*] ye'll/Seem *N.C.S.*

237. *Persever*] stressed persèver.
   sad] serious.
   239. *Wink ... other*] tip each other
the wink; cf. *H5,* v. ii. 324.
   240. *carried*] managed; *OED* 22,
its earliest instance.
   chronicled] recorded in history.
   242. *argument*] theme; here, for
mockery.
   250. *prayers*] Theobald noted the
need for an antithesis to 'threats'.

Q1's 'praise' may come from misreading 'praiers' written with an er
curl.
   254.] Cf. Chaucer, below, p. 130,
at n. 15.
   257. *Ethiope*] blackamoor: strictly,
Ethiopian, from Abyssinia (cf. *Rom.,*
I. v. 44). Like 'tawny' (l. 263) a gibe
at Hermia as a dark lady (see Introduction, pp. lxxx, cxiii).
   257–9.] 'he'll / Seem' would be

Seem to break loose—[*To Lysander.*] take on as you would
     follow,
But yet come not! You are a tame man, go!
Lys. Hang off, thou cat, thou burr! Vile thing, let loose,   260
     Or I will shake thee from me like a serpent.
Her. Why are you grown so rude? What change is this,
     Sweet love?
Lys.   Thy love? Out, tawny Tartar, out!
     Out, loathed medicine! O hated potion, hence!
Her. Do you not jest?
Hel.   Yes sooth, and so do you.   265
Lys. Demetrius, I will keep my word with thee.
Dem. I would I had your bond, for I perceive
     A weak bond holds you; I'll not trust your word.
Lys. What, should I hurt her, strike her, kill her dead?
     Although I hate her, I'll not harm her so.   270
Her. What, can you do me greater harm than hate?
     Hate me? Wherefor? O me! what news, my love?
     Am not I Hermia? Are not you Lysander?
     I am as fair now as I was erewhile.
     Since night you lov'd me; yet since night you left me.
     Why, then you left me—O the gods forbid!—   276

258. loose—[*To Lysander.*] take . . . you] *This edn after Q1* (loose: take . . . you)*;*
loose;/Take . . . you *Q2,F; loose*: take . . . he *Pope* (away *for* loose), *Sisson².*
262-3. Why . . . Sweet love?] *As Q1;* Why . . . rude?/What . . . sweete Love?
Q2,F. this,/Sweet love?] *Qq,F* (*subst.*)*;* this?/Sweet love,—*Camb.*   264. potion]
Q1; poison *Q2,F.*

obelized as corrupt, if it were Arden
practice so to mark a crux for which
no sufficiently acceptable solution
has been proposed (see Appendix II
3). An actor might adopt Martin
Wright's version: 'No, no. / Seem to
break loose, take on as you would
follow . . .'
     258. *take on*] rant and rage; cf. our
colloquial: 'she does take on so!'
     259. *go!*] away with you! Cf. *Rom.*,
I. v. 84: 'you are a princox, go!'
     260. *Hang off . . . thou burr*] In Peele,
Old Wives Tale (ll. 223 f.), Lampriscus
complains that his handsome daughter
'hangs on me like a burre'. Cf. *Meas.*,
IV. iii. 177: to stick like burrs is

proverbial (Tilley, B724). They are
the fruiting heads of the burdock,
and stick by means of their hooked
spines (cf. cats' claws).
     261.] Cf. Acts, xxviii. 5: a snake
having fastened on St Paul's hand,
'he shooke off the Viper into the fire';
Bishops' Bible, 1585, quoted R.
Noble, p. 160.
     262. *rude*] rough, uncivil.
     263. *tawny*] tan-coloured, swart: in
complexion, Hermia is a nut-brown
maid.
     267-8. *bond . . . bond*] (1) signed
contract; (2) ligament.
     272. *Wherefor*] stressed 'wherefòr':
Abbott, § 490.

In earnest, shall I say?

Lys. Ay, by my life!
And never did desire to see thee more.
Therefore, be out of hope, of question, of doubt;
Be certain, nothing truer; 'tis no jest   280
That I do hate thee, and love Helena.

Her. O me! [*To Helena.*] You juggler! You canker-blossom!
You thief of love! What, have you come by night
And stol'n my love's heart from him?

Hel.   Fine, i'faith!
Have you no modesty, no maiden shame,   285
No touch of bashfulness? What, will you tear
Impatient answers from my gentle tongue?
Fie, fie, you counterfeit! You puppet you!

Her. 'Puppet'! Why, so? Ay, that way goes the game!
Now I perceive that she hath made compare   290
Between our statures; she hath urg'd her height;
And with her personage, her tall personage,
Her height, forsooth, she hath prevail'd with him.
And are you grown so high in his esteem
Because I am so dwarfish and so low?   295

---

279. of doubt] *Qq,F;* doubt *Pope.*   289. Why, so?] *This edn;* why so?
Qq,F; why, so: *Theobald;* why so! *Rann;* why, so! *Kittredge.*

---

279. *be . . . hope*] abandon hope;
'out of', destitute of.

of doubt] The emphasis with which
Lysander dwells on each of the three
parallel phrases carries and is even
helped by the disturbance this 'of'
makes in the metre. Pope's smoothing
might be defended on the plea that
Q1 had mistakenly assimilated the
third phrase to the two preceding;
but his reading is hardly natural
English.

282. *juggler*] trickster; a glide-vowel
makes the word trisyllabic.

canker-blossom] grub that ruins
(cankers) 'the blossom (of love)'
(Wells).

288-98.] Stature (cf. also ll. 305,
325 f., 328-30, 343) is the argument
of Scintilla and Favilla's quarrel (with

two youths present) in *Endimion,* II.
ii. 19 ff.: '*Favil . . .* because your
Pantables bee higher with corke,
therefore your foote must needs be
higher in the insteppes: you will be
mine elder, because you stande upon
a stoole, and I on the floore . . .
Scint. I am not angry, but it spited me
to see howe short she was.' See Introduction, p. lxxx.

289. *Why, so?*] O indeed, so that's
how it is? (Kittredge, subst.). Hermia
is unlikely to ask 'Why so?' (Why do
you term me 'puppet'?): she knows
the excuse for the insult only too well.

292. *personage*] For 'personage' as
an allurement (though to the reverse
sex) cf. Lyly, *Euphues and his England,*
II. 119. 7: 'all woemenne are not
allured with personage'.

How low am I, thou painted maypole? Speak:
How low am I? I am not yet so low
But that my nails can reach unto thine eyes.
Hel. I pray you, though you mock me, gentlemen,
Let her not hurt me. I was never curst;   300
I have no gift at all in shrewishness;
I am a right maid for my cowardice;
Let her not strike me. You perhaps may think,
Because she is something lower than myself,
That I can match her.
Her.   'Lower'? Hark, again!   305
Hel. Good Hermia, do not be so bitter with me.
I evermore did love you, Hermia,
Did ever keep your counsels, never wrong'd you,
Save that, in love unto Demetrius,
I told him of your stealth unto this wood.   310
He follow'd you; for love I follow'd him;
But he hath chid me hence, and threaten'd me
To strike me, spurn me, nay, to kill me too:
And now, so you will let me quiet go,
To Athens will I bear my folly back,   315
And follow you no further. Let me go:
You see how simple and how fond I am.
Her. Why, get you gone! Who is't that hinders you?
Hel. A foolish heart that I leave here behind.
Her. What! with Lysander?
Hel.   With Demetrius.   320
Lys. Be not afraid; she shall not harm thee, Helena.
Dem. No sir, she shall not, though you take her part.

299. gentlemen] *Q2,F;* gentleman *Qr.*   320. *Hel.*] *Qq;* Her. *F.*

296. *painted maypole*] two insults in one image. 'Maypole' was proverbial for someone skinny and overtall: Tilley, N778. Any mention of painting in the same breath as female looks carried the customary aspersion; cf. *Ham.,* III. i. 147, *Tw.N.,* I. v. 239.

300. *curst*] Cf. 'Kate the curst' (shrewish); *Shr.,* II. i. 185.

302. *right*] proper, real.

305. *can match*] am a match for.

310. *stealth*] furtively stealing away; cf. *OED* †3, its earliest instance.

312. *chid me hence*] tried to drive me away by scolding; *OED*'s earliest instance.

315–16.] With Helena's repentance that she ever entered the wood cf. the hero's in *Huon* (below, p. 146, at n. 154. Cf. Bottom, III. i. 143–6.

Hel. O, when she is angry, she is keen and shrewd;
       She was a vixen when she went to school,
       And though she be but little, she is fierce.   325
Her. 'Little' again? Nothing but 'low' and 'little'?
       Why will you suffer her to flout me thus?
       Let me come to her!
Lys.   Get you gone, you dwarf;
       You minimus, of hindering knot-grass made;
       You bead, you acorn.
Dem.   You are too officious   330
       In her behalf that scorns your services.
       Let her alone; speak not of Helena;
       Take not her part; for if thou dost intend
       Never so little show of love to her,
       Thou shalt aby it.
Lys.   Now she holds me not: 335
       Now follow, if thou dar'st, to try whose right,
       Of thine or mine, is most in Helena.
Dem. Follow? Nay, I'll go with thee, cheek by jowl.
                              Exeunt Lysander and Demetrius.
Her. You, mistress, all this coil is long of you.
       Nay, go not back.
Hel.   I will not trust you, I,   340
       Nor longer stay in your curst company.
       Your hands than mine are quicker for a fray:
       My legs are longer though, to run away.   *Exit.*

---

323. she is] *Q1; she's Q2,F.*   335. aby] *Qq;* abide *F.*   337. Helena.] *Q1,F;*
Helena. Exit. *Q2.*   338. *Exeunt . . . Demetrius.] F (Exit . . . Demetrius.); not
in Qq.*   341. Nor] *Q1,F;* Not *Q2.*   343. *Exit.] Capell; Exeunt. F (lacking
344); not in Qq.*

323. *shrewd*] malicious.
324. *vixen*] Zantippa, in Peele, *Old
Wives Tale* (ll. 626 f.), is 'a little faire,
but . . . the veriest vixen' (having the
ferocity of the female fox).
329. *minimus*] least of diminutive
creatures.
330–8.] For the rivals' counter-
claims and recriminations in Chaucer,
and (later) their agreement to fight,
see below, p. 131, at nn. 17, 25.

333. *intend*] have in mind, design:
OED's earliest instance.
335. *aby*] See above, l. 175 n.
337. *Of . . . mine*] Cf. *Tp.,* II. i. 27:
'Which, of he or Adrian, . . . first
begins to crow?' (Cuningham).
338. *cheek by jowl*] proverbial: Tilley,
C263.
339. *coil . . . you*] to-do is because
of you.

Her. I am amaz'd, and know not what to say.   *Exit.*

Oberon and Puck come forward.

Obe. This is thy negligence: still thou mistak'st,   345
Or else committ'st thy knaveries wilfully.

Puck. Believe me, king of shadows, I mistook.
Did not you tell me I should know the man
By the Athenian garments he had on?
And so far blameless proves my enterprise   350
That I have 'nointed an Athenian's eyes:
And so far am I glad it so did sort,
As this their jangling I esteem a sport.

Obe. Thou seest these lovers seek a place to fight.
Hie therefore, Robin, overcast the night;   355
The starry welkin cover thou anon
With drooping fog, as black as Acheron,
And lead these testy rivals so astray
As one come not within another's way.
Like to Lysander sometime frame thy tongue,   360
Then stir Demetrius up with bitter wrong;
And sometime rail thou like Demetrius:
And from each other look thou lead them thus,

---

344. *Her. . . . say.*] *Qq; not in F.*   *Exit.*] *Capell; Exeunt. Qq; Exeunt: Herm. pursuing Helena./Theobald (following 343); she follows slowly. N.C.S.; not in F.* S.D. *Oberon and Puck come forward.*] *Wells; Enter Oberon and Pucke. F; not in Qq.* 346. wilfully] *Qq;* willingly *F.*   349. had] *Q1;* hath *Q2,F.*

346. *knaveries*] boyish rogue's tricks: *OED*'s earliest instance of this milder sense.

wilfully] on purpose, of malice prepense.

347. *shadows*] spirits; cf. l. 388 and v. i. 409 and n.

352. *sort*] turn out.

353. *jangling*] discord; cf. *Ham.*, III. ii. 158.

354, 358–9.] Fatal consequences are averted by the fairy ruler's preventing the duel, as in Chaucer by the human ruler's interruption of it: below, p. 132, at n. 32.

355–7.] Cf. Oberon's power, in *Huon* (below, p. 146, at nn. 153–4) to conjure up a black river to frustrate

the mortals. These lines echo Marlowe's 'night deep-drencht in mistie Acheron': *Hero and Leander*, I. 189. Acheron is one of the four rivers of Hades. Sackville, in his Induction in *The Mirror for Magistrates* (ll. 480 f.), makes it a lake that 'boyles and bubs up swelth as blacke as hell'. By synecdoche, Ovid and Virgil call Hades itself Acheron.

356. *welkin*] sky; an acceptable poetic word here, though elsewhere, in prose, it is turned to comic effect by Armado's affected and Feste's 'deliberately inappropriate' use of it (*LLL.*, III. i. 65; *Tw.N.*, III. i. 58–60 and Craik's n.).

360–2.] For ventriloquism (though

Till o'er their brows death-counterfeiting sleep
With leaden legs and batty wings doth creep.   365
Then crush this herb into Lysander's eye,
Whose liquor hath this virtuous property,
To take from thence all error with his might,
And make his eyeballs roll with wonted sight.
When they next wake, all this derision   370
Shall seem a dream and fruitless vision;
And back to Athens shall the lovers wend,
With league whose date till death shall never end.
Whiles I in this affair do thee employ,
I'll to my queen, and beg her Indian boy;   375
And then I will her charmed eye release
From monster's view, and all things shall be peace.
Puck. My fairy lord, this must be done with haste,
For night's swift dragons cut the clouds full fast;
And yonder shines Aurora's harbinger,   380
At whose approach, ghosts wandering here and there
Troop home to churchyards. Damned spirits all,

---

374. employ] *Q1* (imploy); apply *Q2*; imply *F*.   379. night's swift] *Q1*
(nights swift); night swift *Q2*; night-swift *F*.

---

as an impostor's pretended magic)
cf. Scot, *Witchcraft* (below, p. 147, at
n. 163).

364. *death-counterfeiting sleep*] proverbial, and a recurrent concept in
Shakespeare: see Tilley, S527.

365. *leaden*] Cf. 'leaden slumber'.
R3, v. iii. 105; and *Caes.*, IV. iii. 267.

367. *virtuous*] efficacious, by an
innate quality.

373. *date*] term of existence.

379.] Night's dragon-chariot originates from the Moon's in Marlowe
(who may have remembered that of
Ceres): *Hero and Leander*, I. 107 f.:
'yawning dragons draw her thirling
carre / From *Latmos* mount up to the
gloomie skie'. Cf. 'dragon-wing of
night', *Troil.*, v. viii. 17; 'dragons of
the night', *Cym.*, II. ii. 48 and Nos-
worthy's n.

380. *Aurora's harbinger*] Venus
Phosphor, the morning star (N.C.S.),

announcing the approach of the
Dawn-goddess; a harbinger, originally an officer sent ahead to purvey
lodgings for a great personage.

381–4.] Two kinds of ghost are
distinguished: the wandering ghosts
—'walking spirits' (Scot, *Witchcraft*)
is the technical term—departing only
now; and 'Damned spirits', gone already.

381–2. *ghosts . . . churchyards*] Cf.
Scot, *Witchcraft* (below, p. 147, at
nn. 165, 174); cf. v. i. 365–8. Their
bodies lie in consecrated ground.

382–7. *Damned . . . night*] Q1, self-
contradictorily, makes souls already
'Damned' who '*must*' consort with
night, '*wilfully*' exile themselves from
light' by the present act of returning
to their 'wormy beds'. But that is not
an act of their will in the present;
they '*must*'; decision for them is past.
Thirlby's conjecture resolves the con-

That in cross-ways and floods have burial,
Already to their wormy beds are gone,
For fear lest day should look their shames upon: 385
They wilfully themselves exil'd from light,
And must for aye consort with black-brow'd night.
Obe. But we are spirits of another sort:
I with the Morning's love have oft made sport;
And like a forester the groves may tread   390

384-5. gone, . . . upon:] *As Alexander* (upon;); gone: . . . upon, *Qq*; gone;
. . . upon *F*.   386. They] *Qq,F; Obe.* They *conj. Thirlby*   exil'd] *Alexander,
conj. Thirlby;* exile *Qq;* dxile *F.*   388. *Obe.* But] *Qq,F;* But *conj. Thirlby.*

tradiction: they 'exil'd' themselves
from light 'wilfully' by their last act
of will in deciding to kill themselves;
and *therefore* 'must' for ever 'consort
with night'. The emendation assumes
only the misreading, extremely common, of secretary-hand 'd' as 'e'.
Perhaps F's 'dxile' resulted from a
marginal correction, 'd', with the 'd'
then substituted for the wrong 'e'.
With 'exil'd' the punctuation at the
end of ll. 384-5 must be emended;
but once the Q1 compositor had read
the sentence in the sense which 'exile'
gave it, he was bound to punctuate
it as he did, complicating the error.
M. R. Ridley (*Ant.,* Arden edn, pp.
xii f., fn. 2) made, independently,
the same conjecture as Thirlby, who
coupled with his suggestion that
ll. 386 f. belong to Oberon. It may
well be right: Harold Jenkins observes
(privately) that 'the stern explanation
is much more in character for Oberon;
makes a forceful rejoinder to Puck's
merely descriptive lines, and by rein-
forcing the antithesis between *they* and
we, prepares for and gives more point
to "But we are spirits of another
sort" '.
383. *in . . . burial*] not in consecrated ground. Elizabethan suicides
were buried at cross-roads; the bodies
of some who drowned themselves
would not be recovered. Since these
are 'Damned spirits all', the reference,
pace Steevens, Cuningham, and Wells,

cannot be to the superstitition that
want of burial would a long time
deny rest to the souls of even the
accidentally drowned (on whose innocence see the learned opinion of
the First Gravedigger: *Ham.,* v. i.
15-21).
387. *consort*] keep (bad) company;
pejorative, as in *Rom.,* iii. i. 43-4, but
not in *LLL,* ii. i. 178.
black-brow'd night] Cf. *Rom.,* iii. ii.
20: 'come . . . black-brow'd night'
(Cuningham); *John,* v. vi. 17: 'the
black brow of night' (Steevens).
388. *spirits of another sort*] For the
importance of this contrast and its
Spenserian antecedent see Introduction, p. lxxvi. Cf. *Shepheardes Calender,*
June, ll. 23-6: 'Here no night
Ravenes lodge more blacke than
pitche, / Nor elvish ghosts, nor
gastly owles doe flee. / But frendly
Faeries, met with many Graces. / And
lightfote Nymphes can chace the
lingring night . . .' (for possible
further reminiscences of these lines
see above, i. i. 209-10 n., and below,
iv. i. 95, v. i. 362-72, nn.). In *Huon*
(below, p. 146, at n. 156) Oberon
truthfully claims: 'I was never devyll
nor yll creature'.
389.] perhaps 'I have dallied with
Aurora' (N.C.S.). But the personification (if it is one) need not be
mythological.
390-1.] The 'eastern gate' and
'fiery-red' sunrise are inspired by

Even till the eastern gate, all fiery-red,
Opening on Neptune with fair blessed beams,
Turns into yellow gold his salt green streams.
But notwithstanding, haste, make no delay;
We may effect this business yet ere day.   [*Exit.*] 395

Puck.   Up and down, up and down,
          I will lead them up and down;
          I am fear'd in field and town:
          Goblin, lead them up and down.
Here comes one.   400

Enter LYSANDER.

Lys. Where art thou, proud Demetrius? Speak thou now.
Puck. Here, villain, drawn and ready. Where art thou?
Lys. I will be with thee straight.
Puck.   Follow me then
          To plainer ground. [*Exit Lysander, as following the voice.*]

Enter DEMETRIUS.

Dem.   Lysander, speak again.
Thou runaway, thou coward, art thou fled?   405
Speak! In some bush? Where dost thou hide thy head?
Puck. Thou coward, art thou bragging to the stars,
          Telling the bushes that thou look'st for wars,
          And wilt not come? Come, recreant, come thou child!
          I'll whip thee with a rod; he is defil'd   410

---

395. *Exit.*] Rowe (*Exit Oberon*); not in *Qq,F.*   396–9.] *As Pope;* Up . . . down,
I will . . . down./I am. . . town. *Goblin* . . . downe. *Q1;* as prose, *Q2,F.*
402–3. *Puck.*] *Rowe; Rob. Qq,F.*   403–4. Follow . . . ground.] *As Theobald;*
one line, Qq,F.   404. *Exit* . . . *voice.*] *After Capell (Exit Lys. as following the*
Voice, which seems to go off.); not in Qq,F.   406. Speak! In some bush?] *Capell*
(*reading* Speak,), *Collier;* Speak in some bush. *Qq,F (subst.)*   Where dost
thou . . . head?] *Qq,F;* where thou dost . . . head. *Hanmer (reading* Speak in
. . . bush,).   407. *Puck.*] *Rowe; Rob. Qq,F.*

Chaucer's 'orisont' and 'firie Phebus'
in a similarly lyrical passage echoed
also at ll. 418 f., and IV. i. 93; 'the
groves' also has Chaucerian antecedents. See below, pp. 131–2, at nn.
19–22, 24, 30.

402. *drawn*] with drawn sword.
403. *be with*] (1) be beside; perhaps
(2) be even with.
406. *Speak! . . . bush?*] 'Speak.
Are you crept into *some bush?*'
(Capell).

That draws a sword on thee.

Dem.   Yea, art thou there?

Puck. Follow my voice; we'll try no manhood here.   *Exeunt.*

[*Enter* LYSANDER.]

Lys. He goes before me, and still dares me on;
When I come where he calls, then he is gone.
The villain is much lighter-heel'd than I: 415
I follow'd fast; but faster he did fly,
That fallen am I in dark uneven way,
And here will rest me.   *Lies down.*
            Come thou gentle day:
For if but once thou show me thy grey light,
I'll find Demetrius, and revenge this spite.   [*Sleeps.*] 420

Enter PUCK *and* DEMETRIUS.

Puck. Ho, ho, ho! Coward, why com'st thou not?
                            They dodge about the stage.

Dem. Abide me if thou dar'st, for well I wot
Thou runn'st before me, shifting every place,
And dar'st not stand, nor look me in the face.
Where art thou now?

Puck.   Come hither; I am here.   425

412. Puck.] *Rowe; Ro. Qq,F.*   Exeunt.] *Qq; Exit. F.*   412. S.D.] *After
Theobald (Lys. comes back.); not in Qq,F.*   414. he is] *Qr; he's Q2,F.*   418. *Lies
down.*] F (*lye downe./following* day:), *Dyce; not in Qq.*   420. *Sleeps.*] *Capell; not
in Qq,F.*   S.D. Enter] *F; not in Qq.*   Puck and Demetrius.] *Qq,F (Robin for
Puck), Capell.*   421. Puck.] *Rowe; Rob. Qq,F.*   They . . . stage.] *After F
(shifting places/following 416).*   425. thou now?] *Qr; thou? Q2,F.*   Puck.]
Rowe; Rob. Qq,F.

414–21.] F's '*shifting places*', at l.
416, unlike its S.D. at l. 418, is not in
the imperative, and doubtless comes
not from the prompt-book, but (edi-
torially) from 'shifting every place'.
F evidently supposed that this dodging
began where Lysander refers to Puck
eluding him (ll. 413–16) but according to Q1 (412 S.D.) Puck is not
then on stage, and 'I *follow'd* fast;
but faster he *did fly*' points to action
off-stage. Puck and Demetrius' dialogue (ll. 421–5) does seem likely

to imply stage-business.
    417. *fallen . . . in*] got into.
    uneven] not level underfoot.
    418. Lies down] See l. 87 n.
    419. *thy grey light*] Chaucer's 'morwe
gray' (in a passage echoed also at l.
391 and IV. i. 93: see below, p. 131,
at n. 20.
    420. *spite*] bad turn (done me by
malicious fortune).
    421. *Ho, ho, ho!*] Puck's traditional
derisive laughter.
    424. *stand*] await attack.

Dem. Nay, then, thou mock'st me; thou shalt buy this dear
      If ever I thy face by daylight see:
      Now go thy way. Faintness constraineth me
      To measure out my length on this cold bed.   [*Lies down.*]
      By day's approach look to be visited.   [*Sleeps.*] 430

Enter HELENA.

Hel. O weary night, O long and tedious night,
      Abate thy hours! Shine, comforts, from the east,
      That I may back to Athens by daylight,
      From these that my poor company detest.
      And sleep, that sometimes shuts up sorrow's eye,   435
      Steal me awhile from mine own company.
                    [*Lies down and*] *sleeps.*

Puck.   Yet but three? Come one more,
      Two of both kinds makes up four.
      Here she comes, curst and sad:
      Cupid is a knavish lad   440
      Thus to make poor females mad!

Enter HERMIA.

Her. Never so weary, never so in woe,
      Bedabbled with the dew, and torn with briars,

429. *Lies down.*] *Capell; not in Qq,F.*   430. *Sleeps.*] *Capell; Lyes down F4;
Lies down and sleeps. Malone; not in Qq,F.*   432. hours! Shine, comforts,]
Theobald (subst.); houres, shine comforts *Qq,F.*   435. sometimes] *Qq;*
sometime *F.*   436 S.D. *Lies . . . sleeps.*] *Dyce;* Sleeps. *Qq,F.*   437. *Puck.*] *Rowe;*
Rob. Qq,F.   441. S.D.] *As Rowe; Q2,F (following 439); not in Q1.*

428–9. *Faintness constraineth . . . bed*]
Cf. Munday, *John a Kent*, ll. 1396 f.:
'I am growen so faynt / That I must
needes lye downe on meere con-
straynt'.

429. *measure . . . length*] *OED*'s
earliest instance.

432. *Abate . . . hours*] make them
seem shorter.

hours! . . . comforts] assuming
balanced invocations to 'night' and
'comforts'. But if (as Jenkins, privately,
thinks more probable) the sense is
'May comforts shine from the east',
then 'comforts' should have no
commas.

433. *may*] with idiomatic omission
of vb. of motion.

434. *detest*] perhaps: 'by what they
utter, repudiate' (my company). W. S.
Walker brought evidence that in
Shakespeare's time 'detest' retained
from 'detestari' the sense 'of something spoken, not of an affection of
the mind'.

435.] Sleep as respite from sorrow
is proverbial: Tilley, S662.

442, 444. *Never so weary . . . I can
. . . no further go*] Cf. Munday, *John a
Kent*, ll. 1401 f.: 'I never was so
wearie. / . . . I can go no longer'.

442–5.] Though for so natural a

I can no further crawl, no further go;
My legs can keep no pace with my desires.   445
Here will I rest me till the break of day.   [*Lies down.*]
Heavens shield Lysander, if they mean a fray!   [*Sleeps.*]
Puck.   On the ground
                 Sleep sound;
                 I'll apply   450
                 To your eye,
             Gentle lover, remedy.
             [*Squeezes the juice on Lysander's eyelids.*]
                 When thou wak'st,
                 Thou tak'st
                 True delight   455
                 In the sight
             Of thy former lady's eye;
         And the country proverb known,
         That every man should take his own,
         In your waking shall be shown: 460
                 Jack shall have Jill,
                 Nought shall go ill;
The man shall have his mare again, and all shall be well.
                                              [*Exit.*]

446. *Lies down.*] *Rowe; not in Qq,F.*   447. *Sleeps.*] *Capell; not in Qq,F.*
448. *Puck.*] *Rowe; Rob. Qq,F.*   448–52.] *Divided, Warburton; two lines, divided*
sound:/Ile *Qq,F.*   451. To] *Rowe; not in Qq,F.*   452. *Squeezes . . . eyelids.*]
Rowe (eye); not in Qq,F.   453–7.] *Divided, Warburton; two lines, divided* taks't
/True *Qq,F.*   461–2.] *As Johnson; one line, Qq,F.*   463. Exit.] *Rowe*
(*Ex. Puck.*); *They sleep all the Act. F; not in Qq.*

plaint, Shakespeare did not need literary prompting, he will have read in Golding's Ovid (I. 614–17) what Apollo says to the nymph Peneis: 'alas, alas, how would it grieve my heart / To see thee fall among the briers, and that the blood should start / Out of thy tender legges . . .'

452.] The spell is never taken off Demetrius' eyes; without its lasting effect the love-tangle could not be resolved. As in *Huon* (below, p. 146, at n. 157), Oberon's help is indispensable to the happy outcome. See Introduction, pp. lix, ci, cxxxv.

461.] 'Al is wel Jack shal have

gill' (John Heywood, *Proverbes*, 1546); cf. Tilley, A164, M209. *LLL*, v. ii. 865, reverses the proverb: 'Jack hath not Jill'. Jill is Gillian.

463.] 'All is well and the man has his mare again', recorded by Ray in 1678 as proverbial; cf. Tilley, A153, whose instances are all later than the present one; but F. P. Wilson, *Shakespearian and other Studies*, p. 159, adds from Copland, *Jyl of Brentford's Testament, ante* 1548: 'The poore mare shall have his man agayn' (*sic*).

Exit] for F's 'They sleep all the Act', see Introduction, p. xxxii.

ACT IV

[SCENE I]

*Lysander, Demetrius, Helena, and Hermia, still
lying asleep.*

Enter Titania *Queen of Fairies, and* Bottom; Peaseblossom,
Cobweb, Moth, Mustardseed, *and other* Fairies; Oberon
the King, behind [, unseen].

Tita. Come sit thee down upon this flowery bed,
    While I thy amiable cheeks do coy,
    And stick musk-roses in thy sleek smooth head,
    And kiss thy fair large ears, my gentle joy.
Bot. Where's Peaseblossom?   5
Peas. Ready.
Bot. Scratch my head, Peaseblossom. Where's Moun-
    sieur Cobweb?
Cob. Ready.
Bot. Mounsieur Cobweb, good mounsieur, get you your   10
    weapons in your hand, and kill me a red-hipped
    humble-bee on the top of a thistle; and good moun-
    sieur, bring me the honey-bag. Do not fret yourself
    too much in the action, mounsieur; and good moun-
    sieur, have a care the honey-bag break not; I would   15

ACT IV

Scene i

Act IV] F (*Actus Quartus*) not in Qq.   Scene i] Rowe; not in Qq,F. [*Location*]
The Same. Capell. S.D. *Lysander, Demetrius, Helena, and Hermia still lying asleep.*]
Alexander (without 'still'), after Capell (The lovers at a distance, asleep.); not in
Qq,F.   *Enter . . . unseen.*] *Qq,F (Enter Queene of Faieries, and Clowne, and*
Faieries: and the King behind them).   5. *Bot.*] *Rowe; Clown. Qq,F (subst.; so*
throughout scene).   10. you your] *Q1;* your *Q2,F.*

    2. *coy*] caress; from falconry (*OED,*
v¹†2, quoting Turberville, 1575); and
cf. Golding (see l. 121 n. below).

    15. *have a care*] With *LLL,* v. ii. 51,
OED's earliest instances.

be loath to have you overflowen with a honey-bag,
signior. Where's Mounsieur Mustardseed?

Mus. Ready.

Bot. Give me your neaf, Mounsieur Mustardseed. Pray
you, leave your courtesy, good mounsieur.   20

Mus. What's your will?

Bot. Nothing, good mounsieur, but to help Cavalery
Cobweb to scratch. I must to the barber's, mounsieur, for methinks I am marvellous hairy about the
face; and I am such a tender ass, if my hair do but   25
tickle me, I must scratch.

Tita. What, wilt thou hear some music, my sweet love?

Bot. I have a reasonable good ear in music. Let's have
the tongs and the bones.

Tita. Or say, sweet love, what thou desir'st to eat?   30

Bot. Truly, a peck of provender; I could munch your
good dry oats. Methinks I have a great desire to a
bottle of hay: good hay, sweet hay, hath no fellow.

---

20. courtesy] *Q2,F;* curtsie *Q1.*   23. Cobweb] *Qq,F; Pease-blossom/ Rann.*
27. some] *Q1,F;* some some *Q2.*   28. Let's] *Q1* (let's); let us *Q2,F.*
29. bones.] *Qq;* bones. *Musicke Tongs, Rurall Musicke. F.*

16. *overflowen*] flowed over, and (cf.
'overlaid') perhaps suffocated.

19. *neaf*] fist.

20. *leave your courtesy*] Do not stand
bareheaded (out of respectful good
manners). Cf. *LLL.*, v. i. 93 f.:
'remember thy courtesy . . . apparel
thy head'; *Ham.*, v. ii. 92 f., 105 f.

22. *Cavalery*] cavaliero: 'a gay
sprightly military man' (Johnson). Cf.
Wiv., II. iii. 70.

23. *Cobweb*] an error, no doubt
Shakespeare's, for Peaseblossom: see
ll. 7, 10 ff.

29. *tongs and the bones*] *OED*'s earliest
instances. Halliwell quotes Planché
on sketches by Inigo Jones (in the
Duke of Devonshire's library), en-
titled 'Tonges and Key' and
'Knackers'. The tongs were struck
with the key (N.C.S. compares the
modern triangle). The knackers or

bones, clappers of bone or wood,
were held between the fingers of one
hand and rattled together. In recent
times, nigger-minstrels featured 'Mr
Bones' as one of their two corner-
boys.

The F S.D. seems contrary to
Shakespeare's intention: Titania at
once heads Bottom off (Capell). Probably it was concocted on the
suggestion of the text. 'Rurall
Musicke' looks like a duplication:
perhaps an elaboration, in preparing
copy for F, of 'Musicke Tongs' or the
like in the prompt-book (Greg, p.
245).

33. *bottle*] truss: the amount of a
feed 'prescribed by Elizabethan horse-
keepers' (*Shakespeare's England*, I. 350,
quoted N.C.S.).

hath no fellow] there's nothing like
it.

Tita. I have a venturous fairy that shall seek
   The squirrel's hoard, and fetch thee new nuts.   35
Bot. I had rather have a handful or two of dried peas.
   But I pray you, let none of your people stir me:
   I have an exposition of sleep come upon me.
Tita. Sleep thou, and I will wind thee in my arms.
   Fairies, be gone, and be all ways away.   [*Exeunt Fairies.*]
   So doth the woodbine the sweet honeysuckle   41
   Gently entwist; the female ivy so
   Enrings the barky fingers of the elm.
   O how I love thee! How I dote on thee!   [*They sleep.*]

Enter PUCK

Obe. [*Advancing.*] Welcome, good Robin. Seest thou this sweet
   sight?   45

34–5.] *As Hanmer;* I . . . seek the . . . hoard,/And . . . nuts. *Q1;* I . . . Fairy,/That . . . seeke the . . . hoard,/And . . . nuts. *Q2,F.*   35. thee] *Qq, F;* thee thence *Hanmer.*   40. all ways] *Theobald;* alwaies *Qq,F.*   *Exeunt Fairies.*] *Capell; not in Qq,F.*   41. woodbine the . . . honeysuckle] *Knight, conj. Malone;* woodbine, . . . the honeysuckle, *Qq,F.*   44. *They sleep.*] *Capell, not in Qq,F.* 44 S.D. *Puck.*] *Rowe; Robin Goodfellow. Qq; Robin Goodfellow and Oberon. F.* 45. *Advancing.*] *Capell* (*Oberon advances*), *Collier; not in Qq,F.*

38. *exposition*] malapropism for 'disposition'.

40. *be . . . away*] Be off in every direction.

41–2. *So . . . entwist*] The image is parallel with that in ll. 42 f.: as there ivy and elm-twigs stand for Titania and Bottom, so do woodbine and honeysuckle here. Though it is Titania who actively 'entwists', the word calls up a picture of 'two climbing plants' twined 'about each other' (W. A. Wright). Difficulty has been felt because 'woodbine' was undoubtedly another name for 'honeysuckle'. Florio (cited Warburton) and Googe's *Book of Husbandry* (cited Joseph Hunter) make 'the honeysuckle or woodbine' (Googe) alternatives for the same plant. The answer evidently is that 'the name *woodbine* has been applied to several climbing plants' (Nares). Annotating Jonson's *Vision of Delight* (1617), Gifford observed: 'in many of our counties, the woodbine is still the name for the great convolvulus'. His note is on: 'How the blue bindweed doth itself infold / With honeysuckle, and both those intwine / With bryony and jessamine'. The reminiscence of Shakespeare is pretty plain, and, as Gifford said, Jonson's 'bindweed' is Shakespeare's 'woodbine': 'bindweed' certainly does mean 'convolvulus'. No attempt to explain Shakespeare's image in terms of a single plant is satisfactory; not Joseph Hunter's that 'woodbine' and 'honeysuckle' are in apposition, and 'entwist' is intransitive; nor even Johnson's that perhaps the woodbine is the leaves and the honeysuckle the flower, or 'perhaps Shakespeare made a blunder'. Fortunately no such explanation is necessary. (For each reference in this n. see Furness.)

42–3. *female . . . elm*] Cf. *Err.,* II. ii. 174, where, however, the female is the

Her dotage now I do begin to pity;
For, meeting her of late behind the wood
Seeking sweet favours for this hateful fool,
I did upbraid her and fall out with her:
For she his hairy temples then had rounded   50
With coronet of fresh and fragrant flowers;
And that same dew, which sometime on the buds
Was wont to swell like round and orient pearls,
Stood now within the pretty flowerets' eyes
Like tears, that did their own disgrace bewail.   55
When I had at my pleasure taunted her,
And she in mild terms begg'd my patience,
I then did ask of her her changeling child;
Which straight she gave me, and her fairy sent
To bear him to my bower in fairy land.   60
And now I have the boy, I will undo
This hateful imperfection of her eyes.
And gentle Puck, take this transformed scalp
From off the head of this Athenian swain,
That he awaking when the other do,   65
May all to Athens back again repair,
And think no more of this night's accidents
But as the fierce vexation of a dream.

---

48. favours] *Q1;* savors *Q2,F.*   54. flowerets'] *Qq,F* (floweriets).

vine, proverbially and in accordance with Scripture, Ovid, and actual viniculture (Foakes's n., and Tilley, V61). Does Shakespeare deliberately substitute the ivy for the vine (the wife) because Titania's embrace, like that of the ivy in *Err.* (l. 178), is not marital?

46. *dotage*] infatuation.

48. *favours*] Q2 misread the long s.

51–4.] Golding's Ovid and Spenser's *Shepheardes Calender* are in Shakespeare's mind. L. 51 borrows word for word from Golding, II. 33: '. . . with a crowne of fresh and fragrant flowers'. Evidently 'fragrant flowers' acted as an associative link with the *Calender*, which in the December eclogue (ll. 109, 112) has

'fragrant flowers . . . dewed with teares'. In turn the dew on flowers called up the November eclogue, where (ll. 31 f.) 'the kindly dewe drops from the higher tree, / And wets the little plants', and where (l. 83) Spenser's poetical word 'flourets' is picked out by E.K.'s gloss: 'Flouret] a diminutive for a little flower'.

53. *orient*] from the East, and of the purest water; cf. *Ant.,* I. v. 41 and Ridley's n.

63–4.] The 'business' is effected at ll. 79–83. Cf. Scot, *Witchcraft* (below, p. 149, at n. 183) and his heading of bk v, ch. iii.

66. *repair*] return.

68. *vexation*] agitation.

But first I will release the fairy queen.

        [Squeezes the juice on her eyelids.]

    Be as thou wast wont to be;   70

    See as thou wast wont to see:

    Dian's bud o'er Cupid's flower

    Hath such force and blessed power.

Now my Titania, wake you, my sweet queen.

Tita. [*Waking.*] My Oberon! What visions have I seen!   75

Methought I was enamour'd of an ass.

Obe. There lies your love.

Tita.   How came these things to pass?

O how mine eyes do loathe his visage now!

Obe. Silence awhile. Robin, take off this head.

Titania, music call; and strike more dead   80

Than common sleep, of all these five the sense.

Tita. Music ho, music, such as charmeth sleep!   *Soft music.*

69. S.D. *Squeezes . . . eyelids.*] *After Capell* (*touching her eyes with an herb*)*; not in Qq,F.* 70. Be] *Qq;* Be thou *F.* 72. o'er] *Theobald, conj. Thirlby;* or *Qq,F* (*subst.*). 75. *Waking.*] *Wells* (*wakes*)*; not in Qq,F.* 78. do] *Q1;* doth *Q2,F.* 79. this] *Qq;* his *F.* 81. sleep, . . . these five] *Theobald, conj. Thirlby* (sleep *for* sleep,)*;* sleep: . . . these, fine *Qq,F, Rowe³* (*subst.*)*;* sleep . . . these fine *Rowe.* 82. ho] *Q2,F;* howe *Q1.* Soft music.] *N.C.S.; Musick still. F; Still music. Theobald; not in Qq.*

70–1.] 'Be . . . be'; 'See . . . see': a recognized stylistic figure or 'scheme': 'Epanalepsis . . .: or the Eccho sound', Puttenham, quoted Rushton, *Shakespeare Illustrated* (Cuningham).

72. *Dian's bud*] Artemisia (so Onions), which has Diana, as Artemis, in the very name of the herb; or perhaps (Onions, after Steevens) Agnus castus (the chaste tree). *The Flower and the Leaf,* printed in Shakespeare's day with Chaucer's genuine works, speaks of 'Diane, the goddesse of chastitie' who therefore carries the branch 'That *agnus castus* men call properly'.

72–3.] The antidote is a dramatic necessity, prepared for at II. i. 184: it is in keeping, however, with the traditions of love-enchantment. Cupid's golden arrow has its antithesis in his leaden one (cf. not only Golding, but E.K.'s gloss, *Shepheardes*

Calender, March, on l. 79); and as 'Dian's bud' restores Lysander's love of Hermia, so in *Enamoured Diana* Felicia with the help of 'herbes and wordes' restores Syrenus' love, which her philtre had taken away, to Diana (Kennedy, p. 375).

80–1. *strike . . . sleep*] In *Diana,* Felicia's philtres cast Syrenus, Sylvanus, and Selvagia into a sleep unbreakable by ordinary means (Kennedy, p. 186).

81. *five*] the four lovers and Bottom. Q1 has a minim-misreading.

82. S.D.] interpreting *Musick still* (F) as 'still Music' (so Staunton), in the sense it bears in Wilkins, *Painful Adventures of Pericles,* 65. 5–6: 'They should commaund still musicke to sound', which with the direction for 'Still Musicke' at Hymen's entrance (*AYL,* v. iv. 106, S.D.) supports Delius's conj. of 'still' for 'rough'

Puck. [*Taking the ass-head off Bottom.*] Now when thou wak'st,
    with thine own fool's eyes peep.
Obe. Sound, music!   [*Music strikes into a dance.*]
    Come my queen, take hands with me,
    And rock the ground whereon these sleepers be.   85
                [*Oberon and Titania dance.*]
    Now thou and I are new in amity,
    And will to-morrow midnight, solemnly,
    Dance in Duke Theseus' house triumphantly,
    And bless it to all fair prosperity.
    There shall the pairs of faithful lovers be   90
    Wedded, with Theseus, all in jollity.
Puck.   Fairy king, attend and mark:
         I do hear the morning lark.
Obe.   Then my queen, in silence sad,
         Trip we after night's shade: 95

---

83. *Puck.*] *Rowe; Rob. Qq,F.*   *Taking the ass-head off Bottom.*] *After N.C.S.* (peep.
[*he plucks the ass's head from him*]; *not in Qq,F.*   83. Now when] *Q1;* When
Q2,F.   84. *Music strikes into a dance.*] *After N.C.S.* (*the music waxes loud*); *still
musick/Var. '21.; not in Qq,F.*   85. S.D. *Oberon and Titania dance.*] *N.C.S.* (*they
dance*); *not in Qq,F.*   89. prosperity] *Q1;* posterity *Q2,F.*   92. *Puck.*] *Rowe;
Rob. Qq,F.*   Fairy] *Qq;* Faire *F.*   95. night's] *Q1;* the night's *Q2,F.*

music in *Per.*, III. ii. 90 (see Hoeniger's
n.). A specification, 'put last', of the
kind of music, is quoted by Dyce
(*Remarks*, p. 48): 'Trumpets small
above', from Beaumont and Fletcher's
Triumph of Time. Since the music
has not begun, 'Musick still' cannot
be (as one would expect) an instruc-
tion for it to continue; nor for it to be
stilled; nor is it likely, *pace* Dyce, to
bid it be silent until Oberon (l. 84)
seconds Titania's bidding. 'Still music'
here will be associated with the
supernatural and with sleep, as with
recall from apparent death by near-
miraculous healing power in *Painful
Adventures*, and with the supernatural
in *AYL* (cf. Agnes Latham's n., which
mentions J. S. Manifold's opinion
that it would be provided by recorders).

   87. solemnly] in a spirit of festive
ritual; cf. I. i. 11 n.

   88. *triumphantly*] as in a festive
triumph; see I. i. 19 n.

   89. *prosperity*] Q1's authoritative
reading is not to be deserted for F's
'posterity' (an anticipation of v. i.
391 ff.). Oberon and Titania can now
fulfil the purpose which brought him
to Athens: to endow Theseus and
Hippolyta's marriage with joy and
prosperity (II. I. 72). So Malone.

   93. *the morning lark*] Cf. Chaucer, in
the lyrical description echoed also at
III. ii. 391, 419. See below, p. 131, at
n. 19. *Sonn.*, XXIX. ll. 11 f.; and the
serenade in *Cym.*, II. iii. 20 ff.

   94. *silence sad*] sober silence.

   95.] Cf. 'Faeries . . . can chace the
lingring night': Spenser, *Shepheardes
Calender*, June, ll. 25 f.: see above,
III. ii. 388, and below, v. i. 362–72, nn.
For the metre, cf. II. i. 7: 'Swifter than
the moon's sphere'.

We the globe can compass soon,
Swifter than the wandering moon.

Tita.   Come my lord, and in our flight
Tell me how it came this night
That I sleeping here was found   100
With these mortals on the ground.

Exeunt. The four lovers and Bottom still lie asleep.

To the winding of horns [within],
enter THESEUS, HIPPOLYTA, EGEUS, *and* Train.

The.   Go one of you, find out the forester;
For now our observation is perform'd,
And since we have the vaward of the day,
My love shall hear the music of my hounds.   105

101. S.D. *The four lovers and Bottom still lie asleep.*] *After* F (*Sleepers Lye still/at 103); not in Qq.*   101. S.D. *To the winding of horns*] *Alexander; Winde Hornes Qq,F (before 'Enter' F; following 'traine' Qq (Q1 horne)).   within] Capell; not in Qq,F.   Theseus, Hippolyta, Egeus, and*] F (*Theseus, Egeus, Hippolita and all his*); *Theseus and all his Qq.*

102–26.] Theseus' passion for hunting, especially in May, is taken from Chaucer (below, p. 132, at nn. 26–31), where he sets out with Hippolyta, Amazon huntress. His part in the Calydonian boar-hunt is noted by North (below, p. 136, at n. 68) and Golding, VIII. 322 ff.: hence, in l. 125, his reminiscence of hunting in Thessaly. The start at break of day, in Chaucer, associated itself with Hippolytus' similar start, the opening episode of Seneca's play (below, p. 143, at nn. 130–8), and with Kalander's hunting in Sidney's *Arcadia* (ed. Feuillerat, p. 59): 'the sunne . . . could never prevent him with earlines'. Hippolytus' hounds were linked with Actaeon's (in Golding, III. 245 ff.) by the Cretan and Spartan breed among each pack, and by the reverberation of their cry (below, p. 139, at nn. 96–7), which links in turn with the music of Kalander's hounds. Both Hippolytus' hounds and his are uncoupled. Valley and mountain-top figure in Hippoly-

tus' hunting (cf. below, ll. 106 n., 110 n.). And see ll. 119–21, 125, nn.

102. *forester*] the 'officier of [the] forest . . . sworn to preserve the Vert and Venison, . . . and attend upon the wild beasts there' (Manwood, *Lawes of the Forest*, 1598, quoted *OED*).

103. *observation*] observance (of 'the rite of May', l. 132). Cf. also I. i. 167, and for the echoes of Chaucer, n. there.

104. *have the vaward*] command the foremost place (vanguard); as a figurative expression 'vaward' pre-dates *OED*'s earliest example: *2H4*, I. ii. 167.

105.] Choosing hounds for a pack, Elizabethans set great store by its 'music' (cf. ll. 109 f., 112–17, 122–6): the 'crie' of Kalander's (*Arcadia*, p. 60) was 'composed of so well sorted mouthes, that any man would perceive therein some kind of proportion, but the skilful woodman did finde a musick'. With Theseus, that counts

Uncouple in the western valley; let them go;
Dispatch I say, and find the forester.   [*Exit an Attendant.*]
We will, fair queen, up to the mountain's top,
And mark the musical confusion
Of hounds and echo in conjunction.   110
Hip. I was with Hercules and Cadmus once,
When in a wood of Crete they bay'd the bear
With hounds of Sparta; never did I hear

---

107. *Exit . . . Attendant*] *Dyce; not in Qq,F.*   112. bear] *Qq,F;* boar *Hanmer,*
conj. Theobald.

---

more than pace (l. 122). The ideal is
represented by what Gervase Markham prescribes in *Country Contentments*,
1615: 'If you would have your kennell
for sweetnesse of cry, then you must
compound it of some large dogges,
that have deepe solemne mouthes, and
are swift in spending [sc. quick to give
tongue], which must, as it were, beare
the base in the consort, then a double
number of roaring, and loud ringing
mouthes, which must beare the
counter-tenour; then some hollow,
plaine, sweet mouthes, which must
beare the meane or middle part; and
soe with these three partes of musicke
you shall make your cry perfect'.
Markham's is a counsel of perfection,
to which actual packs can hardly have
done more than approximate (so
J. W. Fortescue, in *Shakespeare's
England*, II. 347: cited N.C.S.).

106. *Uncouple*] 'at the side of the
wood . . . the houndes were in couples
staying their comming. . . . The
houndes were straight uncoupled'
(Sidney, *Arcadia*, p. 60). Hippolytus
bids cast off the leashes from one
class of his hounds: below, p. 143, at
n. 132.

110. *hounds and echo*] The hollow
rocks, says Hippolytus, will re-echo to
the bayings of his Spartans (below,
p. 143, at n. 135).; in Golding, the
cry of Actaeon's pack 'did ring
through all the Wood redoubled with
the winde'.

111. *with Hercules*] Cf. North (below,
pp. 134, 135, at nn. 48, 59).
Cadmus] founder of Thebes; in
legend, unheeded by Shakespeare, he
belonged to an earlier epoch than
Theseus and Hercules.
112. *Crete*] where Theseus slew the
Minotaur and, thanks to Ariadne's
thread, escaped from the labyrinth:
cf. Chaucer, *Knight's Tale*, ll. 978–80;
Golding, VII. 225–37; North links
him with Crete (below, pp. 134, 136,
at nn. 50, 64).
bay'd] drove to bay (with barking
hounds).
bear] The authoritative Q1 text is
to be defended, despite the temptation
to emend (claiming an allusion to the
Calydonian boar, as at l. 125 below,
and an easy e : o misreading). In his
Chaucerian source (*Knight's Tale*, l.
1100) Shakespeare read of the hunter
'strangled with the wilde beres'
(Steevens); most likely he knew
Holinshed's statement: 'The beare is
a beast commonly hunted in the East
countrie' (Tollet, Furness, p. 185);
he himself had written of the bear,
besides the boar, as quarry for Adonis
(*Ven.*, l. 883), and was to introduce a
hunted bear in *Wint.* (Malone). The
objection first raised to 'bear', the
unlikelihood of bears in Crete, is
literal-minded and foreign to Shakespeare.
113, 118.] For 'Sparta' and
'Spartan' see l. 125 n.

Such gallant chiding; for, besides the groves,
The skies, the fountains, every region near   115
Seem'd all one mutual cry; I never heard
So musical a discord, such sweet thunder.
The. My hounds are bred out of the Spartan kind,
So flew'd, so sanded; and their heads are hung
With ears that sweep away the morning dew;   120
Crook-knee'd and dewlapp'd like Thessalian bulls;
Slow in pursuit, but match'd in mouth like bells,
Each under each: a cry more tuneable
Was never holla'd to, nor cheer'd with horn,
In Crete, in Sparta, nor in Thessaly.   125
Judge when you hear. But soft, what nymphs are these?
Ege. My lord, this is my daughter here asleep,

116. Seem'd] *F2;* Seeme *Qq,F.*   127. this is] *Q2,F;* this *Q1.*

114. *chiding*] angry noise of hounds:
OED's earliest instance.

115. *fountains*] For 'Lakes, Rivers,
and Fountains' returning an echo
Theobald quotes Virgil, *Aeneid*, XII.
756 '. . . exoritur clamor; ripaeque
lacusque / Responsant circa et coelum
tonat omne tumultu', and Propertius,
Eleg., I. xx. 49, where a name 'ab
extremis fontibus aura refert'.

116. *mutual*] common (*OED* 4,
quoting *Mer.V.*, v. i. 77); the most
frequent sense in Shakespeare, though
now confined to 'reciprocal'.

118. *kind*] strain, lineage.

119. *flew'd*] having large chaps.
Actaeon's Jollyboy was a 'large flewd
hound' (Golding, below, p. 139, at
n. 98).

sanded] sandy-coloured: *OED*'s
earliest instance.

119–20. *heads . . . dew*] Hippolytus'
hounds have their muzzles close to
the dewy earth: below, p. 143, at
nn. 136, 138.

119. *hung*] 'Well-hung' was the
technical epithet for such hounds (in
men, it could signify well-endowed
with tongue, or phallus).

121. *dewlapp'd . . . bulls*] In Golding,
VII. 161, Jason 'coy'd' (cf. l. 2 above)

the 'dangling dewlaps' (folds of loose
skin at the throat) of the bulls he had
tamed. For Thessalian bulls, see
Seneca, *Hippolytus*, ll. 296–8, immediately after the description of
Cupid all armed (p. 142, below).

122.] See l. 105 n.; 'bells', a ring of
bells, from treble to tenor.

123. *cry*] pack (*OED*'s earliest
instance) when giving tongue.

tuneable] harmonious; to a huntsman's ear, melodious.

124. *cheer'd*] encouraged, animated.

125. *Crete . . . Sparta*] Cf. ll. 112 f.,
118. Hippolytus' hounds include
savage Cretans; and Spartans, a breed
bold and eager. Actaeon's Stalker
was Cretan; Blackfoot, Spartan;
Jollyboy and Chorle had a Cretan
sire and Spartan dam: see Seneca and
Golding, below, p. 143, at nn. 133–4,
p. 139, at nn. 96–8.

Thessaly] where Shakespeare locates
the Calydonian boar, 'the boar of
Thessaly', *Ant.*, IV. xiii. 2, though
Calydon is in neighbouring Aetolia.
See ll. 102–26 n.

127. *this is*] Q1's 'this' is either a
mistaken use of the colloquial contraction, authentic in *Lr.*, IV. vi. 185,
'This a good block', or an accidental

And this Lysander; this Demetrius is,
This Helena, old Nedar's Helena.
I wonder of their being here together.   130
The. No doubt they rose up early, to observe
The rite of May; and hearing our intent,
Came here in grace of our solemnity.
But speak, Egeus; is not this the day
That Hermia should give answer of her choice?   135
Ege. It is, my lord.
The. Go, bid the huntsmen wake them with their horns.
                    Shout within; winding of horns.
                    The lovers wake and start up.
Good-morrow friends. Saint Valentine is past:
Begin these wood-birds but to couple now?
Lys. Pardon, my lord.   [*The lovers kneel.*]
The.   I pray you all, stand up.   140
I know you two are rival enemies:
How comes this gentle concord in the world,
That hatred is so far from jealousy
To sleep by hate, and fear no enmity?
Lys. My lord, I shall reply amazedly,   145

---

130. their] *Q1*; this *Q2,F*.   132. rite] *Pope (subst.)*; right *Qq,F*.   137. S.D.
Shout . . . up.] *After Qq,F (Shoute within: they all start up. Winde hornes. Qq;
Hornes and they wake. Shout within, they all start up. F).*   140. The lovers kneel.]
After Capell (He, and the rest, kneel to Theseus); not in Qq,F.

failure to repeat identical letters
(haplography).
   131–2.] See nn. to ll. 102–26, 103,
and I. i. 167.
   132. *rite*] Q1 'right'; our spelling-
distinction was not regularly observed.
Cf. *Oth.,* I. iii. 257 and Ridley's n.
   133. *in grace of*] to grace, honour.
   138–9. *Saint Valentine . . . now*]
Birds were supposed to choose their
mates on St Valentine's Day, 14
February. Chaucer's *Parlement of
Foules* purports to depict a council on
such an occasion. Cf. Surrey, *Poems,*
ed. Emrys Jones, No. 15, ll. 19 f.:
'there might I see . . . the new-

betrothed birdes ycoupled how they
went', and Tilley, S66.
   140. S.D., 140.] Kneeling and
rising were a ready form of meaningful stage-business, founded upon the
significance they had in the rituals of
Elizabethan society. They are used
with supreme effect in *Oth.* (III. iii.
457 ff.), *Lr.* (IV. vii. 60), and *Cor.* (V.
iii. 50 ff.). Here they point the appeal
for mercy, and the grant of a fair
hearing. Chaucer's Theseus honours
the distinction to be made in favour
of those who humble themselves: below, p. 133, at n. 38.
   143. *jealousy*] mistrust.

Half sleep, half waking; but as yet, I swear,
I cannot truly say how I came here.
But as I think—for truly would I speak—
And now I do bethink me, so it is:
I came with Hermia hither; our intent   150
Was to be gone from Athens, where we might,
Without the peril of the Athenian law—
Ege. Enough, enough, my lord; you have enough!
I beg the law, the law upon his head!
They would have stol'n away, they would, Demetrius,
Thereby to have defeated you and me: 156
You of your wife, and me of my consent,
Of my consent that she should be your wife.
Dem. My lord, fair Helen told me of their stealth,
Of this their purpose hither to this wood;   160
And I in fury hither follow'd them,
Fair Helena in fancy following me.
But my good lord, I wot not by what power—
But by some power it is—my love to Hermia,
Melted as the snow, seems to me now   165
As the remembrance of an idle gaud
Which in my childhood I did dote upon;
And all the faith, the virtue of my heart,

151–2. might . . . law—] *Q1* (might . . . lawe), *Dyce* (*Collier subst.*); might be . . . Law. *Q2,F.*   162. following] *Q1;* followed *Q2,F.*   164–6.] *As Pope;* (But . . . is) . . . love/To . . . (melted . . . snow),/ Seems . . . gaude, *Qq,F.*   165. Melted] *Qq,F;* Is melted *Pope.*

146. *Half . . . waking*] perhaps 'being half of me (possessed by) sleep, half of me waking'. But W. A. Wright (followed by Furness, Kittredge, and N.C.S.) took both 'sleep' and 'waking' as nouns (Lysander's reply will half of it be sleep, and half of it waking). He compared 'I shall reply . . . half sleep' to 'He speaks plain cannon-fire' (*John,* II. i. 462). Others have read ' 'sleep' (= asleep), both words adjectival.
152. *Without*] beyond (the reach of).

153–4.] Cf. the first reaction of Chaucer's Theseus to Palamon's story (below, p. 132, at n. 34): to condemn him and Arcite no more is needed. That verdict he rescinds, as Theseus here rejects Egeus' demand.
156. *defeated*] defrauded: legal terminology; *OED v.* 7.
160. *hither*] in coming hither; vb. of motion idiomatically omitted.
168. *faith, . . . heart*] his heart's orientation to fidelity and virtue; 'virtue' meaning also its especial quality (see II. i. 220–6 n.).

The object and the pleasure of mine eye,
Is only Helena. To her, my lord,   170
Was I betroth'd ere I saw Hermia;
But like a sickness did I loathe this food:
But as in health, come to my natural taste,
Now I do wish it, love it, long for it,
And will for evermore be true to it.   175
The. Fair lovers, you are fortunately met;
Of this discourse we more will hear anon.
Egeus, I will overbear your will;
For in the temple, by and by, with us,
These couples shall eternally be knit.   180
And, for the morning now is something worn,
Our purpos'd hunting shall be set aside.
Away, with us, to Athens: three and three,
We'll hold a feast in great solemnity.

---

171. saw] *Steevens;* see *Qq,F.*   173. But] *Qq,F;* Yet *Hanmer;* Now *Cuningham.*
174. I do] *Q1;* do I *Q2,F.*   177. more will hear] *Q1 (reading* here); will hear
more *Q2;* shall hear more *F.*   184-5.] *Q2,F; one line Q1.*

169. *object*] (of the eye): cynosure.
171. *saw*] On Q1's 'see', N.C.S. notes the same anomaly in *LLL,* IV. i. 70-1, and asks 'Can Shakespeare himself have been responsible?' In *LLL,* the compositor may have been set wrong by 'see' (twice, correctly) in l. 72; in *MND,* by the tense of 'Is' in l. 170.
172. *like a sickness*] The sense is clarified by the antithesis between ll. 172 and 173, though the phrase remains difficult. Most likely, because Demetrius seems to speak in personal terms throughout, 'a sickness' = 'a sick man' (perhaps with an implication that he is for the time nothing but his sickness). Kittredge readily adduces Shakespearean parallels for such use of the abstract for the personal: e.g. 'Bring in the admiration', i.e. 'this wonderful person' (*All's W.,* II. i. 87). Alternatively 'a sickness' may = 'a diseased appetite'.

174-5.] Thanks to the love-philtre, Sylvanus in *Diana* can say: 'now since I am safely arrived into a haven of all . . . happinesse, I onely wish I may have harbour . . . there, where my irremoveable . . . love is so firmely placed' (Kennedy, p. 188).
176-80.] Chaucer's Theseus, too, was magnanimous, forgiving the lovers and providing for a happy outcome in marriage (below, pp. 132-134 at nn. 35, 43, 45).
183-4.] Cf. (and with 'in the temple', l. 179, and Oberon's anticipation of dancing 'triumphantly' at the wedding) the end, under Felicia's auspices, of the lovers' troubles in *Diana*: 'riding on their way, they came to *Dianas* Temple. . . . There they were all married with great joy, feasts, and triumphes' (Kennedy, p. 242).
184. *solemnity*] See l. 87, and I. i. 11, and nn.

Come, Hippolyta.   185

Exeunt Theseus, Hippolyta, Egeus, and Train.

Dem. These things seem small and undistinguishable,
   Like far-off mountains turned into clouds.

Her. Methinks I see these things with parted eye,
   When everything seems double.

Hel.   So methinks;
   And I have found Demetrius like a jewel,   190
   Mine own, and not mine own.

Dem.   Are you sure
   That we are awake? It seems to me
   That yet we sleep, we dream. Do not you think
   The Duke was here, and bid us follow him?

Her. Yea, and my father.

Hel.   And Hippolyta.   195

Lys. And he did bid us follow to the temple.

Dem. Why then, we are awake: let's follow him,
   And by the way let us recount our dreams.   *Exeunt.*

Bot. [*Waking.*] When my cue comes, call me and I will
   answer. My next is 'Most fair Pyramus'. Heigh-ho!   200
   Peter Quince? Flute, the bellows-mender? Snout,
   the tinker? Starveling? God's my life! Stolen hence,
   and left me asleep! I have had a most rare vision.
   I have had a dream, past the wit of man to say what
   dream it was. Man is but an ass if he go about to ex-   205

---

185. S.D. *Exeunt . . . Train*] *Capell; Exit Q2; Exeunt Duke and Lords F; not in Q1.*
191–2. Are . . . awake?] *Qq; not in F.*   196. did bid] *Qq;* bid *F.*   197–8.]
As Rowe³; prose, Qq,F.   198. let us] *Q2,F;* let's *Q1.*   Exeunt.] *Rowe; Exit
Q2; Exit Lovers F; not in Q1.*   199. Waking.] *F; not in Qq.*   203. have had]
Qq; had *F.*   205–6. to expound] *Q2,F;* expound *Q1.*

---

188. *parted*] divided (*OED*'s earliest
instance): with the eyes not in focus
with each other.

190. *like a jewel*] 'like a precious
thing found, and therefore of uncertain ownership' (Wells, after
Malone).

193. *we dream*] In *Enamoured Diana*,
a company of lovers, thanks to Felicia
about to be united, 'thought they
were in a dreame, standing like en-
chanted persons, and not believing

their own eies' (Kennedy, p. 376).

200. *Heigh-ho*] a great yawn.

201. *Quince?*] Q1's question-marks
indicate the note of 'where are you?'
in Bottom's shouts: they are not
instances of a compositor's using '?'
for '!'.

202. *God's my life!*] Good lord!
(*OED*'s earliest instance).

204. *wit of man*] power of the
human mind.

205. *go about*] should start trying.

pound this dream. Methought I was—there is no
man can tell what. Methought I was—and methought I had—but man is but a patched fool if he
will offer to say what methought I had. The eye of
man hath not heard, the ear of man hath not seen, 210
man's hand is not able to taste, his tongue to conceive, nor his heart to report, what my dream was. I
will get Peter Quince to write a ballad of this
dream: it shall be called 'Bottom's Dream', because
it hath no bottom; and I will sing it in the latter end 215
of a play, before the Duke. Peradventure, to make it
the more gracious, I shall sing it at her death.   *Exit.*

---

208. a patched] *F;* patched a *Qq.*   213. ballad] *Qq,F* (ballet), *F4.*   216. a
play] *Qq,F;* the play *Hanmer;* our play *Walker.*   217. at her] *Qq,F;* after
Theobald.   Exit.] *Q2,F; not in Q1.*

208. *a . . . fool*] Q1's 'patcht a foole'
(proclaimed—by his patches—a fool)
might be accepted (*praestat difficilior
lectio*) as the reading less likely to have
arisen from its specious appeal to a
copyist. If he had 'a patched fool'
before him, he would have no motive
for a normalizing change, whether
conscious or subconscious. But even
without such motive, the transposition
could easily have been made inadvertently. The Q1 phrase does not,
to my mind, satisfy the criterion of
sitting naturally in its context.
    patched] The fool commonly wore
a child's long coat: parti-coloured,
but, as Hotson showed in *Shakespeare's
Motley,* 1952, not in quarters but in
the weave. It was left to E. W. Ives
(in *Sh.S.* 13, 1960, pp. 90 ff.) to
correct Hotson's idea that the colours
were mingled as in modern tweeds:
that requires advanced manufacturing
techniques. They were arranged in
simple patterns, stripes or checks for
example, which could be produced
with yarns of two colours on the hand-

loom: hence the patched or pied
look. (This account is from Agnes
Latham's fuller one, in her edn of *As
You Like It,* p. lv.) From the dress,
Wolsey's fool was named Patch,
which strengthened the association.
    209–12. *The eye . . . was*] at once con-
fusion of perceptual functions (cf. III. i.
86, v. i. 190 f.) and burlesque of Scripture: 1 Corinthians, ii. 9: 'The eye
hath not seene, and the eare hath not
heard, neyther have entered into the
heart of man' those things God has
prepared (Bishops' Bible, R. Noble,
p. 161).
    213. *ballad*] a topical narrative set
to a popular tune, like those printed
as black-letter broadsides.
    215. *because . . . bottom*] For the mul-
tiple joke, see Introduction, p. cxvii.
    216. *a play*] Emendations to 'the
play', 'our play' are false to Bottom's
only half-focused state of mind, and
curtail the poetic flight of his (and
Shakespeare's) imagination. See Introduction, *loc. cit.*
    217. *gracious*] appealing.

[SCENE II]

Enter QUINCE, FLUTE, SNOUT, *and* STARVELING.

Quin. Have you sent to Bottom's house? Is he come
home yet?

Star. He cannot be heard of. Out of doubt he is transported.

Flu. If he come not, then the play is marred: it goes not   5
forward, doth it?

Quin. It is not possible. You have not a man in all Athens
able to discharge Pyramus but he.

Flu. No, he hath simply the best wit of any handicraft
man in Athens.   10

Quin. Yea, and the best person too; and he is a very
paramour for a sweet voice.

Flu. You must say paragon. A paramour is, God bless
us, a thing of naught.

Scene II

SCENE II] *Capell; not in Qq,F.*   [*Location*] *Changes to the Towne. Theobald; A
Room in Quince's House. Capell; not in Qq,F.* S.D.] *F (reading 'Flute, Thisby,'),
Rowe³; Enter Quince, Flute, Thisby, and the rabble. Qq.*   3. *Star.*] *F (staru.);
Flut. Qq.*   5. *Flu.*] *Rowe³ (Flute.); Thys. Qq,F. (so throughout scene).*   14.
naught] *F2; nought Qq,F.*

S.D.] 'and the rabble' (instead of
Snout and Starveling) by its in-
definiteness marks the Q1 S.D. as the
author's: hence it is he who names
Flute and his role Thisbe as though
they were two persons, at ll. 3, 5
makes *Thys.* answer *Flut.*, and continues with *Thys.* (or *This.*) in the
speech-heads.

3. *Star.*] Q1's *Flut.* cannot stand
(see previous n.): the speaker must
be either Snout or Starveling, and
F's *Star.* may have been recovered
from the prompt-book.

transported] Starveling conflates, I
believe, his erroneous word for
Bottom transmogrified, and a normal
one for his being 'conveyed away' by
whoever shifted his shape—not by
death, as Schmidt thought, drawing
too exact a parallel with *Meas.*, IV.
iii. 72, where 'transport = send from

this world to the next': but the
parallel is not so irrelevant as Furness,
and more dogmatically Cuningham,
made out. Bottom *was* conveyed to
another realm: Starveling's conviction has only just ceased to be true in
both particulars.

7-10.] For Athenian handicrafts-
men as a social class see I. ii. 0 n.

11. *person*] personal appearance,
presence.

13. *paragon . . . paramour*] The
malapropism may have been suggested
by Mouffet's calling Pyramus a
'paragon' (Muir², p. 74). Shakespeare
first uses the word in *Gent.* (II. iv. 41),
perhaps from *Diana* (Kennedy, p.
152 and elsewhere; 'paragoned', p.
129).

14. *a . . . naught*] a shameful thing;
not respectable.

Enter SNUG *the Joiner.*

Snug. Masters, the Duke is coming from the temple, and   15
there is two or three lords and ladies more married.
If our sport had gone forward, we had all been
made men.

Flu. O sweet bully Bottom! Thus hath he lost sixpence a
day during his life; he could not have 'scaped six-   20
pence a day. And the Duke had not given him sixpence a day for playing Pyramus, I'll be hanged.
He would have deserved it: sixpence a day in Pyramus, or nothing.

Enter BOTTOM.

Bot. Where are these lads? Where are these hearts?   25
Quin. Bottom! O most courageous day! O most happy
hour!
Bot. Masters, I am to discourse wonders: but ask me not
what; for if I tell you, I am not true Athenian. I will
tell you everything, right as it fell out.   30

29. not] *Qq;* no F.   30. right as] *Qq;* as *F.*

18. *made men*] men with our fortunes made; cf. Pres. E., 'self-made man'.

19. *sweet bully*] that dear fine fellow; cf. *H5*, IV. i. 44, 48, and above, III. i. 7 and n.

19–20. *sixpence a day*] a joiner (cf. Snug) in 1595 at the Lancs. rate 'received fourpence a day and also his food: without meat and drink his pay was eightpence': M. St. Clare Byrne, *Elizabethan Life*, p. 168; on p. 169 she reckons a master-carpenter's annual earnings, given an average four days' work a week, as £6.18.8. Bottom's daily pension would have come to more than twice as much.

21. *And*] If.

25. *hearts*] grand-hearted chaps; in Lancs., 'gradely lads'.

26. *courageous*] Quince means 'brave' = splendid (N.C.S.). Scots 'braw' keeps the Elizabethan sense, 'fine'.

28–32. *I am . . . tell you*] 'Bottom's anxiety at once to tell his tale and keep up the mystery of it is very humorous' (E. K. Chambers). Rather, the comedy (apart from the involuntary tantalizing of his comrades) lies in his refusals to tell being cover for not being able to: every time he means to burst out with the story he is sure he is full of, he finds the memory has faded even further than when he awoke and could not pin down what 'Methought I was'. Dreams do fade like this: but the fairy magic which (IV. i. 67 f.) was to prevent recollection of 'this night's accidents' as real events no doubt ensures the complete block. Inconsistently, between IV. i and V. i, the lovers, off-stage, have been able to report their experiences with an awareness of fairy participation they never possessed at the time; but where

Quin. Let us hear, sweet Bottom.

Bot. Not a word of me. All that I will tell you is, that the
Duke hath dined. Get your apparel together, good
strings to your beards, new ribbons to your pumps;
meet presently at the palace; every man look o'er   35
his part: for the short and the long is, our play is
preferred. In any case, let Thisbe have clean linen;
and let not him that plays the lion pare his nails, for
they shall hang out for the lion's claws. And most
dear actors, eat no onions nor garlic, for we are to   40
utter sweet breath; and I do not doubt but to hear
them say, it is a sweet comedy. No more words.
Away! Go, away!   *Exeunt.*

42–3. words. Away!] *Q1* (Away,); words: away, *Q2,F.*   43. Go, away!]
Theobald (away.); go away. *Qq,F*   *Exeunt.*] *F; not in Qq.*

dramatic or poetic advantage is to
be had, Shakespeare pays no heed to
inconsistencies which will not trouble
the audience.

34. *strings . . . beards*] the strings tie
the false beards on.

35. *presently*] 'without a moment's
delay' (Kittredge).

36. *the short . . . is*] a colloquial

idiom: five more instances in Shakespeare; cf. Tilley, L419.

37. *preferred*] put forward for
acceptance: characteristically, Bottom considers it as good as chosen. It
has not yet been given the final
preference: at v. i. 42 it has reached
the list of entertainments which are
ready.

ACT V

[SCENE I]

Enter THESEUS, HIPPOLYTA; Lords *and* Attendants,
among them PHILOSTRATE.

Hip. 'Tis strange, my Theseus, that these lovers speak of.
The. More strange than true. I never may believe
 These antique fables, nor these fairy toys.
 Lovers and madmen have such seething brains,
 Such shaping fantasies, that apprehend   5
 More than cool reason ever comprehends.
 The lunatic, the lover, and the poet
 Are of imagination all compact:
 One sees more devils than vast hell can hold;
 That is the madman: the lover, all as frantic,   10

ACT V

Scene 1

ACT V] F (*Actus Quintus*); *not in Qq*. SCENE I] *Rowe; not in Qq,F*. [*Location*]
The Palace. Theobald; A State-Room in Theseus's Palace. Capell; not in Qq,F S.D.
Lords . . . Philostrate.] and Philostrate Qq; Egeus and his Lords F. 3. antique]
Q1; anticke *Q2,F.* 5–6. apprehend/More than] *Theobald;* apprehend
more/Then *Qq,F.* 6–8.] *As Q2,F;* Then . . . lunatick,/ . . . compact. *Q1.*

2–3. *More . . . fables*] Lyly opened
the last Act of *Endimion* with the like
comment on the foregoing magical
adventures: '*Eumenides* hath tolde
such strange tales as I may well
wonder at them, but never beleeve
them'.

3. *antique*] antique, 'ancient'; but
also 'grotesque' (antic): implying
'nowadays recognizably absurd'.

4–8, 21.] Cf. in Scot, *Witchcraft*
(below, p. 147, at nn. 166–7, 173),
his scorn of night-fears and of belief
in fairies and assorted bugbears,
sprung from the vain dreams of

the weak in mind and body.

4. *seething*] on the boil.

5–8.] For Q1's mislined verse here,
at ll. 12–17, and in six further
passages up to ll. 82 f., pointing to
marginal insertions by Shakespeare
in his foul papers, see Introduction,
pp. xl f., and Appendix III.

5–6. *apprehend . . . comprehends*]
apprehend = conceive: Hotspur
(*1H4*, I. iii. 207) 'apprehends a world
of figures here' (Humphreys's gloss is
'snatches at'); 'comprehends' = gets
a grasp of, understands.

8. *all compact*] entirely made up.

103

Sees Helen's beauty in a brow of Egypt:
The poet's eye, in a fine frenzy rolling,
Doth glance from heaven to earth, from earth to heaven;
And as imagination bodies forth
The forms of things unknown, the poet's pen   15
Turns them to shapes, and gives to airy nothing
A local habitation and a name.
Such tricks hath strong imagination,
That if it would but apprehend some joy,
It comprehends some bringer of that joy: 20
Or, in the night, imagining some fear,
How easy is a bush suppos'd a bear!
Hip. But all the story of the night told over,

12–13.] *As Rowe;* The . . . glance/ . . . as/*Q1;* The glance/ . . . to heaven.
Q2,F.   14.] *As Rowe³;* Imagination . . . things *Q1;* And as . . . things
Q2,F.   15–18.] *As Rowe³;* Unknowne; . . . shapes,/ . . . habitation,/ . . .
imagination, *Qq,F.*   16. airy] *Qq;* aire *F.*

11. *of Egypt*] i.e. a gipsy's.

12. *fine frenzy*] the famous *furor poeticus*: see Introduction, p. cxl, and Tilley, W579.

13. *heaven*] Cf. Sidney on 'that high flying liberty of conceit proper to the poet', which 'did seeme to have some dyvine force in it' (*Apologie for Poetrie,* p. 6).

14. *bodies forth*] embodies in forms which the mind's eye, ear, etc. can take in; find (in T. S. Eliot's phrase) an 'objective correlative' for.

18–20.] The 'trick' is perfectly exemplified in the self-deception of Chaucer's Troilus (*Troilus and Criseyde,* v. 1115 ff., 1157 ff.). 'Strong imagination' is Apelles' phrase in Lyly, *Campaspe,* IV. iv. 12 f., though he is not taking himself in. From Campaspe's 'professed faith' he apprehends a joy, making her picture the bringer of an instalment of it: her avowal 'wil cause me to imbrace thy shadow continually in my armes, of the which by strong imagination I will make a substance'.

21–2.] Cf., in combination, Scot, *Witchcraft,* below, p. 147, at nn.

173–4): at night men will frighten themselves into taking a shorn sheep for a ghost; and the proverbial 'Think every bush a bug-bear', be 'afraid of every bush', Tilley, B738, 737. For the like effect attributed to conscience cf. *Lucr.,* l. 971, *3H6,* v. vi. 11, Tilley, T112; and to guilt *Mirror,* p. 325 (Sackville, *Complaint of Buckingham,* ll. 202 ff.): 'the felon . . . pursued by night / Startes at eche bush'. The appeal to proverbial wisdom confirms and rounds off Theseus' observations: by critics who fail to appreciate this the couplet has been thought weak.

21. *some fear*] something to be afraid of.

23–6.] Kittredge paraphrases: 'But the whole story of the night, when told in all its details—especially the fact that the minds of all of them were thus changed and deluded at the same time—testifies that there is something more in the affair than mere pictures of the imagination, and works out into a highly consistent narrative of actual experience!'

And all their minds transfigur'd so together,
More witnesseth than fancy's images,   25
And grows to something of great constancy;
But howsoever, strange and admirable.

Enter the lovers: LYSANDER, DEMETRIUS, HERMIA, *and* HELENA.

The. Here come the lovers, full of joy and mirth.
    Joy, gentle friends, joy and fresh days of love
    Accompany your hearts!
Lys.   More than to us   30
    Wait in your royal walks, your board, your bed!
The. Come now; what masques, what dances shall we have,
    To wear away this long age of three hours
    Between our after-supper and bed-time?
    Where is our usual manager of mirth?   35
    What revels are in hand? Is there no play
    To ease the anguish of a torturing hour?
    Call Philostrate.
Phil. [*Advancing.*]   Here, mighty Theseus.

27. S.D.] *Qq,F* (*Enter Lovers; . . . Helena*).   29–30.] *As F2;* Joy . . . dayes/
. . . hearts. *Qq,F.*   30–1. More . . . bed!] *As F2; prose, Qq,F.*   33–6.] *As
Q2,F;* To . . . betweene/ . . . manager/ . . . play *Q1.*   34. our] *F;* or *Qq.*
37–8. To . . . Philostrate] *As Q2,F; one line Q1.*   38. Philostrate] *Qq;*
Egeus *F.*   38. *Phil.*] *Qq;* Ege. *F* (*so, subst., throughout scene*)   Advancing.]
This edn; not in Qq,F.

25. *fancy's*] 'fancy' here = the
imagination of lovers.
26. *constancy*] (1) self-consistency
(and therefore to be relied on); (2)
able to stand all tests. Cf. *OED*
'consist' 1 and 2.
27. *howsoever . . . admirable*] anyway,
outside normal experience, and to be
wondered at (from Lat. *admiror*).
27. S.D.] Perhaps Shakespeare
wrote 'the lovers' and the specification
is the bookholder's (N.C.S.). If so,
the latter had annotated the foul
papers used as copy for Q1, in readiness for transcribing the prompt-
book from them.
28–31.] Cf. the bliss and melody at
Palamon's marriage (Chaucer, below,
p. 134, at n. 46).
34.] Q1's 'or' is a misreading of o*r*
(= our).

after-supper] dessert, following supper, not rere-supper: 'the court would
hardly wait up three hours after a
rere-supper' (N.C.S.), taken, according to Harrison's *Description of England*
(quoted Cuningham), 'when it was
time to go to rest'.
35–6. *manager . . . revels*] Philostrate
(l. 38) is Theseus' Master of the
Revels; Queen Elizabeth's, at this
period Sir Edmund Tilney, perused
and saw in rehearsal (cf. l. 68) plays
submitted by available companies, in
order to select those to be acted before her (E. K. Chambers, *Elizabethan
Stage*, I. 223 f.). For F's *Egeus*, see
Introduction, p. xxxii and n. 1.
36, 40, 41. *revels . . . play . . . masque
. . . delight*] Cf. Marlowe, *Hero and
Leander*, 1. 299–302: '. . . The rites / In
which loves beauteous Empresse most

The. Say, what abridgement have you for this evening,
    What masque, what music? How shall we beguile   40
    The lazy time, if not with some delight?
Phil. There is a brief how many sports are ripe:
    Make choice of which your Highness will see first.
                                       [Giving a paper.]
The. [*Reads.*] 'The battle with the Centaurs, to be sung
    By an Athenian eunuch to the harp'?   45
    We'll none of that; that have I told my love
    In glory of my kinsman Hercules.
    [*Reads.*] 'The riot of the tipsy Bacchanals,
    Tearing the Thracian singer in their rage'?
    That is an old device, and it was play'd   50

42. *Phil.*] *Qq; Ege.* F.   ripe] *Q1;* rife *Q2,F.*   43. S.D. *Giving a paper.*]
Theobald; Giving a paper which Theseus hands to Lysander to read. Halliwell; not in
Qq,F.   44. *Reads.*] *Theobald; not in Qq,F.*   The] *Qq; Lis.* The *F.*   46. We'll]
Qq; The. We'll *F.*   48. *Reads.*] *Theobald; not in Qq,F.*   The] *Qq; Lis.* The *F.*
50. That] *Qq; The.* That *F.*

delights / Are . . . midnight revell, /
Plaies, maskes . . .'

39. *abridgement*] perhaps embracing
(so Hulme, p. 308) both possible
meanings: (1) pastime, to shorten or
while away the time; (2) a representation in miniature (short or shortened):
for both see *OED.* The context shows
(1) is the primary sense. That the
pastime is to be an Interlude is not
yet determined; but abridgement, for
Shakespeare, may have been associated with drama: in *Ham.,* II. ii.
415, it means 'what will cut me short',
but the abridging agent is the arrival
of the Players (Hulme).

40-1. *How . . . delight?*] Cf. Spenser,
Shepheardes Calender, October, ll. 2 f.:
'. . . let us cast with what delight to
chace, / And weary thys long lingring
Phoebus race' (with which compare
also l. 33 above). This eclogue may
be part of the context of Shakespeare's thought at ll. 52-4, since
according to E.K. it 'is made in
imitation of Theocritus his XVI.
Idilion, wherein he reproved the
Tyranne Hero of Syracuse for his
nigardise towards Poetes. . . . And the
lyke also is in Mantuane'.

41. *lazy*] sluggish.

42. *brief*] short list.

ripe] ready; earlier than *OED*'s
earliest instance, *Caes.,* IV. iii. 215.

43. S.D., 44-60.] In F's version,
evidently from prompt-copy, Theseus,
on receiving the scroll, must hand it
to Lysander: for Lysander reads the
items. The actors, like some editors,
may have seen theatrical advantage
in breaking up Theseus' longish
speech; but Q1 testifies that this was
not Shakespeare's original intention,
and F can yield no assurance that he
changed his mind.

45. *harp?*] Here and below, Theseus
reads the titles in a tone which enquires 'will this do?' Hence Q1's question marks.

47.] For Theseus' pride in his
cousin Hercules see North (below, p.
134, at n. 48; cf. p. 135, at n.
59).

48-9.] For the death of 'the
Thracian Poet', Orpheus, at the hands
of 'Bacchus drunken rout', the
Maenads, see Golding, XI. 1-42.

50. *device*] viz. devised for dramatic
representation: cf. *LLL,* V. ii. 653 f.,
OED's earliest instance.

When I from Thebes came last a conqueror.
[*Reads.*] 'The thrice three Muses mourning for the death
Of learning, late deceas'd in beggary'?
That is some satire, keen and critical,
Not sorting with a nuptial ceremony.   55
[*Reads.*] 'A tedious brief scene of young Pyramus
And his love Thisbe, very tragical mirth'?
Merry and tragical? Tedious and brief?
That is hot ice, and wondrous strange snow!
How shall we find the concord of this discord?   60

52. *Reads.*] *Theobald; not in Qq,F.*   The] *Qq; Lis.* The *F.*   54. That] *Qq; The.* That *F.*   56. *Reads.*] *Theobald; not in Qq,F.*   A] *Qq; Lis.* A *F.* 58. Merry] *Qq; The.* Merry *F.*   58–60.] *As Theobald;* Merry . . . Ise,/And . . . cōcord/ . . . discord? *Q1; prose, Q2,F (Q2 begins 59* And).

52. *thrice . . . mourning*] That Shakespeare intended a recognizable allusion to Spenser's *Teares of the Muses*, 1591, is not now believed; but on the fair likelihood that he himself had it in mind see Introduction, p. xxxix. W. A. Wright conceded that the title may have helped to suggest the present one.
53. *learning . . . beggary*] reminiscent of Marlowe, *Hero and Leander*, I. 470: the Destinies' curse on 'Learning' 'That he and Povertie should alwaies kiss'. From classical and Renaissance Latin authors, the sentiment is illustrated in Burton on 'The Miseries of Scholars' (*Anatomy of Melancholy*, I. 2.3.15); cf. Tilley, M1316. If 'late deceas'd' is nevertheless a topical allusion, it would (as Knight suggested) fit Robert Greene, M.A. of both Universities, whose death in destitution was notorious especially from his last letters to his deserted wife, printed in 1592, one in *Greenes Groats-worth of witte*, and two versions of another in *The Repentance of Robert Greene Maister of Artes* and Gabriel Harvey's *Foure Letters*. Harvey's pamphlet provoked Nashe, and their quarrel (which has echoes in *LLL*) not ending till 1597, might keep the earlier circumstances in the public mind, as Greene's attack, in the *Groats-worth*, upon Shakespeare, and Chettle's amends in *Kinde-Hartes Dreame*, 1592, must have kept them in Shakespeare's.
54. *critical*] censorious.
57. *very tragical mirth*] not solely a general hit at the earlier Elizabethan dramas condemned by Sidney as 'neither right Tragedies, nor right Comedies: mingling Kings and Clownes not because the matter so carrieth it' (Shakespeare contrives that the matter shall); but no doubt alluding specifically to Thomas Preston's *Cambises*, of which the title begins: 'A Lamentable Tragedie mixed full of plesant mirth'. 'King Cambyses' vein' is proposed as a style for mock-heroics in *1H4*, II. iv. 382: in that scene, ll. 386–9, as in the present one, ll. 319, 323 f., 327 f., *Cambises* seems a target.
59. *strange*] unjustifiably emended by many editors who expected an oxymoron (e.g. 'black snow') parallel with 'hot ice'. Even 'extraordinarily odd snow' would be an acceptable meaning. But in Shakespeare, the Cowden-Clarkes observe, 'strange' can signify 'unnatural', 'prodigious'. The phrase here may be equivalent to 'hot ice, and snow no less wondrously unnatural' (so Knight).

Phil. A play there is, my lord, some ten words long,
    Which is as brief as I have known a play;
    But by ten words, my lord, it is too long,
    Which makes it tedious; for in all the play
    There is not one word apt, one player fitted.   65
    And tragical, my noble lord, it is,
    For Pyramus therein doth kill himself;
    Which, when I saw rehears'd, I must confess
    Made mine eyes water; but more merry tears
    The passion of loud laughter never shed.   70
The. What are they that do play it?
Phil. Hard-handed men that work in Athens here,
    Which never labour'd in their minds till now;
    And now have toil'd their unbreath'd memories
    With this same play, against your nuptial.   75
The. And we will hear it.
Phil.   No, my noble lord,
    It is not for you: I have heard it over,
    And it is nothing, nothing in the world;
    Unless you can find sport in their intents,
    Extremely stretch'd and conn'd with cruel pain   80
    To do you service.
The.   I will hear that play;
    For never anything can be amiss
    When simpleness and duty tender it.
    Go bring them in; and take your places, ladies.
                                    [*Exit Philostrate.*]
Hip. I love not to see wretchedness o'er-charg'd,   85
    And duty in his service perishing.
The. Why, gentle sweet, you shall see no such thing.
Hip. He says they can do nothing in this kind.

61. *Phil.*] *Qq; Ege. F.*   66–70.] *As F2;* And . . . *Pyramus*/ . . . saw/ . . . water;/
. . . laughter/ . . . shed *Qq,F.*   72. *Phil.*] *Qq; Ege. F.*   76–8. No . . . world;]
As Rowe³; No . . . heard/ . . . world; *Qq,F.*   81–3. I . . . it.] *As Rowe³;* I . . .
any thing/ . . . it. *Qq,F.*   84. S.D. *Exit Philostrate.*] *Pope;* not in *Qq,F.*

72–3.] Cf. I. ii. S.D. and n.
74. *toil'd*] taxed.
unbreath'd] unexercised, unpractised.
79–80. *intents . . . conn'd*] ' "Intents"
here, as the subject of . . . "stretch'd"

and "conn'd", is used both for *endeavour* and for *the object of endeavour*'
(R. G. White²).
83. *simpleness*] artless sincerity (Kittredge).

The. The kinder we, to give them thanks for nothing.
Our sport shall be to take what they mistake: 90
And what poor duty cannot do, noble respect
Takes it in might, not merit.
Where I have come, great clerks have purposed
To greet me with premeditated welcomes;
Where I have seen them shiver and look pale,   95
Make periods in the midst of sentences,
Throttle their practis'd accent in their fears,
And, in conclusion, dumbly have broke off,
Not paying me a welcome. Trust me, sweet,
Out of this silence yet I pick'd a welcome,   100
And in the modesty of fearful duty
I read as much as from the rattling tongue
Of saucy and audacious eloquence.
Love, therefore, and tongue-tied simplicity
In least speak most, to my capacity.   105

[*Enter* PHILOSTRATE.]

Phil. So please your grace, the Prologue is address'd.

91–2. duty...Takes] *Qq,F;* (willing) duty...do,/Noble...takes *Theobald.*
105. S.D.] *Pope; not in Qq,F.*   106. Phil.] *Qq; Ege. F.*

91. *noble respect*] the noble way of
looking at it.
92, 93–103.] The short line closes
the preceding movement of Theseus'
speech, so that he can modulate into
the key of his reminiscence, which
(see Introduction, pp. lxvi f.) is also a
tribute to Elizabeth's behaviour on
like occasions.
92.] accepts it, not at its actual
value, but with respect to the power,
the resources, of those who offer it. So
(Matthew, xii. 42) is the widow's
mite assessed; and Eliza's shilling, in
Pygmalion, as 'the biggest offer'
Higgins ever had. 'The will for the
deed' is proverbial: Tilley, W393,

S730, especially his quotations from
Pettie (1576) and Porter.
93. *great clerks*] men of deep learning.
101.] 'modesty' = deferential feeling; 'fearful' = timorous.
104–5.] Cf. Tilley, L165, T416: he
quotes Pettie, *Petite Palace* (1576), 'As
I have heard, those that love most
speak least', and Lyly, *Euphues and
his England*, 'True love lacketh a
tongue'.
105. *to my capacity*] to the best of my
power to take things in; the tone is
that of our 'unless I am very much
mistaken'.
106. *address'd*] poised to begin.

The. Let him approach.

Flourish of trumpets.

Enter QUINCE *for the* Prologue.

Pro. *If we offend, it is with our good will.*
    That you should think, we come not to offend,
    But with good will. To show our simple skill,   110
    That is the true beginning of our end.
    Consider then, we come but in despite.
    We do not come, as minding to content you,
    Our true intent is. All for your delight,
    We are not here. That you should here repent you,   115
    The actors are at hand; and by their show,
    You shall know all, that you are like to know.

The. This fellow doth not stand upon points.

Lys. He hath rid his prologue like a rough colt; he knows
    not the stop. A good moral, my lord: it is not enough 120
    to speak, but to speak true.

Hip. Indeed he hath played on this prologue like a child

---

107. *The.*] *Qq,F* (*Duke*).   S.D. *Flourish of trumpets.*] *F* (*Flor. Trum.*)*; not in Qq*.
107. S.D.] *F* (*Enter the Prologue. Quince.*)*, Rowe; Enter the Prologue Qq*.   122.
this] *Qq;* his *F*.

---

107. S.D. Flourish of trumpets] It was regular practice, we learn from Dekker, *Guls Hornbook* (1609), for 'the prologue . . . to give the trumpets their cue, that hees upon point to enter' (Cuningham).

108–17.] In Udall's *Ralph Roister Doister*, Merrygreek, by mischievous mispunctuation in delivery, turns into insult that hero's letter of courtship. The garbled letter gained wide circulation through inclusion in Thomas Wilson's *Rule of Reason* (1533), 3rd edn, 'a popular textbook of logic' (Kittredge). Barnabe Riche's *Farewell to Military Profession* (1581). which Shakespeare knew at least by the time he wrote *Twelfth Night*, contains a similar trick. Malpunctuation (lack of it) had been used for Machiavellian ambiguity in Marlowe's *Edward II*, ll. 2238–48.

For right punctuation of Quince's Prologue, see Appendix IV.
110. But] with correct punctuation, 'on the contrary'; with Quince's, 'except'. The absurdity resembles the one Jonson was to impute to Shakespeare: 'Caesar doth not wrong but with just cause'.
112. in despite] to be vexatious.
118. *stand upon points*] (1) take much stock in punctuation; (2) stick at trifles.
119. *rid*] conducted (with imperfect control, like the rider's); *OED*'s earliest example of this figurative use.
120. *the stop*] (1) mark of punctuation; (2) in the 'manage' (equestrianism) the sudden checking of a horse at full gallop, throwing it on its haunches. Cf. Madden, p. 198 (cited Cuningham).

on a recorder; a sound, but not in government.

The. His speech was like a tangled chain; nothing im-
paired, but all disordered. Who is next?   125

Enter, with a Trumpeter before them, [BOTTOM *as*] PYRAMUS *and*
[FLUTE *as*] THISBE, *and* [SNOUT *as*] WALL, *and* [STARVELING
as] MOONSHINE, *and* [SNUG *as*] LION.

Pro. Gentles, perchance you wonder at this show;
But wonder on, till truth make all things plain.
This man is Pyramus, if you would know;
This beauteous lady Thisbe is certain.
This man, with lime and rough-cast, doth present   130
Wall, that vile wall which did these lovers sunder;
And through Wall's chink, poor souls, they are content
To whisper. At the which let no man wonder.
This man, with lantern, dog, and bush of thorn,
Presenteth Moonshine; for, if you will know,   135
By moonshine did these lovers think no scorn

125. S.D. *Enter, with a Trumpeter before them,*] F (*Tawyer with a Trumpet before them.*/
preceding *Enter*), Alexander (*Trumpet*); not in Qq.   Bottom as . . . Flute as . . . Snout
as . . . Starveling as . . . Snug as] Wells; not in Qq,F.   Thisbe, and . . . Wall,
and] Q1; Thisby, . . . Wall, Q2,F.

123. *recorder*] pipe of the whistle
family: see Edgar Hunt, *The Recorder
and its Music.* Renaissance recorders
are described and illustrated by David
Munrow, *Instruments of the Middle
Ages and Renaissance* (pp. 56–8 of the
book accompanying the discs, which
exemplify the music on Side III, No.
10). The idea of the recorder in
hands unable to play it is used to
great dramatic effect in *Ham.*, III. ii.
387 ff.
in government] under control. Re-
vived by Arnold Dolmetsch, the
recorder, in simplified forms, is now
often 'governed' by schoolchildren.
125. S.D. a Trumpeter] The
prompt-book used in preparing copy
for F named him as Tawyer (William
Tawyer, in the pay of John Heminge,
Shakespeare's fellow actor). Tawyer,
then, was the Trumpeter at least in
the revival that prompt-book seems
to reflect. See Introduction, p. xxx.

127. *till . . . plain*] proverbial:
Tilley, T591, cf. T324; he quotes
Erasmus, *Adagia*; Kyd, *Spanish Tragedy*: 'Time is the author . . . of
trueth . . . / And time will bring
this treacherie to light', and *Lucr.*,
939.
129. *certain*] For the wrenched
accent (archaic by that time) cf. J.
Thomson's Pyramus poem in *A
Handfull of Pleasant Delites* (Muir²,
p. 72).
130, 160.] 'lime' and 'stone' here
and in ll. 164, 189 are from Chaucer's
version of the story in *The Legend of
Good Women*, ll. 764 f.: 'thow sufferest
for to gon / Oure wordes thourgh thy
lym and ek thy ston'.
131.] Cf. ll. 178, 198; Golding,
below, p. 150, at n. 190.
132. *poor souls*] Thisbe is 'poor
soul' in Mouffet (Muir², p. 74).
136. *By moonshine*] See III. i. 50 f.
and n.

To meet at Ninus' tomb, there, there to woo.
This grisly beast, which Lion hight by name,
The trusty Thisbe, coming first by night,
Did scare away, or rather did affright;   140
And as she fled, her mantle she did fall,
Which Lion vile with bloody mouth did stain.
Anon comes Pyramus, sweet youth and tall,
And finds his trusty Thisbe's mantle slain;
Whereat with blade, with bloody blameful blade,   145
He bravely broach'd his boiling bloody breast;
And Thisbe, tarrying in mulberry shade,
His dagger drew, and died. For all the rest.
Let Lion, Moonshine, Wall, and lovers twain
At large discourse, while here they do remain.   150

          Exeunt Prologue, Pyramus, Thisbe, Lion,
                                      and Moonshine.

144. *his trusty*] *Qq;* his *F.*   150. S.D. *Exeunt . . . Moonshine.*] *F* (*Exit all but Wall.*); *Exit Lyon, Thysby, and Mooneshine. Qq,F* (*following 153*).

137. Ninus' tomb] from Golding; see III. i. 92 and n. Despite Quince's correction there, Flute here (at l. 252) repeats his old mistake, and so (at l. 200) does Bottom.

138–40.] The quatrain is defective, lacking a line to rhyme with 138; but the sense hardly admits of one having been lost. The oversight was no doubt Shakespeare's; if he noticed it, he could reckon on it passing muster, with anyone else who did, as characteristic of Quince.

138. grisly . . . Lion] The lioness is 'grisly', and 'lions' are classed as 'fell' (cf. l. 219 below), in Mouffet (Muir², p. 74): cf. 'grieslie ghostes' in Spenser, *Shepheardes Calender*, November, l. 55.

hight by name] Cf. the 'elegant variation "name" and "hight" in successive lines' of the Pyramus poem (anonymous) in *A Gorgious Gallery* (Muir², p. 72).

142. with bloody mouth] from Chaucer: 'With blody mouth . . . with hire blody mouth' (*Legend of Good Women*, ll. 807, 820); cf. Golding: 'with bloudie teeth' and 'with blood / About the chappes' (below, p. 151, at nn. 204, 201).

143. tall] tall youth = fine young fellow; cf. Cotgrave: 'Talle . . . *bel* as bel hom[m]e'.

144. mantle] from Golding (below, p. 151, at n. 203).

146. broach'd] pierced: tapping the liquor as from a cask. Only in Mouffet's version does Ovid's image of the blood squirting like water from a fractured pipe acquire an equivalent to 'broach'd'. Mouffet's pipe is 'goog'd with punch or cheesil slit' (Muir², p. 76).

boiling bloody breast] Cf. the 'boyling brest' of the Calydonian boar in Golding, VIII. 478. In *LLL*, IV. ii. 55, through Holofernes, Shakespeare ridicules poetasters who 'affect the letter'.

147. tarrying . . . shade] In Golding, the lovers agree to 'tarie' beneath a 'Mulberie' (below, p. 150, at nn. 198–9).

The. I wonder if the lion be to speak?

Dem. No wonder, my lord; one lion may when many
     asses do.

Wall. In this same interlude it doth befall
          That I, one Snout by name, present a wall;   155
          And such a wall as I would have you think
          That had in it a crannied hole, or chink,
          Through which the lovers, Pyramus and Thisbe,
          Did whisper often, very secretly.
          This loam, this rough-cast, and this stone doth show   160
          That I am that same wall; the truth is so:
          And this the cranny is, right and sinister,
          Through which the fearful lovers are to whisper.

The. Would you desire lime and hair to speak better?

Dem. It is the wittiest partition that ever I heard dis-   165
     course, my lord.

Enter PYRAMUS.

The. Pyramus draws near the wall; silence!

Pyr. O grim-look'd night! O night with hue so black!
          O night, which ever art when day is not!
          O night, O night, alack, alack, alack,   170
          I fear my Thisbe's promise is forgot!
          And thou, O wall, O sweet, O lovely wall,

---

155. *Snout*] *F; Flute Qq.*   166. S.D.] *F (following 167): not in Qq.*   172. *O
sweet, O*] *Qq;* thou sweet and *F.*

---

155. Snout] Q1's impossible 'Flute'
is probably Shakespeare's error, perhaps because Thisbe, whom he has
just brought on, is in his mind. Cf.
Cobweb for Peaseblossom, IV. i. 23.

157. crannied] with 'cranny' (l.
162), from Golding (below, p. 150,
at n. 186).

hole, or chink] Cf. ll. 132, 175.
Mouffet's wall is 'chinckt'; it has 'a
rift / Or chincke' (Muir², p. 74).

159.] In Golding, the pair talk
'secretly', with 'loving whisprings'
through the cranny (below, p. 150,
at nn. 187–8).

162. cranny] Golding's word (below, p. 150, at n. 186).

right and sinister] echoing, in
farcical vein, Chaucer's 'Upon that o
syde of the wal stod he, / And on that
other side stod Thesbe' (*Legend of Good
Women*, ll. 750 f.). Cf. Golding, below,
p. 150, at n. 189. 'Sinister' was the
normal stress; what is comic is the
assonance, instead of rhyme, with
'whisper'.

163. the fearful lovers] who in
Chaucer converse 'At every tyme
whan they durste so' (*Legend of Good
Women*, l. 749).

165. *wittiest*] most intelligent.

partition] (1) structure which sepa-
rates: wall; (2) section of a learned
book (Burton's *Anatomy of Melancholy*

> That stand'st between her father's ground and mine;
> Thou wall, O wall, O sweet and lovely wall,
> Show me thy chink, to blink through with mine eyne.   175
> > [*Wall stretches out his fingers.*]
> Thanks, courteous wall: Jove shield thee well for this!
> But what see I? No Thisbe do I see.
> O wicked wall, through whom I see no bliss,
> Curs'd be thy stones for thus deceiving me!

The. The wall, methinks, being sensible, should curse   180
again.

Pyr. No, in truth sir, he should not. 'Deceiving me' is
Thisbe's cue: she is to enter now, and I am to spy
her through the wall. You shall see it will fall pat as
I told you: yonder she comes.   185

Enter THISBE.

This. O wall, full often hast thou heard my moans,
> For parting my fair Pyramus and me!
> My cherry lips have often kiss'd thy stones,
> Thy stones with lime and hair knit up in thee.

173. *stand'st*] *Q1*; stands *Q2,F.*   175. S.D. *Wall stretches out his fingers.*] *After Capell* (*Wall holds up his fingers*); *not in Qq,F.*   182–5.] *As Pope*; No . . . me,/ Is . . . spy/Her . . . fall/Pat . . . comes. *Qq,F* (*verse*).   185. S.D.] *Qq* (*following* comes.); *F* (*following* fall *subst.*).   189. *up in thee*] *F*; now againe *Qq*.

is divided into Partitions, subdivided into Sections, Members, Subsections).

175. blink] In *A Gorgious Gallery*, Thisbe gets a 'blink' through the crack (Muir², p. 72).

176. Thanks, courteous wall] In Golding, the lovers express gratitude for this 'piece of courtesie' (below, p. 150, at n. 192).

178. O wicked wall] The lovers in Chaucer cry: 'Alas, thow wikkede wal!' (*Legend of Good Women*, l. 756).

180–1. *being . . . again*] having sensibility, should swear back.

186. full . . . moans] Golding has 'after much complaint and mone' (below, p. 150, at n. 196).

188.] Cf. Chaucer (*Legend of Good Women*, l. 768): 'The colde wal they wolden kysse of ston'; the wall will not 'ones lat us mete / Or ones that

we myghte kissen swete' (ll. 760–1): cf. below, l. 199.

189. hair] to help bind the plaster.

knit up in thee] so F; either an authentic reading, recovered via the prompt-book; or else a remarkably apt guess, without the least authority. See Introduction, pp. xxxi f., correlating it with 'merit' (I. i. 139), 'passionate' (III. ii. 220), and 'morall downe' (v. i. 204). Q's 'now againe' is neither rhyme nor reason; but is hard to account for unless like the equally nonsensical 'Moon vsed' (l. 204) it was an attempt to decipher the handwriting of Shakespeare's phrase in the foul papers. If so, the phrase cannot have been 'knit up in thee', which no compositor would decipher as 'now againe'.

Pyr. *I see a voice; now will I to the chink,*   190
    To spy and I can hear my Thisbe's face.
    Thisbe?
This.   *My love thou art, my love I think!*
Pyr. *Think what thou wilt, I am thy lover's grace;*
    And like Limander am I trusty still.
This. *And I like Helen, till the Fates me kill.*   195
Pyr. *Not Shafalus to Procrus was so true.*
This. *As Shafalus to Procrus, I to you.*
Pyr. *O kiss me through the hole of this vile wall.*
This. *I kiss the wall's hole, not your lips at all.*
Pyr. *Wilt thou at Ninny's tomb meet me straightway?*   200
This. *'Tide life, 'tide death, I come without delay.*

            Exeunt Pyramus and Thisbe [, *severally*].

Wall. *Thus have I, Wall, my part discharged so;*
    And, being done, thus Wall away doth go.   *Exit.*
The. Now is the mure rased between the two neighbours.

191.] *As Rowe³; To . . . face. Thysby? Qq,F.*   192. *Thisbe?| This. My . . . think!*] *As Wells, after Rowe³; Thys. My . . . thinke? Qq,F.*   195. *I like*] *Qq;* like *F.*   201. S.D. *Exeunt . . . Thisbe*] *Dyce; not in Qq,F.*   *severally*] *This edn; not in Qq,F.*   203. *Exit.*] *F (Exit Clow.); Exit Wall, Pyramus, and Thisbe. Capell; not in Qq.*   204. *The.*] *Qq,F (Duk./subst., Rowe; so to end of play).* mure rased] *This edn;* Moon used *Qq;* morall downe *F;* mure all down *Hanmer,* conj. *Theobald;* Mural downe *Pope²;* wall downe *Collier MS.;* Moon to see *Sisson².*

---

190. see a voice] Cf. l. 339 f., III. i. 86, and especially IV. i. 209–12.

191. and] if, whether.

193. Think . . . wilt] a cliché: Tilley, T27.

thy . . . grace] comic version of an honorific title: a duke might be styled 'my lord's grace'.

194–7.] Limander is Bottom's blunder for Leander; Helen, Flute's for Hero; Shafalus and Procrus their blunders for Cephalus and Procris (Johnson). The stories are told, respectively, by Marlowe (from Musaeus) in his poem, and Ovid (Golding, VII. 885 f.). Abducted by Aurora, Cephalus remained unyieldingly faithful to Procris, his wife, to whom Aurora had to relinquish him. *Procris and Cephalus,* a poem by Henry Chute, was entered in the Stationers Register in 1593, and subsequently published (Malone, Halliwell).

199.] Cf. Golding, below, p. 150, at n. 191; above, l. 188 n. (from *The Legend of Good Women*); and, still closer in tone, Mouffet: their 'kisses staide . . . seel'd to the wal with lips' (Muir², p. 74).

200, 252. Ninny's tomb] See l. 137 and n.

201. 'Tide . . . death] whether life or death betide (befall).

204. *mure rased*] For the grounds of the emendation see Appendix II. 4.

Dem. No remedy my lord, when walls are so wilful to   205
    hear without warning.
Hip. This is the silliest stuff that ever I heard.
The. The best in this kind are but shadows; and the
    worst are no worse, if imagination amend them.
Hip. It must be your imagination then, and not theirs.   210
The. If we imagine no worse of them than they of them-
    selves, they may pass for excellent men. Here come
    two noble beasts in, a man and a lion.

Enter LION *and* MOONSHINE.

Lion. *You ladies, you whose gentle hearts do fear*
    The smallest monstrous mouse that creeps on floor,   215
    May now, perchance, both quake and tremble here,
    When lion rough in wildest rage doth roar.
    Then know that I as Snug the joiner am
    A lion fell, nor else no lion's dam;
    For if I should as lion come in strife   220
    Into this place, 'twere pity on my life.
The. A very gentle beast, and of a good conscience.
Dem. The very best at a beast, my lord, that e'er I saw.
Lys. This lion is a very fox for his valour.
The. True; and a goose for his discretion.   225
Dem. Not so, my lord, for his valour cannot carry his
    discretion; and the fox carries the goose.
The. His discretion, I am sure, cannot carry his valour;
    for the goose carries not the fox. It is well: leave it to

205. *Hip.*] *Qq,F* (*Dutch./subst.*), *Rowe* (*so to end of play*). ever] *Q1*; ere *Q2,F.*
213. beasts in, a] *Rowe³*; beasts, in a *Qq,F.*   218. *as*] *Qq*; one *F.*   221. *on*]
Qq; of *F.*

205-6. *walls . . . hear*] 'Walls have
ears' is proverbial: Tilley, W19;
'wilful' = 'forward'.
    214-21.] See III. i. 29-30 n.; *ibid.*,
ll. 26-44.
    215. smallest monstrous] monstrous
= (1) enormous; yet to the ladies the
smallest mouse is (2) like a terrifying
monster.
    218-19. I . . . dam] It is as Snug

that he is a lion, and in no other way
is he a lion's dam.
    224-9.] This lion is found wanting
as a king of beasts: princes, wrote
Machiavelli, should combine the
qualities of lion and fox. For this
criterion in Shakespeare, see Tillyard,
Shakespeare's History Plays, pp. 186,
227.

his discretion, and let us listen to the moon.   230

Moon. This lantern doth the horned moon present—

Dem. He should have worn the horns on his head.

The. He is no crescent, and his horns are invisible within
    the circumference.

Moon. This lantern doth the horned moon present;   235
    Myself the Man i' th' Moon do seem to be.

The. This is the greatest error of all the rest; the man
    should be put into the lantern. How is it else the Man
    i'the Moon?

Dem. He dares not come there for the candle; for you see 240
    it is already in snuff.

Hip. I am aweary of this moon. Would he would change!

The. It appears by his small light of discretion that he is
    in the wane; but yet in courtesy, in all reason, we
    must stay the time.   245

Lys. Proceed, Moon.

Moon. All that I have to say is, to tell you that the lan-
    tern is the moon; I the Man i'th'Moon; this thorn-
    bush my thorn-bush; and this dog my dog.

Dem. Why, all these should be in the lantern, for all these 250
    are in the moon. But silence: here comes Thisbe.

Enter THISBE.

---

230. listen] *Q1;* hearken *Q2,F.*   235–6.] *As Qq; prose, F.*   236. *do*] *Qq;*
doth F.   242. aweary] *Q1;* weary *Q2,F.*   248. i'th'] *Qq* (ith)*;* in the *F.*
250. for all these] *Q1;* for they *Q2,F.*

232.] the well-worn 'cuckold's
horns' joke: Tilley, H625.

233. *no crescent*] punning on his
want of growth, as a Starveling. See
ll. 237–8 n. below.

236.] The markings on the moon
were seen as delineating a man; the
uneducated ('the rude people', Hall's
Chronicle, Richard III) said a man
was there. Caliban, told Stephano
was once 'the Man i'th'Moon', replies 'I have seen thee in her'. Cf.
Tilley, M240; Chaucer, *Troilus and*

Criseyde, I. 1024.

237–8. the . . . *lantern*] The quip is
the more apt because Starveling is a
thin-man part.

241. *in snuff*] (1) needing to be
snuffed; to have the burnt-out part
of the wick removed; but (2) 'to take
in snuff' was an idiom for to resent,
take in anger; Tilley, S598.

243. *small . . . discretion*] Cf. *LLL*,
v. ii. 714 f., and David's n.

244. *in all reason*] as is only reasonable.

This. *This is old Ninny's tomb. Where is my love?*
Lion. *O—!*   *The Lion roars. Thisbe* [, *dropping*
                                        her mantle,] *runs off.*
Dem. Well roared, Lion!
The. Well run, Thisbe!   255
Hip. Well shone, Moon! Truly, the moon shines with a
    good grace.   [*The Lion worries the mantle, and exit.*]
The. Well moused, Lion!
Dem. And then came Pyramus—
Lys. And so the lion vanished.   260

Enter PYRAMUS.

Pyr. *Sweet Moon, I thank thee for thy sunny beams;*
    I thank thee, Moon, for shining now so bright;
    For by thy gracious, golden, glittering gleams,
    I trust to take of truest Thisbe sight.

252-3. *love?/Lion. O—!*] *Qq* (love? Lyon. Oh.), *F* (love?/Lyon. Oh.) *Theobald*
(*reading* Oh—!).   253. S.D. *The . . . off.*] *After F* (*The Lion roars. Thisbe runs*
off.); *not in Qq.*   *dropping her mantle*] *This edn; casts her mantle from her N.C.S.;*
not in Qq,F.   257. *The . . . exit.*] *After Capell* (*Lion shakes Thisbe's mantle, and*
Exit.); *not in Qq,F.*   263. *gleams*] *Staunton, conj. Knight; beams Qq,F* (*subst.*);
streams F2.   264. *take*] *Qq;* taste *F.*   *Thisbe*] *Qq; Thisbies F.*

258. *Well moused*] in treating the
mantle as a cat treats a mouse.
    261.] This absurdity, except for
being unconscious, resembles the one
Petruchio makes Kate accept, *Shr.*,
IV. v. 2 ff.
    262-4.] Cf. Chaucer's account
(*Legend of Good Women*, l. 825): 'The
mone shon, and he myghte wel yse'.
    263. *golden, glittering gleams*] The
compositor, catching 'beames' from
l. 261 above (cf. *AYL*, v. ii. 97). has
obliterated all trace of authority for
Shakespeare's word. It must have
been a rhyming monosyllable; probably it alliterated. Support, all but
decisive, for 'gleams' can now be
adduced from the probability that a
phrase and its context in *Enamoured*
Diana (Kennedy, p. 280) stuck in
Shakespeare's head: 'golden gleames
of glittering haire and face' there

shine from 'this star Diana', 'restoring
to [Berardus'] eies a day so bright'.
That a star, named for the moon-
goddess, should restore bright day
probably helped to suggest the moon's
'sunny beams' (l. 261 above). These
associations may have been strengthened by 'gladsome glittering gleams'
(l. 8) and 'beames of Beautie' (l. 6) in
Blennerhasset, *Second Part of the Mirror*
for Magistrates, 1578 (*Mirror, Parts*
Added, p. 435). See my appendix in
the Arden *Cym.* for Shakespeare's
knowledge of Blennerhasset; his
'Guidericus', by 'I dare what dare be
done', may also have furnished a hint
for *Mac.*, I. vii. 46 f.
    264. take . . . sight] get sight. F's
'taste' might conceivably be the true
reading, one more instance of the
comic confusion of the senses. But to
adopt it would not be justified: it

            But stay! O spite!   265
            But mark, poor knight,
        What dreadful dole is here?
          Eyes, do you see?
           How can it be?
        O dainty duck! O dear!   270
            Thy mantle good,
        What! Stain'd with blood?
        Approach, ye Furies fell!
         O Fates, come, come!
          Cut thread and thrum: 275
      Quail, crush, conclude, and quell.

The. This passion, and the death of a dear friend, would
    go near to make a man look sad.

Hip. Beshrew my heart, but I pity the man.

Pyr. O wherefore, Nature, didst thou lions frame,   280
    Since lion vile hath here deflower'd my dear?

265-76.] *Divided, Pope; But . . . Knight,| . . . here?| . . . bee!| . . . deare!| . . . blood?|
. . .fell,| . . . thrumme,| . . . quell. Qq,F (subst.).*   273.*ye*] *Qq;* you *F.*   277-8.]
As Qq (prose); This . . . friend,/Would . . . sad F (verse).

may just as well be an assimilation by
the compositor to 'trus*t*' and 'true*st*';
and Q1 yields good sense.

265-76.] The stanza-form of the
laments is a version, with internal
rhyme, of 'eight and six' (cf. III. i.
23). It is likely to have been suggested
by Thomson's use of it, *op. cit.* (Muir², pp. 70 f.).

273. Furies] featured in Seneca
(see *Medea*, ll. 13-15, *Hercules Furens*,
ll. 86-8, *Agamemnon*, ll. 759-65,
Thyestes, prologos) and English
Senecal tragedies; primarily, Alecto,
Megaera, and Tisiphone, but often
(even in Greek tragedy) more
numerous. Natives of Tartarus, with
snakes in their hair, eyes dripping
blood, and armed with torches and
scourges, they hounded the guilty
and exacted vengeance in life and
after death.

274-6.] The Fates (Sisters Three,
l. 323) are Clotho, who spins the
thread of life; Lachesis who draws it

out; and Atropos who cuts it. Cf.
Spenser, *Shepheardes Calender*, November, ll. 148 f.: 'The fatall sisters eke
repent / Her vitall thread so soon is
spent'; *Locrine* (M.S.R., l. 2228,
probably echoed in *2H4*, II. iv. 193-5,
see Humphreys's n.): 'Sweet *Atropos*,
cut off my fatall thred'; *Diana*
(Kennedy, p. 112), where death, and
perhaps her 'destinies', 'cut asunder'
Florida's 'vitall thred'; and in
Thomson (Muir², p. 76) 'fatall death'
and '*Atropos* threed'. Mouffet, con-
cerning Thisbe's death, in successive
lines has 'quell' and 'the sisters three'
(*op. cit.*, p. 74; Muir¹, p. 43).

275. thread and thrum] The thrum
is the tufted end of a weaver's warp,
left attached to the loom when the
web is cut and removed. Its aptness
to Bottom's trade turns to burlesque
the classical thread of life.

276.] 'quail', overpower (cf. *Ant.*,
v. ii. 85); 'quell', slay.

Which is—no, no—which was the fairest dame
That liv'd, that lov'd, that lik'd, that look'd with cheer.
                    Come tears, confound!
                    Out sword, and wound   285
                The pap of Pyramus;
                    Ay, that left pap,
                        Where heart doth hop: [*Stabs himself.*]
                Thus die I, thus, thus, thus!
                        Now am I dead,   290
                        Now am I fled;
                My soul is in the sky.
                    Tongue, lose thy light;
                        Moon, take thy flight! [*Exit Moonshine.*]
                Now die, die, die, die, die.   [*Dies.*] 295

Dem. No die, but an ace for him; for he is but one.

Lys. Less than an ace, man; for he is dead, he is nothing.

The. With the help of a surgeon he might yet recover, and prove an ass.

Hip. How chance Moonshine is gone, before Thisbe 300 comes back and finds her lover?

284–95.] *Divided, Johnson; Come . . . wound/ . . . Pyramus;/ . . . hoppe./ . . . thus./ . . . sky./ . . . flight,/ . . . dy. Qq,F.*   288. *Stabs himself.*] *Dyce; not in Qq,F.*
294. *Exit Moonshine.*] *Capell (following 295 Dies.); not in Qq,F.*   295. *Dies.*]
Theobald; not in Qq,F.   299. prove] *Q2,F; yet prove Q1.*   300. gone,
before Thisbe] *Rowe (gone before Thisbe); gone before? Thisbe Qq,F.*

282. is—no, no—] combines aposiopesis (stopping short of what was about to be said) and epanorthosis, 'when any thing passed is called backe' (Abraham Fraunce, *The Arcadian Rhetorike*, 1588, see caps. 28, 29, and in his example from Sidney, 'there was . . . a Prince, no, no Prince').

283. look'd with cheer] Cf. Mouffet's Thisbe over dead Pyramus: 'these heavie lookers cheere' (Muir², p. 75).

286, 287. pap] In *A Gorgious Gallery*, Thisbe thrusts the sword 'beneath her pap'. By giving the word to Pyramus, Shakespeare makes it more ludicrous (so Muir², p. 72). Muir is probably right, though Yong

uses it of a knight, in a serious context (*Diana*, Kennedy, p. 238): Felismena planted an arrow 'under his left pap, and so . . . smot his hart'. Did Shakespeare perhaps find this comic, too?

293. Tongue] for eye.

296–7.] Two dies make a pair of dice; the 'one' is the 'ace', the lowest throw with a single die. 'He is not a whole die, only a one-spot' (Kittredge).

298. *With . . . recover*] Does Theseus aptly recall the Mummers' Play of St George (also performed by artisans), with its Turkish Knight resuscitated by its Doctor?

299. *prove*] Q1's 'yet' is caught from 'yet recover'.

The. She will find him by starlight.

Enter THISBE.

Here she comes, and her passion ends the play.

Hip. Methinks she should not use a long one for such a
Pyramus; I hope she will be brief.   305

Dem. A mote will turn the balance, which Pyramus,
which Thisbe, is the better: he for a man, God warrant us; she for a woman, God bless us!

Lys. She hath spied him already with those sweet eyes.

Dem. And thus she means, videlicet—   310

This.   *Asleep, my love?*

What, dead, my dove?

O Pyramus, arise!

Speak, speak! Quite dumb?

Dead, dead? A tomb   315

Must cover thy sweet eyes.

These lily lips,

302. S.D.] *F (following 301); not in Qq.*   306. mote] *Qq,F* (Moth), *Steevens,
conj. Heath.*   307–8. he . . . us!] *Qq; not in F.*   307. warrant] *Qq* (warnd),
Collier.   311–34.] *Divided, Pope; A sleepe . . . dove?/ . . . arise,/ . . . tumbe/ . . . eyes./
. . . nose,/ . . . cheekes/ . . . mone./ . . . leekes./ . . . mee,/ . . . milke,/ . . . shore/ . . .
silke./ . . . sword,/ . . . imbrew:/ . . . ends:/ . . . adieu. Qq,F.*   317. lips] *Qq,F;*
brows *Theobald.*

303. *passion*] (1) suffering: cf.
'Christ's passion'; (2) passionate
speech.

306. *mote*] minute particle, cf. *Ham.*,
I. i. 112; Matthew, vii. 3.

307–8. *he . . . us!*] cut in the
prompt-copy drawn upon for F to
conform with the statute of 1606
against actors profanely using the
name of God.

307. *warrant*] preserve.

310. *means*] moans, laments the
dead. For N.C.S. 'videlicet' suggests
a quibble on the legal sense: 'lodges a
formal complaint; after 15th century,
chiefly Scottish' (*OED*).

313–14. O . . . speak!] 'O spek, my
Pyramus!' exclaims Chaucer's Tisbe
(*Legend of Good Women*, l. 880); cf.
Mouffet: 'Speake love, O speake'
(Muir², p. 75). Cf. 'tumbe', Golding,
below, pp. 150–3, at nn. 197, 200, 211.

317–20, 322.] Even cherry lips (cf.
l. 188 above) and lily cheeks would
befit a heroine rather than a hero.
The two epithets are misassigned
rather like the senses at ll. 190 f., and
earlier. With the pale lips, high-
coloured nose, absurd hues, and out-
of-place comparisons, cf. Lyly, *Endimion*, v. ii. 95 ff.: Sir Topas exclaims:
'What a sight would it be to embrace
one whose hayre were as orient as the
pearle! Whose teeth shal be so pure
a watchet, that they shall staine the
truest Turkis! Whose nose shall
throwe more beames from it then the
fierie carbuncle! Whose eyes shall be
environd about with rednesse exceed-
ing the deepest Coral! And whose
lippes might compare with silver for
palenesse!'

317. lily lips] includes, no doubt, a
derisive glance at *Cambises*, where

> *This cherry nose,*
> *These yellow cowslip cheeks,*
> *Are gone, are gone!*   320
> *Lovers, make moan ;*
> *His eyes were green as leeks.*
> *O Sisters Three,*
> *Come, come to me,*
> *With hands as pale as milk ;*   325
> *Lay them in gore,*
> *Since you have shore*
> *With shears his thread of silk.*
> *Tongue, not a word :*
> *Come, trusty sword,*   330
> *Come, blade, my breast imbrue!*   *[Stabs herself.]*
> *And farewell, friends ;*
> *Thus Thisbe ends :*
> *Adieu, adieu, adieu!*   *[Dies.]*

---

331. *Stabs herself.*] *Dyce; not in Qq,F.*   334. *Dies.*] *Theobald; not in Qq,F.*

among the beauties of a lamented son were lips of 'pleasant white' (Muir[2], p. 76).

321. make moan] Cf. Thomson, *op. cit.*, 'Then made he mone' (Muir[2], p. 72 and n. 21).

322. green . . . leeks] proverbial: Tilley, L176. Though the comparison is ludicrous, a green eye was not: in *Rom.*, III. ii. 221 (cited N.C.S.), Paris is recommended for his 'green, quick' eye: expressive, that is, of youthful, lively vigour.

323. Sisters Three] the Fates (see ll. 274–6 n.). Cf. Launcelot Gobbo's bantering reference and Pistol's bombastic one; *Mer.V.*, II. ii. 60, *2H4*, II. iv. 195. The phrase is a commonplace: cf., besides Tilley, S490, *Shepheardes Calender* (quoted ll. 274–6 n.); and *Cambises*, Howell's Sephalus in *A Handfull of Plesant Delites*, and Mouffet (all three quoted Muir[1], pp. 36 f., 43; Muir[2], pp. 76, 296 n., 20).

323–8.] Cf. *Cambises*, Prologue: 'sisters three had wrought to sheer his vital thread' (Muir[2], p. 76); *A Hand-*

full of Plesant Delites, quoted Tilley, S490: 'sisters three did full agree, my fatall thread to sheer'. The thread is cut by Atropos in *Locrine* (see ll. 274–6 n.); cf. Thomson (Muir[2], p. 71).

325. pale as milk] 'The milk-white hand' of a *lady* is a ballad-tag. 'As white as milk' is proverbial (Tilley, M931) and Chaucerian (*Canterbury Tales*, I (A), 358).

331. imbrue] pierce (*OED*'s earliest instance, †3b, is Sidney, *c.* 1580, in the sense of a weapon piercing a part). The word is used by Mouffet; 'Imbrude' by Howell's Sephalus (Cephalus), and 'embrude' in *A Gorgious Gallery*: all cited in Muir[1], pp. 36, 38 n. 1, 43. Cf. Pistol's bombastic 'shall we imbrue?' (*2H4*, II. iv. 192).

331.] As something his Blackfriars audience would recollect, Edward Sharpham alludes in *The Fleire* to burlesque stage-business with the stab: 'Like *Thisbe* in the play, a has almost kil'd himselfe with the scabberd' (Halliwell). Chambers, *Elizabethan Stage*, III. 490, dates *The*

The. Moonshine and Lion are left to bury the dead.   335
Dem. Ay, and Wall too.
Bot. [*Starting up.*] No, I assure you; the wall is down that
    parted their fathers. [*Flute rises.*] Will it please you to
    see the epilogue, or to hear a Bergomask dance
    between two of our company?   340
The. No epilogue, I pray you; for your play needs no
    excuse. Never excuse; for when the players are all
    dead, there need none to be blamed. Marry, if he
    that writ it had played Pyramus, and hanged him-
    self in Thisbe's garter, it would have been a fine 345
    tragedy—and so it is, truly, and very notably dis-
    charged. But come, your Bergomask; let your epi-
    logue alone.

    [*Enter* QUINCE, SNUG, SNOUT, *and* STARVELING, *two of whom*
        dance a Bergamask. Then exeunt handicraftsmen, including
                                            Flute and Bottom.]

    The iron tongue of midnight hath told twelve.
    Lovers, to bed; 'tis almost fairy time.   350
    I fear we shall outsleep the coming morn

335–6.] *Qq,F;* (*prefaced by: Enter Lion, Moonshine, and Wall N.C.S.*).   337. *Bot.*]
F; Lyon Qq.   starting up] *Capell; not in Qq,F.*   338. [*Flute rises.*] *This edn;*
not in Qq,F.   344. hanged] *Qq;* hung *F.*   348. S.D. *Enter . . . Starveling,*]
This edn; Enter Lion, Moonshine and Wall (after 334) N.C.S.; not in Qq,F.   two . . .
Bergamask.] After *Rowe* (Here a dance of Clowns.), *Grant White* (A dance by two of the
Clowns.), *N.C.S.* (Moonshine and Wall dance the Bergomask); *not in Qq,F.*   Then
. . . *Bottom.*] After *Capell* (Exeunt Clowns); *not in Qq,F.*

Fleire 1606; entered that May in S.R.,
it was printed 1607.

335. *left*] viz. left alive; not, *pace*
N.C.S., as present on the stage.

337. *Bot.*] Q1's *Lion* was evidently
induced by the mention in l. 335. The
speech can never have been meant
for Snug; it is in character only for
Bottom.

339, 347. *Bergomask*] a dance after
the manner of the people of Bergamo,
commonly ridiculed for their rusticity
(*OED*'s sole instance).

344–5. *hanged . . . garter*] To 'hang
thyselfe in thine owne garters' (Harington, *Orlando Furioso*, 1591, x. 37,

quoted F. P. Wilson, *Shakespearian . . .*
Studies, p. 164) was proverbial: cf.
Tilley, G42.

349. *iron . . . midnight*] Cf. *John*, III.
iii. 37–9 (Arden edn, III. ii. 47–9).

told] counted (in this instance,
aloud); cf. *R3*, v. iii. 276.

350. *fairy time*] which can extend,
pace N.C.S. and *Shakespeare's England*,
I. 356, beyond the rising of the
morning star: Oberon in III. ii. 388–
93 corrected Puck, on whom they
rely.

351. *outsleep*] *OED*'s earliest instance.

As much as we this night have overwatch'd.
This palpable-gross play hath well beguil'd
The heavy gait of night. Sweet friends, to bed.
A fortnight hold we this solemnity   355
In nightly revels and new jollity.   *Exeunt.*

Enter PUCK.

Puck.   Now the hungry lion roars,
                And the wolf behowls the moon;
                Whilst the heavy ploughman snores,
                All with weary task fordone.   360
                Now the wasted brands do glow,
                Whilst the screech-owl, screeching loud,
                Puts the wretch that lies in woe
                In remembrance of a shroud.
                Now it is the time of night   365
                That the graves, all gaping wide,

353. palpable-gross] *Capell;* palpable grosse *Qq,F.*   354. gait] *Qq,F* (gate),
Johnson.   357. lion] *Rowe;* Lyons *Qq,F.*   358. behowls] *Theobald, conj.*
Warburton; beholds *Qq,F.*

352. *overwatch'd*] stayed awake after
normal hours.
353. *palpable-gross*] obviously un-
couth, in (to use Johnson's language)
its 'unresisting imbecility'.
354. *heavy gait*] laggard walk: *OED*
heavy 19b. (earliest instance).
358. *behowls*] Although the word
does not occur elsewhere in Shakespeare, he has at least thirty 'be-'
compounds: cf. 'be-rhyme', *Rom.*, II.
iv. 39: Warburton's emendation presumes the common e : d misreading,
and is decisively supported by Shakespeare's familiarity with Lyly, who has
'eager Wolves bark at the Moone'
(*Euphues and his England*, II. 150, 12)
and 'many wolves barking at thee,
Cynthia' (*Endimion*, v. i. 120); and by
AYL, v. ii. 110 f., 'the howling of
Irish wolves against the moon', and
Caes., IV. iii. 27 (the dog that bays the
moon). Cf. Tilley, D449.
360. *fordone*] tired out (Lat. *con-
fectus*).

361. *wasted brands*] logs almost
burnt-out.
362–72.] As in Spenser, *Shepheardes
Calender*, June, ll. 23–6 (quoted above,
III. ii. 388 n.), owls, ghosts, and fairies
are successively evoked. Fairies 'following darkness', as when tripping
'after night's shade' (above, IV. i. 95
and n.), are probably reminiscent of
Spenser's, who 'chace the lingring
night' (though his are chasing it
away).
362–4.] Cf. *Phoen.*, ll. 5–7: 'thou
shrieking harbinger / Foul precursor
of the fiend, / Augur of the fever's
end'; Golding's 'deathful owle' and
'Screeche owle sent from hell' to
presage Caesar's death (x. 521, xv.
887); Scot, *Witchcraft* (below, pp. 147–
148, at nn. 166, 176): 'night owles,
and shreeke owles', and the fears of
'sicke folke'.
365–8.] Cf. III. ii. 381–2 and n.,
citing Scot, *Witchcraft* (his reference
to the traditional night-terrors of

Every one lets forth his sprite
In the church-way paths to glide.
And we fairies, that do run
By the triple Hecate's team   370
From the presence of the sun,
Following darkness like a dream,
Now are frolic; not a mouse
Shall disturb this hallow'd house.
I am sent with broom before   375
To sweep the dust behind the door.

Enter OBERON *and* TITANIA *the King and Queen of Fairies,
with all their* Train.

Obe.   Through the house give glimmering light
                By the dead and drowsy fire;

376. S.D.] *Qq,F* (*Enter King and Queene of Fairies with all their traine. Q1 ; Enter . . .
with their traine. Q2,F*).

ghosts and churchyards is, however, dismissive); and *Ham.*, III. ii. 378–80.

370. *triple Hecate's team*] 'Hecate's' is dissyllabic. Golding has 'triple Hecate's holie rites' and 'three formed Goddesse' in Medea's invocation (VII. 136, 142), a favourite episode with Shakespeare. At the like point in *Medea*, Seneca refers to Trivia's (sc. Hecate's) chariot, and all her forms; in *Hippolytus* she is 'Hecate triformis' (below, pp. 140, 144, at nn. 110, 139, 143). Cf. also *Aeneid*, IV. 511 (Kittredge). She was Hecate (or Proserpina) in Hades; Diana (and occasionally Lucina) on earth; and Luna (or Phoebe or Cynthia) in the heavens.

373. *Now . . . frolic*] have now our time for frolicking.

375–6.] In popular belief 'sweeping the house at midnight' (Scot, *Witchcraft*, below, p. 146, at n. 160) was one of Robin's good turns. Did he sweep the dust 'behind the door', where it would not tread about, leaving the rest of the floor clean (so Farmer)? Or is that at odds with the standard of cleanliness set by the fairies for maid-

servants, and did he sweep the dust *from* behind the door, where it had been left to be 'out of sight, out of mind' (so Halliwell, Cuningham, Kittredge, N.C.S.)? Yet that seems a limited task.

375. *broom*] Seen here (and in Jonson's masque, *Love Restored*, 1612), this was an attribute of Robin's, like those which identify saints, e.g. Catherine's wheel.

377. *give glimmering light*] not, as some editors would have it, light given by the drowsy fire; an interpretation they fail to reconcile convincingly with the text. The plain sense of 'give' is a command to the fairy train. Accepting this, N.C.S. finds in *Wiv.*, v. v, a likely explanation of what the command requires. There (l. 37) the S.D. of the Bad Quarto, probably descriptive of performance, has the pretended fairies enter 'with waxen tapers on their heads'. Such lights fixed in a headband, notes N.C.S., would leave Oberon's fairies free to dance 'Hand in hand' (l. 385). One may add that Puck probably entered with his tra-

	Every elf and fairy sprite	
	Hop as light as bird from briar;	380
	And this ditty after me	
	Sing, and dance it trippingly.	
Tita.	First rehearse your song by rote,	
	To each word a warbling note;	
	Hand in hand, with fairy grace,	385
	Will we sing, and bless this place.	

> [*Oberon leading, the Fairies sing and dance.*]

	Now, until the break of day,	
Obe.		
	Through this house each fairy stray.	
	To the best bride-bed will we,	
	Which by us shall blessed be;	390
	And the issue there create	
	Ever shall be fortunate.	
	So shall all the couples three	
	Ever true in loving be;	
	And the blots of Nature's hand	395
	Shall not in their issue stand:	
	Never mole, hare-lip, nor scar,	
	Nor mark prodigious, such as are	
	Despised in nativity,	
	Shall upon their children be.	400
	With this field-dew consecrate,	
	Every fairy take his gait,	
	And each several chamber bless	
	Through this palace with sweet peace;	

381-2.] *As Rowe*[3]; *one line*, Qq (. . . mee, Sing . . .), F (. . . me, sing . . .).
383. your] *Q1*; this Q2,F.   386. S.D.] *Alexander; Song and Dance. Capell; The Song. F; not in Qq.*   387. Obe. Now] *Qq; Now* F.   387-406.] *Qq* (*in roman*); *F* (*in italic, as The Song*).   402. gait] *Qq,F* (gate), *Johnson.*

ditional candle, giving the cue, perhaps, for a taper-lit scene.

380. *as . . . briar*] 'as bird on brier' is a frequent alliterative phrase in M.E. poetry, instanced by Steevens from Minet.

386. S.D.] On 'the series of the scene' (Johnson), and the song or songs indicated by ll. 381 f., 383-6, and (rightly or wrongly) by F's

heading *The Song* to ll. 387-408, which it italicizes, see Introduction, p. cxxiii, n. 3.

398. *mark prodigious*] portentous, ominous birthmark. Cf. *John*, iii. i. 45 (Cuningham).

401. *field-dew consecrate*] 'consecrated field-dew', 'fairy holy-water' (Dyce[2]).

402. *take . . . gait*] go on his way: good Yorkshire still.

And the owner of it blest,   405
Ever shall in safety rest.
Trip away; make no stay;
Meet me all by break of day.

Exeunt [all but Puck].

Puck. [To the audience.] If we shadows have offended,
Think but this, and all is mended,   410
That you have but slumber'd here
While these visions did appear.
And this weak and idle theme,
No more yielding but a dream,
Gentles, do not reprehend: 415
If you pardon, we will mend.
And, as I am an honest Puck,
If we have unearned luck
Now to 'scape the serpent's tongue,
We will make amends ere long;   420
Else the Puck a liar call.
So, goodnight unto you all.

405–6.] *As Staunton, conj. Singer;* Ever . . . rest,/And . . . blest. *Qq,F (subst.).*
408. S.D. *Exeunt . . . Puck.*] *Alexander; Exeunt. Qq; Exeunt King, Queen and Train. Capell; not in F.*   409. *To the audience.*] *Wells; not in Qq,F.*

405–6.] evidently transposed in the printing of Q: the emendation, required by the sense, is further supported by its conforming this couplet to the pattern, noted by Keightley, of ll. 391 f., 401 f.: the second line beginning with 'Ever' or 'Every'.

409. *shadows*] Even this degree of reality is denied them by E.K.: 'The opinion of Fairies and elfes is very old. But . . . there be no such thinges, nor yet the shadows of the thinges': a gloss on Spenser's 'frendly Faeries', *Shepheardes Calender*, June, l. 25, which Shakespeare (see above III. ii. 388, IV. i. 95, V. i. 362–72 nn.) will have

read. Puck has called the fairies 'shadows' at III. ii. 347.

410–14.] Cf. Lyly, *The Woman in the Moon* (? 1593–4; before Sept. 1595), prologue: 'If many faults escape in her discourse / Remember all is but a poet's dreame' (Kittredge). Cf. Introduction, p. cxlii.

416. *mend*] do better in future. The promise could only be addressed to the company's regular audience in the public theatre, for whom it is plain the epilogue was written.

419. *'scape . . . tongue*] 'be dismissed without hisses' (Johnson); cf. *LLL*, v. i. 132–4 (Cuningham).

Give me your hands, if we be friends,
And Robin shall restore amends.   [*Exit.*]

424. *Exit.*] *Capell; not in Qq,F.*

423. *Give . . . hands*] applaud, by clapping.

424. *restore amends*] make amends in return; cf. l. 416.

FINIS

APPENDIX I

SOURCE MATERIALS

1. Geoffrey Chaucer, *The Canterbury Tales*.

From *The Knight's Tale*.[1] Ll. 1–37, 47–52, 185–7, 220–312, 632–48, 815–967, 2236–48.

> Whylom, as olde stories tellen us
> There was a Duke[2] that hight Theseus
> Of Athenes he was lorde and gouernour
> And in his tyme suche a conquerour
> That greater was non under the son
> Ful many a riche countrey had he won
> What with his wisedome, and his chevalry
> He conquered all the reigne of Feminy[3]
> That whylom was icleped Cythea
> And wedded the quene Ipolita[4]
> And brought her home with him, into his contre
> With mykell glory and solempnyte[5]
> And eke her yonge suster Emelye.
>
> And thus with victory and melody
> Let I this worthy duke to Athenes ride ...
>
> And certes, if it nere to longe to here
> I woulde have tolde fully the manere
> How wonnen was the reigne of Feminy
> By Theseus, and by his chevalry
>
> And of the great bataile for the nones
> Betwene Athenes and Amasones
>
> And how beseged was Ipolita
> The yonge hardy quene of Cithea[6]
>
> And of the feest, that was at her wedding[7]
> And of the tempest at her home comming. . .
> This duke. . .

1. Text from *The Woorkes of Geffrey Chaucer* (ed. William Thynne, with additions ed. John Stow) 1561. It here varies from Thynne's first edition, 1532, only in minor misprints.

2. I. i. 20.	3. I. i. 16.	4. I. i. 1.	5. I. i. 11, IV. i. 87, 184.
6. I. i. 16–17.	7. I. i. 18–19.		

In all his wele and his most pride[8]

[is halted by women in mourning, who petition him. He enquires:—]

What folke be ye, that at myn home comming
Perturben so my feest with cryeng . . .
Or who hath you misbode, or offended?[9]
Nowe telleth me, if it maie be amended.

[Two young Theban princes, Palamon and Arcite, are held captive by Theseus. Their prison looks out on a garden, where Emelye walks in springtime.]

The seson pricketh every gentell herte. . .
And saythe arise, and do May observaunce.[10]

[From the prison-window, Palamon casts eyes on her.]

And therwith he blent, and cried, ha.[11]
As though he stongen were to the herte.[12]
      And with that crie Arcite anon up sterte
And sayd, cosyn myne, what eyleth the . . .?
      This Palamon answered, and sayde agayn:..
. . . I was hurt right now through myn ey
Into mine hert,[13] that woll my bane be
The fayrnesse of a lady that I se
Yonde in the gardyn, roming to and fro
Is cause of al my cryeng and wo
      I not wher she be woman or goddesse[14]
But Venus it is, sothly as I gesse . . .
      And with that worde Arcite gan espy
Where as the lady romed to and fro
And with that sight her bewte hurt him so
That if that Palamon were wounded sore
Arcite was hurt as moche as he, or more[15]
And with a sighe he said pitously
      The freshe beutie sleeth me sodenly
Of her that rometh in yonder[16] place
And but I have her mercy and her grace . . .
I nam but deed, there nys no more to say. . .
      This Palamon gan knit his browes twey
It were (quod he) to the no great honour

8. I. i. 19, 19 S.D., 22.   9. I. i. 22.   10. I. i. 167, IV. i. 103, 131–2.
11. II. ii. 102, III. ii. 137.   12. III. ii. 59.   13. II. i. 170–2, II. ii. 67–8.
14. III. ii. 137, 226–7.   15. III. ii. 254.   16. the yonder 1532.

To be false, ne for to be traytour
To me, that am thy cosyn and thy brother
Isworne full depe, and eche of us to other
That never for to dyen in the payne
Till that the deth departe us twayne
Neither of us in love to hindre other
Ne in none other case my leve brother. . .
And nowe thou woldest falsly ben aboute
To love my lady, whom I love and serve. . .[17]
   This Arcite full proudly spake againe,
Thou shalt (quod he) be rather false than I
And thou art false I tell the utterly.
For paramour I loved her first or thou
What wilt thou sain, thou wist it not or now
Whether she be womman or goddesse. . .
   Suppose that thou lovedst her byforne
Wost thou not well the olde clerkes sawe?
That who shal give a lover any lawe?
Love is a gretter lawe by my pan
Than may be yeven to any erthly man. . .
A man mote nedes love maugre his heed
He may nat fleen it though he shuld be deed.

[Arcite, banished on pain of death, but returning in disguise, has won favour in Theseus' court.]

The merie Larke, messanger of the daie[19]
Saleweth in her song the morowe graie[20]
And firie Phebus riseth[21] up so bright
That all the orisont laugheth of the sight. . .[22]
And Arcite, that in the court reall
With Theseus his[23] squier principall
Is risen, and looketh on the merie daie
And for to doen his observaunces to Maie. . .
Is riden. . .
And to the grove of which I you tolde[24]
By adventure, his waie he gan holde.
[There Palamon, escaped from prison, is hiding. As rivals, they agree to meet in mortal combat,[25] and do so. Meanwhile:]

17. III. ii. 174–5, 330–7, etc.   18. *cancelled.*   19. IV. i. 93; of day *1532.*
20. III. ii. 418–19.   21. aryseth *1532.* 22. III. ii. 391. 23. Correctly, 'is'.
24. I. i. 165–7, IV. i. 103, 131–2; III. ii. 390.   25. III. ii. 336–8.

... mightie Theseus
... for to hunt is so desirous
And namely at the greate Hart in Maie[26]
That in his bedde there daweth him [no] daie
That he nis clad, and redy for to ride[27]
With hunt and horne, and houndes him beside...[28]
For after Mars, he serveth now Diane...
With his Ipolita, the faire quene[29]
And Emelie, iclothen all in grene
An huntyng been thei ridden rially
And to the grove, that stoode there fast by[30]
In which ther was an Hart, as men him told...
This duke woll have a cours at him or tweie
With houndes, soche as him list commaunde[31]
... and ... anon
He was ware of Arcite and Palamon
That foughten breme, as it were bulles two...
And at a start he was betwixt hem two
And pulled out his sworde, and cried, ho
No more,[32] on paine of lesyng your[33] hedde...
But telleth me, what mister men ye been
That been so hardie for to fighten here
Without judge or other officere
As though it were in listes riall[y]
This Palamon aunswered hastely
And saied: sir, what nedeth wordes mo
We have the death deserved bothe two...

This worthy duke aunswered anon again
And saied, this is a short conclusion
Your owne mouthe, by your confession
Hath damned you,[34] and I woll it recorde
Ye shall be dedde by mightie Mars the redde.

[Ipolyta, Emelye, and the ladies pray Theseus to spare
the lovers.]

And in his gentle harte he thought anone
And soft unto hymself he saied: fie
Upon a lorde that woll have no mercie...[35]
That lorde hath little of discrecion

26. IV. i. 101 S.D., 102 ff.   27. IV. i. 104.   28. IV. i. 101 S.D., 110.
29. IV. i. 101 S.D., 118.   30. III. ii. 390, IV. i. 107, 114.   31. IV. i. 18–26.
32. III. ii. 354, 358–9.   33. of your *1532*.   34. IV. i. 153–4.
35. IV. i. 178, 180.

That in soche case can no [division]³⁶
But waieth pride and humbleness³⁷ after one. . .
He gan to looken up with iyen light³⁸
And spake these wordes all one hight.
    The God of love, ah benedicite
How mightie, and how greate a l rde is he
Again his might there gaineth no obstacles
He maie be cleaped a God for his miracles
For he can maken at his owne gise
Of everich harte, as hym list devise.
    Lo here this Arcite, and this Palamon. . .
That . . . might have lived in Thebes rially. . .
And yet hath love, maugre her iyen two
Brought hem hither bothe for to die
Now loketh, is not this a greate folie?
Who maie be a foole, but if he love? . .³⁹
And yet thei wenen to be full wise
That serve love,⁴⁰ for ought⁴¹ that maie befall
But yet is this the best game of all
That she, for whom thei have this joilite.
Can hem therefore, as moche thanke as me
She wote no more of all this hote fare
By God, than wote a Cokowe or an Hare
But all mote been assaied hote and cold
A man mote been a foole other yong or old
I wotte it by my self full yore agone
For in my tyme, a servaunt was I one
And therefore sith I knowe of loves pain
I wote how sore it can a man distrain
As he that oft hath be caught in her laas⁴²
I you foryeve all hoolly this trespaas.⁴³

[He takes Palamon and Arcite and their rivalry under his patronage. Had his plan for deciding it determined the outcome,⁴⁴ Arcite would have won the lady. The intervention of Venus and Saturn bestows her on Palamon. The tale ends with Theseus making the match.]

36. diffynition *1532*; diffinicioun *1561*.   37. humblesse *1532*.
38. IV. i. 140.   39. III. ii. 114-15.   40. II. ii. 114-15.
41. aught *1532*.   42. cf. North (below), at n. 70.   43. IV. i. 178, 180.
44. See Introduction, p. cv.

Bitwixt hem was maked anon the bond
That hight Matrimonie or mariage. . .[45]
And thus with all blisse and melodie[46]
Hath Palamon iwedded Emelie. . .
And Emelie hym loveth so tenderlie
And he her serveth so gentellie
That never was ther no word hem bitwene
Of jelousie, or of any other tene.

2. Sir Thomas North, *The Lives of the Noble Grecians and Romans compared together by . . . Plutarke, . . . translated.* 1579. Edition of 1595.

From The Life of Theseus, pp. 4–5, 10–16. Shoulder-notes are given in pointed brackets.

⟨*Aegeus the father of Theseus.*[47]⟩

Now *Hercules*, travelling abroade in the world, drave away many of those wicked theevish murderers, and some of them he slew . . . [The] fame and glory of *Hercules* noble deedes, had . . . secretly set [*Theseus*] heart on fire, so that hee . . . lovingly hearkened unto those . . . which had seene him, and beene in his companie, when he had sayde or done any thing worthy of memorie . . . [He] determined with himselfe one day to doe the like, and the rather, because they were neere kinsemen, being cosins remooved by the mother side. ⟨*Theseus and Hercules near kinsmen*⟩[48]. . . [He] killed another [robber], called *Sinnis* . . . This *Sinnis* had a goodly faire daughter called *Perigouna*, which fled away, when she sawe her father slaine. ⟨*Perigouna Sinnis daughter*⟩[49]. . . But *Theseus* finding her . . . sware by his faith he would . . . doe her no hurt . . . Upon which promise she came out of the bush, and lay with him. . . Afterwards *Theseus* maried her unto one *Deioneus* . . .

[The] kingdome of *Creta* fell by inheritance into the hands of . . . *Ariadne.* ⟨*How Ariadne fell in love with Theseus.*⟩ Theseus made league with her . . . and concluded peace . . . betweene the *Athenians* and the *Cretans.* . .[50] They report many things also touching this matter, and specially of *Ariadne* ⟨*Divers opinions of Ariadne*⟩: but there is no troth nor certaintie in it.[51] For some say, that *Ariadne* hung her selfe for sorrow, when she saw that *Theseus* had cast her off. Other write, that she was transported by mariners into the Ile of *Naxos,* . . and

45. IV. i. 179–80.   46. V. i. 28–32.   47. I. i. 19 S.D., 23.
48. V. i. 44, 47.   49. II. i. 79.   50. IV. i. 111–13, 125.   51. II. i. 81.

they thinke that *Theseus* left her, because he was in love with another, as by these verses should appeare.

> *Aegles the Nymphe, was loved of Theseus*[52]
> *who was the daughter of Panopeus.*

Now what things are found seemely in Poets fables,[53] there is none but doth in manner sing them. But one *Paenon* . . . reciteth this cleane after another sort, and contrarie to all other:[54] saying, that *Theseus* by tempest was driven with the Ile of *Cyprus*, having with him *Ariadne*, which was great with childe, and so sore sea sicke, that she was not able to abide it. ⟨*Theseus leaveth Ariadne in Cyprus.*⟩ In so much as he was forced to put her a land, and him selfe afterwards returning abourd . . . was forthwith compelled to loose into the sea. . . And yet there are of the *Naxians*, that report this otherwise,[55] saying, there were two . . . *Ariadnees.* ⟨. . . *two Ariadnes*⟩.

[He] brought all the inhabitants of the whole province of *Attica*, to be within the cittie of Athens ⟨*Theseus brought the inhabitants of the countrie of Attica into one cittie*⟩, and made them all one corporation . . . promising that it should be a common wealth and not subject to the power of any sole prince, but rather a popular state. In which he would only reserve to himselfe the charge of the warres, and the preservation of the lawes. . . .[56] Yet for all that, he suffered not the great multitude that came thither tagge and ragge, to be without distinction of degrees and orders. For he first divided the noble men, from husbandmen and artificers,[57] appointing the noble men as judges and magistrates . . . to determine the law. ⟨*Theseus maketh difference of states and degrees in his commonweale.*⟩ And as the noblemen did passe the other in honour: even so the artificers exceeded them in number, and the husbandmen them in profit. . . .[58]

Touching the voyage he made by the sea Maior . . . some . . . holde opinion, that he went thither with *Hercules* against the *Amazones*: and that to honor his valiantnes, *Hercules* gave him *Antiopa* the *Amazone*.[59] But the more part of the other Historiographers . . . doe write, that *Theseus* went thither alone, after *Hercules* voyage, and that he tooke this *Amazone* prisoner,[60] which is likeliest to be true. ⟨*Antiopa the Amazone ravished by Theseus.*⟩[61] For we do not find that any other that went this jorney with him, had taken any *Amazone* prisoner besides him selfe. [The Amazons came] valiantly to assayle the citie of *Athens* . . . *Theseus* . . . gave them

52. II. i. 79.   53, 54, 55. II. i. 81.   56. I. i. 119–20.   57. I. ii. S.D.
58. IV. ii. 17–24, v. i. 72.   59. II. i. 80.   60. I. i. 16, 17.
61. II. i. 78, 80.

battell⁶² ⟨*Theseus fighteth a battell with the Amazones.*⟩ . . . and slew a great number of them. Afterwards, at the end of foure moneths, peace was taken betweene them by meanes of one of the women called *Hyppolita.* ⟨*Peace concluded at foure moneths ende by meanes of Hyppolita.*⟩ For this Historiographer calleth the *Amazone* which *Theseus* maried, *Hyppolita,* and not *Antiopa.*⁶³ . . . Howsoever it was, it is most certain that this war was ended by agreement. . . It is very true, that after the death of *Antiopa, Theseus* maried *Phaedra,* having had before of *Antiopa* a sonne called *Hippolytus* ⟨*Hippolytus Theseus sonne by Antiopa. Phaedra Theseus wife and Minos daughter King of Crete.*⟩⁶⁴ . . . And yet we finde manie other reportes touching the mariages of *Theseus,* whose beginnings had no great good honest ground, neither fell out their endes verie fortunate. . . For we read that he tooke away *Anaxo* the *Troezenian,* and that after he had killed *Sinnis* and *Cercyon,* he tooke their daughters perforce:⁶⁵ and that he did also marie *Peribea,* the mother of *Ajax,* and afterwards *Pherebaea,* and *Joppa* the daughter of *Iphicles.* And they blame him much also for that he so lightly forsooke his wife *Ariadne,* for the love of *Aegles* the daughter of *Panopœus,* as we have recited before.⁶⁶ Lastly, he tooke away *Hellen.* . .

Albeit in his time other princes of *Grece* had done many goodly and notable exploits in the warres, yet *Herodotus* is of opinion, that *Theseus* was never in any one of them: saving that he was at the battell of the *Lapithae* against the *Centauri.*⁶⁷ Others say to the contrary, that he was at the jorney of *Cholchide* with *Jason,* and that he did helpe *Meleager* to kill the wilde Bore of *Calydonia.*⁶⁸

From the comparison of Theseus with Romulus, p. 43.

. . . *Theseus* faultes touching women and ravishments,⁶⁹ of the twaine, had the lesse shadowe and colour of honestie ⟨*Theseus detected for his ravishments of women*⟩.⁷⁰ Because *Theseus* did attempt it very often: for he stole away *Ariadne, Antiope,*⁷¹ and *Anaxo* the *Troezenian.* Againe being stepped in yeares, and . . . past mariage: he stole awaye *Helen* in her minoritie, being nothing neere to consent to marrye. Then his taking of the daughters of the *Troezenians,* of the *Lacedaemonians,* and the *Amazones* . . . did give men occasion to suspect that his womanishenes was rather to satisfie lust, then of any great love. *Romulus* now in a contrarie manner, when his people had

62. I. i. 16.   63. I. i. I.   64. IV. i. 111–12.   65. II. i. 77–8.
66. II. i. 79–80.   67. V. i. 44.   68. IV. i. 102 ff.   69, 70. II. i. 78.
71. II. i. 80.

taken eight hundred, or thereaboutes, of the *Sabine* women to ravish them, kept but onely one for himselfe . . . and delivered the rest to his best and most honest cittizens. ⟨*Romulus ravishment of women excused.*⟩ Afterwardes by the honour, love and good entertainment that he caused them to have . . . of their husbands, he changed this violent force of ravishment, into a most perfect bond and league of amitie. . . Furthermore, time hath given a good testimonie of the love, reverence, constancie, kindnesse, and all matrimoniall offices that he established by that meanes, betwixt man and wife.

3. Arthur Golding, *The XV Books of P. Ovidius Naso, entytuled Metamorphosis, translated . . . into English meeter.* 1567.

From Book I. Deucalion's Flood. Ll. 285, 312 ff. Compare this and the following four extracts with Titania on cosmic disorder in II. i.

The king of Gods . . .
. . . set at large the Southerne winde, who straight with watry wings
And dreadfull face as blacke as pitch, forth out of prison flings . . .
His ugly forehead wrinckled was with foggie mistes full thicke, . . .[72]
Assoone as he betweene his hands the hanging cloudes had crusht,
With ratling noyse adowne from heaven the raine full sadly gusht.
The Rainbow *Junos* messenger bedect in sundrie hue,
To maintaine moysture in the cloudes, great waters thither drue.[73]
The corne was beaten to the grounde, the Tilmans hope of gaine,
For which he toyled all the yeare, lay drowned in the raine.[74]
Joves indignation and his wrath[75] began to grow so hot,
That for to quench the rage thereof, his Heaven suffisde not
His brother *Neptune* with his waves was faine to doe him ease:
Who straight assembling all the streames, that fall into the seas,[76]
Said to them . . .
. . . from your open springs, your streames with flowing waters sende . . .
And to the Sea with flowing streames yswolne above their bankes,[77]
One rolling in anothers necke, they rushed forth by rankes . . .
The flouds at randon where they list, through all the fields did stray,[78]

Except for nn. 96–8 (and 89 in part), nn. 72–108 all refer to II. i. See headnotes to extracts 3 and 4.
72. Ll. 88–90.   73. Ll. 89–91, 104.   74. Ll. 94–6.   75. L. 104.
76. L. 91.   77. Ll. 91–2.   78. L. 96.

Men, beastes, trees, corne, and with their gods, were Churches
washt away.

From Book v. Ceres' curse makes Sicily a waste land. Ll. 591,
593 ff.

She curst all landes . . .
But bitterly above the rest she banned *Sicilie* . . .
And therefore there with cruell hand the earing ploughes she
brake,
And man and beast that tilde the grounde[79] to death in anger
strake.
. . . the corne was killed in the blade:[80]
Now too much drought, now too much wet did make it for to fade.
The starres and blasting windes[81] did hurt . . .

From Book vii. King Aeneus describes the Plague of Aegina,
sent by offended Juno. Ll. 678 ff.

. . . First the Aire with foggie stinking reeke
Did daily overdreepe the earth:[82] and close culme Clouds did
make
The wether faint: and while the Moone[83] foure times hir light did
take . . .
The warme South windes[84] with deadly heate continually did
blow.
Infected were the Springs, and Ponds, and streames that ebbe and
flow . . .
The wretched Plowman[85] was amazde to see his sturdie Steeres
Amid the forrow sinking downe ere halfe his worke was donne.
Whole flocks of sheepe did faintly bleate, and therewithall
begonne
Their fleeces for to fall away and leave the naked skin,
And all their bodies with the rot attainted were within.
. . . In wayes, in woods, in plaines
The filthie carions lay, whose stinche the Ayre it selfe distaines.[86]

From Book xv. The fourth quarter of the year. Ll. 233–5.

. . . Then ugly winter last
Like age steales on with trembling steppes, all bald, or overcast
With shirle thinne heare[87] as whyght as snowe.[88]

---

79. Ll. 93–4.   80. Ll. 94–5.   81. L. 88.   82. L. 90.   83. L. 103.
84. Ll. 88–90   85. L. 94.   86. L. 97.   87. L. 109.   88. L. 109.

From Book II. The seasons. Ll. 33–39.[89]

There stoode the springtime with a crowne[90] of fresh and fragrant
  floures:[91]
There wayted Sommer naked starke all save a wheaten Hat:
And Autumne smerde with treading grapes late at the pressing Fat.
And lastly quaking for the colde, stood Winter all forlorne,
With rugged heade as white as Dove,[92] and garments all to torne,
Forladen with the Isycles[93] that dangled up and downe
Uppon his gray and hoarie bearde[94] and snowie frozen crowne.[95]

From Book III. Actaeon's hounds. Ll. 250, 267–9.

... three good houndes comne all of *Arcas* kinde ...
... with other twaine that had a Syre of *Crete*[96]
And Dam of *Sparta*:[97] Tone of them callde Jollyboy, a great
And large flewd hound.[98]

4. Seneca, *Oedipus*, *Medea* and *Hippolytus*: passages in modern and
   Elizabethan translation.

From *Oedipus*: The Plague of Thebes. Ll. 36–185 *passim*. Compare Titania on cosmic disorder, II. i.

(a) Translated by F. J. Miller (Loeb Classical Library, 1917).

I have made heaven pestilent. . . With paling light glides
Phoebus' sister athwart the sky,[99] and the gloomy heavens are wan
in the lowering day . . ., a heavy, black fog broods o'er the
lands. . .[100] The ripened corn withholds its fruitful harvest, and
though the golden crop waves high its wheaten ears, the grain dies
shrivelled on its parched stalk. . .[101] First the plague struck the slow-
moving sheep; to their bane did the woolly flock crop the rich her-
bage. . .[102] The abandoned cattle lie stricken in the fields; the bull
pines away amidst his dying kine . . . all things have felt our plague
. . .[103] [The] sickly cheeks burn red; small spots overspread the
face. Then hot vapours search the body's very citadel. . .[104]

(b) Translated by Alexander Nevile (in *Seneca His Tenne
   Tragedies*, ed. Thomas Newton, 1581).

89. Ll. 107–14 (especially 111–13).   90. L. 109.
91. Ll. 108, 110; and IV. i. 51.   92. L. 107.   93. L. 109.   94. L. 107.
95. L. 109.   96. IV. i. 112, 125.   97. IV. i. 113, 118, 125.   98. IV. i. 119.
99. L. 104.   100. L. 90.   101. Ll. 94–5.   102. L. 97.   103. Ll. 93–4.
104. L. 105.

Thou, thou, infected hast the ayre . . .[105]
The Moone with clowds quight over cast, all sadly forth she glides,
And dolefull darksom shades of night, the whole worlde overhides.
. . . black and hellike hue
Hath overshaded all the Skyes, whence deadly mists ensue.[106]
The corne that wonted was to growe and fruitfully to springe,
Now to the voyded Barnes nought els, but empty stalkes doth
    bring . . .
The sheepe of rot by heapes as thick, as dogges doe fall and dye,
And belching out their wasted lunges, on grounde doe sprawling
    lye . . .
Nothing (alas) remaynes at all, in wonted old estate,
But all are turned topset downe,[107] quight voyd and desolate . . .
The Bull for lacke of foode and meate in field all faintyng lyes.
. . . All things are quight out of their Que . . .
What shal I say? all things (alas) are writhen out of course.[108]
. . . Botch and blane of sundry kindes . . . sothern blasts do blow.

From *Hippolytus*: Diana, regent of moonlit woods, is petitioned
to change Hippolytus' disdain to love. Ll. 406–17.

(a) Translated F. J. Miller.

O queen of groves . . . O great goddess of the woods and groves,
bright orb of heaven, glory of the night,[109] by whose changing
beams the universe shines clear, O three-formed Hecate . . .[110]
Conquer the unbending soul of stern Hippolytus . . . may he learn
to love, may he feel answering flames. Ensnare his mind . . . may
he turn him back unto the fealty of love.[111]

(b) Translated by John Studley (in *Seneca His Tenne Tragedies*,
     ed. Thomas Newton, 1581).

O Goddesse greate of Woods . . .
O Goddesse that in forestes wyld and groves obtaynest might,
O shyning lampe of heaven, and then the Diamon of the Night,
O threefold shapen Heccate . . .
O mollify Hippolytus his stubborne hardned hart
And let him learne the pangues of love and tast like bitter smart
. . . entreate his brutish breast,
And chaunge his mynd, in Venus boundes compel him once to rest.

---

105. L. 104.   106. L. 90.   107, 108. Ll. 106–7, 111–14.
109. i. i. 209–14.   110. v. i. 370.   111. iii. ii. 172–3; cf. iv. i. 169–76.

Phaedra resolves on infatuated pursuit of Hippolytus, heeding no obstacle; and would welcome death at his hand. Ll. 233–241, 699–712.

(a) Translated by F. J. Miller.

Though he keep him to the peaks of snowy hills, though he course swiftly 'mongst the ragged rocks, still through the deep forests, over the mountains, 'tis my resolve to follow him.[112] *Nurse.* Will he stop for thee and yield himself to thy caresses? . . . Will he give up his hate for thee[113] when 'tis for hate of thee, perchance, that he repels all women? . . . He will flee away. *Phaedra.* Though he flee through the very seas, still will I follow.[114] [She pleads with Hippolytus.] I am not mistress of myself.[115] Thee even through fire, through the mad sea will I pursue, yes, over crags and rivers, swollen by torrent streams; where'er thou shalt direct thy steps, there will I madly rush.[116] Once more, proud man, I grovel at thy feet.[117] Hippolytus, now dost thou grant me fulfilment of my prayer; thou healest me of my madness. This is beyond my prayer, that, . . . 'tis by thy hands I die.[118]

(b) Translated by Studley.

To follow him even through the hilles, the Forrest thycke and wood,
That keepes among the clottred clives besmeard with silver Snow,
Whose nimble heeles on craggy rockes are frisking to and froe:
I wysh. Nu. He will resist and not be dalyed with nor coyd, . . .
And turne perhaps his cankred hate to light on thee alone,
That now he beares to all. . .
Hee'le runne away.[119] Ph. If by the Seas he flie, I on the same
Will follow him. [She pleads with Hippolytus.]
. . . it is not in my might
To rule my selfe: through burning fire runne after thee I shall,
Through raging Seas, and craggy Rocks, through fleeting Ryvers all,
Which boyling waters ruffling rayse, what way so goe thou will,
I bedlem Wight with frantick fits will follow, follow still.
O stately Lorde before thy feete yet fall I once agayne.
Hip. . . . Draw, draw my sword, with stripes deservde Ile pay her on the skin . . .
Ph. Hippolytus, now dost thou graunt to mee mine owne desire,

---

112. I. i. 247–8, 250–1; II. i. 206–7.   113. II. i. 211.   114. II. i. 227, 230.
115. I. i. 107–9; II. i. 195.   116. II. i. 206–7, 230.   117. II. i. 203, 205.
118. II. i. 243–4.   119. II. i. 227.

Thou cooles my ramping rage, this is much more than I require,
That . . . I may be geven to death,
By bloudy stroke received of thy hand to loose my breath.

Cupid all armed, in sky and seascape. Ll. 192–203, 331–7, 351,
294–5.

(a) Translated by F. J. Miller.

Phoebus himself, who guides with sure aim his arrows from the bow-string, a boy of more sure aim pierces with the flying shaft,[120] and flits about, baneful alike to heaven and to earth.[121] *Nurse.* 'Tis base and sin-mad lust that has made love into a god, and, to enjoy more liberty, has given to passion the title of an unreal divinity. The goddess of Eryx sends her son, forsooth, wandering through all lands, and he, flying through heavens void,[122] wields wanton weapons in his boyish hands,[123] and though least of gods, still holds such mighty empire. 'Tis love-mad souls that have adopted these vain conceits and have feigned Venus' divinity and a god's archery . . . *Chorus* . . . Where the land is encircled by the briny deep, where the bright stars course through heaven itself, over these realms the pitiless boy holds sovereignty,[124] whose shafts are felt in the lowest depths by the sea-blue throng of Nereids, nor can they ease their heat by ocean's waters . . . Love sways the monsters of the raging sea[125] . . . [Cupid] bids the very gods leave heaven and dwell on earth.

(b) Translated by Studley.

And Phoebe himselfe that weldes his dart upon his twanging
    string,
With aymed shaft[126] directlie driven the wimpled Ladde doth
    sting.
With powre he scoures along the Earth and Marble Skye amayne.
Lust favoring folly filthily did falsly forge and fayne
Love for a God: and that he might hys freedome more attayne.
Ascribes the name of fayned God to shittle beldame rage.
Erycina about the world doth send her roving page,
Who glyding through the Azure skies with slender joynted arme
His perlous weapons wieldes at will, and working grievous harme,
Of bones and stature beyng least great might he doth display
Upon the Gods, compelling them to crouch and him obey.
Some Brainsicke head did attribute these things unto himselfe,

120. II. i. 159.   121, 122. II. i. 156.   123. II. i. 157.   124. II. i. 149–56.
125. II. i. 150, 152.   126. II. i. 157–9.

And Venus Godhead with the bow of Cupid little elfe...
> CHORUS

Whereas the Land by Seas embraced round,
Where twinkling Starres doe start in Welkin bright[127]
This peevish Elfe the Countreys all doth keepe,
Whose quarrels sting the Marble faced rout
Of water Nimphes, that with the Waters deepe
The brand that burnes in breast cannot quench out...
The Dolphin of the raging Sea doth love...[128]
Cupid... doth compell
The Gods descending downe from starry Sky,[129]
... to dwell
Upon the Earth.

At early dawn, Hippolytus gives directions to his huntsmen. Ll. 1–6, 31–43.

(a) Translated by F. J. Miller.

Go, girdle the shadowy woods and the topmost ridges of the mount, [130] ye sons of Cecrops!.. scour the coverts that lie... in the vale of Thria...[131] But do you cast off the leashes from the dogs[132] that hunt in silence;... let the savage Cretans[133] tug on the stout bonds with well-worn necks. But the Spartans[134] (for their breed is bold and eager for the prey) hold in carefully with a tighter knot. The time will come when the hollow rocks will re-echo with their bayings;[135] now, with heads low-hung,[136] let them... with muzzles to the earth quest through the forest haunts, while the light is still dim,[137] while the dewy ground[138] still retains the well-marked trail.

(b) Translated by Studley.

Goe raunge about the shady Woods...
About, about, the craggy crests of high Cecropes hill...
... with coursing wander still...
That... in Dale below doth lurke,
... let slip, let slip your Houndes,
But in your leashes Syrs keepe up your eiger Mastifs yet,
Keepe on their Collers still, that doe their galled neckes yfret.
The Spartayne Dogges eiger of pray and of couragious kynd...

127. II. i. 153.   128. II. i. 150.   129. II. i. 153.   130. IV. i. 108.
131. IV. i. 106.   132. IV. i. 106.   133. IV. i. 112, 125.
134. IV. i. 113, 118, 125.   135. IV. i. 105, 109–10, 113–17.
136. IV. i. 119–20   137. IV. i. 104.   138. IV. i. 120.

Tye shorter up within your leash: to passe tyme shall it bring,
That with the youlping noyse of houndes the hollow rockes shal
    ring.
Now let the Houndes goe fynd of it with Nosthrell good of sent,
And trace unto the uglye den ere dawning day be spent.
Whyle in the dewish s[l]abby ground the pricke of cleaze doth
    sticke. . . .

From *Medea*: The Enchantress, invoking Hecate, recounts the
cosmic disorder her spells have created; and bids her come,
wan and vengeful. Ll. 750–69, 787–94 *passim*.

(a) Translated by F. J. Miller.

Now . . . do thou, orb of night, put on thy most evil face and come,
threatening in all thy forms.[139] For thee . . . with heaven's law con-
founded . . . [the] order of the seasons have I changed:[140] the
summer land has blossomed 'neath my magic song, and by my
compelling Ceres has seen harvest in winter-time. . .[141] [The]
Hyades, moved by my incantations, totter to their fall . . .[142] I see
Trivia's swift gliding car . . . as when . . . she drives ghastly, with
mournful aspect . . . so do thou wanly shed from thy torch a gloomy
light through air;[143] terrify the peoples with a new dread.[144]

(b) Translated by John Studley.

And thou, . . . O torch and lampe of night,
Approche O Lady myne with most deformed vysage dight:
O threefolde shapen Dame[145] that knitst more threatning browes
    then one, . . .
Through me . . .
The heavens with wrong disturbed course and out of order
    quight, . . .
The framed course of roaming time racte out of frame I have.
So my enchauntments have it wrought that when the flaming
    sunne
In sommer bakes the parched soyle then hath the twigges
    begunne,
With sprowting blossom fresh to blome, and hasty winter corne
Hath out of harvest seene the fruite to barnes on sudden borne . . .
Eke at my charme the watry flocks of *Hyaedes* went to glade . . .

139. II. i. 104.   140. II. i. 106–7.   141. II. i. 109–11.
142. II. i. 153.   143, 144. II. i. 104, 113.   145. V. i. 370.

I see Dianaes waggon swif[t]e . . .
. . . when with heavy cheare
With dusky shimmering wanny globe, her lampe doth pale
 appeare . . .[146]
So with thy dumpish dulled blase, thy cloudy faynting lyght,
Sende out, amid the lowring sky, the heart of people smyght
Wyth agonies of suddeyne dread . . .

5. *The Boke of Duke Huon of Burdeux*, translated by Lord Berners.
  Printed by Wynkyn de Worde about 1534. Edited S. L. Lee.[147]

  From Chapters xxi–xxiv.

Whan Huon had herde Gerames, than he demaundyd forther of
hym yf he coude go to Babylon, 'ye, syr', quod Gerames, . . . 'But . . .
yf ye take the shorter way ye most passe throwout a wood a .xvi.
leges of lenght;[148] but the way is so full of the fayrey and straunge
thynges, that suche as passe that way are lost,[149] for in that wood
abydyth a kynge of the fayrey namyd Oberon,[150] he is of heyght
but of .iii. fote and crokyd shulderyd, but yet he hath an aungelyke
vysage . . . and ye shall no soner be enteryd in to that wood, . . . he
wyll fynde the maner to speke with you, and yf ye speke to hym ye
are lost for ever, and ye shall ever fynde hym before you . . . and yf
he se that ye wyll not speke a word to hym, Than he wyll be sore
dyspleasyd with you, and or ye can gete out of the wood he wyll
cause reyne and wynd, hayle, and snowe, and wyll make mervelous
tempestes with thonder and lyghtenynges, so that it shall seme to
you that all the worlde sholde pereshe, and he shall make to seme
before you a grete rynnynge river, blacke and depe. But . . . all is but
fantesey and enchauntementes that the dwarfe shall make[151] . . .
Huon . . . had grete desyre in hym selfe to se that dwarfe kynge of
the fayrey, and the straunge adventures that were in that wood . . .
'Syr', quod Gerames, '. . . whiche so ever way ye take . . . I shall
brynge you to Babylone . . . and when ye be come thether ye shall
se there a damesell, . . . the fayrest creature in all Inde. . .
  [Huon and Gerames enter the wood.]
where as kynge Oberon hauntyd most . . . [The] dwarfe of the fayre
kynge Oberon, came rydynge by. . . . Than kynge Oberon, who . . .
hade sen the .xiiii. compagnyons, . . . set hys horne to his mouth and
blewe so melodious a blast that the .xiiii. compagnyons, beyng

146. II. i. 104.   147. Text from E.E.T.S. e.s. 1882, 1883, pp. 63–9, 71.
148. I. i. 159, 165.   149. II. ii. 34–5.   150. II. i. 18, 20.
151. III. ii. 355–7.

under the tre, had so parfayte a joy at there hertes that they al rose up and begane to synge and daunse . . .

[The] dwarfe, seynge howe that they rode awey and wolde not speke, he was sorowfull and angry, than he sette one of his fyngers on his horne out of the whiche issuyd out suche wynde and tempest so horryble to here that it bare downe trees . . . [The] beestys in the wodes brayed and cryed.[152] [Than] sodeynly aperyd before them a grete ryver . . . and the water was so blacke and so perrelous, and made such a noyse that it myght be herde .x. leges of.[153] 'Alas', quod Huon, 'I se well now we all be all loste. . . I repent me that ever I enteryd into this wode'[154] . . . 'Syr', quod Gerames, 'dysmay you not, for all this is done by the dwerfe of the Fayrey', 'well', quod Huon, . . . 'I thynke we shall never skape fro hense . . .'[155]

[Oberon confronts them again.]

Huon sawe hym fyrst, and sayd, 'I se the devyll who hath done us so myche trouble.' Oberon herde hym, and sayde 'frende, thou doest me injurey without cause, for I was never devyll nor yll creature . . .'[156]

[Later, Oberon declares his help indispensable in solving Huon's problem:] sodenly Oberon aperyd to them, and sayd . . . I knowe the message that Charlemayn hath chargyd the to say to the admyrall Gaudys, the which thing is impossyble . . . without myne ayed, speke to me and I shall do the that courtesy that I shall cause the to acheve thyne enterpryce, the which is impossyble without me.[157]

6. Reginald Scot, *The discoverie of witchcraft*, 1584.

From Book IV, chapter x, p. 85.

In deede your grandams maides were woont to set a boll of milke before . . . Robin good-fellow,[158] for grinding of malt or mustard,[159] and sweeping the house at midnight:[160] and you have also heard that he would chafe exceedingly, if the maid or good-wife of the house, having compassion of his nakednes, laid anie clothes for him, beesides his messe of white bread and milke, which was his

---

152. III. i. 97 S.D., 194.   153. III. ii. 355-7.
154. III. . 143-5, III. ii. 314-16.   155. III. i. 145-6.
156. III. ii. 388; II. i. 245, 260-3; III. ii. 354, 358-9, 366-73.
157. III. ii. 94-5, 99, 101 S.D.; cf. 452 n.
158. II. i. 33-4; in Q1, II. i. S.D., III. ii. S.D.; Robin frequently in S.D.s and S.H.s. Scot's use of the name elsewhere (see further extracts) is not footnoted.
159. II. i. 36.
160. V. i. 375-6; II. i. 41.

standing fee. For in that case he saith: What have we here?[161]
Hemton hamten, here will I never more tread nor stampen.[162]

> From Book VII, chapter ii, p. 131. How the lewd practise of the
> Pythonist of Westwell came to light . . . and that all her
> diabolicall speach was but ventriloquie and plaine cousenage.[163]

. . . heretofore Robin goodfellow, and Hob gobblin were as
terrible, and also as credible to the people, as hags and witches be
now: and in time to come, a witch will be as much derided and
contemned, and as plainlie perceived, as the illusion and knaverie
of Robin goodfellow.[164] And in truth, they that mainteine walking
spirits,[165] with their transformation, &c: have no reason to denie
Robin goodfellow, upon whom there hath gone as manie and as
credible tales, as upon witches; saving that it hath not pleased the
translators of the Bible, to call spirits by the name of Robin goodfellow, as they have termed divinors, soothsaiers, poisoners and
couseners by the name of witches.

> From Book VII, chapter xv, pp. 152–3.

But certeinlie, some one knave in a white sheete hath cousened
and abused manie thousands . . .; speciallie when Robin goodfellow kept such a coile in the countrie. But . . . these bugs speciallie
are spied and feared of sicke folke, children, women, and cowards,
which through weaknesse of mind and bodie, are shaken with
vaine dreames and continuall feare. . .[166] But in our childhood
our mothers maids have so . . . fraied us with bull beggers, spirits,
witches, urchins, elves, hags, fairies,[167] satyrs, pans, faunes,
sylens,[168] kit with the cansticke,[169] tritons, centaurs, dwarfes,
giants, imps, calcars, conjurors, nymphes, changlings,[170] *Incubus*,
Robin good-fellowe, the spoorne, the mare, the man in the oke, the
hell waine, the fierdrake, the puckle,[171] Tom thombe, hob gobblin,[172] Tom tumbler, boneles, and such other bugs, that we are
afraid of our owne shadowes: in so much as some never feare the
divell, but in a darke night;[173] and then a polled sheepe is a
perillous beast, and manie times is taken for our fathers soule,
speciallie in a churchyard,[174] where a right hardie man heretofore
scant durst passe by night, but his haire would stand upright. For
right grave writers report, that spirits most often . . . take the shape

---

161. III. i. 73.   162. III. ii. 25.   163. III. ii. 360–2.   164. II. i. 40.
165. III. ii. 381.   166. V. i. 4–8, 21–2, 362–4.   167. II. i. S.D. etc.
168. Viz. Silenuses.   169. cf. *IH4*, II. i. 125.   170. II. i. 23.
171. Puck, II. i. 40 etc.   172. II. i. 40.
173. V. i. 21, 365–6, III. ii. 382, 387.   174. V. i. 22, 367–8, III. ii. 381–2.

of women . . .; and of beasts . . .;[175] of fowles, as crowes, night
owles, and shreeke owles.[176]

From Book XIII, chapter xix, pp. 315–16.

If I affirme, that with certeine charmes and popish praiers I can
set an horsse or an asses head upon a mans shoulders,[177] I shall not
be beleeved; or if I doo it, I shall be thought a witch. And yet if *I.
Bap. Neap.* experiments be true, it is no difficult matter to make it
seeme so. ⟨To set an horsses or an asses head on a mans neck and
shoulders⟩[178] Cut off the head of a horsse or an asse (before they be
dead) otherwise the vertue or strength thereof will be the lesse
effectuall, and make an earthen vessel of fit capacitie to conteine
the same, and let it be filled with the oile and fatte therof; cover it
close, and dawbe it over with lome: let it boile over a soft fier three
daies continuallie, that the flesh boiled may run into oile, so as the
bare bones may be seene: beate the haire into powder, and mingle
the same with the oile; and annoint the heads of the standers by,
and they shall seeme to have horsses or asses heads. . .[179] It is also
written, that if [the] *Sperma* in anie beast be burned, and any bodies
face therewithall annointed, he shall seeme to have the like face as
the beast had.

From Book v, chapter iii, pp. 94–6.

Of a man turned into an asse, and returned againe to a man,
by one of Bodins witches.

It happened in the citie of *Salamin*, in the kingdome of *Cyprus*, . . .
that a ship . . . staied there for a short space. [One of those aboard],
a certaine English man ⟨What the divel should the witch meane to
make chois of the English man?⟩ . . . went to a womans house . . . to
see whether she had anie egs to sell. Who perceiving him to be a
lustie yoong fellowe, . . . and farre from his countrie (so as upon the
losse of him there would be the lesse . . . inquirie) she considered
with hir selfe how to destroie him . . . [A]fter some detracting of
time, she brought him a few egs, willing him to return to hir, if his
ship were gone when he came . . . [B]efore he went aboord, hee
would needs eate an eg . . . and within short space he became dumb
and out of his wits . . . When he would have entred into the ship,
the marriners beat him backe . . . saieng; What a murren lacks the
asse? Whither the divell will this asse? The asse or yoong man (I
cannot tell by which name I should terme him) ⟨A strange meta-

morphosis, of bodie, but not of mind⟩[180], . . . understanding their
words that called him asse, considering that he could speake never
a word,[181] and yet could understand everie bodie, he thought that
he was bewitched by the woman, at whose house he was . . . And
therefore . . . he remembred the witches words, and the words of his
owne fellowes that called him asse,[182] and returned to the witches
house, in whose service hee remained . . . three yeares . . . [carrying]
such burthens as she laied on his backe; having onelie this comfort,
that although he were reputed an asse among strangers and beasts,
yet . . . this witch and all other witches knew him to be a man.

[After three years, by falling to his devotions in a churchyard in
service-time, he draws attention to his bewitchment. The witch is
compelled to restore him to his old shape.][183] . . . [N]otwithstanding
they apprehended hir againe, and burned hir: and the yoong man
returned into his countrie with a joifull and merrie hart.

7. Arthur Golding: Ovid, *Metamorphoses*, translated, 1567.

From Book IV. Pyramus and Thisbe. Ll. 67–201. (Main source
of Quince's Interlude, v. i. 127 ff.)

Within the towne (of whose huge walles so monstrous high and
    thicke
The fame is given *Semyramis* for making them of bricke)
Dwelt hard together two yong folke in houses joynde so nere
That under all one roofe well nie both twaine conveyed were.
The name of him was *Pyramus*, and *Thisbe* calde was she.
So faire a man in all the East was none alive as he,
Nor nere a woman maide nor wife in beautie like to hir.[184]
This neighbrod bred acquaintance first, this neyghbrod first did
    stirre
The secret sparkes, this neighbrod first an entrance in did showe,
For love to come to that to which it afterward did growe.
And if that right had taken place, they had bene man and wife,
But still their Parents went about to let which (for their life)
They could not let. For both their hearts with equall flame did
    burne.
No man was privie to their thoughts. And for to serve their turne
In steade of talke they used signes: the closelier they supprest

180. III. i. 98, 113–14 ff. See Introduction, p. ci f., cv.   181. III. i. 194.
182. III. i. 109–12.   183. IV. i. 63–4, 79, 83.
Notes 184–211 refer to v. i., except where otherwise indicated.
184. L. 129.

The fire of love, the fiercer still it raged in their brest.
The wall that parted house from house[185] had riven therein a crany[186]
Which shronke at making of the wall. This fault not markt of any
Of many hundred yeares before (what doth not love espie?)
These lovers first of all found out, and made a way whereby
To talke togither secretly,[187] and through the same did goe
Their loving whisprings verie light and safely to and fro.[188]
Now as a toneside *Pyramus* and *Thisbe* on the tother
Stoode often[189] drawing one of them the pleasant breath from other,
O thou envious wall (they sayd), why letst thou lovers thus?[190]
What matter were it if that thou permitted both of us
In armes eche other to embrace? Or if thou thinke that this
Were overmuch, yet mightest thou at least make roume to kisse.[191]
And yet thou shall not finde us churles: we thinke our selves in det
For the same piece of courtesie,[192] in vouching safe to let
Our sayings to our friendly eares thus freely come and goe.
Thus having where they stoode in vaine complayned of their woe,[193]
When night drew nere, they bade adew and eche gave kisses sweete
Unto the parget on their side, the which did never meete.[194]
Next morning with hir cherefull light had driven the starres asyde
And *Phebus* with his burning beames[195] the dewie grasse had dride.
These lovers at their wonted place by foreappointment met.
Where after much complaint and mone[196] they covenanted to get
Away from such as watched them, and in the Evening late
To steale out of their fathers house and eke the Citie gate.
And to the entent that in the feeldes they strayde not up and downe,
They did agree at *Ninus* Tumb[197] to meete without the towne,
And tarie underneath a tree [198] that by the same did grow
Which was a faire high Mulberie[199] with fruite as white as snow,
Hard by a coole and trickling spring. This bargaine pleasde them both,
And so daylight (which to their thought away but slowly goth)
Did in the Ocean fall to rest: and night from thence doth rise.

185. Ll. 172-3.   186. Ll. 157, 162.   187. L. 159.   188. Ll. 132-3, 159, 163.
189. L. 162.   190. Ll. 131, 178, 198.   191. L. 188.   192. L. 176.
193. L. 186.   194. Ll. 198, 199.   195. i. ii. 31-2, v. i. 261.   196. L. 186.
197. Ll. 137, 200.   198. L. 147.   199. L. 147.

Assoone as darkenesse once was come, straight *Thisbe* did devise
A shift to wind her out of doores, that none that were within
Perceyved hir: And muffling hir with clothes about hir chin,
That no man might discerne hir face, to *Ninus* Tumb[200] she came
Unto the tree, and sat hir downe there underneath the same.
Love made hir bold. But see the chaunce, there comes besmerde
 with blood,
About the chappes[201] a Lionesse all foming from the wood,
From slaughter lately made of kine, to staunch hir bloudie thurst
With water of the foresaid spring. Whome *Thisbe* spying furst
Afarre by moonelight,[202] thereupon with fearfull steppes gan flie,
And in a darke and yrksome cave did hide hirselfe thereby.
And as she fled away for hast she let hir mantle fall[203]
The whych for feare she left behind not looking backe at all.
Now when the cruell Lionesse hir thurst had stanched well,
In going to the Wood she found the slender weede that fell
From *Thisbe*, which with bloudie teeth[204] in pieces she did teare.
The night was somewhat further spent ere *Pyramus* came there:
Who seeing in this suttle sande the print of Lions paw
Waxt pale for feare. But when also the bloudie cloke he saw[205]
All rent and torne, one night (he sayd) shall lovers two confounde,
Of which long life deserved she of all that live on ground.
My soule deserves of this mischaunce the perill for to beare.
I wretch have bene the death of thee, which to this place of feare
Did cause thee in the night to come, and came not here before.
My wicked limmes and wretched guttes with cruell teeth therfore
Devour ye O ye Lions all that in this rocke doe dwell.
But Cowardes use to wish for death. The slender weede that fell
From *Thisbe* up he takes and streight doth beare it to the tree,
Which was appointed erst the place of meeting for to bee.
And when he had bewept and kist the garment which he knew,
Receyve thou my bloud too (quoth he) and therewithall he drew
His sworde, the which among his guttes he thrust, and by and by
Did draw it from the bleeding wound beginning for to die
And caste himselfe upon his backe. The bloud did spin on hie
As when a Conduite pipe is crackt, the water bursting out
Doth shote itselfe a great way off and pierce the Ayre about.
The leaves that were upon the tree besprincled with his blood
Were dyed blacke. The roote also bestained as it stoode,
A deepe darke purple colour straight upon the Berries cast.[206]

200. L. 252.   201. L. 142.   202. L. 135; cf. iii. i. 47.   203. L. 141.
204. L. 142.   205. Ll. 271-2.   206. ii. i. 167.

Anon scarce ridded of hir feare with which shee was agast,
For doubt of disapointing him commes *Thisbe* forth in hast,
And for hir lover lookes about, rejoycing for to tell
How hardly she had scapt that night the daunger that befell.
And as she knew right well the place and facion of the tree
(As whych she saw so late before:) even so when she did see
The colour of the Berries turnde, shee was uncertaine whither
It were the tree at which they both agreed to meete together.
While in this doubtfull stounde she stood, shee cast hir eye aside
And there beweltred in his bloud hir lover she espide[207]
Lie sprawling with his dying limmes: at which she started backe,
And looked pale as any Box, a shuddring through hir stracke,
Even like the Sea which sodenly with whissing noyse doth move,
When with a little blast of winde it is but toucht above.
But when approching nearer him she knew it was hir love,
She beate hir brest, she shricked out, she tare hir golden heares,
And taking him betweene hir armes did wash his wounds with
     teares.
She meynt hir weeping with his bloud, and kissing all his face
(Which now became as colde as yse) she cride in wofull case
Alas what chaunce my *Pyramus* hath parted thee and mee?
Make aunswere O my *Pyramus*:[208] it is thy *Thisb*, even shee
Whome thou doste love most heartely that speaketh unto thee.
Give eare and rayse thy heavie head. He hearing *Thisbes* name,
Lift up his dying eyes, and having seene hir closde the same.
But when she knew hir mantle there[209] and saw his scabberd lie
Without the swoorde: Unhappy man thy love hath made thee die:
Thy love (she said) hath made thee slea thy selfe. This hand of
     mine
Is strong inough to doe the like. My love no lesse than thine
Shall give me force to worke my wound. I will pursue the dead.
And wretched woman as I am, it shall of me be sed
That like as of thy death I was the only cause and blame,
So am I thy companion eke and partner in the same.
For death which only coulde alas a sunder part us twaine,
Shall never so dissever us but we will meete againe.
And you the Parentes of us both, most wretched folke alyve,
Let this request that I shall make in both our names bylive,
Entreate you to permit that we whome chaste and stedfast love
And whome even death hath joynde in one, may as it doth behove
In one grave be together layd. And thou unhappie tree

207. L. 309.   208. L. 314.   209. L. 144, 271.

Which shroudest now the corse of one, and shalt anon through
   mee
Shroude two, of this same slaughter holde the sicker signes for ay.
Blacke be the colour of thy fruite and mourninglike alway,
Such as the murder of us twaine may ever more bewray.
This said, she tooke the sword yet warme with slaughter of hir love
And setting it beneath hir brest,[210] did too hir heart it shove.
Hir prayer with the Gods and with their Parentes tooke effect.
For when the frute is throughly ripe, the Berrie is bespect
With colour tending to a blacke. And that which after fire
Remained, rested in one Tumbe as *Thisbe* did desire.[211]

210. Ll. 330–1.   211. L. 315.

APPENDIX II

FOUR TEXTUAL CRUCES[1]

1. I. i. 139.

> *Lis.* Or else, it stoode vpon the choyce of friends;
>
> *Q1*; *for* friends, *F reads* merit

Though 'friends' (= kin or guardians) is the more acceptable in the context, the F reading deserves greater consideration than it has had, for when one tries to account for it, it proves hard to avoid concluding that it too is Shakespeare's. (1) The thought of 'choice' determined by 'merit' is Shakespearean: cf. *Troilus and Cressida*, I. iii. 348 f.: 'choice . . . makes merit her election'. (2) Neither 'friends' nor 'merit' can be a copyist's mistake of the one word for the other. (3) 'Friends' makes admirable and easy sense which would not provoke scribe, compositor, or editor to interfere with it. (4) Since 'merit' makes the sense more difficult, it is not an unconscious or a deliberate smoothing: the principle *praestat difficilior lectio* is in its favour. F's variants from Q1 fall into five classes (see the Introduction, pp. xxx–xxxiii). F's 'merit' is not (a) taken over from its main copy, Q2, which reads 'friends'. For reasons 2–4 above, it can hardly be (b) an attempt by sheer guesswork, good or bad, to correct Q2; (c) nor a miscorrection of Q2, generated by the comparison of it with a prompt-book; (d) nor attributable to a copyist's error, at least of any recognizable kind. It must belong, it seems, to the fifth category: readings accurately taken from prompt-copy, as at least some of F's S.D.s must have been. If it stood in the prompt-book with which Q2 was compared (though mainly for S.D.s) in preparing copy for F, how did it get there? An actor was no more likely than a copyist to substitute it for 'friends'; he would equally have had no motive, and would by chance have lit upon what from *Troilus and Cressida* we know to have been a genuinely Shakespearean idea in Shakespearean words. The argument points to 'choice of merit' as having been at some stage, no less than 'choice of friends' at another, Shakespeare's expression. If so, which represents his final intention?—if 'merit', an editor would be bound to adopt it.

---

1. On each I have had the benefit of discussion with Harold Jenkins.

If 'merit' is the revision, Shakespeare might have been revising away from the probable source (in *Euphues and his England*, see above, Commentary, *ad loc.*) ; in revising, authors often move away from their sources. The word makes acceptable sense: Hermia's response,

> Oh hell! to choose love by another's eyes,

shows that the 'merit' consists of qualifications estimated by, in fact, a 'friend' or a parent like Egeus or Old Capulet. What Shakespeare understood here by 'choice of merit' is illustrated precisely by *Rom.*, III. v. 178 ff., where Capulet rehearses the merits of Paris, and storms at Juliet for rejecting the choice he has made of him on their account.

Yet supposing (which I find some reason to suppose) that *Romeo* immediately preceded the *Dream*, this passage may be the source from which Shakespeare moved away. Bearing it in mind, *he* would be clear that such 'choice of merit' was no right ground of love; but until Hermia spoke, an audience would be apt to take 'merit' as good ground. Would he introduce this awkwardness by revising 'friends' to 'merit'? He is more likely to have fallen into it, and then rectified it by revising 'merit' to 'friends', making plain to the audience the objection to this 'choice' which was left latent in his original phrase.

Even if 'friends' is a revision, it must have been in the foul papers from which Q1 was printed. If 'merit' is an earlier, rejected reading, how could it have come to supersede 'friends' in a later text? For that, it must have remained legible in the foul papers. Then, one would postulate, it was wrongly selected, instead of the revised reading, either when the prompt-book was prepared, or if both words survived in that, then in the preparation of copy for F. Such a hypothesis allows us to believe 'friends' the revision, and so to retain it in our text. It is in itself the more satisfactory reading in the context. To abandon it would be rash, even though it is impossible to be certain that Shakespeare did not change it to the less satisfactory one.

2. III. i. 78–80.

> *Pyra.* *Thisby* the flowers of odious sauors sweet.
> *Quin.* Odours, odorous.
> *Py.* Odours sauors sweete.
>   So hath thy breath, my dearest *Thisby* deare,
>
>   Q1 ; F reads Quin. Odours, odours.

In the present edition, the text of ll. 79 f. is regarded as corrupt, and is emended. L. 78 provides no antecedent for 'So hath' in l. 80, and some editors have suspected textual corruption as the cause. It seems likeliest, however, that the lapse is Shakespeare's, and so emendations of those lines have not been accepted in this edition, any more than by Alexander, W. H. Clemen, or Stanley Wells.

(a) Ll. 79 f.

It is hard to view Quince's 'Odours' (Qq, F) as an apposite response to Bottom's howler, though Martin Wright defends it, explaining that he draws Bottom's attention to the root of the proper adjective (not 'odious' from 'odium', but) 'odorous' from 'odours'. This, though attractive in keeping Q1's text, seems more like Holofernes than Quince. If 'Odours' is a corruption, the minimum emendation of the passage is to read ' "Odious" ', with Alexander, or 'Odious?', with N.C.S., assuming 'Odours' to be a misreading of that word. So limiting their emendation, they have Bottom (improbably, as Harold Jenkins points out to me) fail to follow the correction, and without further notice taken by Quince, say 'Odours' instead of 'Odorous'. Whatever Quince's correction is taken to be, Bottom must repeat it: the comedy of his blundering again, if he were intended to do so, would be pointed for the audience, not passed over. It is also necessary that Quince's correction should make tolerable sense of what Bottom should have said in l. 78. That is where trouble arises with the adoption (as by Clemens and Wells) of F's 'Odours, odours' (a reading with little claim to authority: no doubt F made a simple 'correction' by guess, conforming 'odorous' to 'Odours'; it is unlikely the prompt-book was consulted). With 'the flowers of odours savours sweet' as Quince's text, what, one asks, are 'the flowers of odours'?—a question leading to the emendation of 'of' (see (b) below). Unless, by that emendation, a verb is supplied, the verb, if the phrase is complete in itself, must be 'savours', singular in form after a plural subject, without the usual predisposing conditions for that irregularity. Other attempts to complete the sense interpret 'savours' as 'savour's' (the flowers of odorous savours is sweet) or, emending 'flowers', make Bottom apostrophize Thisbe ('Thisbe, the flower of odorous savours, sweet', or 'of odours' savours sweet,'), a hypothesis which requires him, on resuming, to miss out a line of Quince's text. None of these suggestions carries conviction.

With 'odorous' as Quince's correction, and taken straightforwardly as meaning 'the flowers of [viz. possessing] sweet odorous savours', the phrase is interrupted before reaching its verb,

which should have furnished a sense preparatory to the second
term of the comparison 'So hath thy breath'. That Shakespeare
never provided this continuation and its verb is the conclusion now
to be considered.

(b) Ll. 78, 80.

Why in l. 78 as corrected by Quince is there no antecedent for
'So hath' in l. 80? That Shakespeare intended the hiatus, with
Bottom, as he continues from 'savours sweet', incompetently skip-
ping a line of Quince's text, is not plausible. Quince does not pull
him up, and unless he did, such a point would not be taken by the
audience. Collier suspected and Dover Wilson presumed textual
corruption: if in l. 78 we adopt, for 'of', Collier's conjecture 'have'
or the N.C.S. emendation 'ha',' then 'So hath' follows normally. A
copyist carrying words in his head might substitute 'of' for 'have'
through association of two similar-sounding words. In N.C.S., 'of'
is explained as the compositor's misexpansion of ' 'a', Shakespearean abbreviation for 'have'; but though Shakespeare writes
'might 'a been' (*LLL*, v. ii. 17; cf. *Ham.*, IV. v, 64), I do not believe
his ear would have permitted ' 'a odious'. Rowe, in his third
edition, made a different effort to save Shakespeare's consistency,
emending 'so hath' to 'so doth', and apparently finding the needed
antecedent in 'savours' (or 'savour's': already in Rowe[1]) regarded
as a verb. Even Collier's conjecture seems less probable than a
characteristic and negligible lapse on Shakespeare's part. Resuming after the joke on 'odious', Shakespeare would have in mind
the comparison with flowers which he had started, but might easily
ignore the fact that the first term of the comparison had been left
incomplete, so that he was going on to the second before it had been
syntactically prepared for. If he ever noticed his own lapse, he
could be sure that, with the joke intervening, no spectator would;
or if, exceptionally, one or two did, they would accept it as a part
of the fun; for it is in keeping with Bottom's other gaffes, provided
one does not try to work out what this particular gaffe is.

Our reading, 'Odorous, odorous' (l. 79), satisfies both conditions
Quince's interruption has to meet. It is a natural response to
Bottom's 'odious'; and as what he ought to have said, it makes
adequate Quincean sense in 'the flowers of odorous savours
sweet—' (cf. l. 78), a coherent though uncompleted phrase. With
'odours', the phrase needs emendation. Our 'Odorous', since
Bottom must accept it in l. 79, requires emendation of 'Odours'
there; but the compositor, having (*ex hypothesi*) set 'Odours' for

'Odorous' already, would be likely enough to do so again, especially as that would be to copy the word directly above.

3. III. ii. 257–9.

> *Lys.* Away, you Ethiop.
> *Dem.* No, no: heele
> Seeme to breake loose: take on as you would follow;
> But yet come not. You are a tame man, go.

> *Q1; For* No . . . follow; *F reads*:
> No, no, Sir, seeme to breake loose;
> Take on as you would follow,

As the anomalous shortness of these two lines reveals, F is merely smoothing by guess the peccant Quarto text, not recovering a credibly true one. By re-division, and the cavalier substitution of 'Sir' for the problematical 'heele', it removes, as mere smoothers will, the original signs of corruption, which are three. In Q1, l. 257 lacks a foot of the pentameter. To divide 'heele seeme' between two lines is what Shakespeare would hardly have done at this period of his verse. And the abrupt change from 'heele' to 'you', in l. 258, disrupts (as Harold Jenkins emphasizes to me) the proper parallelism and connection of Demetrius' three phrases. Without resort to the desperate remedy of giving 'No, no, heele', with conjectured dash or verbal addition, to Hermia (Cuningham, conj. Joicey), this third trouble can be cured by Pope's emendation of the 'you' to 'he', as Sisson (not citing Pope) argues in *New Readings*, I. 129: 'The change in address', to 'You', then 'comes after a series of sarcastic comments, with the sudden direct insult: "You are a tame man, go" '. If Shakespeare did write 'he' in l. 258, a corruption to 'you' could be attributed to catching by the Q1 compositor from 'You' in the line below. But Sisson is mistaken in supposing that the emendation would solve the whole crux; the hiatus at 'heele/Seem' would remain. Accordingly, we should have to postulate two independent corruptions occurring by coincidence in successive lines and so complicating the crux: the odds against this seem high. Rather, it appears likely that in or next door to 'heele' a deeper corruption lies; so deep perhaps that the true reading is beyond recovery. I am aware of some sixteen different attempts, a dozen of them recorded in Furness. Eight of the dozen I rule out as dependent in one way or another on F's 'Sir'. Cuningham's procedure is drastic. Having abolished the 'heele . . . you' problem by transferring 'No, no heele' to Hermia, he completes the metre and her sense with the invented supplement 'kill thee'. Demetrius then begins 'Seeme . . .', so there is no awkward enjambment. The N.C.S. text gives only 'No, no' to Hermia; solves the 'heele . . .You' problem by emending 'heele' to 'Ye'll' as Demetrius' first word, and leaves the enjambment and too short line no better than before. While Cuningham's emendations are too arbitrary, these stop short of mending what is amiss. Pope, as one expects of him, does mend the versification, reading: 'No, no, he'll seem / To break away, take on as he would follow'; but at the expense of 'loose', which there are no proper grounds for suspecting to be a corruption. A proposal by David Wilson to delete 'No, no, heele' as a fragment of a cancelled passage in Q1's copy, Shakespeare's foul papers, leaves a metrically uncompleted half-line (Lysander's); but though that is not an insuperable objection, the supposition disposes of all the other difficulties perhaps too easily and conveniently. Martin Wright tentatively pursues it to the conclusion that Shakespeare meant 'heele' to be deleted but left it standing, the intended text being: 'No, no,/Seem to break loose, take on as you would follow'— acceptable sense and versification, but again leaving Lysander's line metrically uncompleted. Finally, several scholars give Demetrius, after 'heele', the words they guess as those of the foot missing from the pentameter. Nicholson (*apud* Camb.) conjectures 'he'll but'; and Schmidt, 'he'll not stir' or 'he'll not budge'; Capell, earlier, read: 'he'll not come'. His and Schmidt's additions not only supply acceptable sense and metre, but do away with the objectionable enjambment. If such additions are permissible, I conjecture 'he'll only', with some support from *2H4*, I. i. 197 f., 'their weapons only/Seem'd on our side', which at least shows that 'only/Seem' is not out of keeping with Shakespeare's versification at roughly this period. But neither this remedy, nor any other so far proposed, commands enough confidence for promotion, beyond conjecture, to our text. None points firmly enough to how the corruption arose; and even if any one of them is right, we have no means of assuring ourselves it probably is so.

4. v. i. 204.

> *The.* Now is the mure rased between the two neighbours.
> *For* mure rased (*this edn*) *Qq read* Moon vsed;
> F morall downe

'Moon vsed', though Alexander keeps it (and is right, in my opinion, to reject emendations based on the Folio), is clearly corrupt. 'Now is the Moon vsed betweene the two neighbors' is

Theseus' comment on the exit of Wall (alias Snout). Moon (alias Starveling) has been on stage only during Quince's prologue, and his part in the playlet is still to come. That Theseus spoke of Wall is made doubly certain by Demetrius' reply: 'No remedy, my lord, when walls are so wilful to hear without warning.' That the Quarto reading must be wrong was obvious to the man who annotated a Second Quarto whether for playhouse use, or (much more probably) in preparing copy for the Folio. His alteration on the print cannot have been meant to produce the nonsense 'morall downe'. I conjecture that he wrote 'wall downe', but that the compositor read this as 'rall downe', imagining that 'rall' was intended to turn 'Moon' into 'morall'. The confusion of 'w' and two-stemmed 'r' is well attested (cf., e.g., *Hamlet*, IV. vii. 22, Q2 'arm'd' for 'a wind'); the postulated mistake would be especially natural if a mark cancelling 'Moon' appeared to cancel only the 'on'. Neither 'murall' nor 'mure all' is very convincing as what lay behind F's 'morall': 'all' is otiose or worse in the context, and 'murall' a word not elsewhere used by Shakespeare even in a more ordinary sense than it would have to bear here; whereas 'wall downe' is exactly what an annotator would be bound to think of, if he had to guess the required words from the context. Indeed 'the wall is down' is Bottom's phrase later, at v. i. 357, which may or may not have influenced the annotator, but does not make it likelier that Shakespeare gave almost the same words to the Duke.

Even if 'wall downe' correctly restores the intended reading of the copy for F, this does not give us Shakespeare's original words in the copy for Q1. None of the proposed emendations of the Folio enables one to explain the Q1 corruption: 'Moon vsed' can hardly have arisen from 'wall downe', any more than from 'murall downe' or 'mure all downe'. The attempt to recover Shakespeare's original phrase by emending the Folio disregards the principle that a solution should be sought from the corruption in a text of first-rate lineage rather than from an easier reading in one of inferior authority. The principle may even apply where the superiority of the better text is not great: a classical instance is in *Othello*, I. iii. 330, where both the Folio and the Quarto readings evidently go back to a word hard to decipher. Q guesses the sense correctly, from the context, as 'ballance'; F, making an attempt to read the letters, produces 'braine', which is nonsense, but by pointing to the form of Shakespeare's word, enables us to see that it was 'beame'. Similarly, in the present crux, F can point to the sense, but not to the form of what stood in the foul papers; the form can be conjectured only from Q1, which is therefore our sole guide to what Shakespeare originally wrote. The criteria both of sense and of form are satisfied by 'mure rased', which could well be misread as 'moon vsed'. The misreading would be favoured by the presence of nine minims, including those of two-stemmed 'r'; not improbably by confusion resulting from Shakespeare's occasional 'a' left open at the top (cf., for example, 'vttred' in error for 'altred' in some copies of Q1, *2 Henry IV*, iv. v. 13, which offers a parallel to *v*sed for *r*ased (italics mine); but above all by the compositor's need to interpret the general shape of the unfamiliar 'mure' as some word that he knew. Comparatively rare as 'mure' may be, Shakespeare employs it in *2 Henry IV*, iv. iv. 119, where Prince Humphrey says of the King:

> Th' incessant care and labour of his mind
> Hath wrought the mure that should confine it in
> So thin that life looks through.

In the corresponding passage of the source, namely Daniel's *Civil Wars* (to the relevance of which in this connection Harold Jenkins has drawn my attention), we have:

> Wearing the wall so thin that now the mind
> Might well looke thorow, . . .

Did this wall associate in Shakespeare's brain with another wall that was looked through, and so call up the word 'mure' by which he had designated that?

The passage in *2 Henry IV* is not a particularly mannered one: Shakespeare does not seem to have felt that 'mure' was suited only to a mannered speaker, and this argues against the objection raised (privately) by one of my scholar friends that 'mure rased' is too precious for Theseus' diction. Besides, we must expect something a bit out of the ordinary to lie behind Q1's corruption— something difficult to the compositor, or why should he have blundered over it? This is a third criterion, added to those of form and meaning, which 'mure rased' satisfies. Again, as Geoffrey Tillotson remarked to me, contrast with the clowns' want of mastery over language is proper to the courtly spectators; it is given by the fanciful crackle of their wit playing upon such terms as 'valour', 'discretion', 'crescent', 'circumference', 'die', 'ace', 'means', 'videlicet'; and 'mure rased', without being mannered, is in keeping with this. Demetrius has already styled the wall a 'partition'.

If an editor still hankers after an emendation derived from the Folio reading, he must suggest how that reading comes to have independent authority. It would not be downright impossible to do this. In respect of certain stage-directions the copy for the Folio text of the *Dream* was derived from the playhouse. Faced with an impossible reading in Q2 the annotator may have made his alteration not by guesswork, but by turning to the same source, probably the prompt-book. The playhouse phrase, if it originated while Shakespeare still had a say in the text, might be his own revision, or one he acquiesced in. If so, he was at least willing to agree that his former version was unsatisfactory. Authors have been known to alter their dialogue when an actor protested 'I can't *say* that!'; perhaps the Theseus jibbed at 'mure'. And when 'rased' was spoken at rehearsal or in performance, perhaps it was condemned as indistinguishable from its antonym 'raised'. If each hypothesis in this sequence is correct, then but only then should an editor accept an emendation of the Folio's 'morall downe'—not as the words of Shakespeare's draft, but as superseding those, with at least his consent. Little confidence, however, could be placed in an emendation which required such a chain of suppositions, particularly when the evidence can be explained without even the first of them, since the annotator might easily produce his reading without consulting the prompt-book at all.

If he did consult it, and found 'wall downe' there, I should still not attribute to Shakespeare the departure from the draft version. The actors, I should be forced to admit, were content that after Snout's exit-couplet,

> Thus haue I *Wall*, my part discharged so;
> And being done, thus *Wall* away doth goe,

Theseus should tamely echo the already-repeated 'Wall' with 'Now is the wall downe . . .', and Demetrius follow with a fourth repetition: 'No remedy, my Lord, when walls are so wilfull. . . .' But I should still see small reason to think that Shakespeare had to do with such a revision, or ever meant his Theseus to abandon the words assigned him originally in the draft. These I have given reasons for conjecturally restoring as 'mure rased', 'mure' being a choice but not affected variation on Snout's emphatic 'Wall', and both words sustaining the tone of urbane amusement appropriate to Theseus here.

APPENDIX III

THE MISLINED VERSE IN Q1, v. i
(Eight passages, between ll. 5 and 83)

Such shaping phantasies, that apprehend more,   5
Then coole reason euer comprehends. The lunatick,
The louer, and the Poet are of imagination all compact.   8

The Poets eye, in a fine frenzy, rolling, doth glance   12
From heauen to earth, from earth to heauen. And as
Imagination bodies forth the formes of things
Vnknowne: the Poets penne turnes them to shapes,
And giues to ayery nothing, a locall habitation
And a name. Such trickes hath strong imagination.   18

Ioy, gentle friends, ioy and fresh daies   29
Of loue accompany your hearts.
Lys. More then to vs, waite in your royall walkes, your
boorde, your bedde.   31

To weare away this long age of three hours, betweene   33
Or after supper, & bed-time? Where is our vsuall manager
Of mirth? What Reuels are in hand? Is there no play,
To ease the anguish of a torturing hower? Call *Philostrate.*   38

Merry, and tragicall? Tedious, and briefe? That is hot
    Ise,   58
And wodrous[1] strange snow. How shall we find the cōcord
Of this discord?   60

And tragicall, my noble Lord, it is, for *Pyramus,*   66
Therein, doth kill himselfe. Which when I saw
Rehearst, I must confesse, made mine eyes water:
But more merry teares the passion of loud laughter   70
Neuer shed.

1. = wōdroys.

Phil. No, my noble Lord, it is not for you. I haue heard   76
    It ouer, and it is nothing, nothing in the world;   78

The. I will heare that play. For neuer any thing   81
    Can be amisse, when simplenesse and duety tender it.   83

APPENDIX IV

QUINCE'S PROLOGUE (v. i. 108–16) RIGHTLY PUNCTUATED

If we offend, it is with our good will
That you should think we come, not to offend,
But with good will to show our simple skill:
That is the true beginning of our end.
Consider then, we come—but in despite
We do not come—as minding to content you;
Our true intent is all for your delight:
We are not here that you should here repent you.
The actors are at hand . . .